Ancient Egypt
in the Popular Imagination

ALSO BY DAVID HUCKVALE
AND FROM MCFARLAND

*Visconti and the German Dream: Romanticism, Wagner
and the Nazi Castastrophe in Film* (2012)

*Touchstones of Gothic Horror: A Film Genealogy
of Eleven Motifs and Images* (2010)

Hammer Film Scores and the Musical Avant-Garde (2008)

*James Bernard, Composer to Count Dracula:
A Critical Biography* (2006; paperback 2012)

Ancient Egypt in the Popular Imagination

Building a Fantasy in Film, Literature, Music and Art

DAVID HUCKVALE

McFarland & Company, Inc., Publishers
Jefferson, North Carolina, and London

LIBRARY OF CONGRESS CATALOGUING-IN-PUBLICATION DATA

Huckvale, David.
Ancient Egypt in the popular imagination : building a fantasy in film, literature, music and art / David Huckvale.
    p.   cm.
Includes bibliographical references and index.

ISBN 978-0-7864-6577-4
softcover : acid free paper ∞

1. Egypt — In motion pictures.   2. Egypt — In mass media.
I. Title.
PN1995.9.E32H84 2012   700'.45832 — dc23   2012009362

BRITISH LIBRARY CATALOGUING DATA ARE AVAILABLE

© 2012 David Huckvale. All rights reserved

No part of this book may be reproduced or transmitted in any form or by any means, electronic or mechanical, including photocopying or recording, or by any information storage and retrieval system, without permission in writing from the publisher.

On the cover: Boris Karloff in *The Mummy*, 1932 (Universal Pictures/Photofest); background © 2012 Shutterstock

Manufactured in the United States of America

*McFarland & Company, Inc., Publishers
Box 611, Jefferson, North Carolina 28640
www.mcfarlandpub.com*

To Anthony Sellors

Acknowledgments

All the photographs are by the author unless otherwise stated. I would like to thank Marcus Hearn for providing many of the Hammer film stills, Dave Hawley for allowing me to use his photographs of Egypt, Simon Harvey Williams for his photograph of the Egyptian House in Penzance, Dez Skinn for the illustrations from *House of Hammer* magazine (courtesy of House of Hammer © Quality Communications 2011, *http://dezskinn.com/warner-williams/*), and the Ministero per i Beni e le Attività Culturali in Rome for granting permission to reproduce the etching by Piranesi. My thanks in general are also extended once again to Gail-Nina Anderson for invaluable help and encouragement.

Table of Contents

Acknowledgments	vi
Introduction	1
One • Films	7
Two • Egyptology	59
Three • Myth and Magic	86
Four • Art	107
Five • Fiction and Fantasy, Part 1	132
Six • Fiction and Fantasy, Part 2	159
Seven • Music	188
Conclusion	218
Filmography	223
Chapter Notes	225
Bibliography	235
Index	239

Introduction

Imagine that you are walking through a wood, surrounded by tall trees, lush bracken, ferns and birdsong. It's a familiar scene: the babbling stream that runs from the lake on the grounds of a large house in the adjoining park. We might allow ourselves to think of the house as slightly sinister, perhaps. Hasn't it just been occupied by a foreign gentlemen who wears a fez? You recall something to that effect. The meandering path that threads its way through the overhanging branches leads you to the dark waters of a somber little pond surrounded by bullrushes. A breeze ripples its silent waters as you pause to watch a couple of startled Mallard ducks fly off. Bubbles rise to the surface as though something is stirring in the depths. With a shudder, you don't wait to find out what has caused them. You move swiftly on. Shafts of light pierce the canopy of leaves overhead, the fresh smell of recent rain rises from the loam at your feet.

But into this sylvan scene, you now perceive a human shape in the distance — a stumbling silhouette emerging from behind a screen of silver birches — an alien presence, bandaged from head to foot, its eyes glaring with demonic malevolence. Perhaps you are one of those people who always laugh at the actors who play such terrors from the tomb in the movies, but you are not laughing now. You are alone in an otherwise tranquil forest with a lumbering, unstoppable horror advancing upon you, dripping water and slime from the dark pond you have just passed. Part of you — the rational part — might think yourself the victim of a grotesque practical joke, but as the figure advances, thrashing the undergrowth from its path with a bandaged hand, your irrational instinct doesn't allow you to wait and see. Frightening though an encounter with a living mummy in an Egyptian tomb would be, it is even more unnerving in this context — a familiar scene, far from the origin of this monster from the ancient, alien past.

The reason for starting our journey in this manner is to stress that mummy movies and the stories that inspired them are motivated by a fear of what we might term "the other." Every mummy movie ever made pits East against West. Either a mummy is reanimated in England or America, or an Englishman or American encounters an ancient evil in Egypt. Frequently, both these things happen. With the exception of *The Night of Counting the Years* (a.k.a. *The Mummy,* dir. Shadi Abdel-Salam, 1969), which is hardly a mummy movie in the accepted sense of the term, a mummy film with a cast consisting entirely of Egyptians has yet to be made. This suggests that mummy movies are a fundamentally racist form of entertainment. According to this view, such films express a fear of religious conflict, cultural infiltration and even invasion. They also express the imperialist desire to dominate and exploit the exotic, not to mention the repressed guilt that accompanies such a desire. After the opening scenes of Hammer's *The Mummy* (dir. Terence Fisher, 1959), which are set in Egypt, we are whisked back to a sylvan English scene. The composer, Franz Reizenstein, supplies bucolic oboes and a pastoral melody to help establish the required sense of familiarity and tranquility after the disturbing events in the tomb of Ananka that open the film. The remainder of the action significantly takes place entirely in England, just as many of the Universal mummy films take place in a small-town American environment that is threatened by the unleashed forces of ancient Egypt. The literary genre that nourished such films took the same approach. Bram Stoker was careful to create an accurate impression of then-contemporary Edwardian London in his novel *The Jewel of Seven Stars* (1903), and at one point in that book, the doctor who has been called to assist the mysteriously stricken Egyptologist, Abel Trelawny, in his Kensington mansion, equates Egypt itself with what is unhealthy and dangerous:

> I am completely ignorant of Egyptian matters, language, writing, history, secrets, medicines, poisons, occult powers — all that go to make up the mystery of that mysterious land. This disease, or condition or whatever it may be called, from which Mr Trelawny is suffering, is in some way connected with Egypt.[1]

Sax Rohmer expressed the same sentiment (although somewhat less elaborately) in his gloriously lurid Egyptian romance, *Brood of the Witch Queen* (1918), in which a reanimated mummy is hellbent on sorcery and revenge. After a description of the excessive heat of a London summer, Rohmer gave one of his characters the line "Egypt is in London ... our fears are well-founded."[2]

But European culture has another kind of fascination with ancient Egypt, motivated not so much by fear as by awe. All that remains of the immense wealth and political power of ancient Egypt now lies in the ruins of its architecture and surviving antiquities. The West's fascination with (and ambition to emulate) all that led to a different, though related kind of film entertainment. The Egyptian epic was sometimes Biblical, as in the two versions of *The Ten Commandments* (dir. Cecil B. DeMille, 1923 and 1956) and sometimes it was of what one might call the pharaonic variety. Good examples of the latter type are the two versions of *Cleopatra* (the first directed by DeMille in 1934; the remake by Joseph L. Mankiewicz in 1963), *The Egyptian* (dir. Michael Curtiz, 1954) and *Land of the Pharaohs* (dir. Howard Hawks, 1955). What mummy movies and pharaonic films have in common is, of course, the glamor and allure of Egyptian art, which both types of film attempt to recreate with varying degrees of success, depending on the scale of their budgets. Egyptologists may take care that antiquities are treated with respect and academic rigor, but the popular imagination has always been fascinated by their splendor. Even Howard Carter, the most respectable and careful of scholarly Egyptologists, spoke (quite understandably) of "the strained expectancy — why not confess it? — of the treasure-seeker"[3] when describing the opening of Tutankhamen's tomb. Indeed, parts of his gripping narrative would not be out of place in any less academically respectable mummy romance:

> I suppose most excavators would confess to a feeling of awe — embarrassment almost — when they break into a chamber closed and sealed by pious hands so many centuries ago. For the moment, time as a factor in human life has lost its meaning. Three thousand, four thousand years maybe, have passed and gone since human feet trod the floor on which you stand, and yet, as you note the signs of recent life around you — the half-filled bowl of mortar for the door, the

blackened lamp, the finger-mark upon the freshly painted surface, the farewell garland dropped upon the threshold — you feel it might have been but yesterday. The very air you breathe, unchanged throughout the centuries, you share with those who laid the mummy to its rest. Time is annihilated by little intimate details such as these, and you feel an intruder.[4]

To the general public, the discovery of a tomb has always been far more about fabulous wealth, beautiful objects and the mystery of the past than historical understanding. This is succinctly summed up in a scene in the 1999 remake of *The Mummy* (dir. Stephen Sommers) when Jonathan Hyde's Dr. Allen Chamberlain uncovers the Book of the Dead that will eventually revive the mummy of Imhotep.

"Who cares about a book?" one of his avaricious cronies asks. "Where the hell's the treasure?"

"This—" Chamberlain replies, "this *is* treasure."

The hard graft of Egyptology as a science, the painstaking reassembly of an ancient culture is not what sells newspapers or attracts audiences to cinemas. Quite the opposite, in fact. Modern civilization (whether it be manifested in popular culture, or "high art") has always recreated the past in general — and ancient Egypt in particular — in its own image. The past is only of psychological use to us if it can help us make sense of the present. This was something deeply understood by Thomas Mann, who discussed the subject of ancient Egypt in *Joseph in Egypt* (1936). The fascinating prelude to the entire tetralogy of Joseph stories of which *Joseph in Egypt* is the third installment is called "Descent into Hell" because fantasies of the past always take us to the underworld of our own culture. In Jungian terms, they plunge us into the ocean of our shared psychological archetypes. Mann (who was instinctively in sympathy with Jung's ideas) suggested that

> the essence of life is its presentness, and only in a mythical sense does its mystery appear in the time-forms of past and future. They are the way, so to speak, in which life reveals itself to the folk; the mystery belongs to the initiate. Let the folk be taught that the soul wanders. But the wise know that this teaching is only the garment of the mystery of the eternal presentness of the soul, and that all life belongs to it, so soon as death shall have broken its solitary prison cell. I taste of death and knowledge when, as story-teller, I adventure into the past; hence my eagerness, hence my fear and pallor.[5]

But if we find ourselves wandering in the past, we also find aspects of ourselves that we might prefer not to encounter, or even acknowledge as belonging to us at all. Howard Carter spoke of "embarrassment," and feeling like an "intruder" when breaking the seal of Tutankhamen's tomb. There is not only a sense of guilt in disturbing the dead, but also a fear that we are disturbing the sediment of our own psychological sump. To counteract this discomfort, we project what we find disturbing about ourselves onto monsters. Mummy movies, in this respect, are like all racist fantasies, deflecting the West's dark shadow — its alter-ego — onto an unnerving, inverted double. The demonization of "the other" in ancient Egyptian fantasies is no different in principle from Wagner's demonization of the Jews in his writings and music-dramas. Wagner presented the Jews as ugly and dangerous, whereas ancient Egypt is usually presented as beautiful and dangerous, but both fantasies express the same unease with "the other." Mummy movies and the fictions on which they feed invariably enforce the dominant cultural values on the alien culture that is perceived to threaten it. In *Brood of the Witch Queen*, Sax Rohmer compounds the evil nature and foreignness of his re-animated mummy with the insinuation that it is also homosexual, or at least bisexual. Even on the hottest days, the mummy in question, who masquerades as the adopted son of a wealthy Egyptologist, wears overcoats extravagantly lined either with the fur of white fox or civet-cat. Also, there is "something revoltingly effeminate" about this creature; a "sort of cat-like grace which had been noticeable in a woman, but which in a man was unnatural, and for some obscure reason, sinister." He even goes so far as to have his unnatural villain describe himself as "a compound of man and woman."[6]

Wagner was rather more tolerant of homosexuals than he was of Jews (though there is continuing speculation with regard to how far he suspected he had Jewish blood running through his own veins, not to mention how gay he was as well).[7] Decadent and neurotic himself, Wagner was convinced that the Jews were undermining a culture that had itself grown weak:

> As long as the separate art of music possessed a really organic need for life, up until the time of Mozart and Beethoven, there were no Jewish composers to be found: it was impossible for an element completely foreign to this living organism to take any part in its growth. Only when a body's inner death is evident can outside elements gain entry, and then only to destroy it. Then the flesh of that body is transformed into a swarming colony of worms.[8]

It's significant that Wagner used the imagery of Gothic horror here to emphasize his grotesque point. Just as reanimated mummies are usually destroyed at the end of the films through which they rampage, Wagner drastically proposed the physical destruction of the Jews as the only way to save his own "threatened" culture. Addressing his enemy, Wagner concludes that "redemption from the curse laid on you can be achieved by only one thing, and that is the redemption of Ahasuerus — decline and fall!"[9] Ahasuerus was the mythical wandering Jew, who laughed in the face of Christ when the Savior was carrying His cross to Calvary, and was condemned, like a reanimated mummy, to eternal, soulless life until Christ's second coming. In his wife's *Diaries*, Wagner is on record as having recommended the "drastic" solution of burning all Jews during a performance of Lessing's *Nathan der Weise*, ironically, a play that advocates religious tolerance.[10] Similarly, mummies are usually "redeemed" by physical violence at the end of the films in which they appear; and if you think my inclusion of Wagner here rather a tenuous link to Egyptian fantasy, it's interesting to listen to Louis Levy's score for *The Ghoul* (dir. T. Hayes Hunter, 1933), an early British horror film with an Egyptian theme. Levy (1894–1957) was a veteran of musical accompaniment in the silent era, and he brought to *The Ghoul* the tradition of compiling a score from existing sources, working with Alfred Hitchcock on *The 39 Steps* (1935) and *The Lady Vanishes* (1938). Most of his source material for the score of the *The Ghoul* was selected from Wagner's music dramas. We hear the motif of Fafner, the dragon from *Siegfried*, throughout, along with the Act I prelude and dragon-slaying music from that opera, as well as music associated with the evil sorceress, Ortrud, from *Lohengrin*. Most striking of all is Levy's interpolation of Siegfried's Funeral March (re-orchestrated for much smaller forces, of course) from *Götterdämmerung*. Levy's approach was also adopted by Hollywood musical directors. The slow movement from Schumann's Piano Quintet, part of Beethoven's Seventh Symphony, the opening of Liszt's B minor piano sonata, and one of Liszt's Hungarian Rhapsodies accompany the Bela Lugosi/Boris Karloff vehicle *The Black Cat* (dir. Edgar G. Ulmer, 1934), a film which, as we shall see in the next chapter, also has loose connections with the mummy genre.

Though we will also be considering the history of Egyptology in this cultural adventure, the only reason for doing so is to discover how fantasy has been influenced by fact. The reality of Egypt ancient or modern is not the issue here. Indeed, "reality," whatever it is, has rarely been as powerful a force as fantasy. Human affairs have largely been propelled by fantasy: idealism, religion, and the many social changes brought about by the conflicts they have caused. Reality, in the context of this book, is merely a starting point — an inspiration for fantasy. Reality is the catalyst, the trigger, but not the chemical reaction or the explosion. Dreams, after all, are the product of everyday experience; but how much more efficiently they reveal to us our drives, preoccupations, anxieties and desires.

As Florence Nightingale wrote in her private diary, written during on her own trip to Egypt in 1849, her imagination "spoiled it all by dreaming." She confessed to being "disappointed with myself and the effect of Egypt on me."[11] It's a problem that's been analyzed by many professional fantasists. The great French symbolist Villiers de L'Isle Adam (1838–1889) pointed out in his play *Axël:*

> You see the external world through your soul, so it dazzles you!... Oh! the external world! Let's not be dupes of that old slave, whom real light shows chained at our feet, and who promises us the keys to a palace of enchantment, when what his black hand hides is a fistful of ashes! A little while ago you spoke of Bagdad, Palmyra, where else? Jerusalem. If you knew what a heap of uninhabitable stones, what a sterile burning soil, what lairs of unclean beasts make up in *reality* these poor wretched towns which appear resplendent with associations in the depths of that Orient you carry within![12]

Famously, the hero of J. K. Huysmans' novel *À Rebours* (1884) plans a trip to London, having been inspired to see for himself the city he has imagined by reading Dickens. After traveling through Paris in a fog truly worthy of a London pea-souper, leafed through travel brochures and a Baedeker guide to London museums, recollected the English paintings he had seen in International Exhibitions and dined in a wine-shop filled with English tourists, he simply hasn't the energy, still less the need, to make the actual trip. He has imagined, far more nourishingly, what would be merely a disappointment in reality. And so, he returns home to dream.

Reality is usually disappointing to the imaginative. To visit Transylvania so as to feel closer to Bram Stoker's *Dracula* is an irrelevant effort and expense. Stoker imagined it all the more successfully by never having gone there himself. Similarly, to those embarking on this book, the experience of Egypt itself— particularly in the tourist-crowded and commercially exploited conditions of the 21st century — would actually be counter-productive. That sort of thing is better left to archeologists. What this book hopes to unearth are the origins of ancient Egyptian fantasies, and as they have much more to do with the West than the East it is actually more productive to stay at home. W. Somerset Maugham observed that "to imagine is to fail; for it is the acknowledgment of defeat in the encounter with reality."[13] In the realm of fantasy, however, it is reality that fails us. Ours dreams never do.

• ONE •

Films

Vengeance is the main motivation of the mummy movie: a tomb has been defiled by an infidel explorer, and the outraged guardian of the tomb reactivates the mummy, sending it out to destroy the desecrators; but the claims of the culture that has been violated by the West are usually overridden by the British or American heroes who triumph over the guardians of the tomb and their mummified strong men. Among the exceptions to this general rule are films such as Universal's *The Mummy* (dir. Karl Freund, 1932) and Hammer's *Blood from the Mummy's Tomb* (dir. Seth Holt, 1972), which are somewhat more metaphysical affairs concerned with reincarnation (a concept that was quite alien to the ancient Egyptians themselves). Both these films nonetheless exploit the traditional fear of "the other."

As film historian Leslie Halliwell has pointed out,[1] ancient Egypt inspired the cinema from its very earliest days. Georges Méliès incorporated sarcophagi in some of his trick films, and two of the earliest supernatural mummy films were, significantly, made in Britain, which had produced a wealth of fantasy literature about ancient Egyptian by the time these films appeared. It was fertile ground and would nourish both Universal and Hammer mummy movies later. The first, *The Vengeance of Egypt*, appeared in 1912. It concerned a mummy's ring, in the form of a scarab, which is stolen by a soldier during Napoleon's Egyptian campaign. Unfortunately, it brings death to all who possess it, but when the mummy is eventually reunited with its stolen property, its eyes glow with mystical satisfaction. *The Avenging Hand* or, to give its original British title, *The Wraith of the Tomb* (dir. Charles Calvert, 1915), was the first full-length British horror film. In it, the spirit of an Egyptian princess scours London in search of her mummified hand—a hand with a murderous life of its own. Both films have certain things in common with Bram Stoker's Egyptian novel, *The Jewel of Seven Stars*. This was only nine years old by the time of *The Vengeance of Egypt*, and may well have provided the inspiration for the idea of a scarab ring in that film, not to mention the severed hand and wandering spirit of an Egyptian princess in *The Avenging Hand*; but, as we shall see later, this latter film may also have been inspired by a tale about a mummy's *foot* by Theophile Gautier.

Perhaps the first movie with the word "mummy" in the title hardly qualifies for the genre of mummy movie at all. Directed by Ernst Lubitsch, *Die Augen der Mumie Ma* (*The Eyes of the Mummy*, 1918) starred Pola Negri as a young girl called Mara, who has been abducted and imprisoned in the tomb of Queen Ma, where her eyes peer out from behind the stone relief of a mummy mask on the wall. She's eventually rescued by a young man

called Albert Wendland (played by Harry Liedtke), who then takes her to London and launches her, rather prosaically (given the exciting title of the film), on a theatrical career. As an example of what we would nowadays expect from a film with the word "mummy" in it, *The Eyes of the Mummy* is bound to disappoint.

Lubitsch's film appeared only a few years before the sensational discovery of Tutankhamen's tomb in 1922, an event that sent shock waves of Egyptomania across the Western world. In his book *The Dead That Walk*, Halliwell usefully quotes from Robert Graves and Alan Hodge's study of the interwar years, *The Long Weekend*, to demonstrate the extent to which ancient Egypt now gripped the modern world:

> Ancient Egypt suddenly became the vogue. In March 1923 the veteran professor Flinders Petrie lectured on Egypt to an entranced Mayfair gathering. Replicas of the jewellery found in the tomb, and hieroglyphic embroideries copied from its walls, were worn on dresses; lotus-flower, scarab and serpent ornaments in vivid colours appeared in hats. Sandy tints were popular, and gowns began to fall stiffly in the Egyptian style. Even the new model Singer sewing machine of that year went Pharaonic, and it was seriously proposed that the new underground extension from Morden to Edgeware, then under construction, should be called Tootencamden, because it passed through Tooting and Camden Town.[2]

Hollywood, of course, had exploited ancient Egypt before. As early as 1912, Helen Gardner had played Cleopatra in a film version of Sardou's Cleopatra play, directed by Charles L. Gaskill. Theda Bara followed in the Fox version of the story in 1917, directed by J. Gordon Edwards. Then, of course, there was Cecil B. DeMille's production of *The Ten Commandments* in 1923, but only the first part of this epic concerns Moses in Egypt. The second part is a morality fable exploring how the ten commandments apply to modern life. However, everything starts off with an impressive shot of a huge sphinx that's being wheeled into position. In front of it stands an Egyptian soldier wielding a whip in an image that sums up the basic propaganda message of Exodus in a single shot, but it obviously wasn't enough for DeMille or his audience. His set designer, Paul Iribe, went to town on some very impressive recreations of ancient Egyptian monuments, while the interior of Pharaoh's palace is dominated by an enormous sphinx that looms threateningly behind the throne. When photographed in heavy shadow during the plagues of Egypt, the sphinx's towering bulk becomes even more oppressive. The sheer magnitude of ancient Egypt and the opportunities it offered to overwhelm was what impressed Hollywood directors most, and it's tempting to ponder the possibility that such a film anticipated the monumentalism that was to dominate Western architecture throughout the 1930s. Such monumentalism would also inform fascist architecture, Hitler's aim in the neo-classical works of Albert Speer being similarly to overwhelm the spectator with architectural spectacle. Could the fashion for Egyptian epics in the 1920s be seen as part of a mood that ultimately led to this? The black marble floors of Pharaoh's palace in *The Ten Commandments* seem, with hindsight, to foreshadow the similarly oppressive interiors of fascist architecture in the 1930s, and Pharaoh's Egypt is certainly presented as a tyrannical and ruthless regime, having more in common with the modern world than the relatively benign reality of ancient Egyptian society. DeMille's dual aim to overwhelm his audience with architectural immensity while

Opposite: Emil Jannings hurls Pola Negri down a short flight of stairs at the end of *The Eyes of the Mummy* (dir. Ernst Lubitsch, 1918). Negri was hurt in the process and might well have died but for the cushions, which softened the blow to her head.

The original "vamp," Theda Bara, in the title role of *Cleopatra* (dir. J. Gordon Edwards, 1917).

simultaneously condoning the authority that built such overbearing monuments is fraught with contradictions, anticipating what Susan Sontag was to define in her famous 1974 essay as "fascinating fascism" in an essay of the same name. Though derived from a variety of styles in the wake of Art Deco, the architecture of the 1930s was also indebted to Egyptian models, and it's useful to regard DeMille's film as being symptomatic of that development in its early stages. It was also all very operatic, deriving, in turn (as we shall see in later chapters), not only from stage design in the 19th century but also 19th-century academic painting.

Despite all that extravagance, Hollywood took a while to latch on to the supernatural potential of ancient Egypt. Having said that, Karloff's ground-breaking performance as Im-ho-tep was in some ways foreshadowed by the entirely non–Egyptian *The Phantom of the Opera* (dir. Rupert Julian, 1925). The cadaverous make-up of Lon Chaney's Phantom, Erik, indeed presents him as a kind of mummy, and the mask he wears is the equivalent of the bandaged visage that would menace so many leading ladies who followed in the wake of Mary Philbin. She had famously pulled off Erik's mask to reveal the horror beneath. "Feast you eyes, glut your soul on my accursed ugliness!" Erik shrieks (silently, of course), in a direct quotation from Gaston Leroux's novel. Moviegoers had never seen anything like it, unless, of course, they had been unfortunate enough to experience the horror of trench warfare in World War I. Chaney's make-up indeed resembles the horrific disfigurements

Theodore Roberts as Moses and Charles de Rochefort as Rameses, the Magnificent in Pharaoh's Hall in *The Ten Commandments* (dir. Cecil B. DeMille, 1923).

suffered by French war veterans. Buried fears of those living nightmares no doubt rumbled around the sub-conscious of *The Phantom*'s first audiences, and a more general fear of death — and burial alive — was a significant part of the mummy's unnerving allure.

Mummies also share the Phantom's loneliness, along with his desire to possess the female who inspires him, and though Erik isn't technically dead like his fellow monsters, he is as good as dead. In Julian's film, he appears as the Red Death incarnate at the Opera Ball. Indeed, Gaston Leroux describes Erik's face as a kind of mummy: "But imagine, if you can, Red Death's mask suddenly coming to life in order to express, with the four black holes of its eyes, its nose, and its mouth, the extreme anger, the mighty fury of a demon; *and not a ray of light from the sockets.*"[3] What else is a mummy than a death mask come to life, expressing a similar fury? And does not Leroux's description of the black holes of the Phantom's eye sockets suggest what the makers of *The Mummy's Hand* did to the eyes of Tom Tyler's Kharis, which were similarly blacked out and turned into depthless chasms of malevolence?

Lon Chaney never played the mummy, but his son eventually (though reluctantly) would. That, however, lay some years in the future. Having triumphed with *Dracula* (dir. Tod Browning, 1931) and *Frankenstein* (dir. James Whale, 1931), Universal Studios looked around for another horror vehicle for Karloff and pondered the possibility of a scenario about Cagliostro. This had been submitted to them by Nina Wilcox Putnam (1888–1962), a prolific author of stories, novels and the Sunny Funny Bunny comic books for children. Having also co-authored the original *Dracula* play on which the Bela Lugosi film was later based, she also acquired a reputation for gothic horror. Her *Cagliostro* proposal, however, had little to do with the 18th-century occultist, Count Alessandro Cagliostro, though it was to some extent influenced by Cagliostro's interest in Egyptian magic, along with his own sensational claims to immortality. As we shall see, Cagliostro, whatever his actual identity, certainly existed and developed a Masonic rite purporting to be based on ancient Egyptian beliefs. He also claimed to have personally known Pontius Pilate and Jesus Christ, an acquaintance which aroused the interest of the Inquisition; but as Philippa Faulks and Robert L.D. Cooper suggest, Cagliostro may not have meant this to have been taken seriously. He may have said, "Of Jesus Christ. I knew him well," which could be interpreted as merely being familiar with Christ's word and mission.[4]

Putnam's Cagliostro was an ancient Egyptian magician who has kept himself alive for over 3,000 years by means of nitrate injections. He spends his time pursuing various women who resemble the woman who betrayed him in the ancient past. These he dispatches in increasingly macabre ways. Mercifully, this idea was not pursued, but from such an unpromising basis, John L. Balderston's script for *The Mummy* emerged as a set of Egyptian variations on the themes of Universal's previous horror films dealing with death, resurrection, love and immortality.

The refreshing thing about the first Universal mummy movie is that Karloff's mummy, the resurrected High Priest, Im-ho-tep, isn't at all interested in avenging himself on those who have desecrated his tomb. In fact, he must have been rather grateful to young Bramwell Fletcher's archeologist, Norton, for reading the Scroll of Thoth and inadvertently bringing him back to life, for without such an intervention he would never have had the chance to reunite himself with the reincarnation of his long-lost love. "He went for a little walk!" Norton shrieks, but he's the only one to see it. The director, Karl Freund, exercised considerable restraint by leaving that experience to the audience's imagination. When we next encounter the mummy he has removed his bandages, to reveal a face transformed by make-up artist Jack P. Pierce to create the required effect of fragile antiquity. As photographed by Charles Stumar, this visage of death reanimated has never been bettered. Pierce's make-up made Karloff's already cadaverous features even more sunken, pinched and shriveled. Like two stagnant pools in the desert moonlight, Karloff's eyes stare out at us across the centuries.

Karloff's ghoulish gaze in *The Mummy* (dir. Karl Freund, 1932).

Im-ho-tep also dislikes to be touched, giving the impression that if he was, he would collapse into a heap of dust.

No, it is not revenge he seeks, nor mere sexual conquest like Dracula. Im-ho-tep desires, rather, the reincarnation of Anck-es-en-amon, his long-lost love. Unlike Christopher Lee's Kharis, he does not discover his princess by accident while stomping over the living room carpet. Im-ho-tep sets out deliberately to find her. He lures her to the Museum of Antiquities in Cairo and hopes ultimately to embalm her, like himself, before resurrecting her for all time. In this respect he strongly resembles Dracula who also seeks an immortal consort, but here the affection is genuine and moving.

> IM-HO-TEP: It was not only this body I loved — it was thy soul, O Princess — I destroy this lifeless thing — for but a few moments *thou shalt take its place*— and then rise again as I have risen.... For thy love I was buried alive — I ask of thee only a moment of agony — only *so* can we be united.[5]

Even the domestic settings of *The Mummy* and the positions of the actors within them resemble Tod Browning's *Dracula*. The scene which shows Zita Johann lying on a sofa when Karloff comes to call recalls the similar situation of Helen Chandler when Lugosi did the same thing in the earlier film; and, of course, Edward Van Sloan appears in both *Dracula* and *The Mummy* as the monsters' nemesis, not to mention having been the voice of reason in James Whale's *Frankenstein*. Both Lugosi's Dracula and Karloff's mummy also have hypnotically penetrating eyes, of course, but despite the similarities between the two characters, only Karloff achieved the accolade of being billed by his surname alone — a distinction previously unique to Garbo. If Garbo had been persuaded to perform Zita Johann's role in *The Mummy*, her status might well have ensured the survival of film's reincarnation scenes. Cut from the finished print, as they were thought to slow down the story, they seem, from the surviving stills, to have been miniature historical epics in their own right. If they had survived we would have treated to the sight of Zita Johann in her various past lives as a Christian martyr being fed to the lions, a suicidal eighth-century barbarian queen, a medieval queen bidding farewell to her dutiful crusaders, and an aristocrat in 18th-century France who was presumably guillotined during the Revolution. Sadly, Universal guillotined them all, and today are considered lost.

Balderston also intended another subtle effect. When Bramwell Fletcher's Norton first examines the Scroll of Thoth, the screenplay asks for "two little blue flames" to "dance on the ends of the scroll which is to his left. From these flames," it continues, "a peculiar vapor rises, curling into the still air. It is important that this effect should be very slight and that the light should be dimmed only a little, because we don't want an effect so striking that Norton would notice it."[6] In the event, no one is able to notice these flames as they weren't included, presumably because they presented too much of a technical challenge. Balderston's script also contains evidence of his archeological and occult interests. The statue of the god Amon, for example, is bathed in moonlight that streams through a small hole in the roof above, and Balderston took the trouble to point out that "this effect is genuine. There is a shrine at Karnak now which has its statue and the hole for the moonlight."[7] This is, in fact, the black granite statue of Sekhmet in the Sanctuary of Ptah at Karnak. Balderston also draws the outline of an ankh in the screenplay at one point, explaining that it is the "crux ansata, or the symbol of life," and during his description of the film's dénouement adds that the crux ansata held by the statue of Isis which ultimately destroys Im-ho-tep "is fashioned in the form of the hieroglyph meaning 'millions of millions of years.'"[8]

Karloff had no desire to endure the agonies of playing the mummy again. "Physical exhaustion was nothing compared to the nervous exhaustion I suffered," he confessed. "I am glad it is over!"[9] But his involvement with ancient Egypt wasn't. He returned to his native England the following year to film *The Ghoul*. Despite the Wagnerian leitmotifs of Louis Levy's score and the atmospheric input of its three German set designers, Heinrich Heitfeld, Günther Krampf and Alfred Junge, this is unfortunately a typical example of the slow, lumbering nature of many British movies made during the 1930s. First-class British actors such as Ralph Richardson (here making his screen debut), Cedric Hardwicke and Ernest Thesiger are all rather wasted as T. Hayes Hunter laboriously unfolds his predictable story about an Egyptologist (Karloff) who lies dying in a bedroom that already resembles a tomb with its statue of Anubis in one corner. (Perhaps the screenwriters had Stoker's *The Jewel of Seven Stars* in mind, the Egyptologist of which similarly lies in a bedroom filled with Egyptian curios.) Karloff's character leaves instructions with his Scottish manservant (Thesiger) that he should be buried clutching a life-giving ancient jewel called the Eternal Light (the interment scene is when we hear Siegfried's Funeral March), and, sure enough, he eventually emerges from his beautifully designed Egyptian mausoleum to seek vengeance

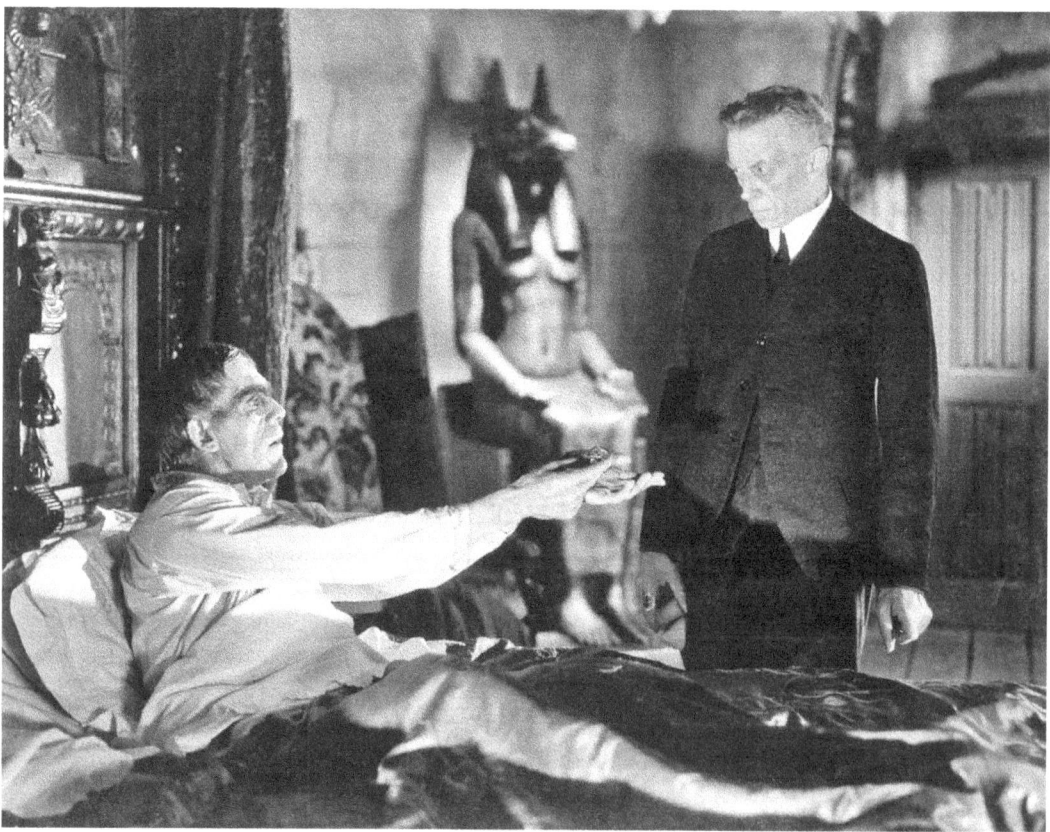

Anubis in the room. Boris Karloff (left) and Ernest Thesiger in *The Ghoul* (dir. T. Hayes Hunter, 1933).

on Thesiger who has let the secret out. As Jonathan Rigby observes,[10] the shot of Karloff wrenching the iron bars from a window before attacking the cringing Thesiger anticipates the scene in Hammer's *The Mummy*, when Christopher Lee's Kharis breaks into the padded cell of Felix Aylmer's stricken Egyptologist, Stephen Banning. (It's during Karloff's murder of Thesiger, incidentally, that we hear Levy's arrangement of the dragon-slaying music from Wagner's *Siegfried*!)

Back in Hollywood, James Whale was still riding the crest of the horror tsunami he had created with *Frankenstein* and now turned his attention to H. G. Wells's *The Invisible Man* (1933). Though not mummified, Claude Rains' research scientist, Jack Griffen, certainly looks like a mummy, wrapped up in all those bandages — though, admittedly, no ancient Egyptian ever wore goggles. The film made Rains into a star — proof that what you don't see really is far more frightening than what you do see. Like the Phantom before him, the mystery of what Griffen actually looks like is the secret of the character's horrible appeal. Like a mummy, there seems to be nothing behind the bandages, as though the figure is animated by pure spirit alone — a spirit that, also like the mummy, becomes increasingly malevolent as Griffen realizes the true extent of his power over others. "Even the moon is frightened of me," he shouts, "frightened to death! The whole world is frightened to death!"— and, indeed, Rains' performance, even though we can't see more than the clothes he's wearing, is actually more frightening than any dusty old mummy (with the possible exception of Karloff's example). Rains, of course, had the supreme advantage of being allowed to use his velvet voice. Excepting Karloff's Im-ho-tep, this was a privilege denied to every other ancient Egyptian horror until the appearance of Arnold Vosloo as a positively loquacious Imhotep in the 1999 remake. Reminiscent of both Claude Rains' Invisible Man and Lon Chaney's masked Phantom, Vosloo at one point (in fact when he is only half reconstituted) invites his next victim to tea. He sits behind a sinister mask of his own and two elegant tea cups stand on the table before him, reminding one of the behind-the-scenes stills of Karloff taking his very British tea breaks during the filming of his horror classics. It is during this particular scene that the line about Im-ho-tep not liking to be touched is reprised. The line is not, however, given the dignity of Karloff's utterance, being delivered on Imhotep's behalf by his seedy sidekick, Beni Gabor (played by Kevin J. O'Connor). Anyway, we don't have to wait long for him to pull off the mask for a classic "reveal," his half-reconstituted face combining the vacuity of the Invisible Man with the cadaverous horror of the Phantom of the Opera, but with nothing of their eerie power.

Cats being the guardians of the underworld, Vosloo's Imhotep lives in fear of them until he is fully regenerated. This is why he is terrified of the charming white cat which innocently walks over the keys of a grand piano; but it was a *black* cat that inspired Karloff's next movie with mummy connotations. Made one year after *The Ghoul*, on Karloff's return to Hollywood in 1934, *The Black Cat* might seem at first sight to be a long way from ancient Egypt. It's set in Hungary for a start, and features Bauhaus-inspired set designs rather than hieroglyphics and ancient tombs; but, when viewed closely, the streamlined aesthetic of Bauhaus has a fair amount in common with the comparably streamlined aesthetic of ancient Egyptian architecture. The story of the film was also, in part, inspired by the example of the occultist Aleister Crowley, who was much in the news at the time, and, as we shall see, Crowley had a particular interest of his own in ancient Egypt. Black cats also have an association with the ancient Egyptian goddess Bast. *The Black Cat* also contains a variant of the

Invisible mummy. Claude Rains under the bandages in *The Invisible Man* (dir. James Whale, 1933).

mummy theme in the series of perfectly preserved female corpses which are displayed in glass cases in the cellar of Karloff's cellar. Karloff, who plays a satanically deranged architect, Hjalmar Poelzig, also keeps the embalmed body of his adversary's wife, whom he has murdered — and that adversary is played, of course, by Bela Lugosi. The spirit of the equally well-preserved Queen Tera in Stoker's *The Jewel of Seven Stars* isn't so very far away here, though the finished film almost entirely removed the screenplay's original intention of

Lugosi (left) and Karloff confront one another in *The Black Cat* (dir. Edgar G. Ulmer, 1934). Karloff's character, Hans Poelzig, keeps the embalmed body of his wife, Karen Werdegast Poelzig, played by Lucille Lund, in the cellar of his creepy Bauhaus mansion. Her distinctly Nefertiti-inspired hairstyle anticipated that of Elsa Lanchester's "Bride" in *The Bride of Frankenstein* (dir. James Whale, 1935).

suggesting that the evil soul of the eponymous black cat has entered the body of the film's heroine, Joan (played by Jacqueline Wells). If more had been made of that, the film would have had even more in common with Stoker's novel.

Ancient Egypt burst onto the screen in no uncertain manner the same year with Cecil B. DeMille's *Cleopatra,* starring Claudette Colbert in the title role. *The Black Cat* had presented Art Deco in a severely modernist style but *Cleopatra* drew hedonistically on Art Deco's love affair with Egyptiana in Hans Dreier's astonishing sets. As one might expect in a DeMille production, no expense was spared in this department, and in the scene set on Cleopatra's barge, double rows of ram-headed oars move in balletic synchronization as dancing girls cavort beneath confetti and waving fans. We then cut to a shot of the barge elegiacally floating off down the moonlit Nile. White peacocks stalk Cleopatra's throne room, a pet leopard falls asleep on her silken couch and DeMille even shows us the army of asses who provide the milk for Cleopatra's bath. Her cats can't resist lapping this up, and, these being pre–Hays Code days, DeMille enjoys showing the milk lapping around Colbert's bare breasts, and almost (but not quite) revealing the nipples. Cleopatra's servant then strips off (but we see only her bare legs) to join her in the frothing foam.

In a sense, *The Bride of Frankenstein* (1935), James Whale's sequel to *Frankenstein,* also has its Egyptian influence. The famous portrait bust of Nefertiti, now in the Neues Museum in Berlin, inspired the towering hairstyle of the female monster, played by Elsa Lanchester, but screenwriter Balderston had also referred to Nefertiti in his earlier script for *The Mummy,* suggesting there that Zita Johann's Helen Grosvenor should resemble "the well-known bust of Nefertiti in the Berlin Museum" while simultaneously pointing out, in scholarly manner, that "this Nefertiti in real life was probably the mother of the real Anck-es-en-amon."[11] However, audiences had to wait until 1940 for a follow-up to *The Mummy* with *The Mummy's Hand* (dir. Christy Cabanne). By that time, Universal's movie monsters were becoming a convenient shorthand for real and perceived threats from abroad. Universal Studios became not so much a dream factory as a conveyor belt of nightmares, unleashing restive aspects of the collective American Id, with its troubled memories of European oppression and patrician decadence.

The British, who had been repelling foreign invaders since the days of the Spanish Armada, had their own fears along similar lines, of course. After all, it had been British writers who had created so many classic horror characters in the first place. One of these was Manchester-born Sax Rohmer, the creator of Fu Manchu, whom Karloff played for MGM in *The Mask of Fu Manchu* (dir. Charles Brabin, 1932). This film significantly places Chinese coolies inside Egyptian mummy cases in the British Museum. One of them stares out through eye-holes in the mummy mask, and the others even wear mummy costumes when leaping out of their sarcophagi to overcome Lawrence Grant's Sir Lionel Barton with chloroform. Similarly, *Charlie Chan in Egypt* (dir. Louis King, 1935) has the famous Chinese detective (played by Warner Oland) investigating the theft of antiquities from an Egyptian tomb. Such films eloquently demonstrate how the East in general was regarded as a melting pot of interchangeable exotic menace for the Western imagination. As Edward Said put it, the point of orientalism is "to characterize the Orient as alien and to incorporate it schematically on a theatrical stage whose audience, manager and actors are *for* Europe, and only for Europe."[12] When confronted in the British Museum by the suavely effeminate and entirely evil mummy of Rohmer's *Brood of the Witch Queen*, the hero, Robert Cairn, says in a savagely

Claudette Colbert in *Cleopatra* (dir. Cecil B. DeMille, 1934).

hoarse voice, "Before God! I will throttle the life from you!"[13] One can't help wondering if this resonantly racist revulsion was behind the similar line in Balderston's screenplay for *The Mummy* when Edward Van Sloan's Dr. Muller snarls at Im-ho-tep: "If I could get my hands on you I could *break your dried flesh to pieces*!" Both Rohmer and Balderston also mention the strange and unnerving effect on Westerners of incense and even orchids, which latter play a highly sinister role in *Brood of the Witch Queen*:

"I don't approve of orchids," jerked Cairn doggedly. "They are parodies of what a flower should be. Place an Odontoglossum beside a rose, and what a distorted unholy thing it looks!"

"Unholy?" laughed Myra.

"Unholy,—yes!—they are products of feverish swamps and deathly jungles. I hate orchids."[14]

(Rohmer's fear of exotic flora, incidentally, was shared by the makers of *The Werewolf of London* [dir. Stewart Walker, 1935], which features a frog-eating plant, whose means of mastication vaguely resembles the female reproductive organ, perhaps combining xenophobia with misogyny.)

The *Mummy's Hand*, coming, as it did, at a time when Europe was at war with Germany, presented a rather cruder set of propositions than had been the case with *The Mummy*. The heroes of the film are no-nonsense Americans (one rather more intellectual than the other) played by Dick Foran and Wallace Ford respectively, who in many ways anticipate Lou Costello and Bud Abbott's later encounters with Universal's mummy. After a good deal of exposition, featuring comedy dialogue and a stage magician (played by Cecil Kellaway) who eventually agrees to fund their expedition, they all set off to discover the tomb of the Princess Ananka. However, they're quite unaware that this has been guarded by the mummy of Kharis, which has been kept alive in a state of suspended animation for over two thousand years, waiting to destroy anyone disturbing the tomb. Kharis, we learn in a subsequent flashback, had fallen in love with the Princess Ananka, and as a punishment for this sacrilege had been buried alive, his tongue having been cut out beforehand to prevent him blaspheming against the gods. Kharis was played by Western star Tom Tyler (in his only horror film), but the real villain of the piece is George Zucco's Professor Andoheb. Andoheb's day job is curator of the Cairo Museum, but he is also the High Priest in charge of Ananka's tomb, so it's his responsibility to make sure that the desecrators of it are duly punished. He revives Kharis with an infusion of sacred Tana leaves and, together, they set to work.

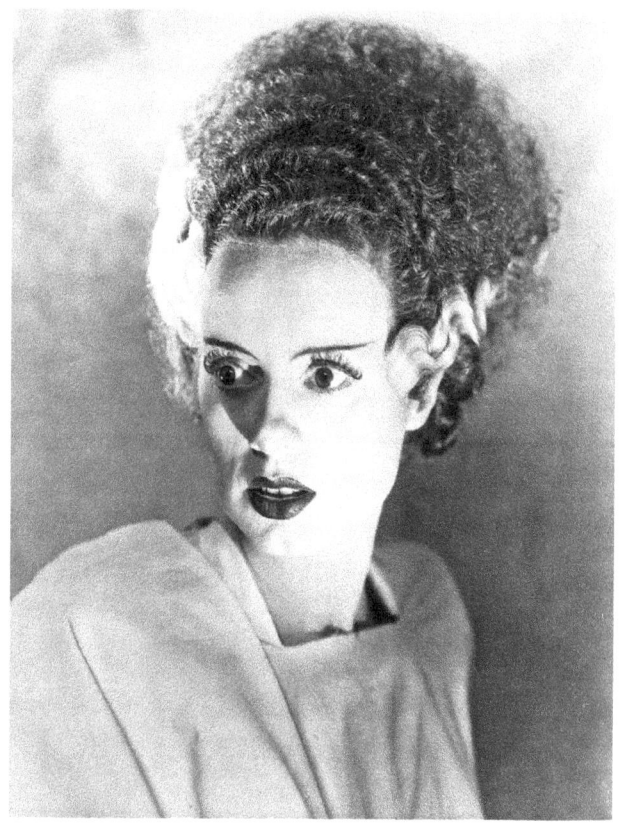

Elsa Lanchester in her Nefertiti-inspired make-up for *The Bride of Frankenstein* (dir. James Whale, 1935).

Eventually, of course, our heroes overcome both Andoheb and Kharis. The former is dispatched by the less intelligent of the two heroes, Babe Jenson (Wallace Ford), who threatens him, Wild West style, with his revolver. Ford's line "What are you doing here? Selling real estate?" tells us all we need to know about the level of the dialogue, but no matter how

Tom Tyler, as Kharis, carries Peggy Moran in *The Mummy's Hand* (dir. Christy Cabanne, 1940).

absurd the script may be, Zucco, like Peter Cushing after him, makes every word sound like Shakespeare. With his sepulchral timbre, physical stillness and inky-black, glittering eyes he is surely the best thing in the film. Supremely calm and collected, Andoheb doesn't flinch from Babe's revolver, but when he's shot he tumbles down an immense flight of steps and expires, gasping, "Mighty Isis, forgive me!"

The second best thing about *The Mummy's Hand* is Tyler's performance as Kharis, whose eyes were blanked out after the film was finished (he found the intended contact lenses too painful to wear). This process transformed his eyes into black holes of swirling, eldrich oblivion, far more frightening than the eyes of any subsequent mummy. Combined with his lurching limp, this Kharis is still the stuff of nightmares, and back inside the tomb (the decor of which we'll be returning to in a later chapter), the other hero, Steve Banning (played by Dick Foran) is about to come face to face with him. Peggy Moran's heroine, Marta Solvani (daughter of the magician who financed the trip), has been secured to an altar by Andoheb. Andoheb had planned to inject himself and her with enough Tana leaf fluid to make them both immortal, but with Andoheb dead, Kharis has no one to control him, and like a man dying of thirst in the desert he now makes his way slowly and painfully (Tyler had arthritis at the time, which no doubt only helped his performance) to the boiling bowl of Tana fluid. If he drinks it all in one draught he'll become a monster such as the world has never seen, but Banning manages to crush the life out of him before the final credits roll, to the relief of all concerned.

This basic formula continued throughout all three of Universal's succeeding mummy movies (*Abbott and Costello Meet the Mummy,* directed by Charles Lamont in 1955 was very much an afterthought), adding very little along the way. With America now enmeshed in World War II, the action of these films was rooted firmly on decent, dependable but distinctly xenophobic American soil (the respectable, if wholly fictional New England town of Mapleton), and the mummy became even more a mindless, robotic bogeyman with hardly any humanity about it. Lon Chaney, Jr., hated playing the character for that very reason, his predicament not helped by the inexpressive mask he was forced to wear, which prevented any characterization from seeping through.

It's revealing to compare the way in which Universal promoted their wartime mummy movies with government propaganda posters. The latter often share similar "horror" imagery, presenting the enemy as an inhuman monster. Clutching, shadowy hands, alternately emblazoned with a swastika and a rising sun threaten an American woman and child in G. J. Odell's incentivizing poster to "Buy the New Victory Bonds." The cover of Collier's Magazine for December 12, 1942, shows Arthur Szyk's image of a Japanese vampire bat, its epaulettes emblazoned with swastikas, about to drop a bomb on Pearl Harbor. But perhaps the most filmic poster of all is Bert Yates's two-headed monster attacking the Statue of Liberty, in an image reminiscent of King Kong assaulting the Empire State Building. One head is a helmeted Nazi with a Hitler mustache and bloody dagger in his hand. The other is a sneering Japanese with blood dripping from his fangs. "Stop this monster that stops at nothing!" the slogan urges beneath. "Murdering!" "Destroying!" similarly shriek the titles in Universal's trailer for *The Mummy's Ghost* (dir. Reginald Le Borg, 1944). "Nothing human tore through that wall," continues the dialogue. Universal's publicists had chosen to include the line "We've got to run it down!" for the earlier trailer to *The Mummy's Tomb.* "STOP *HIM* AND THE JOB'S DONE," urged another well-known poster from the same year (1942), showing a Japanese soldier taking aim at the viewer with his rifle. The line concerning "the bodies of freshly murdered men," included in the trailer for *The Mummy's Curse*, clearly resonated with what was going on in the real world at the time.

The Mummy's Tomb (dir. Harold Young, 1942) was quite correctly called an "arrant potboiler" by Leslie Halliwell,[15] but fortunately, George Zucco was still involved (he was only wounded, not killed by Babe's bullet in the previous film, we learn). However, by this time he's become so infirm that he's been forced to call on the services of a new priest, played by Turhan Bey, to do his dirty work for him. This is the origin of the character Mehemet Bey, who was to be resurrected by Hammer in their first mummy feature, along with the name of Banning, the legend of Ananka, and Kharis, of course. Steve Banning also appears in *The Mummy's Tomb* as does Babe (whose surname is now Hanson for some reason), but both of them are killed off by Kharis to avenge their desecration in the previous film.

Lon Chaney, Jr., in *The Mummy's Tomb* (dir. Harold Young, 1942).

Mehemet next takes a fancy to the innocent white girl who is due to be married to Banning's son. This segment of the story doubtless grew out of deep-seated fears of interracial marriage. Racial discrimination was still widespread in the United States at this time, and in England the threat of being raped by an Indian was still regarded as a fate worse than death. (Think of E. M. Forster's novel *A Passage to India* [1924] and the *Raj Quartet* of Paul Scott [1965–75], the action of which begins in the year *The Mummy's Tomb* was first released. Both novels have the rape of a white girl by an Indian as the principal motivation of their respective plots.) Anyway, Mehemet sends Kharis off to collect the girl for him, but the outraged people of Mapleton force the mummy and his victim to the Banning family home, which promptly goes up in flames. Somehow the girl survives, and so too does Kharis, for he still had two more movies to make.

The Mummy's Ghost followed two years later. In this one, Ananka's spirit is reincarnated in the body of Amina Mansouri (played by Ramsay Ames). She's a local girl, despite her name, who is convinced that something odd happened to her during a trip to Egypt; but it's not as odd as what happens to her in *The Mummy's Ghost*. John Carradine plays Yousef Bey, the latest disciple of Zucco's Andoheb, who certainly needs help as he is by now utterly decrepit and almost a mummy himself. Still mourning his lost love, Kharis carries off Amina, convinced she is the reincarnation of Ananka. The trouble is that Yousef Bey also wants to spend eternity with Amina, and Kharis is jealous. He quickly dispatches his rival and then tries to escape the (still) outraged people of Mapleton, who chase him and Amina to a swamp (another of Hammer's later borrowings), where he drowns and Amina disintegrates — so was she Ananka all along?

The final film in the cycle, *The Mummy's Curse* (dir. Leslie Goodwins, 1944), only confuses the matter. Continuing the swampy ending of *Ghost*, *Curse* now takes us to the swamps of Louisina. Somehow the New England swamp has oozed into a different state and Kharis with it. Andoheb has died, but his latest disciple, Dr. Ilzor Zandaab (Peter Coe), has discovered where Kharis languishes and has brought him back to life. Together, they set up home in a deserted monastery. Another weary flashback from the original mummy film reminds us of what no one surely needs reminding of again. Then, in the film's best scene, Ananka herself rises from the mud and Kharis sets out to gather her to his dusty bosom. The fact that we saw the mummy of Ananka crumble to dust in the previous film isn't something we should concern ourselves about too much. Perhaps this revenant is meant to be Amina? But she's played by a different actor anyway (Virginia Christine). Obviously, we're not invited to analyze the proceedings too rigorously at this point. She herself confesses that "sometimes I feel as though it's all part of a strange dream." How true. Ananka seems frightened by Kharis at any rate and runs away from him when he appears before her, but eventually Kharis manages to grab her and take her back to the monastery. Although Dr. Zandaab is delighted, his joy doesn't last long, as his sidekick, Ragheb (Martin Kosleck), stabs him, whereupon Kharis goes berserk and pulls the ruins of the monastery down around them.

Mummy's girl. Virginia Christine takes care of Lon Chaney, Jr., between takes for *The Mummy's Curse* (dir. Leslie Goodwins, 1945).

While this somewhat confusing Egyptian fantasy was being filmed, a much grander Egyptian epic was in preparation far across the Atlantic in England, where wartime conditions and the extravagance of its director, Gabriel Pascal, made what should have been a dream come true into something of a nightmare. Pascal had suggested a film version of George Bernard Shaw's play, *Cæsar and Cleopatra,* in 1943 as an ideal way for the British film industry to compete with Hollywood epics like DeMille's first version of *The Ten Commandments.* Such was Shaw's immense reputation at the time, J. Arthur Rank readily agreed. (It's well-nigh impossible to think of any film company contemplating a Shaw production today, so rapidly has his significance been eclipsed by the economic and political forces he spent his life attempting to overthrow. A remake of *My Fair Lady* perhaps? But what would be the point of trying to improve perfection?) Unfortunately, Rank didn't quite realize how expensive Pascal's suggestion would turn out to be. Its spiraling costs indeed anticipated the money-maelstrom of the Elizabeth Taylor *Cleopatra* twenty years later. Shaw himself predicted it would cost a million pounds.[16] In the end it cost Rank half as much again. Along with the staggeringly impressive Egyptian sets, the appearance of Ernest Thesiger as Theodotus provided another connection with the mummy genre, his performance in Shaw's play being no less eccentric than the one he gave for T. Hayes Hunter in *The Ghoul.* Vivien Leigh was an annoyingly coy and childish Cleopatra, initially under the thumb of her sharp-tongued nurse, Ftatateeta, played by Flora Robson, who would later appear in a couple of horror films, though, sadly, not of the mummy variety. The then-recently invisible and velvet-voiced Claude Rains was Caesar. Stewart Granger, who would discover King Solomon's Mines in 1950, played the rather contrasting role of the foppish carpet merchant, Apollodorus, and even the young Roger Moore, much later to wander around the ruins of Abu Simnel as 007 in *The Spy Who Loved Me* (dir. Lewis Gilbert, 1977), had a walk-on role as a spear-carrier.

Vivien Leigh as Cleopatra in *Caesar and Cleopatra* (dir. Gabriel Pascal, 1945).

Despite the stars on parade in Pascal's visually splendid though dramatically rather stodgy film, the real stars are the sets. This is somewhat ironic, as Shaw was always more interested in ideas than spectacle, and his play would have worked just as well — perhaps even better — if performed along stylized Brechtian lines. He himself had insisted to Pascal: "In Heaven's name, no Egyptian music,"[17] which is why we have what Shaw described as the "almost Handelian"[18] music of Georges Auric. If Shaw didn't want "Egyptian" music

Publicity poster for *Abbott and Costello Meet the Mummy* (dir. Charles Lamont, 1955).

one wonders why he put up with Pascal's outrageously ostentatious but carefully researched Egyptian sets. Built at Denham Studios in Buckinghamshire, they covered 28,000 feet. Thousands of extras were imported to populate the steps and colonnades, giving a sense of scale to the immense statues and buildings. Pascal also had his heart set on populating Cleopatra's garden with white peacocks but had to make do with the normal variety when he was told that the owners of the white variety refused to travel up to Denham with them for fear of air raids.[19] The huge Sphinx which opens the picture was actually constructed from papier-mâché, and very impressive it looks before its backdrop of astronomically accurate stars. (An astronomer was indeed employed to ensure that the constellations were correct.) Pascal even imported sand from Egypt, an absurd extravagance which became even more pointless when the delays caused by bad weather and the dangers of Hitler's V2 rockets made filming at Denham so difficult that Pascal took the entire production to Egypt itself. There, the fish-glue that varnished the soldiers' papier-mâché shields proved irresistible to the extras, who promptly ate them.[20] To have undergone all this during the latter stages of World War II is proof, if any is needed, of Shaw's overriding importance at the time; but the film was an immense flop. Even Pascal himself thought it boring.

Back in the Hollywood that Shaw loathed even more than conservative politicians in England, no one would ever have dreamt that such immense amounts of money could ever be spent on that much more modest Egyptian entertainment: the humble mummy movie. This proved to be a failure of the imagination, of course, but Brendan Fraser and the computer-generated images of Universal's remake of *The Mummy* (dir. Stephen Sommers, 1999) were a long way in the future. The mummy's appearance with Abbott and Costello in 1955 only proved that Universal had well and truly run out of ideas. With stereotype sinister Egyptians blowing poison darts, the dialogue rarely rises above the most minimal requirements, though there are some exceptions:

> BUD: I overheard Dr. Zoomer say he needed a couple of men to accompany his mummy back to the States.
> LOU: Is she afraid to travel by herself?
> BUD: His mummy is a he.
> LOU: [gasps]
> BUD: What's wrong with that? Some mummies are men, some mummies are women.
> LOU: It's a strange country.

The set designers, Alexander Golitzen and Bill Newberry, did at least come up with an attractive temple set in which dancers perform rather elegantly (though what they dance is typically Orientalist in the combination of a multi-armed Hindu god with elements of Turkish whirling dervish style). The priest who presides over this ceremony then administers what we presume to be distilled Tana leaves to the mummy of Klaris (no longer Kharis), who has been reduced to pantomime status.

It seemed that Kharis (let alone Imhotep) would ever come back to life again. That, as we know, was not to be the case, but before Christopher Lee's Kharis stirred from the ghoulishly green light of Ananka's tomb in Hammer's all-color version in 1959, Hollywood began to take a different approach to the subject of ancient Egypt. This was partly due to the political climate of the time, which was sullied by Senator McCarthy's Communist witch-hunts. Hollywood trembled as accusations of conspiracy and collusion with the perceived Soviet threat deprived many of Hollywood's great and good of their livelihoods. This sorry state of affairs was to have an unexpected benefit for Hammer films when the blacklisted director, Joseph Losey, was forced to seek refuge in England. There he made *The Damned* for Hammer in 1963 before going on to make a string of Dirk Bogarde classics; but for those left behind

Yul Brynner as Pharaoh in *The Ten Commandments* (dir. Cecil B. DeMille, 1956).

in Hollywood things became so strained and paranoia so intense that producers looked to safe subjects, and what safer subject could there be than the Bible? Hence the reappearance of the lavish Biblical epic. DeMille's lavish remake of *The Ten Commandments* is perhaps the most Egyptian of these, this time devoting its entire running time to the conflict between Moses and Pharaoh, as outlined in Exodus. Charlton Heston, who was later to return to Egypt in *The Awakening* (dir. Mike Newell, 1980), builds many a monument for Cedric Hardwicke's Pharaoh before leading the Jews to freedom as Moses, while Yul Brynner's perplexed and frustrated Rameses II tries to stop him. Despite the excellence of its stars, it is, again, the film's special effects, sets and costumes which steal the show. Inspired by the Victorian artists, Sir Edward John Poynter (1836–1919) and Sir Lawrence Alma-Tadema (1836–1912), such production values brought DeMille's earlier black-and-white vision of ancient Egypt to life in a series of Technicolor tableaux.

Some of the sets used in *The Ten Commandments* had actually been built two years earlier for *The Egyptian* (dir. Michael Curtiz, 1954), the only film adaptation of Mika Waltari's 1945 best-selling novel about Sinhue, an Egyptian physician who begins life as an orphan, abandoned in a reed basket on the Nile like Moses, and eventually becomes Pharaoh's brain surgeon. There are aspects to the production that make *The Egyptian* slightly different from standard Egyptian Epic fare. For a start, the film begins with shots of Egyptian antiquities as they were in 1954, effectively establishing a melancholy mood before cutting to a reconstruction of the pyramids and Sphinx at Giza. We are then shown a variety of street scenes, unusually depicting everyday ancient Egyptians going about their business amid domestic, vernacular architecture.

Sinhue (played in the film by Edmund Purdom) is a fictional character, though Waltari named him after an Egyptian text known as *The Story of Sinhue*, and the story is a pessimistic one in keeping with the war-weary mood of the time in which the novel was written. Having played Yousef Bey in *The Mummy's Ghost*, John Carradine now appears as a grave robber, and promoted from her small role as harp player in *Caesar and Cleopatra*, Jean Simmons has a much more substantial role as Meret, Sinhue's long-suffering girl friend. Unfortunately, she has a dangerous rival in Nefer, a scheming courtesan (played by Bella Darvi) who persuades Sinhue to give her not only all his own earthly goods but also to steal his parents' property and give that to her as well. She places his gifts and deeds in a coffer with a cat's head, symbolic of her catlike nature, and for all the laudable attempts at historical authenticity, the gathering at which Sinhue first meets her resembles a rather trendy 1950s house-party with low sofas, plenty to drink and plenty of sex going on discretely in dark corners. Shamed by his actions and full of self-loathing, Sinhue goes into exile with his servant (played by Peter Ustinov, in a similarly shifty though distinctly less regal role to that of Nero in *Quo Vadis* three years earlier); but Sinhue's skills as a wandering doctor bring him fame and fortune, so much so that the new pharaoh, Akhnaten (a softly-spoken Michael Wilding), becomes his patron. Akhnaten's pacifist views and forgiving nature exasperate his military commander, Horemheb (played by Victor Mature). However, Akhnaten refuses to allow Horemheb to attack the Hittites, who threaten Egypt, so Horemheb plots to overthrow him and destroy Akhnaten's visionary ideal of peace and brotherhood under one god. After the carnage and death of Akhnaten, Sinue is exiled for life by his old friend, now Pharaoh Horemheb.

The year 1954 also saw MGM take a less solemn approach to the commercial potential of ancient Egypt in *Valley of the Kings* (dir. Robert Pirosh). The trailer tells us all we really

Publicity poster for *The Egyptian* (dir. Michael Curtiz, 1954).

need to know. "MGM Goes to Egypt — Hollywood's first venture into the exotic land of the Pharaohs." That, at least, was true. No studio back lot or Californian scrub-land for this picture. *Valley of the Kings* was filmed "in the shadows of the pyramids." Inaccurately, the main title of the film is superimposed over a shot of the temple at Abu Simnel, but no one was really bothered too much about that. "One girl [Eleanor Parker] in a caravan of *men*," the trailer continues, teasingly. There's a "man of intrigue" (Carlos Thompson, with a cigarette), a "mysterious stranger" (Kirt Kaszna, in a turban) and a "desert chieftan" (Victor Jory, with a black silk face mask like the Red Shadow in *The Desert Song*). The voice-over continues:

> Ancient Egypt — birthplace of civilization, provides the spectacular setting for the years' wonder-show: *Valley of the Kings!* Here is a land: dangerous, mysterious, beautiful. In the crowded back alleys and age-old streets of its colorful cities begins the suspenseful search to discover a secret buried centuries ago during the time of the Bible. Into its vast desert burning sands rode a caravan led by a handsome adventurer and a flame-haired beauty. One girl among bold men, each desiring their own treasure — rare, forbidden.

ROBERT TAYLOR: You know what they say? Egypt is like a man without a woman.
ELEANOR PARKER: Why do they say that?
ROBERT TAYLOR: Hot by day, cold by night.
ELEANOR PARKER: That could apply just as well to a woman without a man.

They fight their hazardous way through intrigue and danger to learn the secret hidden in the tomb of a lost pharaoh. What was this secret — and how did it all start?

To encourage us to find out, the trailer lists the menu of Egyptian delights on offer: a desert sandstorm, a camel stampede, duels to the death, a "Dance of the Houri" performed by Egyptian belly-dancer Samia Gamal, and the "fabulous burial vault of the lost Pharoah" — all filmed in glorious Eastman Color. As Mendelssohn once said of Meyerbeer's opera, *Robert le diable*, there's "etwas für jeden" (something for everyone).[21]

In *Land of the Pharaohs* (dir. Howard Hawks, 1956), which was filmed partly in Egypt and partly in the Titanus film studios in Rome, Joan Collins played Princess Nellifer, who becomes the second wife of Pharaoh Khufu (a somewhat miscast Jack Hawkins). Khufu is obsessed with building an immense pyramid (also known as the Pyramid of Cheops) in which he intends to place all his treasure after he dies, but Nellifer has other ideas. First, she murders the queen and then does away with Pharaoh himself so that she can steal his treasure and be sole ruler of Egypt. Unfortunately, her crimes are discovered and, when she is invited by the High Priest to give the order to seal Khufu's mummy in its sarcophagus, she finds that she has also set in motion a sand-operated trap in the pyramid itself which seals all the exits from the tomb. Like Aida, Nellifer is buried alive, but unlike the priests in Verdi's opera, who walk about in the temple above Aida's tomb, the priests in the film are buried alive with Nellifer. Being mutes they are horribly silent as they stare accusingly at the cringing, desperate girl: a truly nasty way to die for an actress who would later play a similarly scheming role in *Dynasty*, the popular 1980s TV soap. It's a truly macabre moment, in which aspects of the traditional horror film combine with lavish Hollywood spectacle, pointing the way towards the *Indiana Jones* films and the resurrection of Universal's mummy franchise in 1999. The claustrophobic finale is undoubtedly the best part of the film, in which the actors merely provide an excuse for magnificent sets and costumes; but previous scenes spare no expense to bring us extras filling the screen like ants as they construct the pyramid. They wave their arms in the air and clap their hands to welcome the Pharaoh, maidens throw flowers in his path, soldiers blow war trumpets (their raucous bellowing appropriately replicated by Dimitri Tiomkin's poster-paint score), camels wander about looking rather bored, Pharaoh fights a bull, dancers entertain him and his queen, and there's a good old-fashioned

Bikini meanie. Joan Collins publicizing *Land of the Pharaohs* (dir. Howard Hawks, 1955).

sword fight between Pharaoh and his traitorous captain of the guard. When Pharaoh eventually dies, a gigantic bell in the shape of an ankh is struck, which mournfully announces, at last, the moment we've all been waiting for. Sand gushes from the ingenious engineering project of James Robertson Justice's architect, Vishtar, activating mighty blocks of stone to seal the burial chamber, and Joan Collins, in her figure-hugging, gold lamé robe, shrieks, "I don't want to die!" One thing worth remembering from the dialogue (and there's not much that's memorable in that department) are the words Nellifer uses to describe the "gift" she gives to Pharaoh's son Xenon (Piero Giagnoni). She calls it a "magic flute," and encourages Xenon to learn how to play it so that eventually a snake will be lured by its Oriental melody and, thus, dispose of Pharaoh's queen (who falls on it to protect her child). It's extremely unlikely that anyone had Mozart's opera, *The Magic Flute,* in mind when giving those words to the curvaceous Miss Collins, but they do set up a resonance with the Egyptian setting of that opera, the significance of which we will be exploring later. From the point of view of good old-fashioned Orientalism, however, it's appropriate that we also have a snake-charmer (and snake-charmer music) as part of the general mix. Tiomkin provides just what's needed here, and, indeed, attempts a somewhat operatic approach in general to the music, which includes choral music, clapping, marches (*Aida*-style) for the military parades and a good deal of general sonic *swagger.*

Thus was Hollywood's way with ancient Egypt in the mid–1950s. Back in England, it was inevitable that Hammer Films, having made such an impact with *Dracula* and *The Curse of Frankenstein,* should next turn its attention to *The Mummy*; but instead of following the Karloff/Freund approach, they took most of their inspiration from the Universal sequels. Crucially, though, they placed the action in the 1890s and most of it takes place in England, thus making clear the genre's debt to late–Victorian/Edwardian fiction, and distancing its approach from the American models in terms of overall style, if nothing else. Stephen Banning was now played by Felix Aylmer, and his son, John, by Peter Cushing. Joseph Whemple (Raymond Huntley) also turns up and together they discover the tomb of Ananka (again). Ignoring the warnings of fez-wearing Mehemet Bey (George Pastell) that death will visit all who desecrate the tomb, they press on. Once inside the tomb, Stephen Banning reads the words of life, the mummy (Christopher Lee) is revived (though we don't actually see this happening until a later flashback) and Banning is understandably driven insane by the shock. Quite why Mehemet doesn't have done with Banning there and then, instead of going to all the trouble of following him back to England and only then getting Kharis to do what he could so easily have done in the tomb, is one of the plot's unanswered questions; but that's exactly what happens. Mehemet raises Kharis from the swamp into which he's fallen, thanks to a couple of drunk and nervous carters, and then crashes through the windows of Banning's padded cell (a situation that Hammer would repeat in *Blood from the Mummy's Tomb*) before stomping back to Mehemet's sinister residence to await his next murderous mission.

Meanwhile, John Banning sorts through his father's papers in the elegant family home (a set remarkably dressed by the ever-resourceful production designer Bernard Robinson and lit to perfection by Hammer's brilliant cinematographer Jack Asher). He tells the legend of the Princess Ananka to Whemple (and any members of the audience who never saw the Universal films), which leads to the first flashback, taking us back to ancient Egypt. There, in sumptuous Eastman Color, Kharis, distraught with grief, dares to resurrect the dead

Christopher Lee's Kharis consigns the handmaidens of Ananka to death in *The Mummy* (dir. Terence Fisher, 1959).

princess for whom he grieves. Hammer didn't actually show his tongue being cut out (the camera observes the process from behind Lee's back), but we do see him being mummified and entombed alive.

The rather pointless revenge plot continues when Whemple is finished off, and then the only person left is Banning himself. The mummy's first attempt is foiled when it's distracted by the similarity of Banning's wife, Isobel (played by Yvonne Furneaux), to the Princess Ananka. "She was considered the most beautiful woman in the world," Banning explains. "Mind you," he adds, "the world wasn't so big then." And so, he lays in wait for the mummy to return, which it surely does, carrying off Isobel, whom it takes back to the swamp, though quite what it plans to do with her is left to the imagination. (Lee himself pondered "the impossibility of such a poor old monster having a love life, owing to the bandages and his mouth bring sewn up."[22]) Banning and the police follow frantically, and though Kharis previously survived being skewered by a spear (Cushing felt that the publicity poster showing a beam of light shining through a hole in the monster's chest needed explaining, and so incorporated this bit of business into the proceedings himself), the mummy can't withstand an assault of gun fire. Expiring more from a broken heart than any bullet, having been rejected by Furneaux' Isobel/Ananka, he sinks beneath the swamp never to return.

Visually, *The Mummy* is one of Hammer's most sumptuous productions. Its elaborate sets (in particular the Egyptian tomb of Ananka and Banning's elegant study) set a very high standard, but it's not perhaps Hammer's most engaging film in terms of plot, as it's really no more than a series of murders committed by Christopher Lee's mummy, whom Leslie Halliwell summed up as "a muddy expressionless creature which moves rather faster than usual."[22] That's not really fair to Lee, who manages to combine an unnerving sense of something having been reanimated and now quite unstoppable (rather than the usual impression in other mummies, that it's just an actor in bandages) and his eyes are the most expressive eyes of any movie mummy after Karloff's. Apparently, the eye-holes of his skin-hugging make-up were the only orifices through which he could breathe, perhaps adding an extra element of desperation to his expression.[23] Having said that, the plot lacks momentum, as much of it is spent rather pointlessly second-guessing Eddie Byrne's policeman who has the thankless task of solving a mystery that's no mystery at all to the audience. We all know that the mummy is the murderer, so Byrne's role is largely redundant. George Pastell, in the role of Mehemet Bey, is also nowhere near as sinister as George Zucco's Andoheb, and his conversation with Cushing's Banning comes rather late in the plot (such as it is) as by this time there's absolutely no doubt that he keeps a reanimated mummy in his living room. Even so, in terms of performance alone, this atmospheric and elegantly performed duel of words is one of the most interesting scenes in the film:

BANNING: I made an extensive study of this so-called religion. It's based on artificial creeds and beliefs, some of them ludicrous in the extreme.
BEY: Did it ever occur to you that beneath the superficial you've learnt about there could be a great and passionate devotion to this god.
BANNING: It occurred to me but I dismissed it.
BEY: You're intolerant, Mr Banning.
BANNING: Not intolerant, just practical.
BEY: Intolerant. Because you are unable to experience the greatness of a deity, you dismiss it as of no consequence; but believe me, to those who worship and serve Karnak he is all powerful.
BANNING: Surely there can't be people who still have such beliefs?
BEY: Now you talk about something of which you know nothing. You've scratched only the surface and you know nothing. You assume the right to disturb the everlasting peace of the gods. You pry and meddle with unclean hands and eyes. Profanity, blasphemy, religious desecration: all these you are guilty of, but the powers with which you have meddled do not rest easy. I think you will not go unpunished.
BANNING: Punished? By whom?
BEY: There are certain things for which civilization has no answer, but if you choose to meddle thus, then you must be prepared to face the consequences, whatever they are.
BANNING: Consequences? That sounds like a threat.

The Mummy was released on September 25, 1959, by which time only three years had passed since the Suez crisis when British troops had invaded Egypt to help prevent President Nasser's plan of nationalizing the Suez Canal. One can't help feeling that screenwriter Jimmy Sangster had rather more sympathy for Mehemet Bey than the arrogant, interfering and intolerant emissary of the British Empire, John Banning. Just as Kharis in *The Mummy's Hand*, had a limp, it is now Banning who is crippled, a lame dog, still trying to rule the world. Though played with great charm by Peter Cushing, Banning nonetheless proves to be the real villain of the piece. That he emerges triumphant at the end of the film only goes

Cover illustration by Brian Lewis for *Hammer's Halls of Horror* magazine, vol. 2, no. 10, July 1978 (courtesy House of Hammer © Quality Communications 2011).

to reinforce his dominant position, especially as his wife turns out to be a reincarnation of the princess for whom Kharis committed sacrilege, had his tongue cut out and was buried alive. Not only has Banning desecrated Ananka's tomb, he's also stolen the woman for whom Kharis sacrificed everything.

Things might have been more interesting if the script had been filmed as Sangster had originally envisaged it — at least, this is what the British magazine *Hammer's Halls of Horror* suggested in its comic-strip adaptation of the movie. This magazine was always keen to point out that its adaptations were based on the original scripts, not the completed films, so some interesting variations appear in its pages. In the comic-strip version, Banning sensibly visits Mehemet Bey rather earlier on (directly after Stephen Banning is murdered, in fact). The door is not answered by Mehemet but by Kharis, who is unbandaged and dressed in the kind of galabia that Karloff wore in the first Universal mummy film. "What are you doing at the door? Get away from there!" Mehemet shouts from behind,[24] before explaining that his "servant" is a deaf-mute. Artist David Jackson later shows us Mehemet Bey rewrapping Kharis to prepare him for his next murder; but that's not the last we see of the unwrapped mummy. He's there again in part two of the adaptation, wandering about Mehemet's hall in his robe as the doorbell rings, announcing Banning's second visit.

Sadly, this interesting opportunity for Lee to add another dimension to his performance failed to materialize, but the film in general offers other visual compensations. Apart from the general splendor of the sets and costumes, Terence Fisher also managed to create a sense of anguish and terror by the simple device of slanting the angle of the camera when Stephen Banning realizes that the mummy is on its way to murder him. It's a device that was sent up in the American *Batman* TV series (1966–68) starring Adam West in the title role, but in 1959 it provided a novel visual *frisson* and still has the power to unnerve. Of course, the other major trump Fisher had up his sleeve was color. There had been plenty of colorful Egyptian epics but there had never been a mummy movie in color before, and Fisher made sure that Ananka's tomb glowed a lurid green, that the swamp was an unhealthy shade of rust and blood, and that all the golden artifacts on display glittered as never seen in a horror film before.

Hammer's *The Mummy* no doubt drew some of its life from the popularity of the Egyptian epics we've already mentioned, but it also initiated a new wave of movie Egyptiana. Just after the release of *The Mummy*, an Italian epic purported to tell the story of Cleopatra's daughter, but even in the prologue immediately after the main title of this film it's obvious how much we're about to fly in the face of historical fact:

> Cleopatra, after the civil war that followed the assassination of Caesar met Anthony in Syria where they planned the defense of Egypt against the Romans. Before leaving, Cleopatra entrusted her young daughter, Shila, to the rulers of Assyria to be brought up as their own. After Marc Antony's defeat and Cleopatra's death, Egypt for the next twenty years was torn apart and ruled by a youthful Pharaoh Nemorat, with his despot Queen Mother, Tegi, who desired to strengthen both kingdoms and strengthen her son's rule by conquering Assyria and making Shila, now a beautiful woman, his queen.

It's true that Cleopatra had a daughter. In all, she had four children: Caesarian (with Caesar) and (by Marc Antony) Cleopatra Selene, Alexander Helios and Ptolemy Philadelphus, but there was no Shila, despite Debra Paget's performance of her. (In fact, Cleopatra Selene and Alexander and Ptolemy were taken to Rome after their mother's suicide and cared for

A frame from the comic strip adaptation of *The Mummy* (dir. Terence Fisher, 1959) by Steve Moore, with artwork by David Jackson from *Hammer's Halls of Horror* magazine, vol. 2, no. 10, July 1978 (courtesy House of Hammer © Quality Communications 2011).

by Marc Antony's wife. Later Selene married King Juba II of Numibia.) Neither was there a Pharaoh Nemorat (Corrado Pani) at this period of Egyptian history, but the sets and costumes of *Il sepolcro dei re* (a.k.a. *Cleopatra's Daughter*, dir. Fernando Cerchio, 1960) were certainly colorful. In 1961, Cerchio brought us *Nefertiti — Queen of the Nile* in which Edmund Purdom, last seen in an Egyptian setting as Sinhue in *The Egyptian*, is transformed into

Tumos, a sculptor, who falls in love with the daughter of a High Priest called Benakon, who is played with pale-faced severity by none other than Vincent Price. Benakon, however, has other plans for his daughter, eventually to be known as Nefertiti, whom he wants to marry Pharaoh Akhnaten (Amedeo Nazzari). Tumos is therefore thrown into prison, but fortunately is not killed, and so is later able to escape, work his way into the pharaoh's court and eventually sculpt the famous portrait bust of Nefertiti, now in Berlin.

After all that, the stage was well and truly set for that ultimate Hollywood epic, *Cleopatra,* in 1963, which cost Twentieth Century–Fox $44 million. The huge publicity surrounding the affair of the film's principal stars, Elizabeth Taylor and Richard Burton, during the troubled filming of this immense spectacle was of rather more interest to audiences than the love affairs of the characters they played. Originally intended as two films, the resulting four-hour marathon isn't quite what the screenwriters originally had in mind (i.e., one film for Caesar and Cleopatra, another for Cleopatra and Marc Antony) but it's certainly spectacular, which is surely the film's basic *raison d'etre.* Cleopatra's palace, Cleopatra's golden barge, Cleopatra's exotic costumes, and Cleopatra's staggering entry into Rome on a gigantic Sphinx pulled by an army of Nubian slaves have never been bettered in any film since. Of course, it's all a very different proposition to a mummy film, despite the shared Egyptian background, though there are some soothsaying sequences, with priests flaring the flames of sacred fires, which add a superficial element of magic (or at least belief) to the proceedings.

Publicity poster for *Carry on Cleo* (dir. Gerald Thomas, 1964).

Amanda Barry applies her Cleopatra make-up for *Carry on Cleo* (dir. Gerald Thomas, 1964).

With hindsight, it's interesting to see Andrew Keir as Agrippa some eight years before he took over grief-stricken Peter Cushing's role as Professor Fuchs in *Blood from the Mummy's Tomb*, and it's amusing to observe the young Richard O'Sullivan as Ptolemy fondling a white cat much as would Blofeld in the James Bond films (though we can thank Guy Boothby's Dr. Nicola character for the idea of a super-villain with a cat). Rex Harrison's Caesar calls Elizabeth Taylor's Cleopatra a "descendent of inbred mental defectives" but nonetheless falls for her particular charms, as does Richard Burton, of course, in a story too familiar to need much reiteration. The script has some nice touches, even so. When Lotus, one of Cleopatra's servants (played by Jacqui Chan), is discovered having tried to poison the queen, she begs for forgiveness. Cleopatra replies, "I forgive you. Now drink it."

The staggering amount of money that Twentieth Century–Fox spent on *Cleopatra* inspired British producer Peter Rogers to send up the whole affair in *Carry on Cleo* (dir. Gerald Thomas, 1964) for a tiny fraction of the cost and in a mere six weeks. Another major incentive was that all the lavish sets that had been built for the Burton/Taylor epic at Pinewood Studios in Buckinghamshire had been abandoned when Fox took the production to Rome, and Rogers simply couldn't resist making use of them for next to nothing. This good fortune, coupled with another series of sets left over from a failed production of a play about Caligula in London's West End, made *Carry on Cleo* one of the most visually extravagant of all the Carry On films. Classical Rome, of course, vied once more with Egyptian decor in this comic version of the famous story which was released in the year that Hammer started work on their pseudo–Egyptian fantasy, *She* (dir. Robert Day), with its melange of ancient Roman, Assyrian and Egyptian elements. Two years later, Rogers decided to send up Hammer films as well. He and James Carreras, head of Hammer, knew each other well. "You make the comedy," Carreras used to say to him. "I'll make the horror."

"It may have been unfair that I tackled his line of business," Rogers admitted, "but he was perfectly free to put Matron Has Risen From the Grave into production. I certainly wouldn't have minded."[25]

One scene from *Carry on Screaming* briefly sends up the mummy genre. A mummy case (with distinctly Assyrian features) decorates the creepy drawing room of Dr. Orlando Watt (played by Kenneth Williams, who does his very best to impersonate Peter Cushing).[26] When the police come to investigate what's been going on, they stop to admire the ancient artifact.

"Ah, gentlemen," says Williams' Watt, "I see you are admiring my pharaoh. He was the founder of the fourth dynasty you know. King Rubbatity. I've often thought how fascinating it would be to make him live again. I bet he could tell a thing or two, eh?—all those barge orgies on the Nile. No wonder they kept finding things in the bullrushes." Later Rubbatitty does indeed come back to life, his mummy-case struck by lightning, and he drives Watt into the cellar where he drowns in the vat of fluid that transforms young women into shop-dummies, shrieking "Frying tonight!" as he goes under.

Back at Hammer's Bray Studios, they were taking their mummies rather more seriously, but with Kharis shot to pieces in a swamp, and Christopher Lee unwilling to endure the physical discomforts of performing the role of the mummy again, it was left to Dickie Owen to animate the bandages of Hammer's next mummy, Ra-Antef, in *The Curse of the Mummy's Tomb*, which appeared the same year as *Carry on Cleo*. This epic was directed by Michael Carreras, who had even grander ambitions for Hammer than his father, and while his attempts to put them into practice in this film were interesting, something was missing. This turned out, most of the time, to be the mummy itself, which doesn't do anything for quite some considerable time. Set in 1900 (a few years after the action of *The Mummy*), things get off to a flying start. During the main titles, the camera roams around the dusty artifacts of Ra-Antef's tomb, some of them re-cycled from Ananka's tomb in the earlier film, and we're then shown stock footage of a real desert (unlike the obvious studio backdrop of its predecessor). This lasts only a few moments, though, as we soon cut to another of Hammer's studio-bound deserts. Before being murdered, the leader of the expedition, Professor Dubois (Bernard Rebel) has his hand cut off (*Curse of the Mummy's Tomb* is rather partial to severed hands, a motif that would return in *Blood from the Mummy's Tomb*), and when we're introduced to the rest of his expedition team we discover that they've all set up camp in the tomb itself. This, as we shall see, was quite a common thing for 19th-century archeologists to do, from the great explorer Giovanni Belzoni onwards. So far, so good.

We then have the pleasure of watching Hammer stalwart Michael Ripper blacked up and saying, "Hussain, you are too quick. You are your mother's son," when the contents of the tomb are removed prior to their being shipped back to England. The social mores of the time had, of course, no problem with a British actor impersonating an Egyptian. Neither

Michael Carreras (right) consults Egyptologist Andrew Low during the filming of *The Curse of the Mummy's Tomb* (1964).

did it have any problem with actor Ronald Howard (brother of the more famous Leslie) casting racial slurs such as "We know all about your ways" to George Pastell's Hashmi Bey, who, despite the obligatory fez, is no more than a benign red herring in this one. The sarcophagus of Ra-Antef is then raised into a packing case with a pulley-and-rope system similar to that used by Howard Carter in the tomb of Tutankahmen. Indeed, Carter's discovery is obviously the basis of this film. There's a curse (of course) and an aristocrat (Sir Gyles Dalryple, played by Jack Gwillim), who, like Lord Carnarvon, dies halfway through the action. The mummy is also "road-showed," as the brash American impresario Alexander King (Fred Clark) puts it, just, indeed, as Tutankhamen's artifacts were taken on tour in the late 1970s. (Nowadays, reproduction artifacts attract less discerning but no less enthusiastic crowds.)

The ancient Egyptian back-history of *Curse of the Mummy's Tomb* concerns the troubled relationship of two immortal brothers. The mummy of the title is one, while the other masquerades as a wealthy playboy who calls himself Adam Beauchamp (Terence Morgan). He can only find eternal rest by being slain by his bandaged brother. This is why Adam summons the mummy back to life by means of a magical amulet and then keeps him in the cellar of his elegantly appointed London residence. Significantly, like Terence Fisher before him, Michael Carreras went to just as much trouble to recreate the atmosphere of Victorian England as that of ancient Egypt in this film. He lingers on details, such as a sumptuous cut-glass decanter stopper, just as much as he does on the impressive array of Egyptian relics on display. Carreras's penchant for the lavish spectacular might have been limited for budgetary reasons in the Egyptian scenes, but he did manage some lavish camera work on board the ship that brings the artifacts back to England, in which we move from the porthole of Professor Dalrymple's cabin right up to the top of the ship's deck in a single take. There's also an expensive-looking silver punch bowl on display in Adam Beauchamp's London flat, plenty of champagne, and in the early scenes set in the tomb a lavish banquet, complete with candelabra. There are also some satirical moments amid the mayhem and period elegance. A monkey gobbles a box of Turkish Delight (a name we are unsuccessfully persuaded to believe was invented by Alexander King himself), and Ronald Howard's character also pretends to scare the pretty Jeanne Roland by holding out his hands and intoning, "The only real physical danger you may be in is not from the mummy but — from — ME!" (The heroines of Hammer's first two mummy films, incidentally, were both played by French actresses, perhaps in acknowledgment of Napoleon's contribution to Egyptology.) There are also some prescient words about the British education system, when Dalrymple complains that "if money is to be the yardstick by which the value of education is to be assessed, I fear for the future." How true!

Eventually, after more comedy (the carter from the first Hammer mummy film, played by Harold Goodwin, appears as one of King's assistants during rehearsals for the unveiling of the mummy) the mummy itself, at long last reanimated, appears at the top of a flight of steps. Breathing heavily (no other mummy is quite so asthmatic), it attacks King as he is on his way home. The sound of foghorns before the mummy's threatening appearance adds immeasurably to the sinister effect of the swirling yellow fog here. It's a perfect expression of Egyptian Gothic. Yellow, incidentally, is the film's primary color. Adam Beauchamp's underground lair is decorated with golden-yellow wallpaper, and the heroine is seen wearing a golden-yellow dress, all of which suggest something of the decadent "yellow" '90s of late–Victorian England with its *Yellow Book* and penchant for yellow-bound French novels.

More murders happen, as they must. Dalrymple has his head crushed by the mummy, as does Hashmi Bey, who, mortified at the sacrilege, offers himself as a willing sacrifice to the mummy's foot. The heroine is also placed in danger when Adam Beauchamp reveals to her who he really is and then commands his mummified brother to dispatch her as well. But, of course, she is saved in the nick of time and in the expensive sewer set where everyone ends up, the mummy causes the roof to fall in, drowning both itself and his evil brother.

Though the mummies of Hammer's four films on the subject varied, the props often returned (a sensible economic measure), and so in the next film, *The Mummy's Shroud* (dir. John Gilling, 1967), we meet the same amulet we encountered in *Curse*. There it had brought Ra-Antef back to life. In *Shroud* it serves as the royal seal of the pharaohs and permits the head slave Prem (Dickie Owen) eventually to become Pharaoh himself. This is necessary as he has to be mummified somehow, and a slave would hardly have been granted such an honor. Prem has taken the son of Pharaoh into the desert to save him from an insurrection. (The voice-over insists that the desert is a place of scorching heat, but it actually looks rather damp as it was all filmed in a sandpit near Gerrards Cross in Buckinghamshire.)

An unusual still from *The Curse of the Mummy's Tomb* (dir. Michael Carreras, 1964) showing Dickie Owen's mummy being reanimated by Terence Morgan's Adam Beauchamp (actually the mummy's immortal brother, Be).

Unfortunately, the boy dies and Prem buries him in the sand, first placing the shroud of the film's title over the body. This is important, as the shroud has the words of life embroidered upon it, and soon after André Morell's Sir Basil Walden discovers the tomb the shroud is being used to put the mummy to work.

The living Prem is played by Dickie Owen, who had been the mummy in the previous film, but Prem's mummy is played by Eddie Powell — a rather confusing state of affairs. The film also features another Keeper of the Tomb, in this instance played (perhaps with rather too much relish) by Roger Delgado, who turns in a politically incorrect "filthy Arab." No western suit and Fez for him. Instead, the London-born Delgado appears in full desert costume. The only people wearing a fez in this film (apart from the hotel receptionist) are the police — always an encumbrance in horror movies which really can't stand too much ratiocination. Sir Basil is bitten by a snake, Cleopatra style, and later collapses in the Restoration House, where all the artifacts are stored prior to being sent to the museum. There we encounter the mummy case we saw in *The Curse of the Mummy's Tomb* along with a kneeling figure supporting a shallow dish, also from the previous film, which now stands on a table in front of the mummy of Prem. Delgado's Hasmid is soon at work intoning the words on the shroud and sending Prem off to dispatch the desecrators one by one.

Prem's mummy, rather more frightening than the one in *Curse*, was based on a genuine mummy still to be seen in the British Museum, and the curse that propels the plot is again derived from what the world's press concocted when the tomb of Tutankhamen was discovered around the time in which *The Mummy's Shroud* is set. Eventually, the mummy finishes off Michael Ripper's Longbarrow, the put-upon assistant of the expeditions' financier, Stanley Preston (John Phillips). Ripper's performance here provides the film's most moving moment, conveying in under a minute of screen time all the loneliness of home-sickness. He wakes up after an afternoon nap, accidentally breaks his glasses, anxiously splashes water on his face and is then hurled out of the window by Prem in the most brutal manner: an innocent victim of circumstances indeed. Preston's murder soon follows, his head crushed to pulp by the mummy, and Prem eventually crushes his own head to pieces, thanks to a hitherto unspoken passage in the shroud's spell which orders him to commit suicide, if such a thing is technically possible for a reanimated corpse.

Though there's nothing new in the story or underlying meaning of this film, director John Gilling does manage to create a suitably claustrophobic atmosphere by carefully lighting his confined Cairo street sets, shooting them through lattice-screens and from different heights and angles. The set designer also went to some trouble when decorating the den of fortune teller Haiti (played with toothless relish by Catherine Lacey). Here is a gypsy whose very name exudes voodoo associations. She's the proud owner of an expensive crystal ball which rests on a tablecloth embroidered with astrological sigils. There are also tarot cards, a black jackdaw in a cage, incense, a weird skull-like dummy, and a beaded curtain. (It no doubt inspired the decorative scheme of many a student dorm room.) Anyway, in a broom-cupboard adjacent to Haiti's consulting room, Hasmid has a shrine, dominated by the statue of Anubis, which we will later see decorating the hall of Professor Fuchs's London home in Hammer's next, and most interesting, Egyptian fantasy. It's not quite such an impressive broom-cupboard as that of Mehemet Bey in Hammer's first mummy film, but it serves the same purpose. Interestingly, the least impressive set of *Shroud* is the actual tomb of Ra-Antef itself. This is basically no more than an improvised pit in a cave: the "earliest form of mummification," as Sir Basil points out when uncovering the mummy that has been preserved in nothing more than sand for 4,000 years. Much more money must have been spent on the 1920s-style black marble hotel set in which so much of the action takes place.

Hammer's mummy cycle advanced in correct chronological order. By the time of *Blood from the Mummy's Tomb* things were brought completely up to date (as far as the original audiences were concerned), the action having been transported to the 1970s. *The Curse of the Mummy's Tomb* may have accessorized Adam Beauchamp's basement with Egyptian curios, but in *Blood from the Mummy's Tomb* portions of Queen Tera's tomb have been reconstructed in a suburban cellar, and the mummy is there with it. Unlike all the others, this mummy is the perfectly preserved body of an evil Egyptian queen who plans to return to life in modern London. Stoker's story had been rather more faithfully adapted from the novel by British Independent Television in 1970 as part of its *Mystery and Imagination* series, though (presumably for financial reasons) it located the recreation of Tera's tomb not in a cave off the coast of Cornwall, but in Trelawny's London home. (One of the mummy cases on display in Trelawny's study in the ITV production also looks extremely like the one we see in Hammer's *The Curse of the Mummy's Tomb*. One wonders if they had borrowed it.) Entitled *The Curse of the Mummy*, it starred Isobel Black as Margaret Trelawny.

Eddie Powell as the mummy of Prem in *The Mummy's Shroud* (dir. John Gilling, 1966).

(Black had played the thoroughly evil Tania in Don Sharp's *The Kiss of the Vampire* for Hammer in 1963 and would go on to play the entirely good Ingrid Hoffer in John Hough's *Twins of Evil* in 1971. In this Egyptian tale she was called upon to be both good and evil in one character.) Graham Crowden was her father, Abel Trelawny, and Patrick Mower appeared as her fiancé, Malcolm Ross, who has now become a G.P., absorbing the role of Stoker's Dr Winchester. Guy Verney's direction is unfortunately pedestrian, and John Russell Taylor's script is extremely wordy with consequently little action; but Stoker's novel is similarly cerebral, which is no doubt why screenwriter Christopher Wicking felt he had to spice up the action in his adaptation for Hammer. The somewhat confusing prologue of *The Curse of the Mummy*, set in ancient Egypt, suggests that Malcolm Ross is also a reincarnation, as we see Patrick Mower with a shaven head indulging in a kind of Egyptian Liebestod with Tera in a tomb that resembles an Egyptianized London Underground station. At the end of the story, Malcolm has survived the ordeal and is looking forward to marrying Margaret — who we then see standing behind him as Tera in full Egyptian rig, thereby cleverly conflating Stoker's two alternative endings. To date, this version remains the only dramatization of *The Jewel of Seven Stars* that shares the Edwardian setting of Stoker's novel.

When Hammer decided to adapt the same novel the following year, a different title was chosen. According to Christopher Wicking, this was the result of a brainstorming session, in which all the various permutations of mummy titles were put on a list to find the most appropriate and eye-catching combination.²⁷ *Blood from the Mummy's Tomb*, left out the one word which characterized its production for it was a truly cursed picture. As is well known, Peter Cushing, who was to have starred in it, had to withdraw when his wife, Helen, died; Wicking was then banned from the set by producer Howard Brandy; and director Seth Holt, whose first name made him a singularly appropriate choice for a mummy movie, died from a heart attack before the film was finished, forcing Michael Carreras to supervise the missing footage.

Wicking added plot elements of his own, involving three characters who had nothing to do with Stoker's novel. These were the team members of the expedition led by Professor Fuchs (Stoker's Trelawny), who jointly discovered Queen Tera's tomb. They were played by Rosalie Crutchley, George Coulouris and Hugh Burden, each of whom possesses a relic from the tomb, which they guard with their lives until Tera claims them back, killing each one off in turn. Andrew Kier, replacing Peter Cushing at the last minute as Fuchs, isn't sure if Tera's spirit plans to take up permanent residence in Margaret's body or merely return to her own perfectly preserved corpse. At the end of the film, Tera does indeed come back to life and attempts to strangle Margaret, who, it would appear, has been merely a waiting room for Tera's spirit; but Margaret stabs Tera and we're left in some doubt as to which one has survived after the film's final cataclysm, when we are shown a bandaged woman, eyes staring wildly as though buried alive.

Both Tera and Margaret were played with cleavage to the fore by Valerie Leon who was extremely well-qualified in that department, even if not always able to prevent her cleavage from rhythmically rising and falling when playing Tera lying dead in her sarcophagus. This has the unfortunate consequence of suggesting that Tera has come back to life

Queen of Cleavage. Valerie Leon as Queen Tera in *Blood from the Mummy's Tomb* (dir. Seth Holt, 1971).

somewhat prematurely. Leon also has to deliver some of Stoker's original dialogue, which sits rather uncomfortably in the otherwise contemporary setting. To be fair, in this context most actors would have difficulty with this bit of dialogue: "I get a feeling of great loneliness, of her dreaming alone of things far different from those around her. No scheming and malignant priesthood or endless rituals of death: a land where love is the divine position of the soul."

"That'll be the day," her boyfriend, replies, wrenching us back to the present day. Having said that, the boyfriend (played by Mark Edwards) is the namesake of Universal's *Dracula* director, Tod Browning—a backward-looking glance if ever there was one.

At the risk of imitating one of the flashbacks of Universal's mummy series, which kept recycling old shots of Karloff as Im-ho-tep, I'd like briefly to reprise what I've already discussed in my earlier book, *Touchstones of Gothic Horror,* concerning the incestuous theme of *Blood from the Mummy's Tomb.* One shot in particular sums up this subtext. Andrew Keir manages to convey all of Fuchs' pent-up desire in a single expression when, as he leans over Tera's mummy midway through the film, he almost licks his lips in anticipation of the delights to come. He's then struck down by the spirit of the Egyptian queen, who might well be said to represent his own *psychological* guilt, just as Corbeck, played with ruthless charm by James Villiers, represents Fuchs' alter-ego and his desire for power. (Graham Crowden's Trelawny in the TV *Curse of the Mummy* is similarly besotted, kinkily kissing Tera's severed hand before he places it back in its box; and whether intentional, a Freudian slip, or just an actor's mistake, it seems significant that at one stage Donald Churchill's Corbeck refers to Trelawny as "Corbeck.")

Incest is an introverted, secretive passion, so it's appropriate that *Blood from the Mummy's Tomb* so often dwells on confined or secretive places: the padded cells and corridors of a lunatic asylum in which one of Fuchs's expedition party is incarcerated; Fuchs' underground study; the deserted suburban streets with their clipped hedges and dark windows; the dusty, packing case-filled museum room where Hugh Burden's Geoffrey Dandridge works as a curator of Egyptian artifacts. Even the empty house occupied by Corbeck is locked up, boarded up and put up for sale (courtesy of "Neame and Skeggs"—the names of the film's two producers, masquerading as otherwise unseen estate agents). Together, these creepily confined spaces create an appropriately claustrophobic atmosphere that's a perfect metaphor for this incestuous tale.

Fuchs is obsessed with his secret passion. Only Corbeck is brave enough to contemplate the sexual forces he's unleashed. Corbeck accuses Fuchs of being too frightened to face up to his true feelings, fascinated by the source and nature of Tera's power whilst trying to keep the evil bottled up. "All you've done is sit in here and play games," he says. "Wouldn't it be fun if it were all true? Well, it is true, undeniably so, and you are scared. Every waking moment you are scared; but she's made you see, hasn't she? Tera has given you a warning: 'Don't let me down. Don't try and back out or you are dead.'" (The TV production presented a completely reversed state of affairs. Trelawny is the crazed fanatical figure, while Corbeck desperately wants to escape. At the climax of the proceedings he even holds up a crucifix over Tera's mummy!)

Only when it's too late does Fuchs face up to the truth: that Margaret, under the influence of Tera, is responsible for the death of her own boyfriend, Tod. The unfortunate Tod has intruded on the love affair between father and daughter/ancient queen, and must, therefore, pay the price. Neither Margaret nor Fuchs want to accept the truth about their incestuous feelings for one another. When Tera comes to life at the end of the film, Margaret tries to kill her, but she's really killing herself; and then Tera kills Fuchs. Significantly, Margaret's mother dies in childbirth. Her only function, it seems, was to give birth to the daughter Fuchs loves so much more than her. Although Margaret's mother survives childbirth in *The Awakening*, Mike Newell's very underrated version of the same novel, her psychological redundancy is made crystal clear. When Margaret is born in Newell's film, her mother (played by Jill Townsend) realizes all too clearly how little she counts in the scheme of things. "You weren't there," she recalls in the hospital when her husband comes to visit her after a difficult childbirth. Indeed, the professor was simply too busy with Queen Tera (now called Kara) to bother about a merely mortal woman. Newell's version steps up the incestuous undercurrent in a later scene, set in Kara's tomb, which Corbeck and Margaret have visited in order to find the missing canopic jars that are a vital element of the resurrection ceremony. Standing on the vaginal steps that lead down to the womb-like burial chamber, Margaret stares insolently at her father. "She murdered her father, didn't she?" she whispers, the spirit of Queen Kara having temporarily taken her over. "She hated him." Then, she kisses her father passionately on the lips. Understandably, Corbeck is very unnerved.

As if to clarify Hammer's suggestion that Fuchs and Corbeck are two sides of the same coin, Newell's film combines both roles in one. The Egyptologist played by Charlton Heston in *The Awakening*, is called Professor Corbeck (and anyway, by 1980, the name Fuchs would probably have raised knowing titters). Queen Tera also becomes Queen Kara, for less apparent reasons. When Heston's professor enters Kara's tomb, Newell suggests that he is guilty of a kind of rape, especially when he intercuts this scene with shots of Corbeck's wife suffering her first birth pangs.

The Awakening had various problems to solve for a 1980s audience that had moved on from the Edwardian world that still lingered in *Blood from the Mummy's Tomb* for all its then-contemporary setting. In Stoker's 1903 novel, Professor Trelawny has shipped the contents of the tomb to his palatial residence in Kensington Palace Road. That was believable in 1903, when an English Egyptologist had a great deal more power than he would have today. It was always a little difficult to accept that such a thing would have been possible in 1972, as by then the Egyptian authorities would surely never have permitted such a thing; but there's a certain timelessness about Seth Holt's direction of *Blood from the Mummy's Tomb*, despite Mark Edwards' sports car and Valerie Leon's kinky boots. Andrew Kier's Professor Fuchs wears traditional tweed three-piece suits, complete with a watch chain, and the suburban house in which much of the action takes place is sufficiently Edwardian for us to overlook the impossibility of Fuchs ever having been allowed out of Egypt with an entire tomb in his suitcase. Low budgets, after all, never stopped Hammer from mounting costume dramas, so the only explanation for the 20th-century setting of *Blood from the Mummy's Tomb* must have been the desire of the filmmakers to emphasize the juxtaposition of ancient and modern, as well as East and West, which lies at the center of Stoker's complex novel.

This problem is only amplified by the ruthlessly up-to-date 1980s setting of *The Awakening*. To accommodate this with the needs of the story, various changes had to be made. Fuchs is given an ankh-shaped mirror from the tomb he has discovered, as a gesture of appreciation from the Egyptian government, but he *steals* the canopic jars that he needs for the occult ceremony he plans. The ceremony itself takes place neither on the Cornish coast, as in the book, nor in the cellar of a suburban villa, but rather in the British Museum itself where the mummy has more believably been brought for safe keeping. Such details may seem superficial, but they are, in fact, vital, as it is essential that Egypt is brought to England for the story to work.

When Stoker's novel was filmed for the third time in 1997 by Jeffrey Obrow as *Bram Stoker's Legend of the Mummy*, the action was transferred to contemporary America, but confined mostly to the Egyptologist's atmospherically claustrophobic home. This made the likelihood of a house full of Egyptian artifacts in the present day perhaps less believable. However, for all its late–20th-century American context, this version is in many ways more faithful to Stoker's book. The names of many of Stoker's characters are retained, so we have a Sergeant Daw (Mark Lindsay Chapman), who is fond of recalling his days at Scotland Yard; the housekeeper is still called Mrs. Grant (played sympathetically by Mary Jo Catlett); and the Egyptologist is finally known by Stoker's original appellation of Abel Trelawny. Corbeck, however, has become black and, as somewhat manically played by Lou Gossett, Jr., distinctly deranged. In homage to Hammer's version, Aubrey Morris, who played the role of Dr. Putnam in *Blood from the Mummy's Tomb*, reprises the role here, but as Dr. Winchester, again faithfully following Stoker's novel. There are some atmospheric artifacts on display, some effective flashbacks to ancient Egypt and an impressive resurrection scene, but having said all that, Obrow was less successful than Hammer always was in disguising a low budget (a deficiency not helped by the perfunctory electronic score by Rick Cox). There's also a rather hurried pace and some inappropriate comedy scenes involving Richard Karn which, in the final analysis, make the film was rather less successful than either of its two predecessors.

Soon after *Blood from the Mummy's Tomb*, traditional Gothic horror went out of fashion. Hammer bravely updated Dracula on two occasions in the early 1970s and tried new approaches to old subjects, but no one could find a scroll of life to resurrect the movie mummy. Egypt itself became a mere backdrop for increasingly more mainstream genres. When Vincent Price's Dr. Phibes went there in *Dr. Phibes Rises Again!* (dir. Robert Fuest, 1972), he took up residence in the (wholly fictional) Temple of Iviscus, through which flows the river of life. This eventually grants him immortality and restores to life his dead wife, Victoria (played mutely by Caroline Munro). Hugh Griffith, as Harry Ambrose, mentions the Book of the Dead, and Price (in one of his most convincing — though equally high-camp — performances as a completely insane psychopath) resembles a resurrected mummy himself. The Egyptian element, however, is merely decorative, but by transforming the interior of the temple into a kind of Art Deco auditorium, designer Brian Eatwell pointed out yet another connection between Egypt and the cinema in terms of architecture and interior design.

As well as the location work already mentioned with regard to *The Spy Who Loved Me*, production designer Ken Adam came up with a witty set for the interior of an Egyptian tomb in which Military Intelligence have set up an operations base. Lois Maxwell's Miss Moneypenny sits at her desk with ancient Egyptian wall paintings and hieroglyphics behind her. (Valerie Leon even appears at one point as a hotel receptionist, bringing with her an echo of her role as Margaret Fuchs six years earlier.) The Agatha Christie novel, *Death on the Nile,* offered obvious picture-postcard opportunities for John Guillermin's 1978 film

Vincent Price as the hideously disfigured Dr. Anton Phibes in a romantic pose with Virginia North as Vulnavia *The Abominable Dr. Phibes* (dir. Robert Fuest, 1971). The make-up indeed resembles that of many a mummy, a horror role Price never otherwise played.

adaptation with Peter Ustinov as Hercule Poirot, but the story could just as easily have been played out on the Thames for all the relevance it has to ancient Egypt.

BBC television, however, had kept the spirit of ancient Egyptian fantasy alive in a *Doctor Who* serial in the autumn of 1975. Conspiracy theorists have long suggested that the geological phenomena in the shape of pyramids on Mars are evidence of life on that planet, and that the ancient Egyptians were taught how to build pyramids by visiting Martians. *Doctor Who*'s "Pyramids of Mars" took a slightly different approach, arguing that after a cosmic battle, Horus imprisoned Sutekh, or Set, in a pyramid on Mars, thus preventing him from destroying the universe. Both gods belonged to a race known as the Osirians, who were the extraterrestrial inspiration behind ancient Egyptian myth and ritual.

"Pyramids of Mars" in fact reworks many elements of previous mummy movies, and mixed them with a dose of science-fiction. The paralyzed, incarcerated Sutekh (played by Gabriel Woolf) plans to build a missile (in the shape of a pyramid) with the enforced help of a human servant and a gang of three service robots. The missile, built on earth, will be aimed at Mars to destroy the Eye of Horus — a glowing scarlet egg-shaped device that keeps Sutekh in eternal bondage in his pyramidal prison. A Victorian Egyptologist, Marcus Scarman (played by Bernard Archard), is killed by Sutekh, who then reanimates him as his servant. As Tom Baker's doctor puts it, Scarman is an "animated human cadaver," and therefore

Tom Baker as Doctor Who in "Pyramids of Mars" (dir. Paddy Russell, 1975).

something of a mummy himself. Following Sutekh's orders, the service robots (who assist him in the building of the missile) stomp around the surrounding woodland in the guise of bandaged mummies, and terrorize a game-keeper in roughly the same way that the preface to this book describes such an encounter. Much of the action takes place in Scarman's Victorian Gothic mansion (the exteriors of which were actually the Stargroves Estate in Hampshire, then the home of Mick Jagger). Like the residence of any self-respecting archeologist in a Hammer film, this mansion is filled with Egyptian artifacts and adorned with the barley-sugar Solomonic columns so often employed by Hammer's principal set designer, Bernard Robinson. (A further echo of Hammer is provided by Bernard Archard who had played Professor Heiss in *The Horror of Frankenstein* [dir. Jimmy Sangster, 1970].) In the first episode, Scarman's mansion is occupied by an equally creepy Egyptian by the name of Ibrahim Namin (played by Peter Mayock). Like Georges Zucco and Pastell before him, Mayock is togged out in 19th-century Western dress and a distinctive red fez. Namin also proves to be something of an organ virtuoso like the Phantom of the Opera and even Dr. Phibes. As he plays his eerie rhapsody (courtesy of composer Dudley Simpson) at the impressive instrument in the corner of the mansion set, the three mummy robots stomp in to worship the sarcophagus of Sutekh, which is actually a tele-porter device. Unfortunately for him, Sutekh can't avail himself of this useful piece of kit as he's paralyzed, but both Scarman and the doctor pass through it. Eventually, however, when the Eye of Horus is destroyed by means other than the missile (which is successfully sabotaged), Sutekh is released from his bondage and at last enters the tele-porter. Needless to say, the Doctor manages to prevent his entry into the world and thus the universe is saved once again.

"Pyramids of Mars" is an entertaining summation of four decades of mummy movies and an interesting reworking of the Egyptian mythology that inspired them. Certain of its ideas were reworked by Brian Hayles, who had also been a writer for *Doctor Who*, in his screenplay for *Warlords of Atlantis* (dir. Kevin Connor, 1978). In the under-sea world of the Atlanteans, we observe Peter Gilmore's scientist, Charles Aitken, wander through the Egyptian-cum-Aztec architecture of this aquatic master-race in the company of Cyd Charisse and Daniel Massey, who play Atsil and Atraxon, the leaders of the elite. Sadly, Peter Cushing hadn't been available to play Atraxon, but Massey does a perfectly adequate job in explaining how the Atlanteans have inspired humanity to develop its technology. They hope to harness the neutron power that mankind will ultimately develop and thus escape the confines of the Atlantic ocean. Previously, Atsil explained how their predicament came about:

> From our dying planet, we journeyed across space. We brought our cities, our way of life, our power and ambition. A comet wrecked our charted course. Thrown into the gravitational field of your planet, we fell into the life-preserving waters of the ocean above us but we found ourselves trapped, slowly decaying in this alien world — a world so primitive and so retarded that it had barely developed intelligent life forms. Only by ordering the destiny of that world could we have hoped to escape.... We are a master-race. We control, we manipulate. We of the red planet will not soil our hands with blood.

So, these (only vaguely Egyptian) Atlanteans are also Martians. The triangular doorways of their citadel nonetheless suggest they may have had something to do with the construction of the pyramids.

British television had a couple more cards to play along these lines. One of them was Simon Raven's revival of Sexton Blake in a story concerning another ancient Egyptian deity. *Sexton Blake and the Demon God* entertained Sunday tea-time audiences during September and October of 1978 with Blake's quest to find the Marvel — the jewel-encrusted, Gorgon-like mask of an ancient god last seen by an ancient Egyptian soldier called Tu Fu Edas. Tu Fu Edas was present at the parting of the Red Sea when he fell into a cave and discovered the Marvel. Anyone who wears it is given the power of imposing his will and ruling the world. When the mummy of Tu Fu Edas is transported to England by Flinders Petrie and ends up in the British Museum, it attracts the attention of a Levantine millionaire and Egyptologist by the name of Hubba Pasha (played by Derek Francis), who steals it. He forces a young British woman into his traveling harem, intending to sacrifice her to the god. Tinker, Blake's trusty assistant (played by Philip Davis), manages to save her from certain death, and in the nick of time, Tinker is himself saved from being sacrificed by Sexton Blake (Jeremy Clyde), whom the Marvel reveals to be the real Chosen One, not Hubba Pasha. "For endless centuries I have sought the one honest heart," the Marvel explains, after Blake declines to use the mask for world domination. "I thought I had found him more than once — the dragon-slaying George and a king named Arthur, but none could match thy stature and thy deeds, Oh Valiant Sexton Blake."[28]

Sexton Blake and the Demon God signaled the end of the 20-year British dominance of low-budget film and television fantasy. *Star Wars* (dir. George Lucas, 1977) had exploded like an atom bomb the previous year, the cultural fallout of which mutated the film industry forever. Like the Death Star of Peter Cushing's Grand Moff Tarkin, *Star Wars* put an end to the way Hammer, Amicus, the BBC and independent television had been producing fantasy so imaginatively and for so long. In its place, the big-budget, American-made blockbuster ensured that things would never be the same again. Having said that, Egypt continued to inspire films that appeared in this new context. *Raiders of the Lost Ark* (dir. Steven Spielberg, 1981), one of the most interesting of the new breed, featured an Egyptian-style Ark of the Covenant and a race against the Nazis to discover it, in a superior chase movie which nonetheless tackled a long-held scholarly preoccupation concerning the true nature of the Ark and its connection with ancient Egyptian religion. As audiences of *The Ten Commandments* will know, Moses was saved from death at the hands of Pharaoh by being hidden in the bullrushes by his mother. He is discovered by Pharaoh's daughter, who fortuitously (but unknowingly) employs Moses' mother to nurse him. Moses is raised in the court of Pharaoh and presented as the son of Pharaoh's daughter, but he eventually turns against the Egyptians to lead the Jewish people to freedom. The connection between Egypt and Israel personified by Moses (a name of Egyptian origin) is presented in stark terms of good and evil in the Bible. Egypt is considered an abomination and the diametrical opposite of everything for which the Israelites stand. God delivers his ten commandments and then further commands Moses to construct an Ark in which to house them. Exodus XXV describes the Ark in some detail. It is made from "gold, silver and brass, blue, and purple, and scarlet, and fine linen, and goats' *hair,* and rams' skins dyed red, and badgers' skins, and shittim-wood." Onyx-stones and oils are also involved. Measurements are given ("two cubits and a half *shall be* the length thereof, and a cubit and a half the breadth thereof, and a cubit and a half the height thereof. And thou shalt overlay it with pure gold." Staves held in place on each side

The glittering Ark of the Covenant discovered by Harrison Ford's Indiana Jones in *Raiders of the Lost Ark* (dir. Steven Spielberg, 1981).

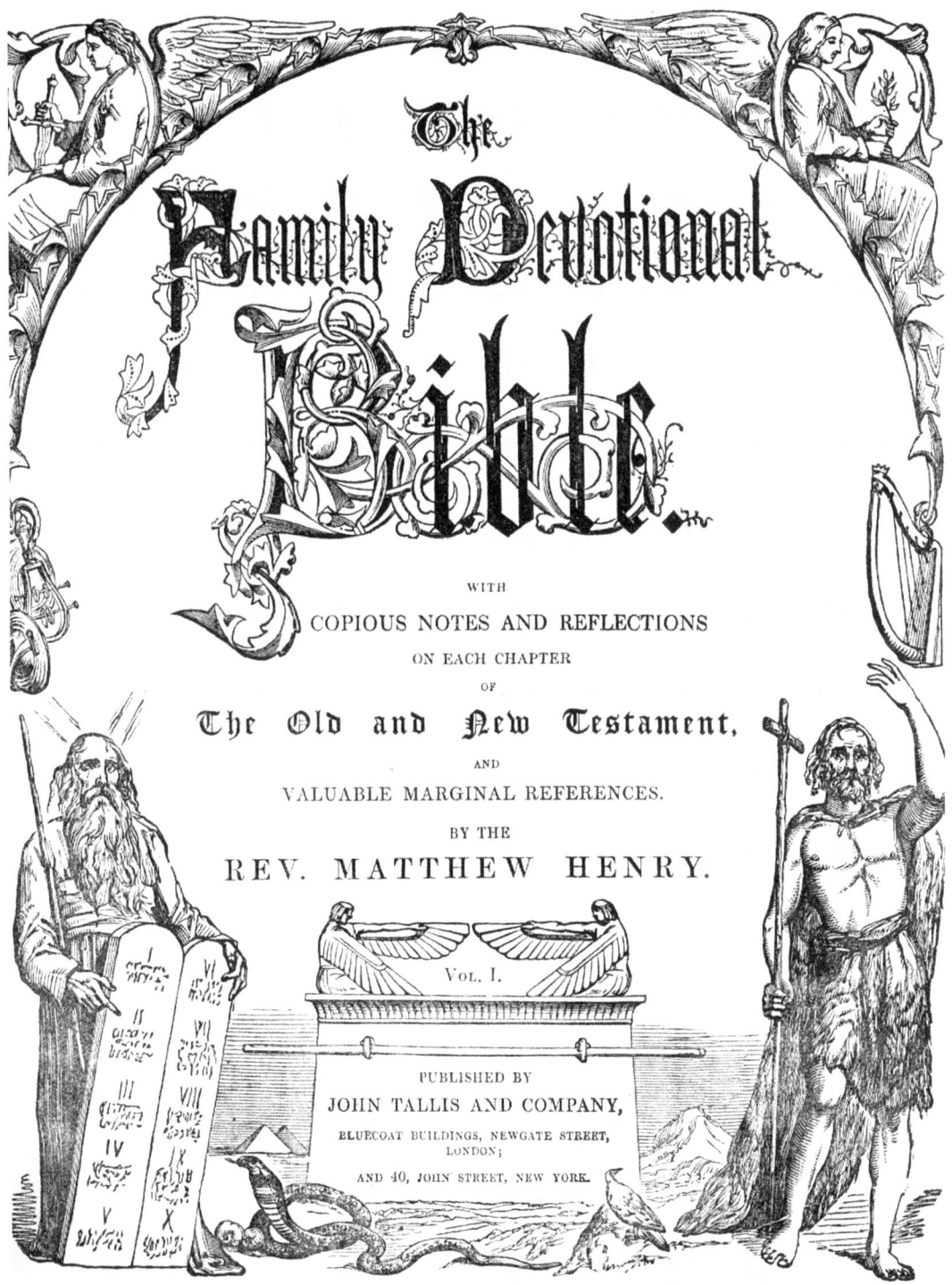

Title page of *The Family Devotional Bible*, edited by the Rev. Matthew Henry (London: John Tallis, 1852).

by gold rings permit it to be carried. There is also a mercy-seat on which stand two cherubs who "stretch forth *their* wings on high, covering the mercy-seat with their wings, and their faces *shall look* one to another." The Bible is not specific with regard to the *style* of the Ark, though it has often been represented in an ancient Egyptian manner. The title page of the Family Devotional Bible, edited by the Rev. Matthew Henry, published in 1852, depicts the Ark in decidedly Egyptian terms, with pyramids in the background and a snake writhing before it. *Raiders of the Lost Ark* similarly represents the Ark as an Egyptian object, and follows what the first-century Jewish philosopher, Philo, had to say about its mystical properties. Philo described the Ark as the abode of God which contained the secrets of creation.[29] As such, it had immense power. It could demolish city walls, spread disease among one's enemies, and kill anyone who touches it inappropriately.[30] Spielberg's Ark similarly has devastating supernatural power. It blasts the Nazis who assemble around it in the film's finale and famously melts the faces of the principal villains.

Given the Nazis' well-documented interest in the occult, the powers of such an Ark, if it could be found, would have been a priority. Of course, there was no such expedition during World War II, as the film suggests, but the Nazis' interest in the concept of Vril — the mystical force invented by Edward Bulwer-Lytton in his 1871 science-fiction novel, *The Coming Race*, suggests a justification for the film's supposition. Willy Ley, the Nazi rocket engineer, described in his article "Pseudoscience in Naziland" (1947) that the "Vril Society" of Berlin were indeed searching for Bulwer's fictional force.[31] Quite how far, if at all, Hitler himself believed in such things is debatable because so little evidence remains. The most serious of the students of Nazi occultism, Nicholas Goodrick-Clarke, dismisses the possibility. Others do not, and films like *Raiders of the Lost Ark* only further fuel the controversy.

Roderick Grierson and Stuart Munro-Hay suggest that Philo may have incorporated elements of the Egyptian Isis cult in his account of how the Ark was used in the Jewish Tabernacle ritual which Philo called the "Mystery of Aaron."[32] This Egyptian connection is further strengthened by the similarity of the Bible's description of the Ark to the rectangular chest with a gabled lid, also designed to be carried on long poles, that was found in the tomb of Tutankhamen. A similar object is depicted in the wall reliefs in the tomb of the grand vizier Mereruka, at Saqquara, discovered by Jacques de Morgan in 1893. Grierson and Munro-Hay even suggest the possibility that Moses, brought up in the Egyptian court of Pharaoh as we know, may have been influenced by the monotheistic worship of Aten, with which Pharaoh Akhnaten had overturned Egyptian society in the 18th dynasty. As the celebrated *Hymn of Akhnaten* has been credited as the basis of Psalm 104, it seems a possibility worth considering. Grierson and Munro-Hay are not alone in such a supposition. The Greek grammarian, Appion, believed that Moses was an Egyptian priest who promulgated the Egyptian sun cult to the Jews. Pompeius Trogus even suggested that Moses brought Egyptian mystery religion to Jerusalem and brought with him "sacred objects of the Egyptians," which may, of course, have included the Ark itself.[33]

Raiders of the Lost Ark certainly has its roots in historical conjecture if not in fact. *Sphinx* (dir. Franklin J. Schaffner, 1981), on the other hand, used Egypt merely as an exotic backdrop in a story that pit archeologist Lesley-Anne Down against black-marketeers in present-day Cairo. *Young Sherlock Holmes* (dir. Barry Levinson, 1985) was much more imaginative, involving an Egyptian cult called the Rametep. This cult is bent on murdering a group of British business men who have shipped the mummies of five princesses to England.

The Egyptian temple set in *Young Sherlock Holmes* (dir. Barry Levinson, 1985).

In revenge, the cult murders four of the five men and builds a gigantic, visually splendid Egyptian temple in London's Wapping district, in which they mummify their female victims. As the girls are wrapped in bandages we are reminded of Boris Karloff and Christopher Lee enduring the same torture as Im-ho-tep and Kharis, respectively. Then, when the embalming fluid flows from its boiling vat through the orifices of a monumental statue, Kenneth Williams' famous line, "Frying tonight," from *Carry On Screaming* also comes to mind. Holmes disrupts the ceremony by sending the central chandelier of the temple set crashing down on the ceremonially robed cult members, echoing the famous chandelier scene in *The Phantom of the Opera*. Director Levinson also manages to include belly dancers, snake charmer music and men in turbans in this affectionate and sensitively made tribute not only to so many Sherlock Holmes movies but also to the horror traditions of Hammer and Universal at their best. (There's even a splendidly Gothic cemetery scene.) Touchingly, Nicholas Rowe, who played Young Sherlock, was interviewed alongside Peter Cushing (a fine Holmes himself) on the BBC TV *Wogan* show on March 19, 1986, further emphasizing the connection between two cinematic eras of Egyptian fantasy and Holmesian detection.

Stargate (dir. Roland Emmerich, 1994), to which we'll be returning in chapter three, revealed, somewhat along the lines of "Pyramids of Mars," that the ancient Egyptians were really extraterrestrials, who arrived on earth through the Stargate of the title, which is a portal through time and space. Taking a similar sci-fi (or rather hi-tec) approach, Thames Television included a five-part ancient Egyptian story, "The Rameses Connection" (dir. Roger Gartland), as part of its relaunched series of *The Tomorrow People* in 1995. Originally a hit in the 1970s, this new series updated the action to the 1990s, though nonetheless relied on tried-and-true formulas. For a start, "The Rameses Connection" featured Christopher Lee in the title role. Dressed in somewhat 18th-century manner, Lee's Rameses masquerades as an industrialist by the name of Sam Rees, much as his Dracula had hidden behind the persona of D. D. Denham in *The Satanic Rites of Dracula* (dir. Alan Gibson, 1974). Also highly reminiscent of D. D. Denham, Sam Rees sits behind a desk in his penthouse at the top of Canary Wharf tower in London. An elevator brings the young hero into his august presence much as it had ushered Peter Cushing's Lorrimer van Helsing into the infernal presence of the arch-vampire in Gibson's film. "I'm not the King of Horror!" Lee later insisted to an interviewer who once suggested that he was, but if Lee ever thought he had escaped his horror image, this series categorically proved that he hadn't. Not only does he dispatch his enemies with fire from his ruby-glowing eyes he also utters lines he hardly needed to memorize, so familiar they must have been to him by then: "You have served me faithfully," You have failed me," "It has begun," "Good evening," "Leave me!" and "You are doomed to die." At the end of the affair we see him enthroned in full pharaoh garb, just as he had been dressed all those years before as Kharis in *The Mummy*. "The Rameses Connection" replays a variety of other mummy film clichés. Everything begins in the British Museum during a thunderstorm. We then visit Cleopatra's Needle on the Thames embankment. (Guy Boothby, as we shall see, was the first to place this landmark in the context of ancient Egyptian fantasy, in his 1898 novel, *Pharos the Egyptian*.) Cleopatra's Needle is more than a backdrop, though. Along with seven other ancient Egyptian obelisks now in various parts of Europe, it forms a kind of transmitter station, echoing the shape of the eight-starred Amtoudi constellation. When these stars come into alignment with the obelisks, immense power from the combined and focused starlight of the constellation will permit Rameses to regenerate his immortality. (Apparently, his immortality requires a bit of a boost, along the lines of Kenneth Williams' Dr. Watt, though it's not advisable to probe the logic of the plot too deeply). Adding one star to Stoker's constellation of seven, and conflating the result with Rider Haggard's *She* is yet another way in which "The Rameses Connection" recapitulates a century of ancient Egyptian fantasies. Rameses, like Queen Tera is wholly evil and aims, again like D. D. Denham/Dracula, to create a new world order with himself very definitely in charge. The teleporting Tomorrow People (enthusiastically played by Kristian Schmid, Christien Tessier and Naomi Harris) are aided by an old woman (Elizabeth Spriggs) and three Alice in Wonderland–style stooges, who form the weirdest part of the proceedings, cavorting, as they do, around the steps of the British Museum dressed in a red raincoat, a Tweedledumesque school uniform and a rag doll costume. It's never explained exactly who they are or why they behave as they do, but they obviously represent the power for good that is an irreverent attitude. Occult theories about pyramid power, fashionable when *The Tomorrow People* was first dreamt up in the 1970s, also form part of the mix. Indeed, the pyramidical roof of Canary Wharf tower is revealed to be Rameses' penthouse headquarters, where he observes plot developments in a pyramidal version of a crystal ball. We teleport over to Cairo for a few scenes and explore a hidden tomb, before eventually finding out that Tutankhamen was apparently a Tomorrow Person himself, desperate to reclaim the mystical crystal in which Rameses hopes to store his star power. ("An intelligent lad," Rameses explains, "but interfering." So he killed him. "It was necessary," Lee intones with a self-justifying shrug.)

As if all that wasn't quite enough for a star wearied unto death by his horror roles, Lee

Patricia Velasquez, as Anck Su Namun, strides through Allan Cameron's spectacular golden setting in *The Mummy* (dir. Stephen Sommers, 1999).

later turned up (if only briefly) in *Talos the Mummy* (dir. Russell Mulcahy, 1998). This once more revived the idea of an ancient curse and a diabolical reanimation. The action was divided between Egypt and London, as of old, but as a whole *Talos* failed to capture the atmosphere of Hammer and Universal at their best; *Prince of Egypt* (dir. Brenda Chapman, Steve Hickner, 1998) told the story of Moses in terms of a DreamWorks animation, and then, of course, Universal remade *The Mummy* with Brendan Fraser in 1999. By that time, the Victorian and Edwardian models which had inspired the original seemed a long way away and post-modern irony took over. The opening scenes set in a gold and glittering ancient Egypt are by far the best, not least due to Arnold Vosloo's magisterial Imhotep, which he played absolutely straight, but this was ancient Egypt for Generation X, packed with CGI effects, little romance, and hardly any attempt at historical accuracy. Among the many historical howlers are claims that the pyramids are situated at Thebes not Giza, that the Book of the Dead was used to reanimate mummies, that there was a corresponding Book of the Living, and that cats were guardians of the underworld, etc., etc. But that's nothing new, as mummy movies have never been exercises in academic Egyptology. In *Brood of the Witch Queen*, Sax Rohmer, after all, had suggested that the Book of Thoth had the power of life and death. What made the inaccuracies of *The Mummy* in 1999 so different to its predecessors, however, was the almost complete lack of belief the film had in its own fantasy.

In 2003 the mummy genre was truly overhauled in Don Coscarelli's *Bubba Ho-Tep* in which Bruce Campbell's Elvis Presley and a character played by Ossie Davis who claims to be John F. Kennedy (apparently not killed by that bullet) take on the eponymous mummy while residing in a nursing home for the elderly. On most levels more absurd than any mummy movie ever made, Coscarelli had, of course, a serious point to make about contemporary society's obsession with youth, its callous indifference to old age and the fact that all of us turn into the living dead in the end. Mummies are, after all, the ultimate old-age pensioners, dependent upon the revenue supplied by the mostly young audiences of their movies if they are to survive in the modern world.

Mummy movies, however, are only the most recent manifestation of the West's troubled fascination with ancient Egypt, and there is much to gain by placing this particular category of horror film in a broader cultural context. Reflecting, as it does, the West's own troubled soul, its anxieties, its guilt and its dreams, the culture of ancient Egypt has offered alternative aesthetic inspiration to architects and art nouveau designers. It has also stimulated artists, stage designers and composers of ballet and opera, while its esoteric wisdom has influenced occultists and theosophists, nearly all of whom interpreted Egypt in ways that would have seemed bizarre to the ancient Egyptians themselves.

All that will come later. To discover what's been going on and *why* it's been going on for so long, we must begin with a few words on the birth of Egyptology itself and the factual events which gave birth to so much fantasy.

Two

Egyptology

Although the study of ancient Egypt gained huge momentum in the 19th century, European fascination with the Valley of the Kings, at least, can be traced back to the writings of the Roman historian Strabo and Greek writer Diodorus Siculus, both of whom were active during the 1st century A.D. Their descriptions of the Valley of the Kings formed the foundation stones of the much later developed science of Egyptology. Strabo also refers to the area as a "spectacle worth seeing,"[1] so one might also claim him as the father of today's mass tourism industry. The rather more obvious fascination of the pyramids and the Sphinx stretches back into prehistory, and both of these ancient monuments have provided ample opportunities for speculation among later writers. Thomas Mann's plunge into the mists of time at the beginning of his Biblical tetralogy, *Joseph and His Brothers,* includes this rumination on the Sphinx:

> At the edge of the Libyan desert, near Memphis, hewn out of the rock, crouched the colossus and hybrid, fifty-three meters high; lion and maid, with a maiden's breasts and the beard of a man, and on its headcloth the kingly serpent rearing itself. The huge paws of its cat's body stretched out before it, its nose was blunted by the tooth of time. It had always crouched there, always with its nose blunted by time; and of an age when its nose had not been blunted, or when it had not couched there, there was no memory at all.[2]

The Bible is notoriously vague about Egypt and it is impossible to identify the particular Pharaohs encountered by Joseph and Moses in Genesis and Exodus. Moses is often said to have served Rameses I and II, but Neferhotep I is also a candidate for this Pharaoh, who refused to let the Israelites go and whose army was drowned in the Red Sea after God parted the waters for Moses and his people. Sobekneferu, the daughter of Amenemhet III, has been suggested as the princess who discovered Moses in the bullrushes, while the Pharaoh whose dreams Joseph famously interpreted could have been Senusret II, Senusret III, or Sesostris III. Thomas Mann opted for Akhnaten who ruled from 1369 B.C. to 1352 B.C., and is celebrated for having established (if only temporarily) a cult of monotheism in Egypt, worshipping the Sun-Disc Aten. There are also those who equate Joseph with the great architect and physician, Imhotep, who is credited with having built the great Step Pyramid of King Djoser at Saqqara. (The later Universal mummy films featuring Boris Karloff in 1932 and Arnold Vosloo in 1999 turned Imhotep into a High Priest. Confusingly, these movie Imhoteps fall in love with a Princess Anck-es-en–Amon, but as we've already seen, *The Mummy's* original screenwriter, John Balderston, know perfectly well that Anck-es-en–Amon was the namesake of Tutankhamen's consort). As far as truly ancient Egypt is con-

"The Sphinx at Midnight." Engraving by M. Sackson, Jr., of a drawing by Frank Dillon from *The Illustrated London News*, July 1862.

cerned there is room for endless speculation, and from the point of view of mythical narratives it doesn't really matter who was who.

Whatever the real identities of these Biblical characters, there is no doubt about the immense wealth and splendor of the Land of the Pharaohs, most of whose tombs were robbed soon after they were sealed. "How great must have been the wealth buried with those ancient Pharaohs!" Carter speculated with regard to the tombs in the Valley of the Kings. "What riches that Valley must once have concealed! Of the 27 monarchs buried there, Tutankhamen was probably of the least importance. How great must have been the temptation to the greed and rapacity of the audacious contemporary tomb robbers! What stronger incentive can be imagined than those vast treasures of gold!"[3] And Carter's account doesn't include the treasures of the pyramids, so long since stripped bare of their splendors.

Naturally, from the point of view of the apparently enslaved Israelites, Exodus is censorious of Pharaoh and Egyptian culture in general, for Pharaoh says, "Who *is* the Lord, that I should obey his voice to let Israel go? I know not the Lord, neither will I let Israel go."[4] The Bible also claims that the Israelites were forced to build Pharaoh's monuments:

> And the children of Israel were fruitful, and increased abundantly, and multiplied, and waxed exceeding mighty; and the land was filled with them. Now there arose up a new king over Egypt, which knew not Joseph. And he said unto his people, Behold, the people of the children of Israel *are* more and mightier than we: Come on, let us deal wisely with them; lest they multiply, and it come to pass, that, when there falleth out any war, they join also unto our enemies, and fight against us, and *so* get them up out of the land. Therefore they did set over them taskmasters, to afflict them with their burdens. And they built for Pharaoh treasure-cities, Pithom and Raamses.[5]

These verses inspired the subject of Sir Edward Poynter's painting, *Israel in Egypt* (1867), which in turn informed DeMille's cinematic images in *The Ten Commandments*; but research since the late 1970s has demonstrated that Poynter and DeMille were wrong, and that the accusation of slavery in Exodus was no more than political propaganda. Slaves certainly existed in ancient Egypt, but the Egyptians relied on professional builders to construct their pyramids. Evidence of animal bones has been discovered, suggesting that enough cows and sheep were slaughtered to feed thousands of people every day, so the men who built the pyramids were extremely well fed and hardly treated in the way that Exodus implies.[6]

Unfair though the Bible may have been to the reputation of ancient Egyptian building methods, there was never any doubt about the overwhelming magnificence of Egyptian architecture. Pliny the Elder, around A.D. 50, anticipated much later censure of what he and others perceived as the wanton extravagance of the Pharaohs. He described those mighty monuments as an "idle and foolish exhibition of royal wealth. For the cause by most assigned for their construction is an intention on the part of those kings to exhaust their treasures, rather than leave them to successors or plotting rivals, or to keep the people from idleness. Great was the vanity of those individuals on this point."[7] The prolific Victorian novelist George Alfred Henty (1832–1902) combined Pliny's opinion with the standard Biblical line on slavery in his children's adventure, *The Cat of Bubastes,* first published in 1889:

> "Vast numbers of slaves captured in war labored at them," the priest replied. "But numerous as these were they were wholly insufficient for the work, and well-nigh half the people of Egypt were forced to leave their homes to labour at them. So great was the burden and distress that even now the builders of these pyramids are never spoken of save with curses; and rightly so, for what might not have been done with the same labour usefully employed! Why, the number of the canals in the country might be doubled and the fertility of the soil vastly increased. Vast tracts might have been reclaimed from the marshes and shallow lakes, and the produce of the land might have been doubled."[8]

Sphinx and pyramids. Photograph by Dave Hawley.

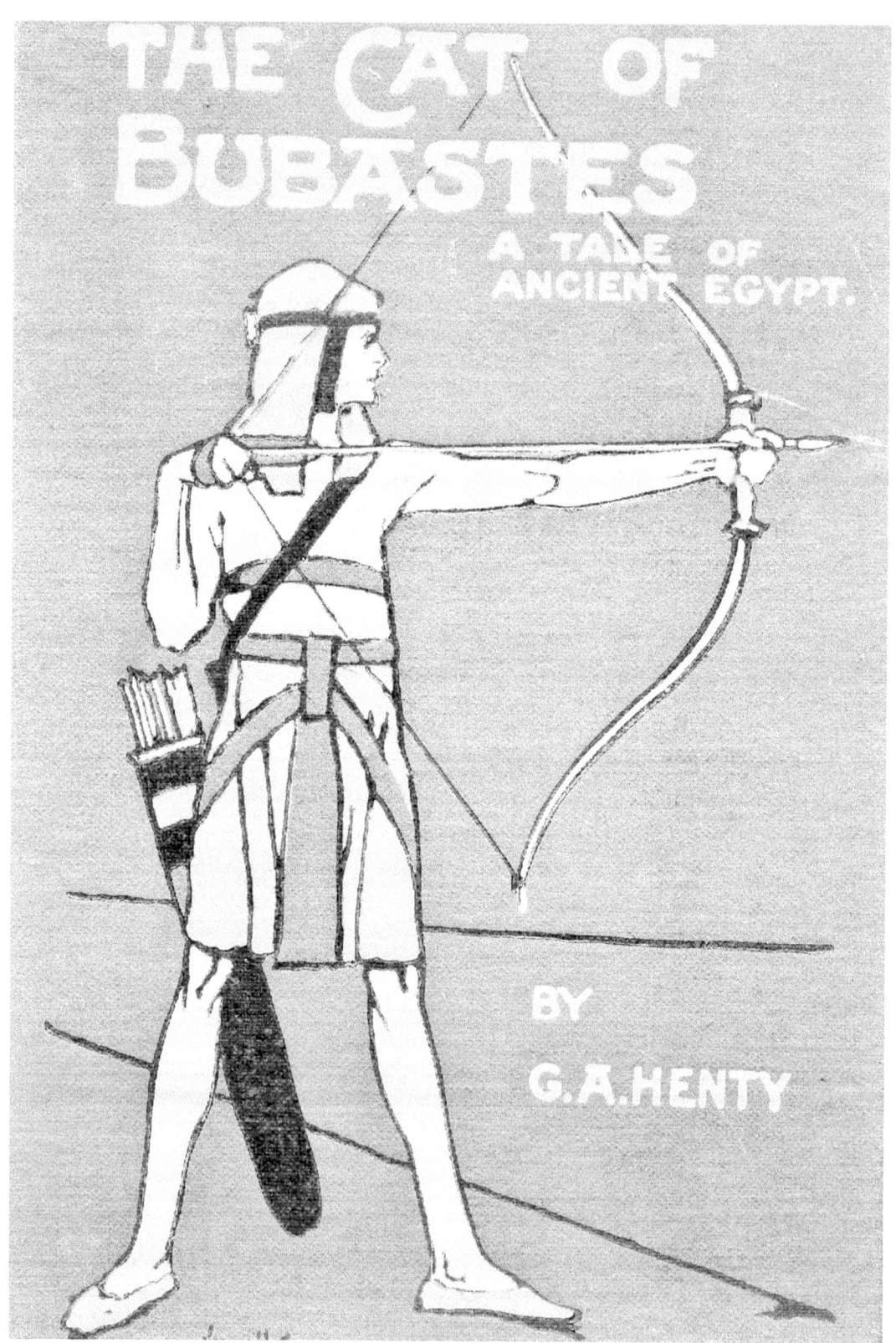

Cover of G. A. Henty's *The Cat of Bubastes* (London: Blackie, 1889).

Contemplating the Great Pyramid, one of Henty's characters says, "What a wonderful structure, but what a frightful waste of human labour!... I know not where his remains rest, but this huge pyramid stands as an eternal monument of the failure of human ambition."[9]

Of course, both Henty and Pliny fell into the trap of reflecting an ancient civilization in the distorting mirror of their own cultural values. As the Egyptologist John Romer has pointed out, this misunderstanding was committed by a much later visitor to the Valley of Kings. Robert Richardson was a doctor who accompanied Lord Belmore on a trip to the Valley of the Kings in the early 19th century. He published his theories in 1822 regarding the "real" purpose of the tombs, but Richardson was a down-to-earth Scotsman whose ideas about what constituted an appropriate burial of the dead were wildly different from those of people whose monuments he attempted to explain. Unable to accept that Egyptian burial customs evolved from a completely different set of ideas about death and the afterlife to his own, and accustomed as he was to much simpler burial customs in his native Scotland, Richardson came to the conclusion that the Pharaohs' tombs were designed for the use of the living rather than the dead:

> Only one sarcophagus in one chamber, and twelve chambers, exclusive of the long corridor, all highly ornamented for nothing! It may have been a subterraneous temple, exhibiting the religious creed of the worshippers, or the rites of initiation ... but never was such a monstrous supposition, or such a superfluous waste, as to fancy that all this was done for the reception of this one sarcophagus.[10]

In 1822, a protestant missionary, the Reverend William Jowett, also expressed the opinion that the tombs were the "scene of idolatrous rites performed in the dark,"[11] an erroneous interpretation that went straight into popular 20th-century occultism. An exemplar of this latter trend was H. C. Randall-Stevens (a.k.a. El Eros), the founder of the Jersey-based Order of the Knights Templar of Aquarius in the 1950s, who claimed not only to be a reincarnation of the Pharaoh Akhnaten but also to have received secret information about ancient Egypt from spiritual entities who had existed in material form during the period of Akhnaten's rule. In his book *Atlantis to the Latter Years* (1966), which includes a reprint of his earlier volume, *A Voice out of Egypt* (1935), he categorically insists that the pyramids were "*never* tombs"[12] but had always formed part of an immense pyramidal masonic initiation complex, built by stranded Atlanteans who had migrated to Egypt after the destruction of Atlantis. This is the occult tradition to which *Warlords of Atlantis* and *Stargate* are both indebted. James Spader, who plays the Egyptologist Daniel Jackson in *Stargate*, discovers, as he translates the hieroglyphics, that

> a traveler from distant stars escaped from a dying world looking for a way to extend his own life. His body decomposing and weak, he couldn't prevent his own demise. Apparently his whole species was becoming extinct, so he traveled — or searched — the galaxy looking for a way to cheat death. Look here! He came to a world rich with life where he countered a primitive race: humans!— a species which, with all his powers and knowledge, he could maintain indefinitely. He realized within a human body he had a chance for a new life. Now, he apparently found a young boy.... It says: as the frightened villagers ran, night became day. Curious and without fear, he walked towards the light. Ra took him and possessed his body like some kind of a parasite looking for a host; and inhabiting this human form he appointed himself ruler. He used the Stargate to bring thousands of people to this planet as workers for the mines.

Stargate is fiction, of course, but El Eros claimed he was writing fact. According to him there are undiscovered subterranean passages and temples beneath the Sphinx connecting the pyramids, along which initiates would work their way towards final enlightenment. Though there is no hint of diabolic intent here (quite the opposite, in fact) one cannot help putting this mystical and apparently heartfelt effusion into its historical context. Randall-Stevens began receiving his spiritual dictations in 1925, only three years after the discovery of Tutankhamen's tomb when Egyptomania was in its second great worldwide flush, and though he claimed to know nothing about Egyptology, popular culture was by that time full of similar theories to those of this self-styled reincarnation of Akhnaten. None of El Eros' ideas were new, however. In Sax Rohmer's study of magic and the occult, *The Romance of Sorcery*, first published in 1914, he makes similar claims regarding the original function of the Great Pyramid:

> The Great Pyramid, in this writer's opinion, is probably by far the oldest structure on earth. Its main purpose was to serve as a temple of initiation for those who were admitted to fellowship with the Atlantean Adepts, established in Egypt more than a hundred thousand years ago![13]

Rohmer carried these personal beliefs into his fiction, thus spreading their influence to a much wider audience. The reanimated mummy in *Brood of the Witch Queen* actually practices his diabolical sorcery in the Pyramid of Méydûm. As the Egyptologist of that novel, Dr. Cairn, puts it: "If I were to publish what I know — not what I imagine, but what I know about the Pyramid of Méydûm I should not only call down upon myself the ridicule of every Egyptologist in Europe; I should be accounted mad by the whole world."[14] Dr. Cairn explains that the mummy, which is discovered lying in an ancient sarcophagus like Count Dracula in his coffin, is "absorbing evil force" from it and adds in a footnote, apparently derived from the eighth volume of what Rohmer refers to as the *Collecteana Hermetica*, that "it seems exceedingly probable that ... the mummy-case [sarcophagus], with its painted presentment of the living person, was the material basis for the preservation of the ... *Khu* [magical powers] of a fully-equipped Adept."[15]

This is indeed a case of Rohmer v. Romer. As a serious Egyptologist, John Romer has little time for this sort of thing, complaining that "a bunch of shoddy mysteries which may rob us of the true sense of wonder and admiration for the civilization of our own remote ancestors is a very poor swap for knowledge hard won by centuries of study."[16] To be fair it is the likes of Randall-Stevens and their attempts to re-write history on mystical lines who are surely the target of Romer's ire here, but Sax Rohmer had no such qualms and gleefully plunged headlong into his excitingly exotic fantasy, not only believing it himself but also very well aware that this sort of thing was exactly what the general public wanted to hear:

> They looked into a square chamber of about the same size as the King's Chamber. In fact, although they did not realize it until later, this second apartment, no doubt, was situated directly above the first.
> The only light was that of a fire burning in a tripod, and by means of this illumination, which rose and fell in a strange manner, it was possible to perceive the details of the place. But, indeed, at the moment they were not concerned with these; they had eyes only for the black-robed figure beside the tripod.
> It was that of a man, who stood with his back towards them, and he chanted monotonously in a tongue unfamiliar to Sime. At certain points in his chant he would raise his arms in such a way that, clad in the black robe, he assumed the appearance of a gigantic bat. Each time that he acted thus the fire in the tripod, as if fanned into new life, would leap up, casting a hellish glare about the place. Then, as the chanter dropped his arms again, the flame would drop also.
> A cloud of reddish vapour floated low in the apartment. There were a number of curiously-

shaped vessels upon the floor, and against the farther wall, only rendered visible when the flames leapt high, was some motionless white object, apparently hung from the roof.

Dr. Cairn drew a hissing breath and grasped Sime's wrist.

"We are too late!" he said strangely.

He spoke at a moment when his companion, peering through the ruddy gloom of the place, had been endeavoring more clearly to perceive that ominous shape which hung, horrible, in the shadow. He spoke, too, at a moment when the man in the black robe, raised his arms — when, as if obedient to his will, the flames leapt up fitfully.[17]

This reanimated mummy, also known as Anthony Ferrara, visits the pyramid to distill a mysterious perfume which he uses in his murderous plan to gain wealth and power. Of course, the best Egyptian fantasies are those that have been thoroughly researched, giving an aura of authenticity to the proceedings, no matter how off-beam they may be with regard to their interpretation of Egyptian beliefs. One of the best from this point of view is Stoker's *The Jewel of Seven Stars*, for which he invented a Dutch explorer, by the name of Nicholas van Huyn of Hoorn. Stoker had Van Huyn claim to have been inspired by the genuine explorer, John Greaves (1602–1652), whose *Pyramidographia* was published in 1646, and Van Huyn's own book is meant to have been published only four years later, in 1650. Stoker correctly identified Greaves as a Fellow of Merton College Oxford. He was also a professor of geometry at Gresham College, London, and during his visit to Egypt in 1637 he made the most accurate surveys of the pyramids that had been achieved at that time. We'll be returning to what the fictional Nicholas van Huyn discovered and what later transpires in Stoker's wonderful novel in due course.

Also in the 17th century, two Jesuit priests (Fathers Protias and François) surveyed the Valley of the Kings. They were followed by another Jesuit (Father Claude Sicard) in 1707, who, by command of the Dauphin, was the first European to document the ancient monuments of the area, publishing the results of his research in Paris in 1717. Sicard was followed by the English clergyman, Richard Pococke (1704–1765), whose *Description of the East*, published in London in 1743 and 1745, was highly praised by Edward Gibbon. An indispensable authority for early explorers, Pococke also provided us with one of the first detailed descriptions of the Valley of the Kings, though we owe the first significant pictures of the Nile monuments to the Danish sea captain, Frederic Louis Norden (1708–1742), who was sent to Egypt by the Danish King Christian VI. His book *Voyage d'Egypte et de Nubie*, published after his death, was advertised by his editor in a manner that resembles the trailer for a Hollywood film:

> Ruins, monuments, magnificent buildings, cataracts, deserts, haunts of wild beasts, or men as they, everything that can attract the eye, or affect the imagination, is exposed to view. In short the reader seems to accompany the author in his voyage, and to share all his pleasures without undergoing the fatigue and dangers.[18]

Norden's account describing a visit to the Pyramids is particularly claustrophobic:

> At the opening of the first Pyramid fire some pistols in order to dislodge the bats, then order the two Arabs to clear away the sand, that almost chokes up the farther entrance to it.
> This done, the next precaution is to strip to your shirt, on account of the excessive heat within the Pyramid; in this trim you get through, each person a bougie [i.e. a candle] in his hand, for in this narrow avenue, it would be dangerous to use flambeaux on account of the suffocating smoke.... At the end of it there is a passage made of force, whose opening is scare one foot and a half high and two broad. And through this hole must curiosity pass, on Belly

Couchant, while the two Arabs who have wriggled themselves through before, seize each leg, and drag their gentlemen through this probation cleft, all covered with filth. Happily this narrow passage is not above two yards long, other wise such tugging would be unsupportable to all ... then a large space opens, where the traveler takes breath, and some refreshments.

The progress continues with great difficulty until at last the traveler reaches a salon "and their past difficulties are swallowed up in admiration."

Here, by way of amusement, pistols are fired, which excite a noise equal to that of thunder.[19]

One wonders if H. Rider Haggard was aware of this account as similar things happen in his 1889 Egyptian novel, *Cleopatra*. The scene in question concerns the Egyptian queen and Harmachis, High Priest of Isis, who together penetrate a pyramid to steal its treasure, but not before being assailed by "a mighty bat, white in colour as though with unreckoned age, and such as I had never seen before for bigness, for his measure was the measure of a hawk."[20] Later, the same bat attacks one of their slaves:

And lo! fixed to his chin, by its hinder claws, hung that grey and mighty bat, which, flying forth when we entered the pyramid, vanished itself to and fro, and we could see the fiery eyes shining in its head.

On discovering this horrible sight, Cleopatra shrieks "till the hollow passages rang with the echoes of her cries, that seemed to grow and double and rush along the depths in volumes of shrill sound."[21]

Sax Rohmer's Pyramid of Méydûm, in *Brood of the Witch Queen*, is also infested with bats, but bats with a difference, as they are a particular breed, as Dr. Cairn explains:

The Cynonycteris, or pyramid bat, has a leaf-like appendage beside the nose. A gland in this secretes a rare oil. This oil is one of the ingredients of the incense which is never named in the magical writings.[22]

The villainous reanimated mummy of the story makes good use of this natural resource and, consequently, the intrepid explorers discover a great many decapitated bat corpses as they make their way farther into the pyramid. They also repeat Norden's acoustic experiment with firearms:

Raising his Browning pistol, he fired — shot after shot — at that bat-like shape which stood between himself and the tripod!
A thousand frightful echoes filled the chamber with a demon mockery, boomed along those subterranean passages beneath, and bore the conflict of sound into the hidden places of the pyramid which had known not sound for untold generations.[23]

John Romer is, of course, quite correct to point out that "only a very few tombs, made late in Egypt's history, ever fulfilled Hollywood's dream of cunning and deadly hydraulic devices that operated with sand."[24] (Romer is obviously referring to the finale of *Land of the Pharaohs* here, but another interesting example of that kind of thing can be seen in *The Awakening*, in which a so-called guardian of a "serdâb" skewers the guide who accompanies Professor Corbek during his search for the canopic jars in Kara's tomb. This serdâb "guardian" — in the film, a baboon-like deity with a sharp dagger — very nearly impales the professor, too, but obviously the spirit of Queen Kara prevents that from happening.) In fact, it was Stoker himself who first popularized this fiendish device in the novel on which that film was based. Corbeck, in chapter twelve of *The Jewel of Seven Stars*, explains what happened:

With a loud click, a metal figure seemed to dart from close to the opening of the serdâb; the stone slowly swung back to its place, and shut with a click. The glimpse which I had of the descending figure appalled me for the moment. It was like that grim guardian which, according to the Arabian historian Ibn Abd Alhokin, the builder of the Pyramids, King Saurid Ibn Salhouk placed in the Western Pyramid to defend its treasure: "A marble figure, upright, with lance in hand; with on his head a serpent wreathed. When any approached, the serpent would bite him on one side, and twining about his throat and killing him, would return again to his place."

I knew well that such a figure was not wrought to pleasantry; and that to brave it was no child's play. The dead Arab at my feet was proof of what could be done! So I examined again along the wall; and found here and there chippings as if someone had been tapping with a heavy hammer. This then had been what happened: The grave-robber, more expert at his work than we had been, and suspecting the presence of a hidden serdâb, had made essay to find it. He had struck the spring by chance; had released the avenging "Treasurer," as the Arabian writer designated him. The issue spoke for itself. I got a piece of wood, and, standing at a safe distance, pressed with the end of it upon the star.

Instantly the stone flew back. The hidden figure within darted forward and thrust out its lance. Then it rose up and disappeared. I thought I might now safely press on the seven stars; and did so. Again the stone rolled back; and the "Treasurer" flashed by to his hidden lair.[25]

As we can see from the parallels so far mentioned between historical accounts and fiction, Egyptian fantasies are not entirely unrelated to fact.

It was the Scottish traveler, James Bruce (1730–1794), who provided Europeans with the first pictures of an Egyptian tomb when he published an account of his Egyptian travels in 1790. At six-foot-four with red hair and a booming voice, Bruce cut a formidable figure. He was also an excellent horseman, an expert marksman, a skilled linguist and immensely rich, so it's perhaps not surprising that he was imbued with a strong sense of his own superiority. In Cairo he dressed as a dervish and his ultimate aim was to explore the Nile, but

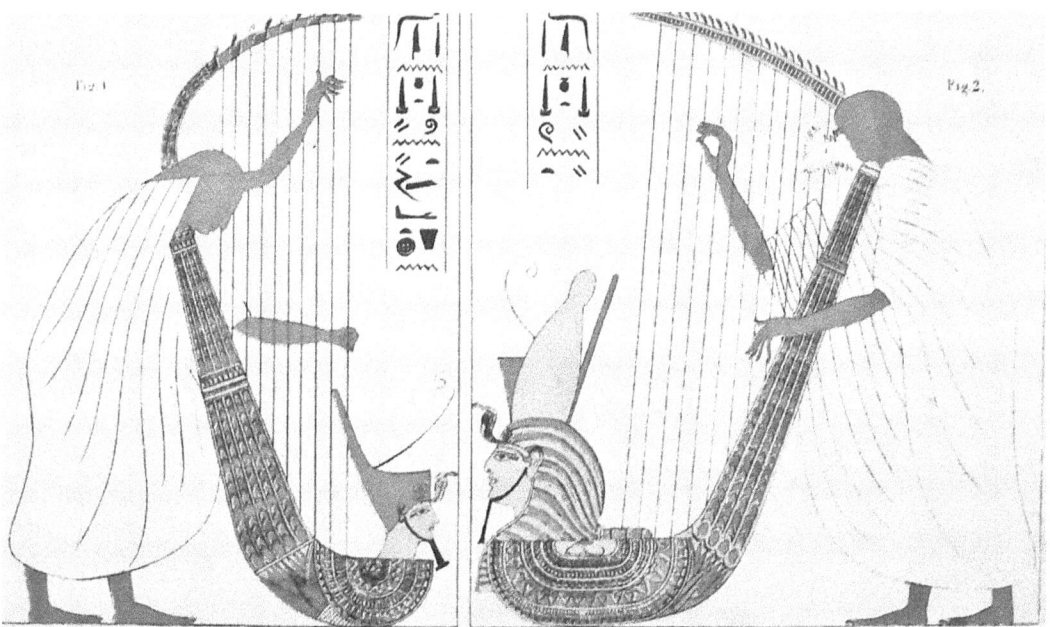

The harpers found in Bruce's tomb from J. Gardner Wilkinson's *The Ancient Egyptians — Their Lives and Customs* (London: John Murray, 1854).

he was also interested in tombs, and his major discovery, when he visited the Valley of the Kings in 1768, was what became known as "Bruce's Tomb." Later research identified the tomb to be that of Rameses III, and Bruce's drawing of two harpers depicted on the walls in the tomb became very well known, even though the engraver of his picture distorted the hieratic style of the ancient Egyptian original into a rather more neo-classical idiom that wasn't to be rectified until the more accurate representation of the English explorer, John Gardner Wilkinson (1797–1875), in the early 19th century. Via the influence this drawing had on later Victorian art, it was eventually to find itself inspiring film set props in *Caesar and Cleopatra*, in which Jean Simmons strums upon one — and also in *Cleopatra*, in which Elizabeth Taylor is entertained in similar manner. As Alan Moorehead points out, there is an atmosphere of "nightmarish fantasy" in Bruce's subsequent descriptions of his travels in Ethiopia, an atmosphere of "*Grand Guignol,* and of medieval melodrama: of horror piled upon horror until everything dissolves into a meaningless welter of brutality and bloodshed. Bruce describes it all in the minutest detail."[26] Bruce was no doubt aware of his readers' appetite for such things, an appetite comparable to the popularity of the Grand Guignol in the horror films of our own time.

All the explorers so far mentioned were private individuals, but gradually things began to change as private exploration and acquisition developed into the academic discipline of Egyptology. Egyptology as a science can really be said to have begun with Napoleon's short-lived occupation of Egypt, which began in 1797. The political justification for this escapade was to inconvenience England. Napoleon believed that if he could subdue Egypt he could use it as a base from which he might eventually be able to expel the British from India. The dream of a Suez canal might also be realizable and thus undermine British sea power; but Napoleon's motivations were not entirely strategic. He was also bored with Europe: "I don't want to stay here, there's nothing to do.... Everything's finished here but I haven't had enough glory. This tiny Europe doesn't provide enough, so I must go east."[27] Napoleon's desire to visit Egypt, it would appear, wasn't so far removed from our own escapist desire to watch a mummy movie on a wet Saturday afternoon. Unfortunately for Napoleon, Nelson eventually sank the French fleet during the Battle of the Nile and, events having turned against him, he characteristically lost interest in the expedition; but culturally, the Egyptian enterprise had highly beneficial consequences, the most

A young Jean Simmons playing a harp modeled on the paintings in Bruce's tomb, in *Caesar and Cleopatra* (dir. Gabriel Pascal, 1945).

"French Soldiers at Karnak in 1798," from *The Illustrated London News*, 1897.

influential of which was a publication whose lengthy title is fully in accord with its exhaustive contents: *"Description de l'Égypte, ou Receuil des Observations et des Recherches qui ont été faites en Égypte" pulblié par les ordres de sa Majesté l'Empereur Napoleon le Grand, à Paris de l'Imprimerie Imperiale.*

This *Description* was divided into three sections dealing with antiquities, modern life and natural history, and was bound in 21 immense folios, filled with astonishingly beautiful and accurate drawings of ancient Egyptian monuments, all explained and annotated in many more supplementary volumes. One of Napoleon's favorites during the Egyptian campaign was the artist and diplomat Dominique-Vivant, Baron de Denon (1747–1825), who now became something of an authority on Egyptian art. He rapidly acquired his own collection of Egyptian curios, the prize object of which was a small mummified foot, the celebrity of which no doubt inspired Théophile Gautier when he came to write his short story "The Mummy's Foot" in 1840 (see page 137). Denon also published his own account of his experiences in *Journey in lower and upper Egypt during the campaigns of general Bonaparte in Egypt* in 1802. In one passage of this, he imagines a funeral procession in the Valley of the Kings much as would a film director in later times.

> Towards the extremity, the opening between the rock even now offers scarcely space enough to pass by the tomb, so that the sumptuous processions which no doubt accompanied the ceremony of royal interment must have produced a striking contrast with the frowning asperity of these wild rocks; if however, they went by this road, it was probably only for the purpose of obtaining a longer space, in which to roll the full tide of the funereal pomp.[28]

The book made Denon a celebrity and he went on to become the Empire's arbiter of Egyptian Style. Just as the Art Deco movement in the 1920s would be influenced by the sensational discovery of Tutankhamen's tomb, so the discoveries made during Napoleon's Egyptian campaign became all the rage in France during the reign of Napoleon, the full impact of which we'll be exploring later. Suffice it to say here that Denon became the art director for the epic "movie" that was Napoleonic Paris. His engravings of Egyptian artifacts inspired Egyptian dinner services, Egyptian clocks, Egyptian cabinets, Egyptian comports, Egyptian handkerchiefs — even Egyptian jam jars. Such commercial manipulation and distortion of the ancient world to meet the requirements (or at least the desires) of the modern world in the West wasn't so far removed from the aesthetic of an Egyptian epic or a mummy movie.

Two other men, Jean-Baptiste Prosper Jollois (1776–1842) and Baron Édouard de Villiers du Terrage (1780–1855), also had their part to play in the history of Egyptology. They claimed to have discovered the tomb of Amenhotep III, though they may not, in fact, have been the first people to do so. More significantly, both were engineers and were the first men to survey the Valley of the Kings on modern principles, preparing precise engineering drawings of the monuments and artifacts that the likes of Denon had only sketched with inevitable artistic license. Beginning with meticulous elevations of the ruins they observed, Jollois and Villiers du Terrage crowned their work by drawing reconstructions of the monuments which suggested how these buildings might originally have appeared. This process of imaginative reconstruction, based on scientific observation, continued with other architects such as Charles-Louis Balzac (1752–1829) and Jean-Baptiste Lepère (1761–1844). Lepère was particularly keen to prepare such restorations, and his impression of the Hypostyle Hall in the temple at Philae, printed in color, became one of the most famous illustrations of the *Description*. Such reconstructions had a considerable impact on the set designs of neo–Egyptian operas, such as Friedrich Schinkel's sets from 1815–16 for Mozart's opera, *Die Zauberflöte,* and later Gustave Doré's illustrations for the Bible, particularly the architecture of the hall in which Moses argues with Pharaoh in Exodus, chapter VII.

Of course, no one could read the hieroglyphs at this time, but even if they could, what really appealed to the consumers of such objects was not so much historical accuracy and understanding as the glamor of a lost civilization, fabulous treasures and the atmosphere of occult mystery such objects and environments suggested. Eventually, in 1822, when Jean-François Champollion (1790–1832) finally broke the code, he revealed the true meaning of the inscriptions that had baffled generations for thousands of years. One of the key moments in Egyptology, therefore, was the discovery of the famous Rosetta Stone, whose bilingual text in three scripts (Greek, Demotic and Egyptian hieroglyphs) was discovered in 1799 by members of Napoleon's expeditionary force, though it was soon taken from the French by the English, which is why it now resides in the British Museum. As we shall see, Champollion was not, in fact, the first person to make sense of Egyptian hieroglyphics, and the Rosetta Stone was not the means by which this was originally achieved.

After the departure of Napoleon, the early years of the 19th century were a difficult period for students of Egyptology. The Turks gained control of the country and it became a very dangerous place to pursue one's interests. Reminiscent of the exploits of Vlad Tepes, the historical model for Bram Stoker's Count Dracula, it was not uncommon to see the severed heads of British prisoners thrust on poles in the thoroughfares of Cairo. But such horrors didn't dissuade two English travelers from visiting the country. One of them, Thomas Legh, was a member of Parliament from Cheshire. The other, Charles Smelt, was a Not-

"Moses Before Pharaoh," Exodus, chapter 7, 1–13. Illustration by Gustave Doré, 1866.

tinghamshire vicar. Together, they explored the Valley of the Kings, carving their names on the tomb of Rameses VI, and Legh later wrote up their adventures in his *Narrative of a Journey in Egypt and the Country Beyond the Cataracts*. It was, however, an Italian strong man and engineer who was to propel the science of Egyptology to new heights.

Giovanni Battista Belzoni (1778–1824) was a professional strong-man who had also organized spectacular waterfall extravaganzas at Covent Garden. A gentle giant, he was the most unlikely candidate to become a major player in the history of Egyptology, and like many success stories, it all happened quite by accident. Having a certain expertise in hydraulics, he decided to apply it to something rather more lucrative (and practical) than the creation of stage waterfalls, so he visited Pasha Mohammed Ali in Cairo in the hope of selling his hydraulic machinery to him. Unfortunately, the pasha wasn't interested, and the journey would have been a complete waste of time and money had not Belzoni subsequently approached the English Consul General at the British Agency in the city to ask if there might be any opportunities for an out-of-work Italian entrepreneur. The consul, one Henry Salt (1780–1827), was determined to exploit as much of Egypt's cultural heritage as possible and was the main competitor of the French consul, Bernardino Drovetti (1776–1852), who had the identical ambition. Drovetti, however, not only had the advantage of a more intimate knowledge of Egypt, having lived there for many years, but was also favored by the pasha. Ali was just as desperate to modernize Egypt as Drovetti and Salt were to pillage its past, so he willingly sold Egypt's heritage to the highest bidder. Drovetti built up three impressive collections of antiquities, one of which went to Turin, the other two to the Louvre and the Berlin Museum. What Salt lacked in personal influence with Mohammed Ali he made up for in greater financial power. He surrounded himself with agents and immediately saw the potential advantage of having Belzoni on his side. When Belzoni explained his situation to him, Salt said there might be work for him if he would be willing to help ship from Thebes to England a colossus which had been presented as a gift from the pasha to the Prince Regent. It was rather an insensitive gift to offer, as the pasha hadn't included its removal expenses, but it unintentionally did Belzoni a very good turn and changed the history of Egyptology. Finding himself to be exactly the right man at the right place and time, Belzoni's particular expertise was just what was needed, and he succeeded in setting the colossus on its journey by moving it from where it lay in the Memnonium to the river bank a couple of miles away.

That particular mission accomplished, Belzoni looked around to see what else ancient Egypt might have to offer. Salt had suggested he should look out for more antiquities to ship back to England, so he visited Bruce's tomb with its celebrated harpists. Having moved a colossus, Belzoni now considered the lucrative possibility of shifting the huge granite sarcophagus of Rameses II in Bruce's tomb. He succeeded in this, too, and the sarcophagus now resides in the Louvre. Belzoni also discovered a coffin lid in the same tomb, which, unfortunately, broke in two during the removal process, but which has since been restored. Today, it forms part of the collection of the Fitzwilliam Museum in Cambridge.

Now fully under the spell of ancient Egypt, Belzoni next discovered the tomb of King Ay, an elderly priest who took over the Egyptian state after the untimely death of Tutankhamen, and played an important role in the court of Akhnaten. Having discovered this tomb (though not the identity of its occupant), Belzoni traveled to Abu Simbel and opened up the famous temple there, which had been obstructed by millennia of sand and debris. Back in the Valley of the Kings, he also entered what is now known as Tomb 25, a mysteriously unfinished burial place, which, much to the horror of contemporary Egyptologists, he famously opened by means of a battering ram. He also explored the tomb of Prince Ramesses Montu-hir-kopesh-ef, wherein he discovered its perfectly preserved wall paintings.

Belzoni then penetrated the tomb of King Rameses I, the decorations of which, like those of the tomb of Ay, show evidence of having been influenced by the "realistic" artistic developments that occurred alongside Akhnaten's religious revolution; but even more exciting was Belzoni's discovery of the spectacular and almost perfectly preserved tomb of Seti I, with its celebrated alabaster coffin, which now resides in the basement of the Sir John Soane Museum in London. Soane bought it for £2,000 (too much, apparently, for the British Museum), and designed a sepulchral space for it as a symbolic foundation stone for his own aesthetic principles. Perhaps Stoker, who knew London well, had Seti's sarcophagus in mind when describing Queen Tera's sarcophagus, which stands with two others in Abel Trelawny's Kensington home in *The Jewel of Seven Stars:*

> The most interesting of the sarcophagi were undoubtedly the three in Mr. Trelawny's room. Of these, two were of dark stone, one of porphyry and the other of a sort of ironstone. These were wrought with some hieroglyphs. But the third was strikingly different. It was of some yellow-brown substance of the dominating colour effect of Mexican onyx, which it resembled in many ways, excepting that the natural pattern of its convolutions was less marked. Here and there were patches almost transparent — certainly translucent. The whole chest, cover and all, was wrought with hundreds, perhaps thousands, of minute hieroglyphics, seemingly in an endless series. Back, front, sides, edges, bottom, all had their quota of the dainty pictures, the deep blue of their colouring showing up fresh and sharply edged in the yellow stone. It was very long, nearly nine feet; and perhaps a yard wide. The sides undulated, so that there was no hard line. Even the corners took such excellent curves that they pleased the eye. "Truly," I said, "this must have been made for a giant!"[29]

Stoker doesn't specify alabaster here, but he does suggest something of the quality of that material with reference to yellow-brown translucency and the qualities of onyx, which can certainly resemble alabaster. Trelawny's solicitors, who are mentioned in a letter to the professor's daughter, Margaret, are "Marvin and Jekes of 27B Lincoln's Inn,"[30] not far away from the Soane museum itself at numbers 12–14 Lincoln's Inn Fields, so it seems highly likely that Stoker would have visited the Soane museum and seen the sarcophagus himself.

Seti's tomb also has a mysterious tunnel situated at the very back of the tomb complex beyond the burial chamber. Until 2010, no one had been able to penetrate this tunnel as it was blocked by debris. When the depths of the tunnel were finally unearthed by a team led by Dr. Zahi Hawass, it proved to be something of an anti-climax. A 54-step staircase was revealed but after 174 meters everything came to a disappointing dead end. Seti may have been attempting to construct a secret tomb for himself, but, unfortunately, this failed to materialize. Dr. Hawass's team did find a false door, however, decorated with hieroglyphic text which, when translated, proved to be no more than very prosaic instructions for the original workmen: "Move the door jamb up and make the passage wider"[31]— not quite the stuff of Egyptian Romance, and no doubt archeologists over the past two centuries have had just as much hope of finding spectacular treasure at the end of this tunnel as the humble readers of novels by Sax Rohmer or Bram Stoker. In *Brood of the Witch-Queen*'s Pyramid of Méydûm, Rohmer was careful not to miss this important ingredient of mystery, as this conversation between Dr. Cairn and his son demonstrates:

> His son was silent for a time; then:
> "According to the guide books," he said, "it is merely an empty tomb."
> "It is empty, certainly," replied Dr. Cairn grimly, "or that apartment known as the King's Chamber is now empty. But even the so-called King's Chamber was not empty once; and there is another chamber in the pyramid which is not empty *now!*"
> "If you know of the existence of such a chamber, sir, why have you kept it secret?"
> "Because I cannot *prove* its existence. I do not know how to enter it, but I know it is there; I

know what it was formerly used for, and I suspect that last night it was used for that same unholy purpose again — after a lapse of perhaps four thousand years!³²

There are further comparisons to make between Belzoni's activities and later Egyptian fantasies when we consider the casts that Belzoni made of the wall decorations in Seti's tomb. Belzoni, it's very important to remember, was also a showman, and in that respect he resembles Fred Clark's Alexander King in *The Curse of the Mummy's Tomb*. Though a far more responsible and sympathetic character than King, Belzoni nonetheless presented the contents of Seti's tomb to the general public in a similar manner. He lived for a year in the tomb and made over four hundred casts and drawings of the walls, which he later assembled at the Egyptian Galleries in London's Piccadilly, where they were fashionably lit by flamboyant gaslight. At the grand opening ceremony, Belzoni theatrically unwrapped a mummy and eventually published an illustrated account of his Egyptian experience in his *Narrative of the operations and recent discoveries within the Pyramids, Temples, Tombs and excavations in Egypt and Nubia*. Belzoni's transportation and re-erection of the wall casts of an ancient tomb in London is also strongly reminiscent of Professor Fuchs' recreation of Queen Tera's tomb in the cellar of his suburban home in *Blood from the Mummy's Tomb*. The Hammer adaptation goes one stage further than Stoker by having Professor Fuchs transport the *actual* walls of Queen Tera's tomb to his cellar. Stoker doesn't go quite this far, relying "merely" on curios and artifacts which are assembled in a cave beneath Professor Trelawny's Jacobean mansion on the coast of Cornwall:

> It was a strange and weird proceeding the placing of those wonderful monuments of a bygone age in that green cavern, which represented in its cutting and purpose and up-to-date mechanism and electric lights both the old world and the new.³³

The way Stoker describes the entrance to this subterranean scene is also reminiscent of the experiences of explorers on entering ancient tombs in the Valley of the Kings:

> In the inside hall we found a whole section of an outstanding angle moved away, and from the cavity saw a great hole dimly dark, and the beginning of a rough staircase cut in the rock. As it was not pitch dark there was manifestly some means of lighting it naturally, so without pause we followed our host as he descended, After some forty or fifty steps cut in a winding passage, we came to a great cave whose further end tapered away into blackness, It was a huge place, dimly lit by a few irregular long slits of eccentric shape.³⁴

Belzoni left Egypt on January 27, 1819, traveling to London via Venice, where, appropriately enough, he met Lord Byron, who left his own contribution to the craze for things Egyptian in the first canto of his poem *Don Juan*. With its *Carry On Screaming*-style reference to a tomb-robber "burglariously" breaking the coffin lid of Cheops' sarcophagus, Byron might have been a slyly referring to what happened to the lid of Rameses' sarcophagus when Belzoni removed it from the tomb:

> What are the hopes of man? Old Egypt's King
> Cheops erected the first pyramid
> And largest, thinking it was just the thing
> To keep his memory whole, and mummy hid;
> But somebody or other rummaging,
> Burglariously broke his coffin's lid:
> Let not a monument give you or me hopes,
> Since not a pinch of dust remains of Cheops.³⁵

Belzoni then presented his native Padua with two black granite statues from Thebes before taking the remainder of his booty to London. He dearly wanted to keep Seti's alabaster coffin but the British Museum confiscated it, despite being too mean actually to purchase it. When Sir John Soane celebrated the coffin's installation in his home, he thew a coffin-warming party at which Belzoni's wife, Sarah, was present, but by that time Belzoni had, sadly, passed away.

The first attempts at decyphering hieroglyphics were based on the (correct) assumption that the characteristic cartouches found on all monumental scripts identified the names of individual Pharaohs. (Cartouches themselves were named after their resemblance to the charges used by French artillery men when loading their cannons.) Eventually, phonetic equivalents for the symbols within these cartouches were worked out, which corresponded to the pronunciation of these ancient names that has come down to us via Greek culture. The original work on this gigantic code-breaking project was carried out by the explorer and Egyptologist, William Bankes (1786–1855), who gathered an extensive collection of antiquities. A fellow student of Byron at Trinity College, Bankes later met the future architect of the Palace of Westminster, Sir Charles Barry, at Abu Simbel in 1819. He began work on his hieroglyphic researches with an obelisk he had discovered at Philae. Today, this stands in the grounds of his ancestral home at Kingston Lacey in Dorset. Unfortunately, Bankes was forced into exile after a homosexual scandal involving a soldier in London's Green Park. He fled to Venice and his important role in the history of hieroglyphics was overlooked. It fell to Champollion to gain the credit for what was, in fact, a joint decoding effort, and Champollion became the first professional Egyptologist. Though his great discovery is usually associated with the Rosetta Stone, he, in fact, initially relied on texts discovered at Abu Simbel.

The next important Egyptologist was John Gardner Wilkinson (1797–1875), who became known as the father of British Egyptology. He was also the first Egyptologist to be knighted (in 1837). Born at Little Missenden in Buckinghamshire — about as far removed from ancient Egypt as is possible to imagine — he was educated at Harrow School and Exeter College, Oxford. Suffering from ill health, he visited Italy for a cure, and it was there that he met the hieroglyphic enthusiast and ex-diplomat, Sir William Gell (1777–1836), who encouraged him to travel to Egypt. (Gell also has the honor of being mentioned by Byron in his poem *English Bards and Scotch Reviewers:* "Of Darden tours let dilettanti tell,/I leave topography to classic Gell." In a footnote, Byron adds, "Mr. Gell's Topography of Troy and Ithaca cannot fail to ensure the approbation of every man possessed of classical taste, as well for the information Mr. G. conveys to the mind of the reader, as for the ability and research the respective works display.")[36]

Wilkinson was also fascinated by hieroglyphics and published various books on Egypt, including *Topography of Thebes and General View of Egypt* (1835) and *Manners and Customs of the Ancient Egyptians* (1837). This latter had over six hundred drawings by Wilkinson, including rather more accurate renderings of Bruce's famous harpers. H. Rider Haggard mentions these harpers in his novel, *Cleopatra*, when, after the exile of his hero, the High Priest Harmachis, who has failed to assassinate the Egyptian queen in his bid to become Pharaoh, takes refuge in the tomb of Rameses III:

> And on the walls of the last chamber — on the left-hand side, looking toward the Hall of the Sarcophagus — are paintings exceeding beautiful, and two blind harpers playing upon their bent harps before the God Mou; and beneath the flooring these harpers, who harp no more, are soft

at sleep. Here, then, in this gloomy place, even in the tomb of the Harpers and the company of the dead, I took up my abode; and here for right long years I worked out my penance and made atonement for my sin.[37]

Perhaps Thomas Mann also had these particular harpers in mind when he described kneeling harp players "with their faces turned heavenwards" in *Joseph in Egypt*.[38] One of Wilkinson's most important achievements was his numbering and dating of the tombs in the Valley of the Kings. When Champollion visited Egypt to gain firsthand experience of the antiquities, he met and worked with Wilkinson, though unfortunately they didn't particularly warm to each other. Another of Wilkinson's colleagues was Edward William Lane (1801–1876), who had traveled to Egypt not only in pursuit of good health but also to study of Arabic. His *Manners and Customs of the Modern Egyptians* (1836) was a kind of companion volume to Wilkinson's *Manner and Customs of the Ancient Egyptians*. (Lane also translated *1001 Nights*, which appeared in three volumes in 1840, and worked on an Arabic-English lexicon.)

After so many years spent in the uncomfortable and dusty environment of ancient tombs, Wilkinson enthusiastically embraced the comforts of modern civilization on his return to England where he gained something of a reputation as a dandy. Always immaculately dressed, he may have been the first in a long line of dapper Egyptologists (and Egyptian villains) in film and fiction: from Sir Joseph Whemple in *The Mummy* (1932) to Professor Fuchs, who wears a full three-piece suit in *Blood from the Mummy's Tomb*. James Villiers is particularly well turned out in that film, with a cane and an extravagant fur collar to his overcoat, which is reminiscent of the evil Antony Ferrara's penchant for coats lined with fox-fur (or civit-cat fur) in *Brood of the Witch Queen*. Terence Morgan's Adam Beauchamp in *Curse of the Mummy's Tomb* also follows Ferrara's example as a very snappily dressed, though in fact very antique dandy. Most mummies are not quite so sartorial, of course.

James Burton (1788–1862) was the son of a successful London builder. After education at Trinity College, Cambridge, he worked for Sir John Soane, at whose home he was no doubt acquainted with the celebrated alabaster coffin of Seti I. In the company of Soane's secretary, Charles Humphreys, he traveled to Egypt where he was introduced to Wilkinson, Lane and Gell. Unsurprisingly, coming as he did from a family of builders, Burton's main interest in Egypt was the architecture of the ancient tombs. One of his exploits again connects us to the much later fiction of Sax Rohmer. While exploring a tomb in a cliff face (now numbered as KV20), Burton had to endure the overpowering combination of extreme heat and the stench of guano left by the bats that infested the tomb. We have already encountered the bats of the Méydûm Pyramid in Sax Rohmer's *Brood of the Witch Queen*. In "The Death-Ring of Sneferu," one of the stories in Rohmer's *Tales of Secret Egypt* (to which we will be returning in more detail later), Rohmer describes a similar situation to the one suffered by Burton in KV20:

> Retreat was impossible; there is but one entrance to the pyramid; and the darkness which now descended upon me was indescribable; it possessed horrific qualities; it seemed palpably to enfold me like the winds of some monstrous bat. The air of the King's Chamber I found to be almost unbearable, and it was no steady hand with which I gripped my pistol.[39]

Scandalously, Burton had also married a Greek slave whom he had originally purchased some years before in Egypt. This was a liaison for which he was disowned by his family when he eventually returned to England along with an exotic entourage of animals, other slaves and antiquities. He indeed resembles the type of exotic explorer one encounters in the pages of fantasy fiction. Significantly, Rohmer included the names of both Burton and Lane in "Breath of Allah," another of his *Tales of Secret Egypt*:

> Rudyard Kipling has trounced the man who inquires too deeply into native life; but if everybody thought with Kipling we should never have had a Lane or a Burton and I should have continued in unbroken scepticism regarding the reality of magic.[40]

Another of Burton's associates was Robert Hay (1799–1863), who was a distant relation. Like Burton, he too married a slave whom he had rescued from a slave market in Alexandria, and, again like his relation, his collection of antiquities eventually made its way to the British Museum where much of it remains. When he was surveying the tomb of Rameses IV, Hay actually set up home in the tomb, as Belzoni had done in the tomb of Seti I. His comforts included carpets, mirrors, bookshelves and even furniture—a home-from-home that we've already seen recreated in Hammer's *Curse of the Mummy's Tomb*, and which is not so far very removed from the combination of modern wash basin, furnace, electric light and desk in Professor Fuchs' subterranean recreation of Queen Tera's tomb in *Blood from the Mummy's Tomb*.

An excellent draftsman, Hay also made many drawings of ancient sites, particularly those in the Valley of the Kings, and he frequently asked other British travelers to help him make visual records. One of these was Owen Jones, who later found fame as the complier of *The Grammar of Ornament* (1856), the most celebrated of 19th-century pattern books. Other publications of this kind included Albert Charles Auguste Racinet's *L'Ornament Polychrome* (1869), Heinrich Dolmetsch's *Ornamentenschaz* (1898), known as *The Treasury of Ornament* in English, and Alexander Speltz's *The Colored Ornament of All Historical Styles* (1915). Both Dolmetsch and Jones included Egyptian style in their highly influential books. Jones, indeed, supervised the layout of the Great Exhibition on 1851, with its spectacular Egyptian Hall (a subject to which we will be returning later). One of the men who helped Jones with the plaster statues of the Crystal Palace Egyptian Court was Joseph Bonomi (1796–1878), a sculptor, well traveled in Egypt. He had formed part of the expedition to the Valley of the Kings in 1844–45 led by the brilliant linguist Richard Lepsius, to whom Sir Arthur Conan Doyle (1859–1930) refers, along with Champollion, in his seminal mummy tale, "The Ring of Thoth" (1890). Bonomi, who was also the curator of the Soane Museum, had personally experienced Belzoni's recreation of Seti I's tomb in the Egyptian Galleries, and so formed an important link between the first commercial exploitation of Egyptian culture in Piccadilly and the Crystal Palace's rather more elaborate, proto-cinematic Egyptian court.

Along with the rapid commercialization of Egyptiana in industrializing 19th-century Europe, Egyptology itself became increasingly scientific, bureaucratic and practically organized. There was concern that the "respectable" looting carried out by antiquarians, not to mention the still-flourishing trade in antiquities, was sending artifacts to disparate collections around the globe. As Nile cruises were also making Egypt more accessible and affordable, the increasing numbers of tourists keen to experience the Land of the Pharaohs threatened the fabric of the tombs themselves. In a time before electric light, the only way to illuminate a tomb so far underground or deep within a stone structure was by means of a naked flame of one sort or another. In some of the more reckless cases, bonfires were lit. Concluding his remarks in a conventionally prejudiced manner, Wilkinson explained in 1847:

> In going into a pyramid [and, of course, much the same thing applied to a tomb in the Valley of the Kings], I need scarcely suggest the necessity of being provided with candles and a lantern,

lucifers, and a supply of water; and a long stick to raise a light upon, in examining the upper part of the rooms, may be useful. I should also recommend a cloak, to put on in coming out, particularly in the evening, which is by no means a bad time for visiting the interior. It may be as well not to intrust it to the care of the Arabs, when not warmed within the Pyramid, as they are not particularly clean.[41]

The possibilities of possessing a personal collection of antiquities to display in one's London home, such as we find in Stoker's *The Jewel of Seven Stars*, was soon to become more restricted with the establishment, by Ishmail Pasha, of the *Service des Antiquitées* in 1858. This was originally under the directorship of Auguste Mariette (1821–1881), a former curator of the Louvre, whose many achievements included having cleared the sand away from the base of the Sphinx, thus revealing the Temple of the Sphinx within. He also discovered the almost-intact tomb of Rameses II's son, Khaemweset, and wrote the original scenario of Verdi's opera *Aida*—yet another way in which academic Egyptology influenced the parallel world of Egyptian fantasy. So celebrated was he that it was almost inevitable that Conan Doyle made a passing reference to him in "The Ring of Thoth."

John Romer quotes a contemporary's description of Mariette as "rather a stern and terrifying figure with his great height, his red tarboosh [fez], his stern face, his staccato talk and his tinted spectacles"[42]—an image which seems to look forward to the various "keepers of the tomb" we encounter in the Universal and Hammer mummy movies, usually played by Georges Zucco and Pastel, respectively. Amid the hard graft and anticlimaxes throughout the history of Egyptology there are always historical events which would not be out of place in such films. Indeed, one of the most sensational finds during this period inspired *The Night of Counting the Years*, Egypt's most significant (but little seen) film. The discovery of a cache of artifacts from a secret tomb at Deir el Bahri in 1881 revealed that it had been being exploited for several years by the inhabitants of a nearby village. After pressure had been brought to bear on the main perpetrators of this nefarious activity (the Abd er Rassul brothers), the tomb was eventually revealed to Emile Brugsch (1842–1930), a German-born Egyptologist who was deputizing for the then-absent head of the *Service*, Gaston Maspero (1846–1916). In a story worthy of a thriller by Agatha Christie (whose name, years later, identified a nearby shortcut to the Valley of the Kings thanks to her having used the setting in *Death on the Nile*), Brugsch was shown an overwhelming cache of royal and priestly mummies, including those of Amenhotep I, Seti I, Rameses II, III and IX, and a wealth of other artifacts. The Abd er Rassul brothers had been selling artifacts from this tomb for about ten years and had made a very handsome profit out of them.

This was the most exciting thing that happened to Brugsch during his time in Egypt, but he has another claim to fame, which has a particular bearing on our own investigation of the influence of ancient Egypt on modern Western fantasies. As the curator of the Bulaq Museum of Antiquities near Cairo, Brugsch entertained many visitors, some of whom were celebrities. In 1886, for example, Rider Haggard, who was planning his Egyptian romance *Cleopatra* at the time, was shown around the museum's treasures by Brugsch in person. The experience made a powerful impression on him, which was increased when he sailed further up the Nile to Luxor and Thebes.[43] Later, in 1904, Brugsch assisted the occultist, Aleister Crowley, by having one of his assistants translate the Stele of Ank-ef-en-Khonsu, also known as The Stele of Revealing, which became an important element in Crowley's seminal work, *The Book of the Law* (1904). This stele had been discovered by Mariette in the mortuary

Obelisk at Luxor. Photograph by Dave Hawley.

chapel of Hatshepsut at Dayr-al-Bahri in 1858 and it formed part of the collection at the Bulaq Museum. Crowley and his wife, Rose, had visited the museum on March 21, 1904, to see if Rose could recognize an image of the god Horus on this painted stele. Coincidentally, the stele bore the catalog number of 666 — the Book of Revelation's number of the Beast with which Crowley so infamously identified. Intrigued by this, Crowley nonetheless "dismissed it as an obvious coincidence."[44] In Crowley's *Equinox of the Gods* (1936), he recorded, in note form, what happened next.

> Brugsch Bey of the Boulak Museum dined with us once to discuss the Stele in his charge, and to arrange for its "abstruction." His French assistant curator, who translated the hieroglyphs on the Stele for us.
> Between March 23 and April 8 the Hieroglyphs on the Stele were evidently translated by the assistant-curator at Boulak, into either French or English — I am almost sure it was French — and versified (as now printed) by me.
> Between these dates, too, my wife must have told me that her informant was not Horus, or Ra Hoor Khuit, but a messenger from Him, named Aiwass.[45]

We will be returning to Crowley's connection with the Stele of Revealing and his revival of Egyptian magic in the next chapter, but there are yet more connections between Brugsch's superior, Gaston Maspero and the rather more sensational extremes of Egyptomania. For a start, Maspero is mentioned in Sax Rohmer's short story "The Death-Ring of Sneferu":

> The death-ring of Sneferu possessed uncomfortable and supernatural properties. So far as I was aware, no example of such a ring (the *lettre de cachet* of the period) was included in any known collection. One dating much after Sneferu, and bearing the cartouche of Apepi II (one of the

Hyksos, or Shepherd Kings) came to light late in the nineteenth century; it was reported to be the ring which, traditionally, Joseph wore as emblematical of the power invested in him by Pharoah. Sir Gaston Maspero and other authorities considered it to be a forgery and it vanished from the ken of connoisseurs. I never learned by what firm it was manufactured.[46]

Maspero took over the running of the *Service* in 1881 and further refined the safeguards of the ancient monuments, introducing admission charges to tourists who wanted to enter the tombs. In 1886, following in Belzoni's footsteps, he unwrapped the mummy of Seti I, revealing the long-preserved serenity of the Pharoah's beautiful face. A later incident would not have been out of place in a mummy movie, for when unwrapping the mummy of Rameses II, the elasticity of the long-dead remains of an arm caused it to spring forward as though it had come to life.[47] It didn't have quite the same effect on him as the appearance of Karloff's Im-ho-tep on Bramwell Fletcher's Ralph Norton, but it nonetheless caused a momentary frisson. Another of the mummies unwrapped by Maspero that year also seemed to share a similar fate as Im-ho-tep. The so-called "Screaming Mummy" indeed presented a shocking sight, for it appeared he had been mummified while screaming in agony. An autopsy carried out with Maspero's consent revealed a contorted stomach, which suggested that "Man E," as he was classified, might have been poisoned. The mummy's identity remained a mystery until 2008 when research led by Dr. Zahi Hawass was able to reveal that the "Screaming Mummy" was in fact the body of Prince Pentewere, elder son of Rameses III, who, with his mother, Tiy, had plotted to assassinate the pharaoh and ascend to the throne himself. The plot exposed, Pentewere was condemned to death but, given his royal status, was granted the honor of being allowed to commit suicide by swallowing poison.[48]

Maspero's immediate successors as head of the *Service* were all similarly Frenchmen: Eugène Grébaut (1846–1915), who filled that office between 1886 and 1892, Jacques de Morgan (1892–1897) and Victor Loret (1897–1899). Again thanks to Mohammed er Rassul, Grébaut discovered a second cache of royal mummies in 1891 containing 160 coffins. De Morgan excavated with the Professor of Egyptology at London University, Sir Flinders Petrie (1853–1942), who, in 1880, became the first scholar accurately to investigate how the pyramids were constructed. Accused of dilettantism by other Egyptologists and tainted due to his commitment to eugenics and other somewhat right-wing views, Petrie nonetheless mentored Howard Carter and founded the Petrie Museum at University College in London's Bloomsbury district, where The British Museum also casts a subtle Egyptian perfume over the somber London streets. The Petrie Museum contains over 80,000 exhibits, including, for example, the earliest pieces of linen from Egypt, a fragment of the first Egyptian calendar, and the first example of metal from Egypt. The building in which the museum is housed in Malet Place also features a deep, dark flight of stone steps, not technically open to the public. It has nothing to do with ancient Egypt but would undoubtedly provide the perfect setting for the appearance of a reanimated mummy.

Victor Loret also experienced a macabre incident relating to his discovery of the tomb of Amenhotep II in 1898:

> I went forward with my candle and, horrible sight, a body lay there upon the boat, all black and hideous its grimacing face turning towards me and looking at me, its long brown hair in sparse bunches around its head.[49]

He wondered if he had come across evidence of a human sacrifice but, as John Romer suggests, it was more likely to have been the mummy of Prince Webenseenu, overseer of the royal chariot horses.

Egyptologists aren't so far removed from grave robbers. Loret later discovered three mummified corpses lying side by side in another part of Amenhotep's tomb:

> We approached the cadavers. The first seemed to be that of a woman. A thick veil covered her forehead and left eye. Her broken arm had been replaced at her side, her nails in the air. Ragged and torn cloth hardly covered her body. Abundant black curled hair spread over the limestone floor on each side of her head. The face was admirably conserved and had a noble and majestic gravity.
>
> The second mummy, in the middle was that of a child about fifteen years. It was naked with the hands joined on the abdomen. First of all the head appeared totally bald, but on closer examination one saw that the head had been shaved except in an area on the right temple from which grew a magnificent tress of black hair. This was the *coiffure* of the royal princes.... The face of the young prince was laughing and mischievous, it did not at all evoke the idea of death.
>
> Lastly the corpse nearest the wall seemed to be that of a man. His head was shaved but a wig lay on the ground not far from him. The face of this person displayed something horrible and something droll at the same time. The mouth was running obliquely from one side nearly to the middle of the cheek, but a pad of linen whose two ends hung from a corner of the lips. The half closed eyes had a strange expression, he could have died choking on a gag but he looked like a young playful cat with a piece of cloth. Death which had respected the severe beauty of the woman and the impish grace of the boy had turned in derision and amused itself with the countenance of the man.
>
> A remarkable fact was that the three corpses, like the one on the boat, had their skulls pierced with a large hole and the breast of each one was opened.[50]

The female mummy described by Loret was actually that of Queen Tiy, wife of Amenhotep III and the mother of Akhnaten, whom Mika Waltari in *The Egyptian* described in fictional terms as short and plump with broad cheekbones and, being by birth a "woman of the people," perhaps with Negro blood in her veins.[51] In the film version, Judith Evelyn's Taia explains how she attracted the attention of Pharaoh:

> He loved me, Sinuhe, because I was strong and lusty — because I was vulgar and unlettered and told him the truth. His other wives, the high-born, delicate ones with their narrow heads: how they hated me! So I swore that I would give him a son to wear the double-crown, and I did; but the gods were perverse. They gave me a son as soft as a woman and a daughter as hard as a man. Baketamon should be Pharaoh, not her brother.

Following in the footsteps of his predecessors as head of the *Service*, Loret found another royal cache of mummies in Amenhotep II's tomb, which included those of Seti II and Tuthmosis IV. Then, in 1898, there was the discovery of the tomb of Tutmosis III which was hidden away in a cleft in the rock high above the Valley of the Kings. This inaccessible location might well have provided Bram Stoker with the idea of placing the tomb of Queen Tera in a similarly vertiginous position in the cliffs of the Valley of the Sorcerer in *The Jewel of Seven Stars*, published four years later. Newall's *The Awakening* provides some very effective location work to dramatize Stoker's eloquent descriptions here:

> In the narrowest part of the valley, on the south side, was a great cliff of rock, rising sheer, of smooth and even surface. Hereon were graven certain cabalistic signs, and many figures of men and animals, fishes, reptiles and birds; suns and stars; and many quaint symbols.... There was something about it so strange, and so different from the other carved rocks which I had visited, that I called a halt and spent the day in examining the rock front as well as I could with my telescope. The Egyptians of my company were terribly afraid, and used every kind of persuasion to induce me to pass on....

When I returned to the valley with these Bedouins, I made effort to climb the face of the rock, but failed, it being of one impenetrable smoothness. The stone, generally flat and smooth by nature, had been chiselled to completeness....

Being thus baffled of winning the tomb from below, and being unprovided with ladders to scale, I found a way by much circuitous journeying to the top of the cliff. Thence I caused myself to be lowered by ropes till I had investigated that portion of the rock face wherein I expected to find the opening. I found that there was an entrance, closed however by a great stone slab. This was cut in the rock more than a hundred feet up, being two-thirds the height of the cliff.[52]

But, of course, the most sensational find of all Egyptology is surely the discovery of Tutankhamen's tomb by Howard Carter in 1922, a discovery that inspired a whole new craze of Egyptiana from jewelry to architecture, not to mention the first wave of mummy movies in Hollywood ten years later. Carter (1874–1939) began his career as an assistant archeological artist, employed to copy hieroglyphics—a very humble beginning for a man who was to outshine all his predecessors. When he was 25 years old, he was appointed Inspector General of Monuments of Upper Egypt and began to make formal records of the Valley of the Kings where things were changing fast. Electric light had been installed in many of the tombs (which, unlike Ananka's tomb in Hammer's *The Mummy*, did not obligingly glow an illuminating shade of green from some unseen source—though, as she see later, something like that apparently happened to Aleister Crowley in the Great Pyramid). Carter also began to tidy the tombs in the Valley, clearing them of rubble and rubbish, and installed handrails to assist visitors along the treacherous flights of steps within.

One of Carter's early financial backers was Theodore M. Davis, a wealthy retired American lawyer. In 1903, the year in which Stoker's *The Jewel of Seven Stars* was published, Carter unearthed the tomb of Tuthmosis IV for Davis. It was one of the most magnificent discoveries in the Valley of the Kings up to that time, revealing superb paintings and artifacts. A fortnight after the discovery, Maspero attended the official opening and described the atmosphere in somewhat cinematic terms:

The electric light does not penetrate the dusty, heavy air very well, and from the corner where I stood my companions looked like vague silhouettes. The dread of the tomb, so lately shut up, and whence the visits of tourists has not banished the impression of death, has invaded them without their knowledge. They speak in whispers, moderate their gestures, walk or rather glide along as noiselessly as possible.[53]

Carter's next discovery for Davis was the tomb of Queen Hatshepsut, the deepest of the tombs in the Valley of the Kings. It proved to be particularly arduous to clear. Altogether, Davis' discoveries form an impressive list, including the tombs of Horemheb, Siptah, and Yuya and Tuya (the great-grandfather and grandmother of Tutankhamen's queen, whose tomb was discovered for Davis by James Quibell, a pupil of Flinders Petrie). In 1914, Davis' concession from the Government to dig in the Valley expired, leaving the field clear for Lord Carnarvon, whose interest in Egyptology had developed as a consequence of wintering in Egypt to improve his health. Davis had retired from the scene, convinced that there were no more tombs to be discovered in the Valley of the Kings. Obviously, he couldn't have been more mistaken. In fact, Davis had found various artifacts connected with Tutankhamen before Carter's discovery of the tomb itself. These included the mummy of Akhnaten, Tutankhamen's father, which had been moved from its tomb in a desolate valley at Amarna to a burial vault in the Valley of the Kings by Tutankhamen himself. This was what convinced

Carter that the boy-king's tomb might be nearby. World War I delayed Carter's activities in this field, but eventually, the miracle happened. In his own account of the discovery, Carter explained:

> The history of the Valley, as I have endeavored to show in former chapters, has never lacked the dramatic element, and in this, the latest episode, it has held to its traditions. For consider the circumstances. This was to be our final season in the Valley. Six full seasons we had excavated there, and season after season had drawn a blank; we had worked for months at a stretch and found nothing, and only an excavator knows how desperately depressing that can be; we had almost made up our minds that we were beaten, and were preparing to leave the Valley and try our luck elsewhere; and then — hardly had we set hoe to ground in our last despairing effort than we made a discovery that far exceeded our wildest dreams. Surely, never before in the whole history of excavation has a full digging season been compressed within the space of five days.[54]

Carter's account has all the excitement and panache of Stoker and Sax Rohmer, not to mention the popular appeal of mummy movies, all of which owe a debt to him in one way or another. Indeed, his famous words on glimpsing the interior of the tomb for the first time, when he shouted that he could see "wonderful things"[55] capture exactly the same emotion any director of a mummy movie would want his audience to feel as well. Carter even included somewhat Gothic elements in his description of the three gilt couches in the form of "monstrous animals":

> Uncanny beasts enough to look upon at any time: seen as we saw them, their brilliant gilded surfaces picked out of the darkness by the electric torch, as though by limelight, their heads throwing grotesque distorted shadows on the wall behind them, they were almost terrifying. Next, on the right, two statues caught and held our attention; two life-sized figures of a king in black, facing each other like sentinels, gold kilted, gold sandaled, armed with mace and staff, the protective sacred cobra upon their foreheads.... I think we slept but little, all of us, that night.[56]

After all that, Hollywood and Hammer mummy movies were surely only a matter of time. Carter had discovered nearly everything such fantasies required. Admittedly, the mummy of Tutankhamen never came to life, but, thanks to a series of unfortunate coincidences and the hyperbole of the press, there was even "evidence" of a curse, which soon caught the public's imagination. The novelist, Marie Corelli (1855–1924), is more responsible than anyone else for having started the rumor of Tutankhamen's curse. As she herself explained: "*All my life* I have been and am a spiritualist in the *highest sense of the word.*"[57] Her series of novels concerning reincarnation, mysticism, astral travel and other aspects of occultism had earned her international fame and an immense fortune. At odds with modern science (and modern society), she lost no time in publishing her fears, prognostications and warnings. In October 1923, the *Manchester City News* published her dire warning about the modern medium of radio. Unlike a guardian of media morality such as Mary Whitehouse in England in the 1970s and 80s, it was not so much the *content* that concerned Corelli as the technology itself:

> Many of the wonders of creation are the result of the "Law of Vibration"— a law which works its way through everything — through which we enjoy the glory of vision, the sense of sound, the ability of speech. Each word we utter, each action we perform, "vibrates"— that is, sets in motion a million responsive tremors, which, like the ripples made in water by a beating oar, spread themselves far and wide and are never lost. Man is at the moment playing with these

vibrations — he has set up his "wireless" and, what is more dangerous, his "broadcasting" apparatus for his own convenience and amusement, utterly forgetful of the fact that he is toying with powers of which he is as ignorant as a new-born child is of the alphabet.

She predicted that all this "cannot fail of disastrous effect in the long run if continued."[58] Her pronouncements about Tutankhamen were, therefore, part of a lifelong preoccupation with occult matters, which old age only accentuated. Two weeks before Carnarvon died, Corelli published an article in the *New York World* newspaper in which she claimed:

I cannot but think some risks are run by breaking into the last rest of a king in Egypt whose tomb is specially and solemnly guarded, and robbing him of his possessions. According to a rare book I possess ... entitled The Egyptian History of the Pyramids ... *the most dire punishment follows any rash intruder into a sealed tomb*. The book names *"secret poisons enclosed in boxes in such wise that those who touch them shall not know how they come to suffer."* That is why I ask, Was it a mosquito bite that has so seriously infected Lord Carnarvon?[60]

The flurry of subsequent theories included the possibility that anthrax spores were present in the tomb, which, having been disturbed, could have been responsible for Carnarvon's illness, as, indeed, they could have caused the plagues of Egypt mentioned in Genesis. More likely, is the simple fact that the blood poisoning caused by the mosquito was complicated by Lord Carnarvon's poor medical condition, which was not improved by the

Anubis. A contemporary souvenir based on a vignette in *The Book of the Dead*.

excitement of the discovery. Whatever the cause, Carnarvon died on April 5, 1923. According to some sources, a power failure plunged Cairo into darkness at the same moment (but power failures were hardly uncommon at that time). Back in England, Carnarvon's dog, Susie, let out a series of dreadful howls at the moment of her master's death, and then expired as well — though there is no evidence for or against this apparent coincidence.

When the news of Lord Carnarvon's death reached him, Sir Arthur Conan Doyle was being interviewed by a reporter from *The Times* newspaper. Asked by the reporter what he made of the coincidence, Conan Doyle casually mooted the opinion that the death could have been caused by a curse. This, too, was reported and further fueled the flames. Inscriptions were fabricated, subsequent deaths, such as that of Lord Carnarvon's brother five months after his own, were implicated, and even the death of Howard Carter's pet canary was considered significant by some. Carter himself was highly skeptical when it came to the subject of ancient Eygptian curses, though in his account of the discovery of the tomb, he does mention an atmospheric encounter with a pair of jackal-like dogs which bore a striking resemblance to Anubis, the god associated with death and the underworld:

> I have witnessed two animals resembling this Anubis form of jackal-like dog. The first example was seen by me during the early spring of 1926, when in the desert of Thebes. I encountered a pair of jackals slinking towards the Nile valley, as is their custom, in the dusk of the evening. One of them was evidently the common jackal *(C. Lupaster)* in spring pelage; but its mate — I was not near enough to tell whether the male or the female — was much larger, of lanky build, and black![61]

Atmospheric though this encounter must have been, it was obviously not a harbinger of doom, as Carter lived another 13 years. What *is* significant, however, is the impact all these supernatural speculations had on popular culture; but in order fully to understand the power they had on the collective imagination we must first explore the religious and magical beliefs of the ancient Egyptians themselves.

Three

Myth and Magic

> This is the Scroll of Thoth. Herein are set down the magic words by which Isis raised Osiris from the dead. Oh! Amon-Ra — Oh! God of Gods — Death is but the doorway to new life —- We live today — we shall live again — in many forms shall we return — Oh Mighty One.

But that, of course, is pure Hollywood. Those words are not a translation from ancient Egyptian. They are from the typewriter of John L. Balderston, who wrote them for *The Mummy* (dir. Karl Freund, 1932). They appear at the beginning of the film, superimposed over production designer Willy Pogany's accomplished (though somewhat simplified) copy of a section from the British Museum's Papyri of Hunefer, one of the several versions of the Egyptian Book of the Dead that have come down to us from the ancient world. In the particular vignette in question, Anubis takes the hand of Hunefer, who, in life, had been the overseer of the royal palace of Seti I, and leads him over the threshold of the Hall of Double Maat in the afterlife, where Hunefer's heart will be weighed. Overhead, 14 gods also sit in judgment. But this scene does not appear in the Scroll of Thoth, for the legendary Scroll of Thoth has never been found, if it ever existed in the first place. Other mystical writings attributed the equally legendary man-god, Thoth, do survive, however, though they were most likely written by an unknown ancient priest in remote antiquity. Thoth, the scribe of the gods and the master of Egyptian magic, was also known as Hermes Trismegistus by the ancient Greeks, who identified Thoth with their own messenger of the gods, Hermes. To distinguish Thoth from that god, they called him "Thrice Great." The Corpus Hermiticum as a whole describes how Thoth became one with Nous — the mind of god — and thereby understood the origin and natural laws of the universe. A major influence on Islam, the Hermeticum was eventually translated into Latin by Marsilio Ficino in 1471, around the same time that interest in the religion of ancient Egypt had begun to grow rapidly.[1] Falsely interpreting what, after all, couldn't be understood at that time, Renaissance thinkers believed that hieroglyphs were a form of secret writing by which priests communed with occult forces. Thus was Hermeticism born, a philosophy which had, in many ways, been anticipated by Pharaoh Akhnaten's monotheistic worship of Aton, as opposed to a panoply of gods that had prevailed in Egypt until his time. In the highly influential second book of the Corpus Hermeticum, known as *The Divine Pymander of Hermes Trismegistus* ("Pymander" means "Shepherd of Men"), the Pymander explains himself to Hermes Trimegistus as follows:

I myself, the Nous, am present with holy men and good, the pure and merciful; men who live piously; and My Presence is a help unto them, and forthwith they know all things, and lovingly propitiate the Father, praising Him, giving Him thanks, singing hymns; being ordinate and intent on Him, with adoration and love.[2]

Though not pantheistic (the Trismegistic writings differentiate between God and the things he creates), the Pymander explains that the Mind of God nonetheless pervades all things:

And all things are full of Soul, and all are moved by it, each in its proper way; some indeed round the Heaven, others around the Earth; see how the right move not unto the left; nor the above below, nor the below above. And that all these are subject to generation, O most beloved Hermes, thou hast no longer need to learn of Me — for they are bodies, have Souls, and are moved. But for all these to come together into one, it is impossible without a principle to gather them into one; therefore there must be such a one, and He is altogether One.[3]

The revival of Egyptian magic in the 18th century, so intimately connected with Rosicrucianism and the Masons, derives from these Hermetic texts, along with the texts of the so-called Emerald Tablet, which is meant to have been inscribed by Hermes Trismegistus himself. No less a figure than Sir Isaac Newton translated this celebrated text about the creation of the world and the nature of the four elements, including the famous alchemical dictum: "That which is below is like that which is above & that which is above is like that which is below to do the miracles of only one thing."[4] Alchemy based its complex quest for the transmutation of lead into gold (and the parallel quest for the purification of the soul) on the words engraved on this emerald, which, if understood correctly and implemented reveal "the glory of the whole world & thereby all obscurity shall fly from you."[5]

The term "alchemy" is thought to have originated from the original name for Egypt: "Kemet" or "Khem," the country in which alchemy was believed to have been most widely practiced. Christopher Lee's Kharis, in *The Mummy*, refers to the Land of Khem during the ritual that accompanies the embalming of Ananka. The word is usually considered to be derived from *khemein* or *khēmia*, meaning "a preparation of black powder." Hence the appellation of "Black Lands" for Egypt — not so much because this was where black magical arts were practiced but because the first stage in alchemy is known as *Nigredo* (blackening) from which ultimate purity is eventually achieved. After *Nigredo*, the intermediary stage, *Cauda pavonis* ("peacock's tail"), symbolizes the many colors that contain the one white color. The second stage, known as *Albedo*, produces the whitening, or cleansing. *Rubedo* (reddening) follows, when the Red and the White (often symbolized by the Queen and the King) reach their greatest heat before unifying in the final stage of the Chemical Wedding. Commonly, this is considered to be the moment when lead is transmuted into gold, but, as Jung has suggested in his study of *Psychology and Alchemy*, it more significantly refers to the achievement of supreme knowledge, the Philosopher's Stone symbolizing psychological integration with the self (or with the *nous*—the mind of God).

But the symbolism of alchemy also has other interpretations connected with the myth of Isis and Osiris. In the film *Chemical Wedding* (dir. Julian Doyle, 2008), John Shrapnel's Aleister Crowley explains the legend of ancient Egypt's two most important gods as follows:

The oldest and most powerful ritual comes to us from Egyptian hieroglyphics. It tells of the murder and betrayal of Osiris by Seth. Seth cut the dead body into fifteen parts and scattered them over the land of Egypt. Isis found most of the pieces and using her magic she fused them together in resurrection, but she was missing the phallus; so, using a reed as a substitute phallus, she performed a wedding rite with Osiris and brought forth a powerful son, Horus.

The basic story is familiar to us already from the account given by Tom Baker in "Pyramids of Mars," but in this reading of the legend, Horus is a magical child, the product of an occult ritual of sexual magic. Crowley himself sometimes referred to such a magical creature as a moonchild. Indeed, he wrote an entire novel about one, called *Moonchild*, in 1917. In Doyle's film the moonchild is presented as an incarnation of Choronzon, the demonic power that represents, as the film's own publicity puts it, the "negative energy of the abyss." (Incidentally, the *Hammer House of Horror* TV episode "Guardian of the Abyss" [dir. Don Sharp, 1980] also dealt with the subject of Choronzon's incarnation at the hands of an occultist played by John Carson, who is obviously modeled on Crowley.) *Chemical Wedding*, in its rather incoherent but visually splendid way, makes the connection between Egyptian myth and Freemasonry clear. Crowley not only performs his ritual in the temple of a Masonic lodge, but the film also shows that Crowley believed himself to be the reincarnation of one of Freemasonry's most influential historical figures, Count Cagliostro.

The original Brotherhood of Masonry first emerged at the end of the 16th century under the auspices of William Schaw, the "Maister o' Wark" under King James VI. In the 18th century, Cagliostro built on these traditions with his Egyptian Rite, which though not specifically Egyptian in its style or reference, was nonetheless indebted to the Hermetic tradition, and so was not, in fact, anything particularly new, as he himself pointed out. He felt that he was merely restoring the ancient teachings to their original importance. This isn't the place to discuss the details of Freemasonry. Readers wishing to pursue this subject at length are directed to Philippa Faulks's and Robert L.D. Cooper's engaging study of Cagliostro's Egyptian Rite, *The Masonic Magician*. More pertinent to the aim of this book is that Cagliostro's interest in the paraphernalia of Egyptology also contributed to the popular conception of ancient Egypt that ultimately resulted in much later mummy movies. After all, as we have already seen, Universal's *The Mummy* began life as a story about Cagliostro. Faulks and Cooper point out that Cagliostro claimed to have received his initiation into the Egyptian Hermetic mysteries in a ritual held inside the Great Pyramid at Giza,[6] and that in 1785 he furnished one of the rooms in his Paris residence in Rue St Claude as a *Chambre Egyptienne*: "Adorned with concave mirrors, statues of Anubis, Isis and the Apis bull and the walls covered in hieroglyphs, it was to create the perfect ambiance for the materialization of the spirits. Cagliostro would appear robed in black silk with hieroglyphs embroidered in red."[7]

Purely for art historical reasons, such a decorative scheme is significant. Along with the Egyptian designs of Cagliostro's slightly older contemporary, Giovanni Battista Piranesi, to which we will return in a later chapter, such décors demonstrate that European interest in Egyptian art predated Napoleon's Egyptian campaign. Faulks and Cooper point out that Cagliostro went so far as to call himself "Grand Copht," a designation for the high priests of ancient Egypt, and they also connect the rituals of Freemasonry with designs found in Egyptian art and architecture. They suggest, for example, that tomb paintings of Rameses II show him wearing what appears to be the apron of a Master Mason, and that the positions adopted by the pharaohs and gods also resemble the postures of stonemasons at work. They argue that ancient Egyptian stonemasons were an organized society, and that aspects of later

Masonic symbolism are directly related to the way in which Egyptian temples were constructed.[8] The pyramid was also a profoundly significant symbol. The four corners of the base represent the four elements, while the fifth point — the tip of the pyramid — represents the spirit which rules the elements. The trials of Fire, Air and Water, which form part of the initiation rituals of Freemasonry, were to play an important role in both Mozart's Masonic and Egyptian *Singspiel*, *Die Zauberflöte*, and Jean Terrasson's influential Masonic novel *The Life of Sethos*, which was a considerable influence on the libretto Mozart set to music.

Terrasson (1670–1750) was an obscure French Abbé, who published his novel in 1731. Despite its apparently biographical title, *The Life of Sethos*, is, in fact, an influential forgery, wholly written by Terrasson himself, concerning the initiation of Sethos, an Egyptian prince, into the mystery religion of Isis and Osiris. Even so, *The Life of Sethos* was originally regarded by many as an authentic document from ancient times. Terrasson claimed that the book was a translation of a text by a Greek author living in Alexandria under the reign of Marcus Aurelius. While simultaneously describing that supposedly original text as a work of fiction, Terrasson claimed that he had also drawn upon sacred Egyptian wisdom, and to increase the sense of occult revelation, he added that the library in which the original text is located is in a foreign country that is "extremely jealous of this sort of treasure."[9] Disguised under such complex veils of dissimulation, it's not surprising that, until well into the 19th century, *Sethos* was believed to be "authentic." It was also believed to be the foundation on which much Masonic ritual was later based, but, in fact, most of the rituals in the book were themselves taken from existing Masonic lore. (Terrasson was himself a mason.) The book nonetheless made a considerable impact on the development of Freemasonry (and according to Faulks and Cooper, Cagliostro may well have been familiar with the novel and based parts of his Egyptian Masonic Rite upon it[10]). It not only provided much of the Masonic ritual we see in *Die Zauberflöte* (1791) but also informed the play, *Thämos, König in Aegypten*, by Tobias von Gebler, for which Mozart wrote incidental music in 1780. *The Life of Sethos*, therefore, seems to be the ultimate source of the veritable Nile-like flood of Egyptian fantasy that culminated in the Universal and Hammer mummy movie cycles of the 20th century. We'll be returning to the influence of *The Life of Sethos* on Mozart and others later, but it's useful to mention here that the novel inaugurated the influential misconception of the ancient Egyptians' belief in reincarnation:

> For, not to mention the Metempsychosis, which Pythagoras was for establishing among them, and which made the souls of men, when freed from the body, pass from one animal to another, till after the space of three thousand years, they again entered into human bodies.[11]

Magic, alchemy and the quest for the philosopher's stone are also mentioned as having originated in Egypt:

> Hermes Trismegistus taught them the secret of transforming all metals into gold, call'd for that reason the Hermetical philosophy. As a proof of which they alledge [sic] the vast extent of their riches, which, say they, one single mine of gold, the only one they knew, could never have furnished.... Besides, wise men don't doubt but this true philosopher's stone, of which Mercury or Hermes was the inventor, was the commerce which this first king of Thebes establish'd in Egypt.[12]

Another misconception, which was to be repeated by the likes of Sax Rohmer nearly two hundred years later, was Terrasson's claim that the pyramids contained subterranean temples "where the priest and priestesses, whose voices he had heard, performed every night different sorts of sacrifices and ceremonies."[13]

This Masonic influence stretched well into the 20th century, even though some of the writers who discussed it claimed to be unaware of the historical processes involved, believing they had received their respective texts by telepathic means from spiritual forces. Perhaps the most famous example of this (in terms of ancient Egypt) is Joan Grant's novel *Winged Pharaoh* (1937), which will be discussed in more detail later. Two years before that novel was published, H. C. Randall-Stevens had published *A Voice out of Egypt* in the seventh chapter of which ("The Hidden Temples") he describes the Masonic initiation rituals for which he claimed the pyramids were built. In his white robes, Randall-Stevens explains, the neophyte must first confront the Sphinx before entering the temple beneath it, which is reached by walking down the flight of steps between its paws. The neophyte is then given a small lamp by a priest and told that he must find his way from the Halls of Matter and Darkness to the Halls of Light before the lamp is extinguished and he is lost forever, abandoned to the powers of Set. He is assailed by phantom visions as he makes his way to the Altar of Purification, where a priest offers him pomegranate juice to drink before moving on to the Halls of Mystery and the Temple of the Lotus. If he can understand the pictures he sees mirrored in the Sacred Water there he may proceed to the next test in the Chamber of Ordeal, which is situated beneath the base of the third pyramid. Some very creative "dreaming" follows during the Ordeal by Suggestion, after which the neophyte finds himself stretched out on the floor of the Chamber of Transmigration from where he is led by another priest to the Temple of Purification, in which he is cleansed by Sacred Water.

Randall-Stevens was adamant (and probably sincerely so) that what he wrote was merely transcribed by him from "the Voice" which dictated such wisdom to him, but it is hard not to draw the conclusion that it is all indebted to Terrasson's *Sethos* and a Masonic tradition derived from ideas that had been built up around the mythical figure of Thoth.

Thoth also played an important role in the story of Isis and Osiris. Set traps his hated brother in a coffer at a magnificent banquet held in Osiris's honor. The coffer is then thrown into the sea where it is eventually washed up in the branches of a sapling on the shores of Byblos. The sapling eventually grows into a noble tree which is then felled to form one of the pillars of the king's palace there. Meanwhile, Osiris's wife and sister, Isis, grief-stricken, locates the pillar and, in the form of a swallow, encircles it at night. After befriending the king and queen of Byblos, she is given the coffer that is discovered to be still intact inside the tree that forms one of the pillars in the palace. She hides it but Set eventually discovers its whereabouts and smashes it. This is the moment when he dismembers the corpse. Isis doesn't search for the pieces alone. She is helped by her sister, Set's wife, Nephthys, and together they reassemble the body of Osiris, thus creating the world's first-ever mummy. Osiris's phallus, which eludes them, has been eaten by an oxyrhynchus fish. (Some commentators have interpreted representations of Set's ears as resembling fins and therefore concluded that the oxyrhynchus fish was, in fact, Set himself, who devoured the offending member in an attempt to make Osiris's immolation absolute.)

Osiris is not resurrected in the sense that we understand the term today. Instead, he becomes what one might term "undead" but without any of the negative connotations such a term might imply thanks to its associations with vampire lore. Isis sings to him (or breathes into him) and calls on Thoth for magical assistance to impel him into this strange dual state. As a mixture of the living and the dead he is installed as the King of the Underworld, but not before he helps Isis conceive a child, Horus, who eventually avenges the death of his father.

Thoth, Isis, Nephthys, Osiris, Set and Horus all make appearances in The Book of the Dead, as, indeed, do Horus's children, Hapi, Mestha, Tuamutef, Quebhsennuf and a host of other gods. The parallels between these mythological characters and those of other religions is obvious to modern eyes, having had the benefit of over a century of studies in comparative religion. Isis and Horus eventually formed the model for the Christian Madonna and Child, Osiris and Set form a parallel for God and Satan. (Indeed, the name Satan is etymologically related to one of Set's alternative names "Setan." In Hebrew "Sâtân" means "adversary.") But Osiris and Set are also related to Cain and Abel, Esau and Jacob, and ultimately, in more secular times, Dr. Jekyll and Mr. Hyde. Set was originally a highly regarded deity, but he became demonized due to political conflict. Upper Egypt remained loyal to Horus while Lower Egypt was ruled by Set. The unification of Egypt sought by the followers of Horus (and Isis and Osiris) in Upper Egypt was resisted by the followers of Set with the consequence that Upper Egypt began to denigrate Set by emphasizing his negative rôle in the legend of Isis and Osiris. (Presumably, these historical events formed the basic idea of Joan Grant's *Eyes of Horus* in which Set's influence is challenged by a group called "Watchers of the Horizon," who work to restore Ra to the whole land of Egypt.) Later, the Greeks equated Set with the storm god Typhon, which is why Set is sometimes referred to as Set-Typhon or Seth-Typhon. (Tom Baker's Doctor Who is keen to inform his companion, Sarah-Jane, of this at the end of "Pyramids of Mars.") In the early pyramid texts, Set was seen as a beneficent god, portrayed as the equal of Horus, who defends the Solar Barque on its voyage through the underworld, but by the time of the Papyrus of Ani, Set is seen in a completely negative light:

> What then is this? It is the day on which Horus fought with Set, who cast filth in the face of Horus, and when Horus destroyed the powers of Set. Thoth did this with his own hand.[14]

Other translations take a less Victorian approach to the translation than Sir E. A. Wallis Budge does here, spelling out that Horus actually crushed the genitals of Set.

The Book of the Dead, despite what to modern ears might sound a rather gloomy title, is not at all a gloomy book. It is, in fact, a wonderfully touching, tender and optimistic document, with nothing of hellfire and damnation in it. The ancient Egyptians were only interested in death to such an extent because they were so interested in life and wanted to ensure that life would continue after death in much the same way as is lived on earth — only better. There are many very moving prayers regarding this:

> Let me have possession of my heart, let me have possession of my whole heart; let me have possession of my mouth, let me have possession of my legs, let me have possession of my arms, let me have possession of my limbs absolutely; let me have possession of my funeral meals, let me have possession of air, let me have possession of water, let me have possession of the stream, let me have possession of the banks.... That which I execrate, I eat it not.[15]

The mystical aura of later religious ideas has rather clouded our understanding of how the Egyptians viewed the afterlife. For them, the Fields of Peace were not an alternative world of angels strumming harps on clouds, but rather an exact replica of the world they knew and loved on earth, where the soul continued to drink, plow, reap, fight, eat and engage in sexual relations. The Book of the Dead contains passages in which the soul pleads not to die a second time and not to become corrupt in the Underworld, nor to perish there and certainly not to be made captive. None of these desires, however, has anything to do with reincarnation. The soul may visit the corpse — its earthly home — but not be reincarnated in the Hindu or Buddhist sense of the term. In this respect the reincarnation element that appears in so many mummy films (and which, of course, is a central aspect of Stoker's *The Jewel of Seven Stars*) is quite alien to ancient Egyptian thought.

It was the purpose of the Book of the Dead to sustain the life of the soul and maintain the rhythms of life. It did not, as suggested by the 1999 remake of *The Mummy*, have the power to resurrect flesh and blood in the material world. Originally the texts were inscribed or painted onto the walls of tombs — first in the pyramids. When the pyramids became unfashionable, the pyramids' texts gave way to coffin texts that were inscribed on the coffins themselves. As ancient Egyptian society gradually became more democratic, papyri began to replace coffin texts, and depending on the wealth of the deceased, the copy of the Book of the Dead buried with them would be more or less elaborately decorated and illustrated. (Even such a sacred, metaphysical text was a commodity with a market price. Sinuhe, in Waltari's *The Egyptian*, describes how he "frittered away" his time making copies of the Book of the Dead and selling them in the courtyard of the House of Life at Thebes.[16] Sinue also writes out a copy of the sacred texts to be lain in his father's tomb: "A fine, fairly written book, though not adorned with colored pictures like those sold in the book court of Ammon's temple."[17]) By means of text and illustrative vignettes, the Book of the Dead explains what will happen to the soul on its journey to the Fields of Peace where it will ride with Re, the sun god, in his solar chariot. It is, indeed, a kind of guide book and phrase book to help the soul accustom itself to the afterlife. On entering the land of Amenta, as the otherworld was known, the heart, or conscience of the departed, must be weighed in the Hall of Double Maat. The concept of Maat represents truth, equilibrium and what is right and just. The texts habitually show the soul of the supplicant observing the weighing of the heart against the feather of Maat, which symbolizes the qualities of Maat. Anubis checks the scales to ensure that there are no mistakes, while the seemingly fearsome (but in practice invariably benign) figure of Ammit, the "Devourer of the Dead," waits patiently beside him (or Thoth) like a grotesque pet dog. Ammit is a typically composite god, part lion and part hippopotamus, with a crocodile's head (an appropriate thing for a devourer of the dead to possess, but, it seems, rarely put to practical use, his object no doubt being to inspire the soul to behave itself and thus pass the test). Thoth, the scribe of the gods — the moon god and master of all magic — stands behind Anubis, inscribing the verdict of the scales. The 12 main other gods also sit in judgment overhead, appeased by a table loaded with offerings. The illustrations of the various versions of the Book of the Dead, particularly those of the royal scribe Ani, the overseer Hunefer and the singer Anhai (all of which are these days in the care of the British Museum) are particularly touching and gentle. The whole process described above is concerned with the care and well-being of the soul, its promotion and ultimate happiness. Next, we see the falcon-headed god, Horus, the son of Isis and Osiris, charmingly holding the hand of the successfully journeying soul, and introducing it to Osiris, who sits enthroned with Isis and her sister Nephthys. This is, in fact, the section of the Book of the Dead that was used to stand in for the Scroll of Thoth in the opening scene of Universal's original version of *The Mummy*. Overhead, the mortuary god, Sokaris, in the form of a hawk's head, is guarded by 12 cobras. As the soul kneels before and venerates Osiris, his wig is drained of color and turns pure white. The solemnity of the funeral procession we see in Hammer's *The Mummy* was no doubt derived from the vignette in Anni's papyrus showing Anni's mummy being drawn by a team of oxen with a priest in a panther-skin presiding over the proceedings, burning incense and sprinkling water. Eight white-clad female mourners follow, while Ani's servants pull a funeral chest on which Anubis is seated, lying on his haunches, his front paws outstretched and his long bushy tail overhanging the back of the chest as we see in the famous Anubis figure discovered in the store chamber or "Innermost Treasury" of Tutankhamen's tomb. The chest is decorated with the Djed column (a symbol associated with Osiris and signifying eternal life), and lotus flowers (symbols of both and morning) surround it. Mourners were paid, as in many other cultures, to provide professional grief, and we see them bare-breasted here along with the touching sight of Ani's wife weeping in genuine grief beside her husband's coffin, which is shown being held by Anubis in a protective, caring manner. Hammer's *The Mummy*, like Universal's 1932 original, also uses interpretations of the Ani papyrus to stand in for its Scroll of Life ("said to have been written by the god Karnak himself," as Peter Cushing's John Banning puts it, though, of course, Karnak is the site of a temple of Amon and was never a god). The funeral cortège of the Princess Ananka as arranged by director Terence Fisher (and "researched" by the film's Egyptology advisor, Andrew Low) contains many elements of ancient Egyptian tradition. Fisher made sure that we see the professional mourners, played by suitably wailing women. Christopher Lee's Kharis is attired in priestly robes replete with the traditional panther skin, and there is what is described in Peter Cushing's narration as "the Sekhmet boat for bearing the spirit of the dead to the afterworld." Some of the boats found in Tutankhamen's tomb had this function, and one of the seven boats of Osiris, which took part in the procession of Osiris is called the Sektet boat, but Sekhmet, the lion-headed goddess, has nothing to do with boats. She ruled the desert, and, as such, had a rather fearsome aspect (the sun disc on her head implies this). Like the Hindu deity, Shiva, she was both a creator and a destroyer, but was fundamentally opposed to evil. (Joan Grant's portrayal of Sekhmet as the consort of the evil Set in *Eyes of Horus* is therefore also incorrect, an inaccuracy that does somewhat undermine her claim to have "remembered" everything from a past life.)

Next in Terence Fisher's wonderful cinematic procession is "The Living God — the personification of the recorder of souls," but this looks more like Anubis, a statue of which, couchant as in the Tutankhamen Anubis mentioned above, follows. The head of Hathor, represented as a cow's head, is carried behind this couchant Anubis. Hathor was the goddess of dance, music and the arts, who also suckles the dead in order to sustain them on their journey to the underworld. Then come maidens bearing ushabti figurines, which are "symbols of mythical power and significance," though Cushing doesn't explain in what way. In fact, the ushabti we find in ancient tombs were designed for the rather prosaic function of doing any manual work which the soul might have to perform in the afterlife. They were mystical robots in that respect.

The royal mummy of Ananka is then pulled on a sledge behind the maidens with the ushabti, supported on a dais replete with somewhat anachronistic violet drapery, complete with tassels — an element at which Andrew Low might well have raised his eye-brows, though as critic Anthony Carthew rightly pointed out when the film first appeared, *The Mummy*, while being "continuously entertaining" was "not intended to be taken seriously."[18] There's enough research, however, to make things as visually convincing as necessary (which is a good deal more than in some of the Universal follow-ups to the original Mummy film of 1932, on which Jimmy Sangster's screenplay is also based). One of the most important rituals of an ancient Egyptian funeral — and one which Hammer included in the temple scenes of *The Mummy*—was that of the "Opening of the Mouth":

> Let my mouth be opened by Ptah, and let the muzzles which are upon my mouth be loosed by the god of my domain. Then let Thoth come, full and equipped with Words of Power, and let him loose the muzzles of Sutu which are upon my mouth, and let Tmu lend a hand to fling them at the assailants.[19]

Christopher Lee's Kharis, as we've seen, ritualistically performs the "Opening of the Mouth" ceremony over the mummy of his beloved Ananka. Just prior to that, when Ananka's body is being embalmed, he says: "And Anubis who sitteth upon the hill hath set thee in order and will fasten thee thy swathings"— a line which seems to be derived from Budge's translation of the Opening of the Mouth ceremony in the Papyrus of Ani:

> THE CHAPTER OF OPENING THE MOUTH OF OSIRIS, THE SCRIBE ANI: "May Ptah open my mouth, and may the god of my town loose the swathings, even the swathings which are over my mouth."[20]

But we see a far more literal treatment of this ceremony in *The Awakening* when Charlton Heston pulls open the jaws of Queen Kara's mummy in the final scene. "Anubis, take away mine eyes," he whispers. "Open thine; Anubis, open thy mouth and fill thy heart." However, it is not the desiccated dust of the mummy that comes to life here. Instead, the reincarnated spirit of the evil queen takes possession of his daughter, who promptly causes a pillar to crush him. This isn't quite what happens in Stoker's novel, which, anyway, has two contrasting endings. The original ending more closely resembles what happens at the end of *The Awakening* and *Blood from the Mummy's Tomb,* and is quite unlike the later, more optimistic ending, forced on Stoker by his publishers for the second edition. In neither ending, however, is the Ceremony of the Opening of the Mouth performed, for the mummy of Stoker's Queen Tera is, as in Hammer's adaptation, perfectly preserved. Stoker's characters do, however, unwrap the mummy to reveal a body "like a statue carven in ivory by the hand of a Praxiteles.... All the pores of the body seemed to have been preserved in some wonderful way. The flesh was full and round, as in a living person; and the skin was as smooth as satin."[21] It is necessary to unwrap Queen Tera because, as Trelawny explains, "I think that under any circumstances it would be necessary to remove the wrappings before she became again a live human being instead of a spiritualized corpse with an astral body. Were her original intention carried out, and did she come to new life within her mummy wrapping, it might be to exchange a coffin for a grave. She would die the death of the buried alive!"[22]

And this leads me on to the ancient Egyptians' somewhat complicated sub-divisions of the soul. Stoker went to considerable pains to root his fantasy in the beliefs of the ancient Egyptians, and quoted Budge in his chapter describing "The Purpose of Queen Tera":

> First there is the "Ka," or "Double," which, as Doctor Budge explains, may be defined as "an abstract individuality of personality" which was imbued with all the characteristic attributes of the individual it represented, and possessed an absolutely independent existence. It was free to move from place to place on earth at will; and it could enter into heaven and hold converse with the gods. Then there was the "Ba," or "soul," which dwelt with the "Ka," and had the power of becoming corporeal or incorporeal at will; "it had both substance and form.... It had power to leave the tomb.... It could revisit the body in the tomb ... and could reincarnate it and hold converse with it." Again there was the "Khu," the "spiritual intelligence," or spirit. It took the form of "a shining, luminous, intangible shape of the body...." Then, again, there was the

"Sekhem," or "power" of a man, his strength or vital force personified. These were the "Khaibit," or "shadow," the "Ren," or "name," the "Khat," or "physical body," and "Ab," the "heart," in which life was seated, went to the full making up of a man.

"Thus you will see, that if this division of functions, spiritual and bodily, ethereal and corporeal, ideal and actual, be accepted as exact, there are all the possibilities and capabilities of corporeal transference, guided always by an unimprisonable will or intelligence."[23]

The quotations within Stoker's text, in fact, derive from Budge's *Egyptian Ideas of the Future Life*, first published in 1899, a copy of which, according to Paul Murray, Stoker owned.[24] Murray says that Stoker's library also contained Budge's nine-volume *History of Egypt*, *Easy Lessons in Egyptian Hieroglyphics* and *The Egyptian Book of the Dead*. Stoker, however, made an important alteration to the passage he quoted from Budge's *Egyptian Ideas of the Future Life*, which lends a false sense of authority to his reincarnation tale. It's agreed among Egyptologists that reincarnation was not a belief shared by the ancient Egyptians themselves. Budge, in *Osiris and the Egyptian Resurrection* (1911), published eight years after Stoker's novel, did briefly consider the possibility of interpreting ancient Egyptian texts in terms of reincarnation, but discounted it:

> There are at least two passages in the Theban Recension of the Book of the Dead which show that the Egyptians believed in the possibility of a "second birth." The first occurs in the LXIV Chapter in which the deceased identifies himself with the "God of the hidden soul, the Creator of the gods," and refers to his second birth, and the second in the CLXXXII Chapter, wherein Osiris is addressed as "he who giveth birth to men and women a second time." The context in the latter case suggests that the new birth or re-birth here referred to did not take place in this world, but in the kingdom of Osiris, and in the former case the new birth of the deceased seems to resemble the re-birth of Ra, the Sun-god, who it was thought was re-born daily. In neither case can the re-birth be considered as reincarnation as the word is understood at the present time.[25]

So Budge did not think, as Stoker suggests he did, that the Egyptians believed in reincarnation. So Stoker simply, but drastically, changed one of the words in the quotations he drew from Budge's *Egyptian Ideas of the Future Life*. In that volume, Budge explained that the Ka "could re-animate it [i.e., "the body"] and hold converse with it." Stoker, by contrast, wrote "could *reincarnate* it and hold converse with it" (my italics). Budge's original paragraph, is as follows:

> The soul was called BA, and the ideas which the Egyptians held concerning it are somewhat difficult to reconcile; the meaning of the word seems to be something like "sublime," "noble," "mighty." The BA dwelt in the KA, and seems to have had the power of becoming corporeal or incorporeal at will; it had both substance and form, and is frequently depicted on the papyri and monuments as a human-headed hawk; in nature and substance it is stated to be ethereal. It had the power to leave the tomb, and to pass up into heaven where it was believed to enjoy an eternal existence in a state of glory; it could, however, and did, revisit the body in the tomb, and from certain texts it seems that it could re-animate it and hold converse with it. Like the heart AB it was, in some respects, the seat of life in man. The souls of the blessed dead dwelt in heaven with the gods, and they partook of all the celestial enjoyments for ever.[26]

"Re-animation" is not at all the same as "reincarnation"— so Stoker is guilty here of falsifying his authority to make it fit his fictional theory.

Dennis Wheatley's occult novel *The Ka of Gifford Hilary* (1956) speaks for many when discussing the complexity of the Egyptians' concept of the soul. In the section of the novel that covers events during Tuesday, September 13, a psychical researcher called Wilfred Tibitts claims that anyone trying to understand this subject would inevitably become "hopelessly confused."[27] As Stoker had done before him, Wheatley then takes us through the various elements: the Ka or Double, the Sahu or Spirit Body, The Khaibit or Shadow, and the Khu or Spirit Soul, adding that the ancient Egyptians "complicated things even further by attributing a separate soul to the Ka, which they called the Ba, and maintaining that the Heart also had independent non-physical qualities.... Having endowed the Ka with a soul they had to protect that, hence the little statues of themselves called Ka figures that they had buried with them in their tombs. The Ka figure was for the Ka soul to live in when it was compelled to leave the physical body at death."[28]

Wheatley is perhaps the only writer of popular fiction to base a tale of Cold War espionage on ancient Egyptian metaphysics. (He's also a rare example of an author who takes the trouble to recommend that any of his readers who do not share his own interest in the political and strategic details of the Soviet threat should skip a few thousand words, assuring them that they will "lose nothing" by doing so!) As for the plot itself, Sir Gifford Hillary of the Ministry of Defence in London, is murdered by his own wife and her lover, who turn a top secret death ray on him. Hillary then discovers that his Ka can now observe the activities of his murderers; but realizing that the Ka dies when the body dies, he begins to wonder if he has become a Ba instead, forced to wander about in a disembodied state forever. In the end he learns that the death ray that he thought had killed him in fact had only "driven the electrons which vitalized my physical being out of it, causing an immediate suspension of animation."[29] Eventually locating his coffin and the only apparently dead body inside it, Hillary's Ka presses its mouth against the body's nostrils and breathes deeply, willing itself back to become one with its own flesh and blood. This, of course, has the unfortunate consequence of Hillary finding himself buried alive, but, as one might expect, he eventually escapes and lives to tell the tale.

The ancient Egyptians themselves did not refer to the pyramid, coffin and later papyri texts as the Book of the Dead. This was a title given to them when they were translated into German in 1842 by Richard Lepsius. His title of *Der Totenbuch* immediately caught the imagination of scholars and public alike and remained as the standard translation of what the ancient Egyptians knew as *Reu nu pert em hru* ("Chapters of coming forth by day"). It is not, in fact, a book at all, but rather a series of spells and prayers with many variants depending on which particular Book of the Dead one is reading. Most of the texts were intended to be spoken by the dead person himself and not by priests in a temple, and so they fulfill a quite different function to later holy books such as the Bible or the Qur'an, which were originally designed for ritualistic use in a church or mosque. The Book of the Dead's original Egyptian title refers to the belief that the departed soul takes all night to reach the world of the afterlife. The soul's "coming forth by day," therefore, refers to its arrival. If the spells are correctly invoked, the soul will enter the other world with the dawn. Religion and magic (which many faiths, particularly Christianity and Islam, prefer to separate) were a unity for the ancient Egyptians, and magic also played an important rôle in everyday life, assisting with such prosaic things as medicine, legal matters and personal protection.

Sax Rohmer's story, "Breath of Allah," another of his *Tales of Secret Egypt*, refers to this everyday use of magic. In this instance it concerns the process of making perfume, a ritual which is traditionally presided over by an *imám*. Admittedly, this is a Moslem ritual, and the story is set in modern (1919) Cairo but the tradition of such an approach to magic is certainly traceable to ancient times:

There is a magical ritual which must be observed in the distillation of the perfume, and each essence is blessed in the name of one of the four archangels, and the whole operation must commence at the hour of midnight on the eve of the Moild en–Nebi.[30]

The most common manifestations of magic were, of course, the many different kinds of amulet in everyday use in ancient Egypt. One writer on the occult, Bernard Bromage, pointed out that great care was taken over the construction of amulets, explaining their magical function as "carriers of supernatural energy." He added that there was "close correspondence between the shaping and the lettering of the image and the actual specific magical, healing, protective equipment of the god. The substance of the image is also important, for, by a law known to occultists as the Law of Properties, certain substances and materials possess in their own nature important occult and magical qualities."[31]

This is rather at odds with the "Far Memory" of Joan Grant in *Eyes of Horus* (1942), in which one her characters, Roidahn, an ancient Egyptian nobleman, explains that the shape of an amulet isn't important. Rather, he points out, it is the power that is stored within them that counts. Roidahn makes Kiyas, the sister of the novel's narrator, Ra-ab, an amulet in the shape of her toy wooden lion, Anilops, explaining that "with children it is usually better to choose a shape they associate with going to sleep."[32] The Life of Ptah can be stored in an amulet just as a bottle stores wine, but "the making of real amulets is a difficult magic, and in these days rare."[33]

Ptah was the most mystical of the Egyptian deities in that he called the world into being. The name means "opener" in the sense of the "Opening of the Mouth" ceremony, which he was also said to have created. Indeed, the name of Egypt comes from the Greek *Aiguptos*, which is derived from the Egyptian *Hwt-Ptah*, meaning "Temple of Ptah." In Act I, scene 2 of Verdi's opera *Aida* there is an atmospheric invocation to this ancient god:

> Immenso Fthà, del mondo
> Spirito animator,
> Noi ti invochiamo!
>
> Immense Fthà, del mondo
> Spirito fecondator,
> Noi ti invochiamo!
>
> Fuoco increato, eterno,
> Onde ebbe luce il sol,
> Noi ti invochiamo!
>
> To che dal nulla hai tratto
> L'onde, la terra e il ciel,
> Noi ti invochiamo!
>
> Nume che del tuo spirito
> Sei figlio e genitor,
> Noi ti invochiamo!
>
> Vita dell' Universo
> Mito di eterno amor,
> Noi ti invochiamo!

> Infinite Ptah,
> Animating spirit of the world,
> We invoke thee!
>
> Infinite Ptah,
> Fecundating spirit of the world,
> We invoke thee!
>
> Fire uncreated, eternal,
> Whence the sun has light,
> We invoke thee!
>
> Though who from nothing
> Made the earth and the heavens,
> We invoke thee!
>
> God, who of thy spirit
> Are son and father,
> We invoke thee!
>
> Life of the Universe
> Gift of eternal love,
> We invoke thee!

The power of Ptah was invested in many different kinds of amulets. Bromage mentions several of the most significant: the Amulet of the Heart (the *Ab*), the heart being "the seat of life itself." "The inscriptions on these amulets," he explains, "referred to the significance of

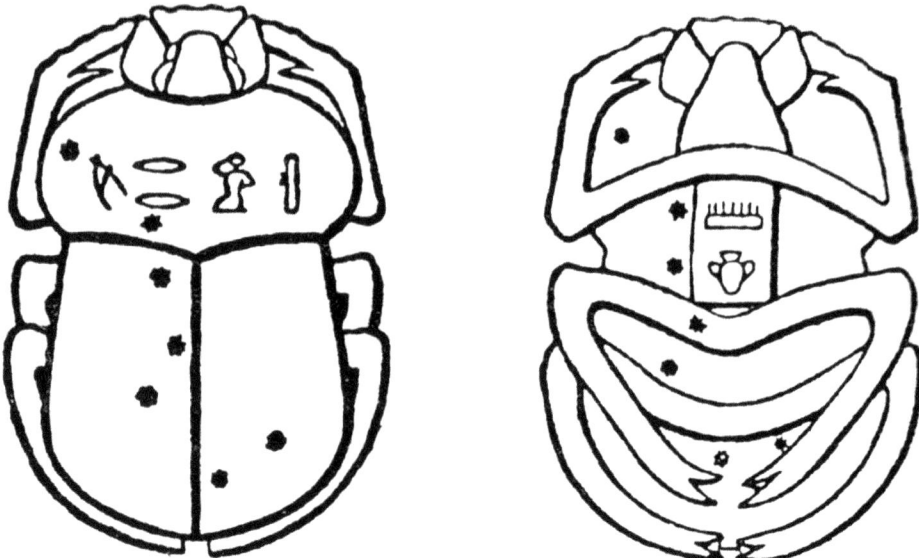

Bram Stoker's design for the Jewel of Seven Stars, from the novel of that name.

the heart: in these words the dead man fervently yearned that his heart might be there to help him when he assumed his various metamorphoses in the Underworld."[34] If the heart didn't support the soul in the Hall of Double Maat where it is weighed by Anubis, the soul's hopes of eternal life would be dashed forever. Bromage also mentions the scarab, which is perhaps the most important of all ancient Egyptian amulets. The scarab, a dung-rolling beetle, represented regeneration and immaculate conception to the ancient Egyptians as it seemed to appear from nowhere. Laying its eggs in the sand, it emerged as if by magic from the earth, and hence appeared particularly magical, especially as it flew in the midday sun, suggesting a kinship with the sun god, Ra. Bromage pointed out that scarab amulets were usually made from green basalt, marble or limestone, but the scarab that is the Jewel of Seven Stars in Stoker's novel is a miraculous ruby, replete with a curious flaw that reproduces exactly the positions of the seven stars of the constellation Ursa Major. (Sadly, none of the film versions present Stoker's jewel as a scarab.) Two hieroglyphs engraved on the reverse mean "abiding of the heart" or "patience," and Queen Tera certainly has plenty of that, having to wait thousands of years for her eventual reincarnation. Stoker's Trelawny explains:

> That Jewel, with its mystic words, and which Queen Tera held under her hand in the sarcophagus, was to be an important factor — probably the most important — in the working out of her resurrection.[35]

Other amulets mentioned by Bromage include the Amulet of the Eye (the Udjat), also known as the Eye of Horus, usually placed over that part of the mummy which had been cut open to remove the internal organs. (Stoker's jewel takes this form in *The Awakening*.) The Udjat was also a very popular personal amulet. If the left eye was used (as was appropriately the case in *The Awakening*), it represented the moon and the power of darkness. The right eye represented the sun, and appropriately, this symbol appeared on the cover of the first edition Joan Grant's *Eyes of Horus*, which concerns the defeat of the evil Set. It was

Set who snatched the eye of Horus. It immediately shattered, and only Thoth could put it back together again. Finally, there is the Ankh, symbol of life, which Christopher Lee's Kharis holds in the temple scenes of *The Mummy*. The mirror from Kara's tomb, which Professor Corbeck presents to his daughter in *The Awakening*, also takes the form of an ankh; and perhaps less appropriately, it is an ankh, held out by a statue of Isis, that destroys Imho-tep at the end of the first Universal mummy film.

There were also magical means to protect oneself again poisonous animals and insects, particularly scorpions. Bromage correctly points out that spells against scorpions were often engraved on granite stelae or wooden plaques and positioned in tombs to protect them. Known as "Cippi of Horus," they are commonly decorated with an image of Horus as a young boy, crushing scorpions and serpents and trampling on crocodiles. One of the most impressive of these stelae is the Metternich Stele, so called as it was presented to the Austrian prince of that name by Mohammed Ali Pasha. Dating from the 13th dynasty during the reign of Nectanebo II, it currently forms part of the Egyptian Collection at the Metropolitan Museum of Art in New York.

The Metternich Stele has a specific magical function to heal those unfortunate enough to have been stung or bitten by a poisonous animal. Water was consecrated by pouring it over the stele, and when the water was swallowed, the magical properties of the stone were passed on to the sufferer. Priests, meanwhile, intoned the appropriate rites and spells. Bromage lists these spells as a conjuration to destroy Apep, the Snake of Snakes; and another addressed to the cat-goddess, Bast. There was also an invocation to Ra to compel Thoth to repel Set, and finally a hymn to Isis. Bromage was convinced that "there is indubitably some tremendous suggestive force working its way through such a power-magnet as the Metternich stele,"[36] and he wasn't the only person to regard the magical power of Egyptian magic and its talismans to be still very much active in the 20th century.

The previous chapter has already mentioned Aleister Crowley with regard to Emile Brugsch and the so-called Stele of Revealing. Serving a similar magical function to the Metternich Stele, the wooden Stele of Revealing was, as we know, originally made for the priest, Ankh-f-na–Khonsu, *circa* 680/70 B.C.. The priest is depicted on it, making an offering to the enthroned god Re-Harakhty ("Re-Horus of the Two Horizons"—a composite of the gods Ra and Horus). The text is a prayer for the safe passage of the priest's soul into the Land of the West. Crowley regarded his encounter with the Stele of Revealing as the most important moment of his life, and explained that the chapter in his *Confessions*, describing the momentous occasion, was "the climax of this book."[37] Indeed, it marked the beginning of Crowley's new religion with the divine dictation to him of *The Book of the Law*, the new Bible of "Crowleyanity." Quite how divine the book is, and quite how much of it was derived from other sources (most notably the 16th-century French writer, François Rabelais, to whom many of the ideas can be traced) is really the subject of another book. It is, however, significant from our point of view that it was an Egyptian artifact (and an Egyptian god) that triggered the whole affair. In fact, it was Crowley's wife, Rose (to whom he referred by the magical name of Ouarda), who brought the stele to Crowley's attention during their visit to Cairo in 1904. Knowing nothing of Egyptology herself, Ouarda one day very mysteriously insisted to him that he had offended the god Horus. She then told him how to invoke Horus, an invocation that apparently worked, before identifying Horus with the Stele of Revealing in the Boulak museum. Neither she nor Crowley had ever seen this particular stele or ever visited the museum, but having "made contact" with it, Crowley was then told by Horus that "the Equinox of the Gods had come,"[38] and that he had been chosen as the conduit between this spiritual force and mankind. Crowley then made a poetic paraphrase from the translations of the stele that he had commissioned from Brugsch's assistant at the museum, and on the 8th, 9th and 10th of April 1904, *The Book of the Law* was dictated to him by an entity called Aiwas, his holy guardian angel. *The Book of the Law* prophesied the Age of Horus — the Crowned and Conquering Child, representing a new age of freedom for mankind. This was certainly a world-shattering event for Crowley, as it transformed him into the world's new Messiah; but whatever magical powers Crowley had or merely professed to have, his interest in and revival of Egyptian magic has to be seen in historical context, for it was part of a more general trend. In fact, it wasn't the first time Crowley himself had had a mystical Egyptian experience. In 1903, during his honeymoon, he entered the King's Chamber in the Great Pyramid with the aim of showing off his magical powers to his wife. During a magical invocation, the interior of the pyramid began to glow mysteriously with what looked like ultra-violet light. Crowley had no idea what was causing the light — if, indeed, it happened at all; but the significant thing is that whatever it was that happened (or didn't happen) took place in an Egyptian context. After all, the story would not have had anywhere near as much resonance if it had taken place in a suburban bedroom.

Crowley returned to the overwhelming revelation of the Stele of Revealing in his short story "Across the Gulf," first published in his magical journal, *The Equinox*, in March 1912. A full analysis of this story awaits us in chapter six, but for the moment it is enough to mention that in the tale Crowley imagines (or indeed believes) himself to be a reincarnation of the priest, Ankh-f-na-Khonsu. The tale concerns the distinctly sado-masochistic adventures of Crowley's ancient alter-ego, who transfers his allegiances between Isis (for whom he becomes a transgender High Priestess in the first part of the story), Osiris (for whom he is a High Priest in the second), and ultimately, Horus, in his 20th century incarnation. He refers to his discovery of the Stele of Revealing at the beginning and the end of this remarkable story. At its outset he recalls that it is five years since he discovered it in the Boulak museum, but adds that it wasn't until experiencing "a certain initiation in the city of Benares last year" (i.e., 1910 — the story was composed in 1911) that he was able to recall "the memory of my life in the Twenty-Sixth Dynasty." [39] At the end of the tale he explains that "Ankh-f-na-khonsu left unto me the stèla 666 with the keys to that knowledge."[40]

Amid the intervening Swinburnian and Wildean excesses which we'll be exploring from a literary point of view later, Crowley also explains the meaning of the three ages personified by Isis, Osiris and Horus. In the first age of Isis, Nature is the center of man's worship. Under Osiris, man "in his suffering and death, man in his purification and perfection" becomes the focus of worship, Osiris being the lord of death. As for Horus:

> I saw also, that as Isis is the Lady of Nature, the living; and as Osiris is the Lord of the Dead, so should Horus come, the Hawk-headed Lord, as a young child, the image of all Nature and all Man raised above Life and Death, under the supreme rule of Hadit that is Force and of Nuit that is Matter — though they are a Matter and a Force that transcend all our human conceptions of these things.[41]

This cycle is apparently continual, as Crowley points out later:

> For he that is born in the years of the power of a God thinks that God to be eternal, one, alone. But he that is born in the hour of the weakness of the God, as the death of one and the birth of

the other, seeth something (though it be little) of the course of things. And for him it is necessary to understand fully that change of office (for the gods neither die nor are reborn, but now one initiates and the other guards, and now one heralds and the other sanctifies) its purpose and meaning in the whole scheme of things.[42]

The revival of interest in Egyptian magic in particular was part of the 19th-century occult revival in general. It began with the birth of spiritualism in the 1840s, which coincided with the appearance of a novel by Dickens' main competitor, Sir Edward Bulwer-Lytton (later Lord Lytton, 1803–1873), who was fascinated, in an admittedly skeptical way, by the history, theory and practice of magic. He knew Éliphas Lévi, the French magus (of whom Crowley later believed himself to be a reincarnation), and Bulwer encouraged Lévi to write his seminal work, *Transcendental Magic—Its Doctrine and Ritual*, in 1855. Bulwer was also the Grand Patron of the Masonic Rosicrucian Society. His Rosicrucian novel, *Zanoni* (1842), was followed by the even more compelling occult novel, *A Strange Story* (1862), and his influential science-fiction story, *The Coming Race* (1871). This trilogy, along with the occult elements in his historical novel, *The Last Days of Pompeii* (1834), had an immense impact on Helena Petrovna Blavatsky (1831–1891), the creator of the Theosophical Society. Her biographer, Peter Washington, claims that it would "be unjust to say that her new religion was virtually manufactured from [Bulwer's] pages,"[43] but it is undoubtedly the case that Bulwer's *Zanoni,* which Blavatsky repeatedly referred to as a profound authority on magical matters, left its mark, and, again according to Washington, it was "almost certainly the main Western source in modern times of Hidden Master mythology."[44] The following passage from Bulwer's introduction to *Zanoni* obviously resonated in Blavatsky's mind and later inspired the title of her first major work, *Isis Unveiled* (1877):

> Who but a Rosicrucian could explain the Rosicrucian mysteries? And can you imagine that any members of that sect, the most jealous of all secret societies, would themselves lift the veil that hides the Isis of their wisdom from the world?[45]

Blavatsky claimed that the ideas of her new theosophical movement had been communicated to her telepathically by Tibetan adepts who had influenced and continued to influence world history and world religion. In fact, she was basically mystifying a fairly straightforward study of comparative religion, comparing the similarities between belief systems and mythologies and explaining these similarities by means of her (manufactured) "Secret Doctrine." These hidden masters, rather like the Atlanteans in *Warlords of Atlantis* have, according to Blavatsky, been guiding the development of mankind towards developing its ultimate capabilities. In *Warlords of Atlantis* that is the power of the neutron bomb, which will unleash the energy the Atlanteans need to take them back to the stars. In Blavatsky's scheme of things, humanity has been evolving and is continuing to evolve through seven "root races" towards ultimate spiritual perfection. Despite, or perhaps because of the extreme nature of her views, Blavatsky's influence was immense, and it attracted many poets, artists and musicians, including W. B. Yeats in Ireland, Piet Mondrian in Holland, Paul Klee in Germany and Alexander Scriabin in Russia. That Bulwer-Lytton was so significant an inspiration to Blavatsky and her worldwide influence is rather ironic, as today his novels are nowhere near as celebrated as those by his friend and rival, Charles Dickens. So often sidelined as merely the man who persuaded Dickens to change the end of *Great Expectations*, Bulwer was much more significant than that.

From our point of view, the references to Egyptian magic in *The Last Days of Pompeii* are perhaps the most immediately significant. Among the extensive cast list of this epic, proto–Hollywood epic, there is an Egyptian priest by the name of Arbaces, who explains

> Egypt ... is the mother of Athens. Her tutelary Minerva is our deity; and her founder, Cecrops, was the fugitive of Egyptian Sais. This have I already taught to her; and in my blood she venerates the eldest dynasties of earth.... Our arts — the arts by which Egypt trained her young novitiates — must be employed.[46]

Bulwer explained in his preface that "the worship of Isis, its existent fane, with its false oracles unveiled — the trade of Pompeii with Alexandria — the associations of the Sarnus with the Nile,— called forth the Egyptian Arbaces."[47] Bulwer was not, of course, the first to be impressed by the evidence of Egyptian religion in Pompeii. In 1780, England's wealthiest man, William Beckford (1760–1844), visited Pompeii and remarked, in his *Dreams, Waking Thoughts and Incidents*, on the remains of the Isis Temple he visited there:

> We were now conducted to the temple, or rather chapel, of Isis. The chief remains are, a covered cloister; the great altar, on which was, probably, exhibited the statue of the goddess; a little edifice to protect the sacred well; the pediment of the chapel, with a symbolical vase in relief; ornaments in stucco on the front of the main-building, consisting of the lotus, the sistrum, representations of gods, Harpocrates, Anubis, and other objects of Egyptian worship.[48]

These Egyptian experiences no doubt later contributed to the Egyptian elements in his oriental Gothic romance, *Vathek*, written three years after this visit, to which we will be returning later.

Blavatsky's *Isis Unveiled* aimed, through its two immense volumes, to compare the similarities of the world's religions, tracing them back to Egyptian mythology. In fact, despite the book's title, Blavatsky spends relatively little time on Egyptian religion, but in her quest to make them racially significant (and this rather dangerously points towards the adoption of Theosophy by later Nazi occultists in the 20th century) she claims that the ancient Egyptians were actually ancient Indians and therefore Aryans.[49] In his screenplay for *Warlords of Atlantis*, Brian Hayles emphasized the connection between Bulwer-Lytton-inspired, Egyptian-flavored theosophy and the Blavatsky-inspired, occult racial program of the Third Reich by combining it with ideas about the Martian origin of the ancient Egyptians, which in turn derive from writers such as Sax Rohmer and occult theorists like Randall-Stevens. "The ruling class must always survive," says Atraxon. "Oh, how very democratic!" derisively replies Peter Gilmore's scientist, Charles Aitken; but when Atraxon places a magical crystal helmet on Aitken's head, Aitken is seduced by the power the Atlanteans offer him. Hayles was quite specific about what he wanted the audience to see during this sequence:

> Under the influence of the helmet, Charles seems to be in quiet ecstasy, throughout the sequence of holographic time-events his mind projects: Brownshirts marching — Swastikas — Street riots — A Jew kicked to death on a door way — The Reichstag ablaze — Nuremberg Rally, 1936 — Nazi banner — Strutting figure of Hitler — At his shoulder, the evil genius of Himmler.... Blitzed ruins of London, Warsaw, Dresden — Bombs — VI doodlebug — V2 rocketry — Mushroom A-Bomb cloud — Polaris missile rising out of sea.[50]

Hayles added in an interview that "the Atlanteans are a master race and it's interesting to note the Nazis, such as Himmler, were convinced that Atlantis and Atlanteans really existed. This theory I worked on about the Great Flood, advanced by the German, Horbiger — his beliefs were taken up by Himmler in his fanatical determination to prove that Germans were the only pure Aryan race on earth ... the only race to be descended directly from the Atlanteans!"[51]

Hayles felt that "the script was almost taking over and producing pieces of knowledge I'd not even read or heard before"[52] but, as we've seen, those ideas are very much a part of the occult literature stretching back to Bulwer-Lytton that was turned into an occult system via Blavatsky's *Isis Unveiled*. So the film is not, perhaps, quite so exclusively "for infants only," as *Halliwell's Film Guide* puts it. Blavatsky eventually lost interest in the Egyptian side of things, turning her attention to Indian mythology and religion (they were, after all, the same thing in her opinion), but the most significant thing about Blavatsky's book is surely its title, for it strikingly advertised an Egyptian origin for everything, promoting the aesthetic of ancient Egypt much as Belzoni had inspired the craze for Egyptiana in Regency London, and Howard Carter would inspire Tutankhamen mania across Europe in the 1920s and 30s. Another link between Blavatsky's interest in the Rosicrucian novels of Bulwer-Lytton and things Egyptian is that the Rosicrucian Society in which Bulwer was reluctantly raised to the level of Grand Patron, was in fact a Masonic society, and, as we have seen, the rituals of the Masons owe a considerable debt to Egyptian magical rituals and names. Indeed, Freemasonry is often alleged to have begun in Egypt.

This connecting thread between Rosicrucianism and Freemasonry now leads us to the foundation at the end of the 19th century of the magical Order of the Golden Dawn, which was originally created by Dr. Wynn Wescott (1848–1925), a surgeon and later coroner who was also a Mason. He claimed to have revived an ancient order but, in fact, he forged the documents on which these claims were based. As Golden Dawn historian Ellic Howe has revealed, these documents "included material drawn from ancient Egyptian texts, but scholars had been unable to read the hieroglyphs until J. F. Champollion deciphered them in c. 1822."[53] No doubt inspired by the example of Blavatsky's validating contacts with hidden masters such as the Tibetan Master Koot Hoomi, Wescott invented a certain Fräulein Sprengel, claiming that she belonged to a non-existent German organization called *Die Goldener Dämmerung*. Blavatsky and her followers had exposed the immense appetite there was in a post–Darwinian industrial age for the mystical and magical worlds which science was undermining, and Wescott was keen to exploit the trend. He joined forces with a retired physician, Dr. William Robert Woodman (1828–1891), and the highly eccentric Samuel MacGreggor Mathers (1858–1918), to create the Order of the Golden Dawn. Wescott was primarily interested in the Jewish Kabbalah, but as he himself explained:

> Even the Rosicrucian revival of mysticism was but a new development of the vaster older wisdom of the Kabbalistic Rabbis, and of that very ancient secret knowledge, the Magic of the Egyptians, in which the Hebrew Pentateuch tells you that Moses, the Founder of the Jewish System, was "learned," i.e. in which he had been initiated.[54]

Hence the Egyptian names of the various temples of the Order of the Golden Dawn: the Isis-Urania temple in London, the "Orisis" in Weston-super-Mare, the "Horus" in Bradford and the "Amen-Ra" in Edinburgh. Some of the robes and insignia used in Golden Dawn ceremonies also paid homage to the Egyptian origins of Kabbalistic magic. The "Mighty Magus of Art" for example, carried in her left hand "the Ankh of Thoth and in her right the Isis Wand."[55] Among the celebrated members of the Golden Dawn were Mrs. Oscar Wilde, Yeats (who transferred his loyalty from the theosophists), and, in the Order's latter years, the writers Arthur Machen and Algernon Blackwood. Another was J. Brodie-Innes, a friend of Bram Stoker and an author himself. Indeed, he dedicated his novel *The Devil's Mistress* (1915) to Stoker, having previously complimented *The Jewel of Seven Stars* with the words: "It is not only a good book — it is a *great* book"[56] — an accolade no doubt due to the mystical "truths" it contained.

Mathers also indulged in a parallel experiment called the "Isis Movement," which was connected formally to the Golden Dawn, and reflected his interest in Egyptian religion. His "Rite of Isis," performed in the Bodinière Theatre in Paris in March 1899, was a hybrid theatrical affair, typical of the times. Indeed, it anticipated by about 12 years, Debussy's and Gabrielle D'Annunzio's theatrical mélange of recitation, dance, ballet and revue that was *Le Martyre de Saint Sebastien*. Ellic Howe quotes from Frederic Lees' account of the Mathers' Egyptian event written for the New York journal *The Humanitarian* in February 1900:

> In the centre of the stage was the figure of Isis, on each side of her were other figures of gods and goddesses, and in front was the little altar, upon which was the ever-burning green stone lamp. The Hierophant Ramses [Mathers], holding in one hand the sistrum, which every now and then he shook, and in the other a spray of lotus, said the prayers before this altar, after which the High Priest Anari [Vestigia] invoked the goddess in penetrating and passionate tones. Then followed the "dance of the four elements" by a young Parisian lady, who, dressed in long white robes, had previously recited some verses in French in honor of Isis. A short time before this lady had become a convert.... Most of the ladies present in the fashionable Parisian audience brought offerings of flowers, whilst the gentlemen threw wheat on the altar. The ceremony was artistic in the extreme.[57]

Karloff in ceremonial robes as the High Priest Im-ho-tep in *The Mummy* (dir. Karl Freund, 1932).

Again, the parallel with Hammer and Hollywood here is obvious. Indeed, a photograph of Mathers in his priestly robes, replete with leopard skin and spray of lotus flowers survives, which bears a strong resemblance to stills of Boris Karloff's Im-ho-tep and Christopher Lee's Kharis in their robes before being so horribly mummified alive.

Mathers's "Rite of Isis" now leads us to the scenes of Egyptian magic we find in Hammer's adaptation of Dennis Wheatley's *The Devil Rides Out*. As is well known, the character of Mocata, the Satanist in this black-magic story, was based in part on Aleister Crowley, whom Wheatley had wined and dined for research purposes, so it's not surprising that elements of Egyptian magic appear in the text. In chapter 25, entitled "The Talisman of Set," Wheatley retells the whole legend of Isis and Osiris in a colorful and engaging manner, describing Set in strikingly modern terms as a "charming but unscrupulous rogue who might have entertained you with lavish hospitality and brilliant conversation yesterday — yet would do you down without the least compulsion if he met you in the street tomorrow."

Samuel Liddell MacGregor Mathers in ceremonial robes.

> He was tall and slim and dark and handsome; a fine athlete and a great hunter, but a cultured, amusing person too, and a boon companion who knew how to carry his wine at table. The type whose lapses men are always ready to condone on account of their delightful personality, and whose wickedness women persuade themselves is only waywardness — while they succumb almost at a glance to that dark male virility.[58]

One can't help wondering if Wheatley was indulging in some wishful thinking here. Mocata's nemesis, the Duc De Richleau, then states that it is imperative that the Satanist is prevented from possessing the Talisman of Set — which he explains is the phallus of Osiris. In Wheatley's account it was not eaten by the oxyrhynchus fish but was embalmed by Set and apparently still survives. To those who find it, unimaginable power is granted.

None of this is included in Richard Matheson's screenplay for the Hammer film adaptation in 1968, but there is a scene, derived from another chapter in Wheatley's book which provides the Egyptian element that is actually missing in the original. The scene concerns the raising of Tanith's spirit to discover the whereabouts of Mocata's coven. In the book, De Richleau performs a magical ceremony over Tanith's body. A spherical blue light hovers above it (Tanith's soul), which gradually increases in intensity and solidity. Much of Wheatley's ensuing dialogue between de Richleau and Tanith's spirit is retained by Matheson, though the film version uses Marie Eaton as a medium for Tanith's voice. (Tanith speaks independently in the novel. Matheson also inserts the resonant line "The sign of Osiris slain. The sign of Osiris risen" for de Richleau to speak. These words are movingly accompanied by Christopher Lee's eloquently performed Egyptian gestures (no doubt recalled from his experience performing Kharis in *The Mummy*). James Bernard's music (utilizing mystically ringing handbells in different pitches) also helps create the illusion of Tanith's soul returning from the dead. This scene is one of the most magical moments in any "horror" film and it gains a great deal of its power from the aura of Egyptian magic that impels it.

In the film's climax, Matheson also includes the name of Set in Mocata's culminating invocation over the hypnotized Peggy, who is about to be sacrificed in the ceremony of "the transference of souls." Set is not mentioned by name in the novel here, but he is present as Mocata wields Set's Talisman, which he places on the forehead of the Goat of Mendes (a demonic manifestation that appears only once in the film version). No doubt the powers-that-were at Hammer felt that a symbolic phallus would have been too much for the censors to tolerate—and, indeed, it would be hard to visualize this without raising unintentional titters in the audience. Instead, Charles Gray's Mocata intones the somber words:

> Almighty and all-powerful Set,
> Father of Darkness, King of Death,
> I pledge this knife to thee
> To do thy work and be thy servant.

By juxtaposing the white and black aspects of Egyptian magic, Wheatley and Matheson demonstrated in graphically dramatic terms what Blavatsky's esoteric studies in comparative religion had drawn to the general public's attention almost a century before; but the influence of ancient Egypt art and architecture made an even more powerful impact on popular Western culture than its myth, magic and history. Before exploring the fiction that fixed so many (often erroneous) ideas about this ancient culture in the popular imagination, we need to explore the visual, theatrical and musical manifestations of Egyptiana that occurred throughout the 19th and early-20th centuries.

Four

Art

The world has always been fascinated by ancient Egypt. Its allure and fascination were only increased by the Bible's often obscure and vague references to it, but lack of artifacts and firsthand experience somewhat limited the application of Egyptian *style* to European artistic needs. There were plenty of medieval Biblical paintings dealing with Egypt but they were understandably executed from an entirely parochial perspective. Even in the 17th century, the Italian Baroque artist Guercino (1591–1666, a.k.a. Giovanni Francesco Barbieri) portrayed Pharaoh in Turkish dress and made no attempt at archeological accuracy. By comparing Guercino's version of Joseph interpreting Pharaoh's dream in Genesis, chapter

Guercino, "Pharaoh's Dream," from *The Family Devotional Bible*, edited by Matthew Henry (London: John Tallis, 1852). Engraving by J. Rogers.

"Joseph interprets Pharaoh's dreams," Genesis, chapter 41, 17–33. Illustration by Gustave Doré, 1866.

XLI with Gustave Doré's 19th-century interpretation of the same moment, we can immediately see how much Europe's fascination with things Egyptian, in the wake of Napoleon's expedition, had developed.

Europe's first wave of Egyptiania didn't really get underway until the 18th century, though there were nonetheless some 17th-century opportunities to stand before Egyptian antiquities and gaze in wonder. The most famous of these is surely Bernini's Fountain of the Four Rivers in the Piazza Navona in Rome, with its central Egyptian-style (though, in fact, Roman) obelisk dating from A.D. 81. According to contemporary accounts, the effect of the *tout ensemble*, when it was unveiled in 1651, was as overwhelming as later film producers hoped their Egyptian epics would be. In the 17th century, England also had its own Egyptian offerings. The *London Gazette* of June 1661, for example, advertised

> an entire Egyptian Mummy with all the hieroglyphics and skutcheons on it ... lately presented to the view of His Majesty ... being not long since brought into England from the Lybean sands near ... Memphis. It is the body of a Princely young lady ... preserved on and with her coffin for 2,500 years without putrefaction.[1]

This mummy would have been regarded as an object of curiosity rather than something necessarily to inspire artistic imitation, but as exploration and exposure to the past increased, the influence of ancient Egyptian style became more pervasive. Vanbrugh, for example, built a pyramid for the gardens at Stowe in Buckinghamshire in the 1720s, anticipating the host of 19th-century Egyptian things to come, not to mention the gigantic pyramid that forms the roof of the Rametep cult's temple in *Young Sherlock Holmes*. Unfortunately, Stowe's pyramid had crumbled to rubble by the end of the 18th-century, but Stowe's house went on to enjoy an Egyptian entrance hall, built in 1803, replete with two sphinxes flanking a flight of steps.

Although it's impossible to state exactly when Egyptian style began to influence European artists and designers, the Egyptian engravings of Giovanni Battista Piranesi (1720–1778) are particularly significant. His designs, based on Egyptian motifs, for murals decorating the Caffè degli Inglesi in Rome, along with a series of "Egyptian" fireplace surrounds, first appeared in his 1769 publication *Diverse Ways of ornamenting chimney-pieces and all other parts of houses taken from Egyptian, Etruscan, and Grecian architecture with an Apologia in defense of Egyptian and Tuscan architecture*. Inspired by the Egyptian artifacts he could study in the Eternal City, it was indeed significant that Piranesi felt the need to defend Egyptian style. By so doing, he broke through the prevailing prejudice in favor of classicism and became the first person to advocate architectural eclecticism. His Egyptian designs show little understanding of the original function of the symbolism he adapted and incorporated into his works. Neither could he have had any idea about the meaning of hieroglyphs as they hadn't been deciphered by that stage. His approach to the art of ancient Egypt was purely decorative, in much the same way that directors of mummy movies create an Egyptian *mood* by decorating their sets with Egyptian motifs, without being too bothered about archeological niceties. *The Mummy's Hand*, for instance, presents its audiences with a very vague impression of Egyptian architecture. The sets, based, as they were, on what was left over from James Whale's major flop, *Green Hell* (1940), made something "Egyptian" out of what had originally been intended to represent primitive South American style. Hence the two lama heads that loom over the interior of Ananka's tomb, which very loosely resemble Anubis. Piranesi did much the same thing in one of his Egyptian fireplace designs

Giovanni Battista Piranesi, design for a fireplace in Egyptian style from *Diverse Mainere d'adornare i Camini* (Rome, 1769) (reproduced courtesy the Ministero per i Beni e le Attività Culturali, Rome).

in which pharaonic heads rest on goats' heads, and monkeys stare out over hieroglyphs. The whole idea of two Egyptian caryatids supporting the proscenium arch over a fire box, as it were, is a striking example of how imagery from a temple was hijacked in the name of domesticity. In such etchings, Piranesi inaugurated the commercialization of Egyptian style and its subsequent transformation into consumable bibelots — the kind of thing, indeed, that often decorates the windows of amusement arcades today, from provincial British towns to the neon swagger and brash theatricality of Las Vegas. Mummy movies, Egyptian epics and Egyptian-inspired adventure films similarly purvey a *style* that has a life of its own far beyond the time, place and function of its architectural and decorative origin.

If Piranesi had helped to create Egyptian style in this sense of the term, it was Napoleon who truly popularized it. Though a military failure, his Egyptian campaign had an immense impact of European art and design, principally due to the publication of the immense *Description de l'Egypte* and Vivant Denon's *Voyage dans la basse et la haute Egypte*, which after its publication in 1802, rapidly became an international bestseller. Though more modest in scope than the *Description* it was perhaps more influential and it wasn't long before a host of objects far removed from the world of ancient Egypt were imitating the designs to be found in Denon's book. Jean-Antoine Lépine (1720–1814), for example, fashioned an elaborate clock based on Denon's depiction of the Temple of Hathor at Dendera, an architectural wonder that Gaston Maspero, who preferred to visit at night, macabrely described in 1902:

A flight of bats envelops us in a circle of short, rapid cries, the pattering of swift claws resounds at our approach, the echoes awake with a hollow noise which does not seem to coincide with our footsteps. A kind of vague presence seems to hover in the gloom, and to pursue us from chamber to chamber. Should we be really astonished if at the turn of a corridor we met a priest come back to his post after centuries of absence if the sound of distant timbrels which announced the theophanies of the goddess began to vibrate in the depths of the sanctuary? In the open air and under the starry vault of heaven the feeling of religious awe remains with us.[2]

Denon, however, being a man of the enlightenment rather than a late Romantic, depicted the temple in a rather more restrained manner; not that there was anything very restrained about the Egyptian dinner service which was also influenced, in part, by Denon's drawing. Most of the pieces in this famous service were decorated with Egyptian views based on those in the *Description*, but Denon's picture of the Dendera temple also formed the basis of the table centerpiece that went with it. Napoleon had originally commissioned the whole thing for himself but he later gave it to Tsar Alexander I, having threatened the Sèvres factory with closure if they failed to achieve what many thought impossible, and deliver the order on time.

Denon found many other ways to occupy his time in Egypt. He watched the Battle of the Pyramids, and in the capacity of unofficial war artist, captured the events of that engagement in further drawings. He was simultaneously intrigued and repelled by belly dancing, and also meticulously copied hieroglyphs. When he returned to France he began designing furniture in Egyptian style, such as an impressive medal cabinet in the shape of an Egyptian pylon with scarab-shaped handles, and a chair with serpents for arm rests. Soon there were sofas supported by sphinxes, sphinxes decorating the pillars of harps, and fruit bowls lifted by Egyptian youths.

In England, Egyptomania was no less fashionable. One of the most influential propagators of the style was the Regency designer, Thomas Hope (1769–1831), who had visited Egypt in 1797, the year before Napoleon's campaign. He also possessed an impressive collection of Egyptian, Roman and Greek antiquities, which included an equivalent to Denon's famous mummified foot, except that Hope's foot was carved from Imperial Egyptian porphyry and of probable Roman origin. There were also, among other things, a late-first century statue of Isis, a Ptolemaic porphyry Lion, a basalt statue of a priest, and two canopic jars, which Hope displayed at his London home in a specially designed Egyptian room. Piranesi was obviously an influence here. Hope's father had bought one of Piranesi's Egyptian fireplaces for his home in Amsterdam,[3] and Hope himself was familiar with Piranesi's Egyptian designs in *Diverse Maniere*, but he was also inspired by Denon and his own travels in the East. The Egyptian room was decorated in "pale yellow and that blueish green which hold so conspicuous a rank among the Egyptian pigments; here and there relieved by masses of black and gold."[4] He designed a plinth on which to place his alabaster figure of a pharaoh, and a glass case for his wooden child's mummy case which stood on another plinth in the shape of an Egyptian pylon. This was guarded by statues of two Egyptian priests which stood on either side, with a winged Isis overhead. The chimney piece was carved from black marble, based on what he had seen in Turkey, rather than Egypt, and as if all that wasn't enough, there were also two couches and four armchairs, painted black with bronzes inspired by Denon's example. Hope's country house at Deepdene in Surrey similarly boasted an Egyptian room, which contained furniture actually designed by Denon, such as an impressive bed with images of Isis and kneeling figures with their arms raised in adoration.⁵ Any set designer would surely envy him.

Surrounded by such wonders, Hope inevitably began to emulate them in his own designs. His chairs began to resemble thrones, their arms in the form of outstretched sphinx wings. A bare-breasted figure of Isis supported a clock, the heads of Egyptian slaves raised candlesticks, Anubis and crouching lions decorated settees. As art historian David Watkin has pointed out, "The 'Egyptian' furniture by Hope and Denon was not an archeological reproduction but the outcome of a synthetic process of design that incorporated echoes from a range of objects. Thus, Hope pointed to a wide variety of sources for the chairs: 'an Egyptian idol in the Vatican ... an Egyptian mummy-case in the Institute [today Museo Civico] at Bologna ... [small canopic vases] imitated from one in the Capitol; and other ornaments are taken from various monuments at Thebes, Tentyris, &c.'"⁶

The first neo–Egyptian building appears to have been the offices of a London newspaper in the Strand, built in 1804 — a highly appropriate arrangement, given the "curses" and other unreliable information about ancient Egypt created by the press over the years. In France, an Egyptian temple in the Place des Victoires appeared around the same time, rapidly followed by P. F. Robinson's Egyptian Hall in London's Piccadilly in 1812. Sadly, this no longer exists, but a building in very similar style still stands in Penzance, Cornwall. This Egyptian House, built around 1835, may well have been designed by the same architect. A riot of Egyptian motifs, it was originally built as a geological museum but can now be

The entrance to the Egyptian Avenue in Highgate Cemetery, London.

The Egyptian House, Penzance. Photograph by Simon Harvey Williams.

rented for holidays. Though the Egyptian Hall lasted considerably less time than its ancient Egyptian models, London has other evocatively macabre examples of Egyptiana which have survived. Highgate Cemetery, for example, with its Egyptian Avenue, opened in 1839. Designed by Stephen Geary, the main entrance to this very Victorian interpretation of ancient Egypt is flanked by two obelisks. Two pairs of stout Egyptian columns frame the pharaonic arch which ushers the visitor to an impressive avenue of death, rather more macabre now than when it was built, due to the intervening growth of vegetation. Though the cemetery was later featured in Hammer's *Taste the Blood of Dracula* (dir. Peter Sasdy, 1970), *Tales from the Crypt* (dir. Freddie Francis, 1972) and the BBC's television adaptation of *Count Dracula* (dir. Philip Saville, 1977), it has so far failed to attract the directors of mummy features. Egyptian style, no doubt due to its obsession with death and the life to come, rapidly became a fashionable motif for 19th-century funerary architecture and monumental masonry, though this wasn't to everyone's taste. The great champion of Gothic

Revivalism, Augustus Welby Pugin (1812–1852), attacked the neo-Egyptian style in his book, *An Apology for the Revival of Christian Architecture in England* (1843), in which he complained that the entrances to commercial cemeteries were

> generally Egyptian, probably from some associations between the word catacombs, which occurs in the prospectus of the company, and the discoveries of Belzoni on the banks of the Nile; and nearly opposite the Green Man and Dog public-house, in the centre of a dead wall (which serves as a cheap medium of advertisement for blacking and shaving-strop manufacturers), a cement caricature of the entrance to an Egyptian temple ... is erected, with convenient lodges for the policeman and his wife, and a neat pair of iron hieroglyphical gates, which would puzzle the most learned to decipher; while to prevent any mistake, some such words as "New Economical Compressed Grave Cemetery Company" are inscribed in Grecian capitals along the frieze, interspersed with hawk-headed divinities, and surmounted by a huge representation of the winged Osiris bearing a gas lamp.[7]

Laman Blanchard, "A Visit to the General Cemetery at Kensal Green," from *Ainsworth's Magazine: A Miscellany of Romance, General Literature & Art,* Vol. II, edited by Harrison Ainsworth (London: Cunningham & Mortimer, 1842). Engraving by W. Alfred Delamotte.

Among the earlier examples of architectural Egyptomania in England is the pyramidical Egyptian Mausoleum at Blickling Hall in Norfolk. This was built in honor of the second Earl of Buckingham, who died in 1793. In fact, it was based on the Tomb of Gaius Caesar in Rome rather than the pyramids at Giza, but the stylistic lineage is clear. It was designed by the Roman-born Joseph Bonomi the elder (1739–1808), father of the remarkable sculptor and Egyptologist Joseph Bonomi the younger (1796–1878). The latter, who joined Robert Hay's expedition to Egypt and illustrated works by James Burton and Sir John Gardner Wilkinson, was an excellent example of a man who combined serious scholarship with flamboyant showmanship. Not only did he arrange the Egyptian exhibits in the British Museum and become curator of the Soane Museum, where he drew the famous Belzoni sarcophagus, he also helped to organized a "Grand Moving Panorama of the Nile" in 1850, and, three years later, assisted Owen Jones with the creation of the Egyptian Court at the Crystal Palace.

Augustus Welby Pugin, "Entrance gateway for a new cemetery," from *An Apology for the Revival of Christian Architecture in England*, 1843.

The Egyptian Court eschewed the relics-and-shards approach of the British Museum, opting instead for full-scale recreation of monumental sculpture and architecture in painted plaster. Scaled-down imitations of antiquities such as the statues of Rameses II from Abu Simbel were placed in the very different High Victorian environment of Joseph Paxton's steel-and-glass structure in Hyde Park. Approached through an avenue of sphinxes, they were surrounded by tropical palms and an ornamental pond filled with lily pads, which had nothing to do with the original desert location of this temple. Such a contextualization of Egyptian style was ultimately to lead to the commercial exploitation of Mohamed Al-Fayad's Egyptian Hall in Harrods, the famous London department store, where sphinx heads with the features of Mr. Al-Fayed himself gazed down upon his bewildered customers. The immense pyramid and sphinx at Las Vegas in the 20th century can also claim an ancestor in the Egyptian Court of the Crystal Palace. Though the intention of Jones and Bonomi was obviously educational, it was simultaneously designed to entertain and overwhelm. They also re-created the portico from the Memnonium at Thebes, with its row of statues representing Osiris. With the benefit of hindsight, the sight of these brightly colored (but not entirely accurate) theatrical reconstructions amid the wrought-iron pillars and gantries of the Crystal Palace strongly suggest the environment of a film studio. And this was really what Jones and Bonomi created. All they lacked was the technology to go with it. Everything was fake and re-contextualized, arranged to create maximum impact and enthuse the crowds. It would have horrified Thomas Hope, who had previously condemned the "modern imitations of those wonders of [Egyptian] antiquity, composed of lath and of plaster, or callico and of paper, [which] offer no one attribute of solidity or grandeur to compensate for their want of elegance and grace, and can only excite ridicule and contempt."[8]

"Crystal Palace — Egyptian Court." Engraving from *The Illustrated London News*, 1854.

An "Egyptian" display in the window of a contemporary amusement arcade.

Egyptiana rapidly spread across the Western world. The gigantic Egyptian-style obelisk of the Washington Monument was designed in 1836 by Robert Mills (1781–1855). New York had its Egyptian-style prison (The Tombs) dating from 1838 (but unfortunately demolished in 1902). Designed by the English-born architect, John Haviland (1792–1852), it too was based on the Temple of Hathor at Dendera — yet another consequence of Denon's influential book. Claude-Nicholas Ledoux's 1785 design for an unbuilt prison at Aix-en-Provence also played a part in the overall effect of The Tombs, which horrified Charles Dickens when he visited New York in 1842:

> What is this dismal-fronted pile of bastard Egyptian, like an enchanted palace in a melodrama!—a famous prison, called The Tombs. Shall we go in?[9]

The Medical College at Richmond Virginia, designed by Philadelphia architect Thomas Somerville Stewart, followed suit in 1845, and churches, custom houses, monuments, bridges and even synagogues across the world increasingly appeared in Egyptian dress. When the distinguished horticulturalist James Bateman (1811–1897) bought Biddulph Grange in Staffordshire in the 1840s he created an unusual Egyptian Folly which combined clipped yew hedges with stone structures and Egyptian-style statuary. In the middle of an eerily dark corridor of yew, the visitor encounters a grotesque stone idol in the form of a monkey: Egypt was increasingly associated with the macabre, an atmosphere which also affected the way in which 19th-century fine art represented the mysterious Land of the Pharaohs.

Some of the earliest origins of later ancient Egyptian film fantasies are the Egyptian set designs Karl Friedrich Schinkel (1781–1841) made for a production of Mozart's *Die Zauberflöte* in 1816. These include designs for the hall of Sarastro's palace in Act II and the garden scene slightly earlier in the same Act, depicting a sphinx bathed in moonlight. Schinkel's spectacular finale has the sun glowing before an immense, shadowy pyramid, and illuminating a statue of Osiris like a halo. These exercises in the sublime (in the sense that they combined fear, awe and spectacle) are certainly proto-cinematic, and contrast with Mozart's considerably more restrained approach to the music, which is rooted in enlightenment, neoclassical aesthetics. Thanks to the more sophisticated technology available to him, Schinkel was able to create rapid changes of scene in a way that anticipated the shock effect of a rapid cut in film. Like any self-respecting production designer, he also researched his Egyptian fantasy designs with care, consulting the works of Denon and the *Description de l'Egypte*, and adapting it to the fairy-tale atmosphere of Emanuel Schikaneder's libretto. The immense sets of the Elizabeth Taylor *Cleopatra* film can certainly be traced back to Schinkel's designs for Mozart's opera. As Michael Snodin explains, "The symmetry of [Schinkel's] compositions and the contrast between geometric structural elements and highly mobile organic forms give these designs a monumental quality,"[10] which is exactly what Joseph L. Mankiewicz had in mind for—and achieved with—his *Cleopatra* film.

Set designers soon had more historical sources to consult as artists became increasingly adventurous and recorded their impressions of Egypt from first-hand experience. The Scottish artist David Roberts (1796–1864) was one. Significantly, he began his career as a set designer, and, like Schinkel before him, he too provided sets for a Mozart opera with an oriental theme. This was for a production of *Die Entführung aus dem Serail* (*The Abduction from the Seraglio*) in 1827, the action of which takes place in Turkey rather than Egypt. His first major painting was *The Departure of the Israelites From Egypt* two years later, a subject that reflected his fascination with the customs and politics of Egypt. When J. M. W. Turner encouraged him to give up his theatre work and become a full-time artist, he embarked for Egypt at the end of August 1838. Soon, he was following in Belzoni's footsteps, visiting Mohammed Ali Pasha and recording the encounter (apparently from memory) in his volume of engravings of Egypt and the Holy Land, for which he is most remembered today. Measuring meticulously as he went, Roberts left visual records of how the famous monuments of ancient Egypt appeared before they were cleared of sand and debris later in the 19th century. One of his views, for example, shows Rameses' temple at Abu Simnel still half buried and, of course, in its original location. Back in England, Roberts negotiated the handsome fee of £3000 from his publisher, the resulting six-folio volumes creating a British equivalent to Napoleon's immense *Description*.

Other British artists continued Roberts' pioneering work. Some of these paintings were straightforward landscapes, like those of Edward Lear (1812–1888), who sailed down the Nile with pre–Raphaelite painter William Holman Hunt in 1854. Lear spent ten days at Karnak feeling "like a cheese mite among such giants"[11] and returned 13 years later to experience the "sad, stern uncompromising landscape"[12] of the Nubian desert. He enjoyed watching the sun rise over the Nile rather more on this occasion, but nonetheless wrote of "the intense deadness of old Egypt" and its "utter silence.... The myriad bees are the only living world here, & where one peeps into those dark death-silent giant halls of columns — a terror pervades the heart & head."[13] He did, however, amuse himself by observing the myriad bird life on the river banks, and composed a "nonsense" rhyme about the pelicans he observed:

> We live on the Nile. The Nile we love.
> By night we sleep on the cliffs above;
> By day we fish, and at eve we stand
> On long bare islands of yellow sand.
> And when the sun sinks slowly down
> And the great rock walls grow dark and brown,
> When the purple river rolls fast and dim
> And the Ivory Ibis starlike skim,
> Wing to wing we dance around,—
> Stamping our feet with a flumpy sound,—
> Opening our mouths as Pelicans ought,
> And this is the song we nightly snort:—
>   Ploffskin, Pluffskin, Pelican jee,—
>   We think no Birds so happy as we!
>   Plumpskin, Ploshskin, Pelican jill,—
>   We think so then, and we thought so still.[14]

At Abu Simbel he was apparently "too astonished & affected to draw"[15] but the many drawings and water colors he did complete were never as fanciful as his nonsense verse. Fantasy impressions of Egypt were the province of others.

As Egypotologist Herman De Meulenaere explains, "All Egyptianizing paintings have one feature in common: the vision of ancient Egypt they wish to transmit is that of a country of splendor, wealth and voluptuousness. Men wear beautiful and expensive garments, the female bodies are either clad in fine transparent clothes or fully exposed, tinting the Pharaonic part with a sense of refined sensuality. In short, Egypt adorns itself with all the seductiveness of a marvelous country of escape."[16] Throughout the 19th century, a wealth of Egyptian fantasies were created by French academicians in which female musicians strum their

Egyptian harps or dance in veils, and Cleopatra watches her slaves die of poison before killing herself. Alexandre Cabanel (1823–1889), Jean-Jules-Antoine Lecomte du Noüy (1842–1923), Jean André Rixens (1846–1924) and Georges Rochegrosse (1859–1938) all contributed to this genre, but the Egyptian fantasies of British painters were actually more influential on subsequent cinematic visions.

Sir Lawrence Alma-Tadema eventually became more associated with ancient Roman scenes, but the earlier part of his career featured a series of ancient Egyptian canvases depicting everyday life. His first attempt at the genre came in 1863 with *Pastimes in Egypt 3,000 Years Ago*. Though he didn't visit Egypt until his old age, Egypt was an obvious artistic destination for him from the start:

> Where else should I have begun ... as soon as I had become acquainted with the life of the ancients? The first thing a child learns of ancient history is about the court of the Pharaohs.[17]

The art historian William Gaunt believed that Alma-Tadema may have been influenced by the publication, in 1864, of *Eine ägyptische Königstochter* (*An Egyptian Princess*), a novel by the German Egyptologist Georg Moritz Ebers (1837–1898). As Gaunt put it, this story "clothed the dry bones of learning with romance,"[18] which exactly mirrored Alma-Tadema's approach to historical painting. Indeed, as though anticipating Alma-Tadema's later speciality of classical scenes, Ebers wrote in his preface:

> To Professor Lepsius, who suggested to me that a tale confined entirely to Egypt and the Egyptians might become wearisome, I owe many thanks; and following his hint, have so arranged the materials supplied by Herodotus as to introduce my reader first into a Greek circle. Here he will feel in a measure at home, and indeed will entirely sympathize with them on one important point, viz.: in their ideas on the Beautiful and on Art. Through this Hellenic portico he reaches Egypt, from thence passes on to Persia and returns finally to the Nile. It has been my desire that the three nations should attract him equally, and I have therefore not centered the entire interest of the plot in one hero, but have endeavored to exhibit each nation in its individual character, by means of a fitting representative. The Egyptian Princess has given her name to the book, only because the weal and woe of all my other characters were decided by her fate, and she must therefore be regarded as the central point of the whole.[19]

In his preface to the fourth edition, Ebers responded to his critics by explaining the appropriate response to a Romance, as opposed to an academic treatise:

> A reply to Monsieur Jules Soury's criticism of "An Egyptian Princess" in the Revue des deux Mondes, Vol. VII, January 1875, might appropriately be introduced into this preface, but would scarcely be possible without entering more deeply into the ever-disputed question, which will be answered elsewhere, whether the historical romance is ever justifiable. Yet I cannot refrain from informing Monsieur Soury here that "An Egyptian Princess" detained me from no other work. I wrote it in my sick-room, before entering upon my academic career, and while composing it, found not only comfort and pleasure, but an opportunity to give dead scientific material a living interest for myself and others.
>
> Monsieur Soury says romance is the mortal enemy of history; but this sentence may have no more justice than the one with which I think myself justified in replying: Landscape painting is the mortal enemy of botany. The historical romance must be enjoyed like any other work of art. No one reads it to study history; but many, the author hopes, may be aroused by his work to make investigations of their own, for which the notes point out the way. Already several persons of excellent mental powers have been attracted to earnest Egyptological researches by "An

Egyptian Princess." In the presence of such experiences, although Monsieur Soury's clever statements appear to contain much that is true, I need not apply his remark that "historical romances injure the cause of science" to the present volume.
Leipzig, April 19, 1875.[20]

This is excellent theory, but Ebers' practice of interspersing his story with a great many lengthy archeological asides is problematic for the modern reader. Obviously, the academic in him was unable to let the raconteur take over completely, but one can see why his novel made such an impression on Alma-Tadema, as it is full to overflowing with elaborate descriptions of settings, props and costumes, of which the following example is fairly representative:

> On this day it was the king's intention to make an especial display of the wealth and splendor of his court, at a festival arranged in honor of his daughter's betrothal.
> The lofty reception-hall opening on to the gardens, with its ceiling sown with thousands of golden stars and supported by gaily-painted columns, presented a magic appearance. Lamps of colored papyrus hung against the walls and threw a strange light on the scene, something like that when the sun's rays strike through colored glass. The space between the columns and the walls was filled with choice plants, palms, oleanders, pomegranates, oranges and roses, behind which an invisible band of harp and flute-players was stationed, who received the guests with strains of monotonous, solemn music.
> The floor of this hall was paved in black and white, and in the middle stood elegant tables covered with dishes of all kinds, cold roast meats, sweets, well-arranged baskets of fruit and cake, golden jugs of wine, glass drinking-cups and artistic flower-vases.
> A multitude of richly-dressed slaves under direction of the high-steward, busied themselves in handing these dishes to the guests, who, either standing around, or reclining on sumptuous seats, entertained themselves in conversation with their friends.
> Both sexes and all ages were to be found in this assembly. As the women entered, they received charming little nosegays from the young priests in the personal service of the king, and many a youth of high degree appeared in the hall with flowers, which he not only offered to her he loved best, but held up for her to smell.
> The Egyptian men, who were dressed as we have already seen them at the reception of the Persian embassy, behaved towards the women with a politeness that might almost be termed submissive. Among the latter few could pretend to remarkable beauty, though there were many bewitching almond-shaped eyes, whose loveliness was heightened by having their lids dyed with the eye-paint called "mestem." The majority wore their hair arranged in the same manner; the wealth of waving brown locks floated back over the shoulders and was brushed behind the ears, one braid being left on each side to hang over the temples to the breast. A broad diadem confined these locks, which as the maids knew, were quite as often the wig-maker's work as Nature's. Many ladies of the court wore above their foreheads a lotus-flower, whose stem drooped on the hair at the back. They carried fans of bright feathers in their delicate hands. These were loaded with rings; the finger-nails were stained red, according to Egyptian custom, and gold or silver bands were worn above the elbow, and at the wrists and ankles.[21]

Alma-Tadema's *Pastimes in Egypt 3,000 Years Ago* depicts a group of musicians and a dancer performing before a wealthy family, with massive columns surmounted by lotus capitals looming behind them. The dancing figure is based on a similar female figure in a wall painting from the tomb of Nebamum, now in the British Museum. Even the chair is copied from an original in the British Museum and the harp is based on an similar instrument in the Louvre to add as much authenticity to the scene as possible.[22] The artist himself explained its history:

"Egypt 3,000 Years Ago." Engraving of the painting by Lawrence Alma-Tadema from *The Art Journal*, 1870, p. 140.

> The picture was painted in 1863 & had its success in Brussels that year. Then the figures were all in white & the background open and in full color. It was exhibited then under the title of How people enjoyed themselves 3,000 years ago. I repainted it as it is now & sent it to the Paris Salon in 1864 under the title of The 18th Dynasty, and had the gold medal for it. Gambart bought it in 1865, and exhibited it in the French Gallery in that year [as An Evening Party at Nineveh]. In 1866 it was very much damaged in the great gas explosion in Gambart's house 62 Avenue Road. It was restored and touched up by myself.[23]

The painting was then exhibited again in 1867 at the Paris Exposition Universelle, where it won a second-class medal. A contemporary critic described the subject as being

> intended to represent an entertainment given in honor of a Nubian ambassador, who is seated in front, and to whom an Egyptian slave is offering some beverage in a cup: on his right, amidst a group of young people, is the host, a priest, named Phtames, the scribe of the great house of the god Phta, at Memphis, whose name appears on the furniture and walls: behind the priest, a little to his right hand, is his standard-bearer: the name of the priest is taken from the column of his tomb, now in the Museum of Leyden. The other leading figures in the composition — musicians and dancer — speak for themselves. The presence of the mummy, in the background on the extreme right, invites the company to be merry, according to the principles of the ancient Egyptians.[24]

The immense success of the painting inspired Alma-Tadema to capitalize on the obvious appeal of Egyptian subjects. *An Egyptian Game* (1865) shows a man and a woman playing chess, while in *An Egyptian at His Doorway* (1865) features a white-robed figure wearing a

"Joseph, Overseer of Pharaoh's Granaries." Engraving of the painting by Lawrence Alma-Tadema from *The Illustrated London News,* October 3, 1874.

green scarab mounted on a gold pendant, leaning nonchalantly against a pillar decorated with the cartouche of Rameses II. As Maarten Raven has pointed out, the scarab jewel, the doorway and the frieze were derived from examples in J. Gardner Wilkinson's book, *Manners and Customs of the Ancient Egyptians.*[25] *The Egyptian Widow* (1872) is an elaborately decorated scene, replete with palms, musicians and a mummified body before which the widow laments. He also depicted *The Death of Pharaoh's First Born* in 1872 before turning his attention to Biblical Egypt in 1874 with *Joseph, Overseer of Pharaoh's Granaries.*

Just as Alma-Tadema's Greco-Roman paintings have been described as "Victorians in togas," one is tempted to categorize his Egyptian scenes in a similar way, for despite the archeological rigor with which he approaches the settings, it could be argued that he portrays the activities involved from the perspective of his own time and culture. As R. J. Barrow points out, "*Pastimes in Ancient Egypt* is remarkable in that it reconciles exoticism and domestication: the inclusion of the word 'pastimes' in the title reassures us of sameness, while, at the same time, the subtitle, 'three thousand years ago,' sets up distance. The painting itself is a genre scene of everyday life, but everyday life in an unfamiliar and exotic setting."[26] Costume dramas such as Mankiewicz's *Cleopatra* film, and the flashback scenes of the various mummy films of Universal and Hammer studios, operate in a similar manner (some admittedly more archeologically correct than others). Alma-Tadema's paintings were indeed the ancestors of such popular 20th-century entertainments, and it's not at all surprising that the artist was also employed as a set and costume designer by the great Victorian actor manager Sir Herbert Beerbohm Tree (1853–1917).

Alma-Tadema returned to Egypt in 1902 when he began *The Finding of Moses*. It was commissioned by the engineer Sir John Aird to commemorate his company's completion of the Aswan Dam. Alma-Tadema had attended the opening ceremony in person (along with Winston Churchill) before returning to London to complete his own Herculean achievement in paint, which took him another two years. Notable for its foreground of exquisite blue delphiniums, *The Finding of Moses* is actually a depiction of the moments immediately after the discovery, when the infant prophet is being taken back to Pharaoh's palace in a reed basket, Pharaoh's daughter being carried by shaven-headed slaves. In the distant background the pyramids loom, as they must.

But Alma-Tadema was not alone. His rival "Olympian" painter, Sir Edward John Poynter (1836–1919), also supplied the Victorian demand for theatrical Egyptian scenes. He began Egyptianizing with a watercolor drawing depicting water carriers. This caught the attention of the Dalziel brothers, who commissioned ten drawings from him for their planned but never published *Illustrated Bible*. This project led to *On Guard in the Time of the Pharaohs* (1864), which shows an Egyptian soldier in his regalia standing on the ramparts of an ancient city port that is spread out below him, with the sea in the distance. *Offerings to Isis* (1866) was another study in perspective, the Egyptian architecture observed this time from eye-level. It provides the backdrop for a young woman on her way to a temple, carrying a slain goose in the basket which she balances on her head. *Adoration to Ra* (1867) shows a high priest, draped with the traditional leopard skin, who gestures before the golden image of a falcon, mounted on a slender column. Incense burns, while in the background we observe the naked breasts of a female figure tying a white cloth around another column. The wall of the temple in which this takes place is highly decorated in the expected Egyptian style.

Poynter's most celebrated Egyptian painting, *Israel in Egypt* (1866), is a spectacular evocation of a temple in the process of being constructed. A large group of slaves pull a monumental lion, while nobles observe the process from behind, protected from the fierce

"Israel in Egypt." Engraving of Edward J. Poynter's painting by W. L. Thomas from *The London Illustrated News*, 1868.

rays of the sun by parasols and fans. Poytner's Christian perspective is obviously critical of Egypt here (though, as we now know, Egyptian monuments were built by professional laborers). To emphasize his moral point, he included a vignette in the center foreground of the scene in which a slave, about to be whipped by an overseer, is ministered by a female figure who offers him water. This detail, along with two passive pylons in the right-hand section of the background (with their murals of war chariots and prancing horses in battle) directly inspired a scene in DeMille's *The Ten Commandments*. For all its apparent historical authenticity, Poynter's painting is, nonetheless, a melange of Egyptian elements (there is even a pyramid in the background). It, in fact, has more in common with the approach taken by the artist of the frontispiece for the Napoleonic *Description*, which similarly (though perhaps less convincingly) conflates various buildings and monuments into a single view. The civil engineer responsible for London's Charing Cross Station, Sir John Hawkshaw, criticized Poynter's painting on engineering lines, complaining that there weren't enough slaves to pull a stone lion of the size Poynter depicted, so Poynter duly obliged him by extending the line of slaves to the edge of the canvas, permitting the viewer to make up as many slaves as he thinks fit for the task in hand.

Frederick Goodall (1822–1904), another Victorian academician, had visited Egypt in 1858, and his Egyptian paintings became immensely popular. As Gaunt records, the first of these fetched £1000, its purchaser, Mr. Duncan Dunbar, referring to it as his "100 guineas-a-foot picture."[27] One can't help equating the immense sums spent on visual fantasy in the Victorian period with the cost of a blockbuster movie today. Indeed, Goodall's *The Finding of Moses* (1885) also influenced DeMille: two naked slaves discover the infant prophet, while the Pharaoh's daughter looks on, attended by a third slave, who, judging by her expression, senses trouble to come. An Ibis, sacred to Isis, paces the quayside. The discovery of Moses in the film is similarly portrayed. Alma-Tadema and Edwin Long (1829–1921) contributed their own versions of this Biblical scene, and other Biblical scenes, of course, proved irresistible to painters with a flair for the spectacular. John Martin (1789–1858) also foreshadowed DeMille in his *Seventh Plague of Egypt* (1823), which depicts a fantasy Egyptian harbor scene replete with pyramids and somewhat Ptolemaic architecture, all of which are threatened by a cataclysmic storm. American artist Frederick Arthur Bridgman (1847–1928), depicted *Pharaoh's Army engulfed by the Red Sea* in 1900, long before DeMille transformed Arnold Friberg's vision of the parting of the Red Sea in the remake of *The Ten Commandments*. Speaking of which, it's also interesting to compare the Danish painter Christoffer Wilhelm Eckersberg's (1783–1853) *The Crossing of the Red Sea* (1813) with the way in which DeMille had Charlton Heston as Moses, urging the Israelites from his vantage point on a rock, raising his arms and pointing towards the waters. Eckersberg's choreography of this moment is yet another possible source for DeMille's image here.

As the Victorian aesthetic movement grew, Egypt began to influence the prevailing fashion for subjectless arrangements of lethargically draped female figures, such as we find in the paintings of Albert Moore (1841–1893). Val Prinsep (1838–1904) followed this trend in *The Death of Cleopatra,* in which the suicidal Egyptian queen seems to be merely asleep, clutching a rose rather than an asp. One of her female slaves has already expired, the basket of figs, in which the asp was hidden, lying on the floor behind her prone figure. The other servant is about to expire herself. The overall atmosphere of this tragic scene, however, is essentially decorative rather than emotional, the hieroglyphs on the walls and columns

Statues of Bast flanking the entrance to the Carreras Building, Mornington Crescent, Camden Town, London. Designed by M.E. & O.H. Collins, 1926.

behind the group forming an equally decorative theatrical backdrop. The aesthetic movement also created its own Anglo-Egyptian style of furniture, thanks mainly to the work of Edward William Godwin (1833–1886). Though based on original artifacts, the furniture in *The Ten Commandments* and other Egyptian epics did not escape the influence of these Victorian recreations of ancient Egyptian models.

The more streamlined approach of Art Deco also inspired major buildings, such as the Carreras Building in Camden, London, which was once the headquarters of the "Black Cat" brand of cigarette. Its original colored paintwork, a solar disc to the Sun-god Ra, and two monumental cats flanking the entrance have now been restored to their former glory and brighten up an otherwise rather dull road in North London. Other splendid examples of the Egyptian Revival style are the Hoover factory on Western Avenue in West London, and William Van Alen's Chrysler Building in New York. The *Daily Telegraph* Building in Fleet Street, designed by Charles Ernest Elcock at the end of the 1920s, also proudly boasts Egyptian columns, but most conspicuous of all were the Egyptian elements of many Art Deco cinemas. The Carlton Cinema in Essex Road, Islington, which opened in 1930, was once a resplendent venue for the enjoyment of cinematic fantasy in its designer George Coles' decorative scheme of cream and green tiles. Edward Albert Stone's Astoria in Streatham also opened in 1930, featuring an Egyptian nude taking her bath in a pool filled with lotuses, while in America, Grauman's Egyptian Theatre on Hollywood Boulevard was built in the

The Carlton Cinema in Essex Road, Islington, London. Designed by George Coles, 1930. Photographed in 2011.

same year that Tutankhamen was discovered. In fact, Sid Grauman beat Howard Carter, who didn't open the tomb until two weeks after the cinema was ready for business. Grauman's was the first-ever venue for a Hollywood film premiere. Sadly, this was not of the Egyptian variety, but rather *Robin Hood*, starring Douglas Fairbanks, but the cinema itself is such a riot of Egyptiana that the screening of a film there is an almost superfluous experience.

Such an Egyptian heritage was perhaps what lay behind the decision in 1985 to build Britain's first multiplex cinema at Milton Keynes, Buckinghamshire, in the shape of a pyramid. Indeed, much of Milton Keynes is indebted to Egyptian inspiration, the geometric simplicity of much of its architecture resembling the Temple of Hatshepsut at Deir el-Bahari. Modernist architecture in general owes much to the ancient Egyptians' love of geometric simplicity and rational elegance, so what better way to commemorate the modernization of the Louvre Museum in Paris than with Ieoh Ming Pei's glass pyramid in the 1990s — a tribute to Napoleon's contribution to Egyptology and the desire of Denon to create just such a museum himself: a palace devoted entirely to the arts.

The set designers of Egyptian epics and mummy movies might not have achieved the fame or distinction of Egyptianizing artists and architects, but their impact on audiences has perhaps been even more powerful. The prolific illustrator Willy Pogany (1882–1955) is well-known for his illustrations for three Wagner operas, *The Ruba'iyat of Omar Khayyám*, and Coleridge's *Rime of the Ancient Mariner*. Though uncredited, his Egyptian sets for

Universal's original version of *The Mummy* were also seen in the reprised flashback scenes of the sequels. Born in Hungary, Pogany emigrated, via London, to America where he became a regular cover artist for *Metropolitan*, *McCall's* magazine and the *American Weekly*. He also did his fair share of advertising work, including a series for Palmolive, which seem deliberately to have echoed the title of Alma-Tadema's first successful Egyptian canvas. They demonstrate various ways of showing how Palmolive was made "3,000 years ago," and one of Pogany's illustrations from 1917 showed an ancient Egyptian scene in this context. A young noble Egyptian woman observes two slaves pouring the ingredients of the soap into a golden bowl. Intriguingly, both the costumes and poses in the design strongly resemble the finale moments in *The Mummy*, when Zita Johann, dressed in ancient robes and headdress, struggles against Karloff's mummy, while slaves stir a bath of natron for her imminent (but thankfully, avoided) embalming.

It was Jack Otterson (1905–1991) who redressed his own sets for James Whale's jungle adventure, *Green Hell*, when designing *The Mummy's Hand*. *Green Hell* had high production values but an appalling script. Vincent Price, who was killed off early in the story, claimed that "about five of the worst pictures ever made were all in that one picture."[28] Although the film was a flop, Otterson's sets were too good to waste. He'd had an impressive flight of ruined steps constructed for *Green Hell*, and he'd also designed the distinctly creepy interior of a ruined Inca temple. Why not make something Egyptian out of all that and use it for *The Mummy's Hand*? Perhaps the reason why not was that a few hieroglyphs do not make an Egyptian tomb, but then again was anyone really paying that much attention?—and how many people knew (or cared) what the inside of an Egyptian tomb actually looks like? Redressed, the Inca sets looked suitably foreign, and anyway, *The Mummy's Hand* was an infinitely better film than *Green Hell* (not that that was hard to achieve).

Otterson returned to design *The Mummy's Tomb*, which required less in the way of Egyptiana as most of the action had shifted to America by then, which is where it stayed for the two further films in the cycle. John Goodman (1901–1991) took over for these, aided by various other designers and set dressers, by which time mummy movies were getting almost as formulaic as ancient Egyptian art itself. The splendor of ancient Egypt now became the province of the epic spectacular. Complemented by Oliver Messel's costumes and interior designs, John Bryan's epic set for the palace at Memphis in Gabriel Pascal's film version of Bernard Shaw's *Cæsar and Cleopatra* were more spectacular than anything before seen in a British film. The British director Ronald Neame was highly complimentary about Bryan's skills, judging him to be the best designer he had ever met:

> He was the cameraman's dream boy, and the director's too. When one proposed a set with him, he would move to a sixteen-by-twelve drawing pad and with a few deft strokes in charcoal he would give you exactly what you had in mind. The moment John began his sketches the film came to life. It was a remarkable talent.[29]

No less remarkable, were the vivid designs of Cecil B. DeMille's art director for *The Ten Commandments*, Arnold Friberg (1913–2010). Friberg designed key sequences such as the parting of the Red Sea, and had been brought to DeMille's attention through the series of paintings commissioned by Adele Cannon Howell, president of the Church of Jesus Christ of Latter Day Saints. Originally published on the covers of its children's magazine, they were highly cinematic in style: naturalistic, with vivid colors, dynamic gestures and a

John Bryan's temple set for *Caesar and Cleopatra* (dir. Gabriel Pascal, 1946).

dramatic evocation of supernatural forces. DeMille faithfully transferred these qualities onto the screen, along with elements drawn from the various 19th-century paintings already discussed.

The legendary Alexandre Trauner (1906–1993) was art director of Howard Hawks' *Land of the Pharaohs.* Born in Hungary, Trauner's most celebrated film was *Les Enfants du Paradis* (dir. Marcel Carné, 1945), but his work for Hawks' rather less respected film is notable for its imaginative evocation of the complex, sand-powered mechanics of Pharaoh's pyramid. Marc Gross goes even further in his reassessment of Hawks' often-maligned movie, and, by implication, Trauner's contribution to it:

> LAND OF THE PHARAOHS is completely different, in both style and feeling, from any other Hollywood production of its period. By evoking the funeral serenity of ancient Egyptian art, and by so doing making explicit the political and personal hubris of a living deity, this film has more in common with Jean-Luc Godard's "neo-realist musical" A WOMAN IS A WOMAN or Roberto Rossellini's THE RISE OF LOUIS XIV than something like BEN HUR. Hawks' film demonstrates, through an amazing rigorousness of cinematic technique and intellectual clarity, the inability of either an individual or a fictional construct such as a motion picture to transcend the ravages of history and time.[30]

With these epic, full-color Egyptian visions in place, Hammer was now in a position to bring an equally colorful, poetic realism to their mummy films. Make-up designer Roy Ashton studied mummies in the British Museum to create a more convincing monster than the somewhat crude make-up for Lon Chaney's mummy had allowed. (Having said that, George Partleton's make-up for the mummy of Prem in *The Mummy's Shroud* was by far the most authentic copy of a genuine Egyptian mummy in any film up to that time, being based on a genuine exhibit in the British Museum which is still on display.) The real star of Hammer's first mummy movie, however, was its production designer, Bernard Robinson (1912–1970) who, along with his wife, Margaret, was largely responsible for making the film the huge success it was. Not only were his designs for the elegant English home of Egyptologist John Banning far more opulent than were strictly necessary, Robinson's way with the tomb of Ananka combined research with poetic license, the whole being flooded with an eerie green glow thanks to Jack Asher's imaginative lighting. The whole effect is rather like a macabre Egyptian bathroom, Ananka's sarcophagus resembling a hieroglyph-inscribed bathtub. In this artfully contrived space, the tomb of Kharis could be a closet filled with Egyptian cotton towels and the "Sekhmet boat" an elaborate dispenser of bath essence. Robinson's interior here is no more accurate than Willy Pogany's. The wall paintings are highly stylized as are the artifacts, despite the watchful eye of Egyptologist Andrew Low, but that was the whole point of Robinson's approach, which aimed to create a heightened realism. In this respect he might be compared to Alexandre Trauner, who believed that an art director "cannot show everything; he chooses the significant elements, the unexpected ones, and these must look true, they must sound right."[31] Like Trauner, Robinson aimed to be convincing but not entirely faithful to his original inspiration. A slavish copy of a real Egyptian tomb would have been neither theatrical enough nor (and this is significant) *domestic* enough. Robinson excelled in domestic spaces into which violence erupts. (This may have had something to do with Hammer's limited space at Bray Studios, but it also reflected Robinson's own meticulous personality and bourgeois approach to his work. As his wife recalled: "His success as a designer was not so much due to his skill as a draughtsman, though it was considerable, but to the mixture of frugality and lavishness that enabled him to enjoy keeping within his budget, dove-tailing and revamping his sets, and yet at the same time sparing nothing on magnificent embellishments.... He prided himself on a businesslike image rather than an arty one.... He couldn't bear ugly things around him and used to collect antique furniture, often finding damaged pieces and lovingly repairing them."[32] Robinson's Castle Dracula, after all, is immaculate: no cobwebs, no drafts, and Dracula's staircase, by the way, is flanked by an Egyptian obelisk. Similarly, Ananka's tomb is clean and tidy, a domestic space, with something nasty in the airing cupboard.

Robinson reused some of the props from the first mummy film in *The Curse of the Mummy's Tomb*, but we see very little of the tomb itself. The tomb in *The Mummy's Shroud* was, as we have seen, humble in the extreme, with a body buried in the sand and simply covered with the sacred shroud. André Morell's performance so eloquently conveys an archeologist's excitement, that there is no need for a host of artifacts and wall paintings. Unfortunately, both these films have their own flashbacks set in ancient Egypt, and these scenes sadly betray the fact that Hammer did not have the resources that were at the disposal of Howard Hawks or Cecil B. DeMille; but like the tableaux in those films, Robinson nonetheless attempted, within his limited means, to recreate the kind of Egyptian fantasy paintings of Alma-Tadema and Poynter.

Scott MacGreggor's work on the production design for *Blood from the Mummy's Tomb*, however, is perhaps the most impressive of all of Hammer's mummy films. The traditional contrast between familiar British domesticity and an ancient culture is made more explicit by having Queen Tera's tomb actually transplanted to the suburban cellar of the Egyptologist, Professor Fuchs. Admittedly, Robinson had done something similar for the final scenes in

The Curse of the Mummy's Tomb, but in that instance he had merely accessorized the cellar of an elegant London home with Egyptian artifacts. Scott MacGreggor's cellar is a much more integrated affair, and very much the workplace of the professor, replete with piles of books, a cluttered desk, a wash basin, and a furnace, which contrast with the mummy, mummy case and hieroglyph-inscribed walls of Queen Tera's tomb. A model of Anubis in the impressive hall of the Fuchs residence is an effective signifier of the Egyptian presence that pervades the entire house, as well, of course, as being a harbinger of death. The tomb scenes set in the time of Queen Tera are also the most convincing of all of Hammer's ancient Egyptian flashback sequences, atmospherically lit by Arthur Grant without the gaudy theatricality of Jack Asher's lurid green light or the unconvincing attempts at grandeur in the ancient Egyptian scenes of *The Curse of the Mummy's Tomb*. The empty house in which James Villiers' Corbeck waits and watches developments in Professor Fuchs' home over the road echoes the abandoned spaces of an Egyptian tomb, as does the corridor of the lunatic asylum in which George Coulouris as Professor Berrigan finds himself incarcerated. Similarly, the dusty museum rooms in which Hugh Burden's Geoffrey Dandridge comes face to face with Margaret Fuchs — or is it Queen Tera herself? — are a place of living death.

The claustrophobic atmosphere, which is so essential an ingredient to this incestuous tale, was largely created by the predominantly studio-bound filming. The few exterior shots of misty (equally deserted) suburban streets were deliberately devoid of pedestrians or traffic and seemed almost as hermetically sealed from the outside world as MacGregor's sets; but by the time Stoker's Egyptian story was filmed again as *The Awakening*, a bigger budget encouraged director Mike Newell to go out on location. We see much more of the tomb and of the desert in which it is situated, and the overall atmosphere is much more naturalistic. Consequently, for all its many excellent features, this version lacks the intense, dream-like qualities of Seth Holt's earlier adaptation. In the age of the blockbuster, the even more lavish budget of the 1999 remake of *The Mummy* only exacerbated this problem. Having said that, Allan Cameron's designs for the opening scenes of this film, set in a very golden ancient Egypt, are undoubtedly the most impressive thing about the entire affair, conveying, as they do, a monumentality that no other mummy movie had hitherto been able to afford. One wonders what Terence Fisher, Michael Carreras, John Gilling and Seth Holt would have made of such resources, and, indeed, if such vast amounts of money would have made their claustrophobic, incestuous and xenophobic Egyptian nightmares any more effective. The money at Stephen Sommers' disposal didn't help his version of *The Mummy* to have any more belief in its own narrative. Perhaps horror films in general — and particularly the Egyptian variety — actually benefit from financial restrictions, describing, as they do, anxiety and fear rather than spectacle and adventure. Low budgets force filmmakers to expand a small space, rather than to contain a vastness — and that is one of the main differences between the epic and the mummy movie, despite their shared concern with ancient Egypt.

Five

Fiction and Fantasy, Part 1

The mummy movies and cinematic Egyptian epics of the 20th century were the culmination of a literary tradition that ultimately stretches back to accounts of the ancient Egyptians in the Bible. This, after all, is where Cecil B. DeMille's *The Ten Commandments* has its origin, but, as we have seen, the Old Testament is notoriously vague about Egyptian life and culture, and European society remained similarly uncertain about it until archeology came to the rescue centuries later. Before that happened, authors were dependent upon what could be gleaned from the Bible and the historical information of Greek historians such as Plutarch, on whose *Life of Antony* and *Life of Pompey* Shakespeare based his play *Antony and Cleopatra*, first performed in 1608. The stage conventions of Shakespeare's day were, of course, very different from the costume dramas of Hollywood, which derived from the archeological obsession of Victorian actors such as Sir Henry Irving (1838–1905). For Irving, who never, in fact, appeared in a production of *Antony and Cleopatra*, "authentic" sets and costumes were perhaps more important than Shakespeare's texts. These he ruthlessly cut in performance. Having said that, Irving's biographer, Laurence Irving, was keen to point out that his grandfather's cuts "were not a work of vandalism by an egotistical actor-manager, but a conscientious adaptation which studied the tastes of the squeamish Victorian audience and made it possible to present the plays within the limits of the theatrical habits and conventions which, for better or worse, prevailed at that time."[1]

It was an approach continued into the Edwardian era by Sir Herbert Beerbohm Tree, who put on a similarly exotic production of *Antony and Cleopatra* in 1906 at His Majesty's Theatre in London. During the scene on the banks of the Nile, which, according to the theatre historian W. MacQueen-Pope "was a marvel of colour, pageantry, and — shall we say — want of costume," the great actor was conscious of someone standing behind him. He turned to discover King Edward VII in top hat and tails who explained that he had been so impressed by this particular scene that he had come in through the stage door as he particularly wanted to see it again. "Do you mind?" he inquired.[2]

Shakespeare, of course, left all that to the imagination. The theater of his day in no way attempted to create authentic locations, and the actors would mainly have been costumed in conventional Elizabethan dress. Indeed, throughout the entirety of *Antony and Cleopatra*, Shakespeare really only provides one poetic description of those splendors of ancient Egypt which were almost the whole point of later cinematic evocations. The speech is so powerful, however, that no more needs to be said. It's delivered by Enobarbus, Antony's friend, who creates a highly synthetic impression of Cleopatra's exotic world, combining

"The most infectious pestilence upon thee!"—Act ii, 5. 61. Anonymous illustration for Shakespeare's *Antony and Cleopatra* from *The Henry Irving Shakespeare,* edited by Sir Henry Irving and Frank A. Marshall (London: Gresham, 1906).

gold, perfume, color, music and sensuality. In fact, it wouldn't be an exaggeration to say that these 121 words became a blueprint for all latter-day set designers working in this field:

> The barge she sat in, like a burnished throne,
> Burn'd on the water: the poop was beaten gold;
> Purple the sails, and so perfumed, that
> The winds were lovesick with them; the oars were silver,
> Which to the tune of flutes kept stroke, and made
> The water which they beat to follow faster,
> As amorous of their strokes. For her own person,
> It beggared all description: she did lie
> In her pavilion,—cloth-of-gold of tissue,—
> O'er-picturing that Venus where we see
> The fancy outwork nature: on each side her
> Stood pretty dimpled boys, like smiling Cupids,
> With divers-colored fans, whose wind did seem
> To glow the delicate cheeks which they did cool,
> And what they undid did.[3]

However, close comparison of Shakespeare's text here with Plutarch revealed that the ancient Greek writer to whom Shakespeare was so indebted was perhaps the true father of the Hollywood epic and the mother of all mummy movies:

Therefore when she was sent unto by divers letters, both from Antonius himself and also from his friends, she made so light of it and mocked Antonius so much that she disdained to set forward otherwise but to take her barge in the river of Cydnus, the poop whereof was of gold, the sails of purple, and the oars of silver, which kept stroke in rowing after the sound of the music of flutes, howboys, citherns, viols, and such other instruments as they played upon in the barge. And now for the person of herself: she was laid under a pavilion of cloth of gold of tissue, appareled and attired like the goddess Venus commonly drawn in picture; and hard by her, on either hand of her, pretty fair boys appareled as painters do set forth god Cupid, with little fans in their hands, with which they fanned wind upon her. Her ladies and gentlewomen also, the fairest of them were appareled like the nymphs Nereides (which are the mermaids of the waters) and like the Graces, some steering the helm, others tending the tackle and ropes of the barge, out of which there came a wonderful passing sweet savour of perfumes, that perfumed the wharf's side, pestered with innumerable multitudes of people.[4]

Despite Shakespeare's lack of Egyptian color, that famous speech and the occasional reference to Isis and the Nile notwithstanding, it was, inevitably, the death of Cleopatra at the end of the play that would resonate through the ages, inspiring poems, paintings, music and film in ways far beyond Shakespeare's wildest dreams:

CLEOPATRA:
[To an asp, which she applies to her breast]
With thy sharp teeth this knot intrinsicate
Of life at once untie; poor venomous fool,
Be angry, and despatch. O, couldst thou speak,
That I might hear thee call great Caesar ass
Unpolicied!

CHARMIAN:
O eastern star!

CLEOPATRA:
Peace, peace!
Dost thou not see my baby at my breast,
That sucks the nurse asleep?

CHARMIAN:
O, break! O, break!

CLEOPATRA:
As sweet as balm, as soft as air, as gentle,—
O Antony!— Nay, I will take thee too.
[Applying another asp to her arm]
What should I stay—
[Dies] [5]

Shakespeare's play is primarily a political, realistic affair. Apart from a soothsayer who tells fortunes, there is no magic and very little myth in this work, which is much more concerned with history, conflict and sexual relationships. If Plutarch and Shakespeare provided the seeds of the Hollywood Egyptian epic, the distant origins of the mummy movie can more convincingly be traced back to Terrasson's *The Life of Sethos*. Terrasson also set the standard for the descriptions of lavish splendor and ceremony that occupied both genres. The novel opens during the last days of Queen Nephte, the mother of Sethos, and describes her subsequent funeral:

The porch of the palace was closed up from all approaches of the sun, and illuminated with lamps: Under it was placed a large chariot with four wheels, all covered over with gold. At the hinder part of the chariot was erected a throne, with an ascent of three steps, covered with a large crown of gold, richly adorned with precious stones, and supported by a sphinx of the same metal, with large wings displayed, upon the head of which the edge of the crown rested. From the top of the crown fell down in large folds, between the sphinx's wings, a cloth of purple in the form of a pavilion, covered with hieroglyphics richly embossed in gold, and representing all the virtues.[6]

Terrasson was also fascinated, as, of course, were his many successors, by the embalming process:

The operation was thirty days in performing. Having, by means of a lateral incision in the body, taken out all the intestines, excepting the heart and reins [sic], they anointed it both outwardly and inwardly with a certain gum composed of cedar, myrrh, cinnamon, and other perfumes; which not only preserved it for several ages, but caused it to diffuse an agreeable odour. They had, besides, the secret of giving a corpse its pristine form; insomuch that the deceased seemed to have retained the air of his countenance, and the port of his person.[7]

The next significant literary event in the history of Egyptian fantasy was the publication in 1786 of a William Beckford's Oriental romance *Vathek*. This is one of the earliest of Gothic novels, though its Oriental setting marks it out as an exception to the general rules of the genre. There are no "Gothick" ruins in *Vathek*, despite the fact that Beckford went on to create the grandest of all Gothic follies in Fonthill Abbey. The Caliph Vathek does, however, enjoy building towers as high as the one that eventually collapsed over Beckford's ill-fated abbey; and Vathek himself is the first Gothic villain in Western literature, anticipating not only the villains of Ann Radcliffe's novels but also the whole cult of the brooding Byronic hero that followed. The mummy movie as a genre within a genre (Egyptian Gothic horror, so to speak) therefore inhabits a space originally put aside for it in Beckford's curious Oriental romance. In the dungeons beneath Vathek's tower, his mother, Carathis, has created the kind of "deep vaulted cell" in which the witches in Purcell's opera, *Dido and Aeneas* (1689), prepared their evil charms:

First she descended, by small steps cut into the thickness of the walls, and known only to her and to Vathek, into mysterious pits which formed the repositories for a number of mummies of the ancient Pharaohs, filched from their tombs. Of these she took a goodly quantity, and then made her way to a gallery where, under the guardianship of fifty dumb negresses, blind in the right eyes, were kept the oil from the most venomous serpents, the tusks of rhinoceroses, and logs cut by magicians in the interior of the Indies, which emitted a suffocating odour; not to mention a thousand other horrible rarities.[8]

Carathis orders the mutes to take the mummies and the other horrible rarities onto the balconies of the tower where she sets fire to them. This causes such a huge cloud of black smoke that Vathek's subjects rush up the tower to extinguish the flames; but so thick is the smoke they do not realize the trap into which they have stumbled. The mutes fall upon them and hang them as a sacrifice to the demonic Giaour, whom Vathek wishes to appease. This is *Vathek's* only specific reference to mummies, but it is significant, grafting, as it does, the Egyptian element (within *Vathek's* overall Arabian context) onto mainstream Gothic.

Written in the wake of Mary Shelley's *Frankenstein* (1818), the extraordinary three-volume epic *The Mummy!* by Jane Webb Loudon (1807–1858) first appeared in 1827. Set in the year 2126, it anticipated television and air-travel and not only reflected ideas about ancient Egypt that were current at the time of the novel's publication but also set the standard for various later mummy movie clichés. Webb repeats the misconceptions about the original function of the pyramids by having the tutor of the novel's hero suggest that they were not mausoleums but temples, a view shared, as we have seen, by the then-contemporary writer on Egypt, Robert Richardson. The tutor also thinks that the corridors inside the pyramid were designed for "penances and personal privations," for "what can be more simple than that the passages the *initiati* had to traverse before they reached the adytum, should be painful and difficult of access."[9]

The descent into the tomb is marvelously described in a manner that inspired all subsequent tomb penetrations, both literary and cinematic:

> The red glare of the torches flashed fearfully on the massive walls of the Pyramid, throwing part of their enormous masses into deep shadow, as they rose in solemn and sublime dignity around, and seemed frowning on the presumptuous mortals who had dared to invade their recesses, whilst the deep pit beneath their feet seemed to yawn wide to engulf them in its abyss.[10]

Plunged into darkness, their path is eventually illuminated by torches held by "two colossal figures who, placed in a sitting posture, seemed guarding an enormous portal, surmounted by the image of a fox, the constant guardian of an Egyptian tomb."[11] By foxes, Webb presumably meant the figure of Anubis; and continuing the diabolical atmosphere, she has the interior of the tomb dedicated to Typhon (or Set). This is decorated with images of ill-omen, such as crocodiles and dragons — an unheard of eventuality in any known Egyptian tomb. Perhaps in honor of Seti I's sarcophagus, which was comfortably established in Sir John Soane's home by the time *The Mummy!* was published, Webb also describes Cheops' sarcophagus as being made of alabaster.

Edric, the hero of *The Mummy!* has gone to all this trouble so that he and his tutor can revive Cheops' mummy, but when it comes to the moment when the revivification is about to take place, he has second thoughts:

> "And what am I," thought he, "weak, feeble worm that I am who dare seek to penetrate into the awful secrets of my Creator? Why should I wish to restore animation to a body now resting in the quiet of the tomb? What right have I to renew the struggles, the pains, the cares, and the anxieties of mortal life? How can I tell the fearful effects that may be produced by the gratification of my earthly longing? May I not revive a creature whose wickedness may involve mankind in misery?"[12]

If we leap forward 172 years to the year 1999, we find exactly the same predicament explored in Stephen Sommers' remake of *The Mummy*, though in the latter case, the consequences are rather more drastic as they unleash the plagues of Egypt. Webb continues to imply the demonic nature of the mummy, describing "the fiend-like expression of the features"[13] (another quality Arnold Vosloo's Imhotep shares with Cheops) which, nonetheless, fail to dissuade Edric from completing his experiment. Although the revivification process itself is obviously inspired by Mary Shelley, it is, in fact, far more interesting and cinematic than Shelley's perfunctory, uninformative lines concerning the creation of the creature. Webb offers a great deal more detail, again anticipating the cinema's love-affair with lab scenes:

> Worked up to desperation, he applied the wires of the battery and put the apparatus in motion, whilst a demoniac laugh of derision appeared to ring in his ears, and the surrounding mummies seemed starting from their places and dancing in unearthly merriment. Thunder now roared in tremendous peals through the Pyramids, shaking their enormous masses to the foundation, and vivid flashes of light darted round in quick succession.

Edric stood aghast amidst this fearful convulsion of nature. A horrid creeping seemed to run through every vein, every nerve feeling as though drawn from its extremity, and wrapped in icy chillness round his heart. Still, he stood immoveable, and gazing intently on the mummy, whose eyes had opened with the shock, and were now fixed on those of Edric, shining with supernatural luster.... Edric saw the mummy stretch out its withered hand, as though to seize him. He saw it rise gradually — he heard the dry, bony fingers rattle as it drew them forth — he felt its tremendous grip — human nature could bear no more — "[14]

Despite this terrifying re-entry into life, the mummy of Cheops is given an emotional and articulate nature, as was Shelley's unfortunate Creature (whom we should never forget is capable of reading Goethe and Milton). Cheops also asks the same big questions: "Where am I? what place is this? Methinks all seems wondrous, new, and strange. Where is my father? And where! oh, where, is Arsinoë? Alas, alas!"[15] In these scenes alone, and building on the foundations laid down by Beckford's *Vathek*, Webb laid the first important courses of the huge pyramid that was to grow up around ancient Egyptian mummy fantasies in the 19th and 20th centuries.

Across the English Channel, the French Romantic author Theophile Gautier (1811–1872), wrote two ancient Egyptian stories. "One of Cleopatra's Nights" (1838) proved to be rather more influential than "The Mummy's Foot" (1840) going on, as it did, to inspire two operas. The first of these operas was by the French composer Victor Massé (1822–1884) in 1885. The second dates from 1920 by the American Henry Kimball Hadley (1871–1937).

"Cleopatra — From a painting by L. Alma-Tadema" in the supplement to *The Illustrated London News*, July 1862.

Gautier's tale also inspired the Diaghilev ballet *Cléopâtre*, the first title of which was *Une nuit d'Egypte*, when it was premiered in 1908 at the Mariinsky Theatre in St. Petersburg, with choreography by Mikhail Fokine, more about which later. "One of Cleopatra's Nights" even informed the film comedy *Due notti con Cleopatra* (dir. Mario Mattoll, 1955) starring "more of Sophia Loren than you've ever seen before," as the trailer teasingly put it.

The story is simple. Cleopatra is bored. A handsome hunter called Meïamoun, obsessed by the queen's beauty, fires an arrow carrying the message "I love you." Cleopatra gives him the option of being killed for his impertinence or trading his life for a night of passion with her. Meïamoun takes the second option, after which Cleopatra rather regrets the conditions she has imposed on this night of passion. The following day, Meïamoun dies from poison nonetheless. As he expires, Antony appears, completely ignoring the unfortunate corpse. The plot, such as it is, is hardly the point of the tale, however, which is far more concerned with atmosphere. Gautier, like the later decadent aesthetic writers he inspired, lists one extravagance after another in much the same way that film directors were to present the opulent props, costumes and sets in their cinematic Egyptian fantasies. So we have exotic descriptions of jewelry; there are lotus flowers "of celestial blue, others of a tender rose-color, like the finger-tips of Isis the great goddess"[16] that decorate Cleopatra's barge, and the sublimity of Egyptian architecture is described as "the vertigo of enormity, the drunkenness of the gigantic, the reckless effort of that pride which would at any cost engrave its name deeply upon the face of the world."[17] It's no surprise, on reading that, that Gautier confessed to having been inspired by the spectacular proto-cinematic paintings of John Martin.

Though there is no overt supernatural theme to Gautier's tale, he does dwell on the ancient Egyptians' fascination with death, albeit from the gloomy perspective of a 19th-century Romantic writer rather than the more cheerful, optimistic approach to death taken by the ancient Egyptians themselves. Gautier describes Egypt as being weighed down with sadness as it was "never aught else than a vast tomb, and in which the living appeared to be solely occupied in the work of burying the dead."[18]

> Mystery and granite — this is Egypt.... Beneath the people lie twenty peoples; each city stands upon twenty layers of necropolis; each generation which passes away leaves a population of mummies to a shadowy city.... Disembowel the sky with gigantic triangles of stone — you cannot thereby lengthen your corpse an inch.[19]

Cleopatra is not only oppressed by these "ghastly terrors of the cities underground,"[20] but is also bored because she's done everything. "To test new poisons upon slaves; to make men fight with tigers, or gladiators with each other; to drink pearls dissolved; to swallow the wealth of a whole province — all these things had become commonplace and insipid."[21] She contemplates awakening "some ancient, bitumen-perfumed pharaoh from his gilded coffin,"[22] and, anticipating many a moviegoer, she wonders what these mummies mutter to each other, "for they still have lips and every ghost would find its body in the same state as when it quitted it if they should all take the fancy to return."[23]

But most significant of all, at least from the point of view of Gautier's influence on *fin de siècle* writers, are the author's repeated reveries on the Sphinx, who is "weary of eternally gazing upon the desert and unable to detach herself from the granite socle upon which she has sharpened her claws for twenty centuries."[24]

Of what invisible flock are those huge sphinxes the guardians, crouching like dogs on the watch, that they never close their eyelids, and forever extend their claws in readiness to seize? Why are their stoney eyes so obstinately fixed upon eternity and infinity? What weird secret do their firmly locked lips retain within their breasts?[25]

Unlike Universal's *The Mummy's Hand*, Gautier's subsequent Egyptian tale, "The Mummy's Foot," turns out to be nothing more dangerous than a whimsical dream. The narrator visits a D'Annunzian antique shop, and, once more, Gautier spends a great deal of time describing its unusual and exotic curiosities (a device much used by Poe in those stories of his where *décor* and props play such a crucial part in the creation of *mood*). Eventually, the narrator decides to purchase the mummy's foot of the title, which he takes home, only to fall asleep while contemplating it. His subsequent dream, heightened by the perfume of ancient gums and embalming fluids that linger in the antiquity, involves the Egyptian princess to whom the foot once belonged. She seems to appear in his room and offers to take him back to ancient Egypt, delighted to have found her foot again. Gautier doesn't explain that all this is a dream until the end of his story, but we hardly need telling. There's no curse, no threat, nothing sinister at all, not even any magic, unless we count the hallucination of the dream as such.

As we have already seen, Edward Bulwer-Lytton contributed to Egyptian fantasy in his best-selling novel, *The Last Days of Pompeii* (1834). Though set, as the title suggests, in Italy, this epic historical romance includes two important Egyptian elements in both its most interesting character, the wicked Egyptian priest-magician Arbaces, and the Egyptian-style settings through which he moves. These include his own apartments and the Temple of Isis at Pompeii. Arbaces proudly claims descent from Rameses, and, as Bulwer explains in one of his footnotes,

> Sylla is said to have transported to Italy the worship of Egyptian Isis. It soon became "the rage," and was peculiarly in vogue with the Roman ladies. Its priesthood were sworn to chastity, and, like all such brotherhoods, were noted for their licentiousness.... The priests of Isis arrogated a knowledge of magic and of the future. Among women of all classes — and among many of the harder sex — the Egyptian sorceries were consulted and revered as oracles.... At the time in which my story is cast, the worship of Isis was, however, in the highest repute; and the wealthy devotees sent even to the Nile, that they might sprinkle its mysterious waters over the altars of the goddess. I have introduced the ibis in the sketch of the temple of Isis, although it had been supposed that that bird languished and died when taken from Egypt. But from various reasons, too long now to enumerate, I incline to believe that the ibis was by no means infrequent in the Italian temples of Isis, though it rarely lived long, and refused to breed in a foreign clime.[26]

The story concerns the fates of six individuals. Glaucus, a Greek, loves Ione, a beautiful young Roman woman. Ione is also loved by Arbaces, the Egyptian priest, who is mentoring Ione's brother, Apæcides (whom he eventually kills). A blind flower-girl, Nydia, also loves Glaucus as does the wealthy and elegant Julia, who seeks a love potion from Arbaces. Eventually, they decide on a potion that will make Glaucus lose his senses, but, of course, the eruption of Vesuvius puts paid to all their machinations and emotional turmoil.

Bulwer's interest in the occult, which was later to flower into three of the most influential occult novels ever written — *Zanoni*, *A Strange Story*, and *The Coming Race* — imbued Arbaces with a compelling character, who is the mouthpiece for much of the novel's philosophical content. Early on in the novel he says: "I love the old recollections of my ancestral land; I love to keep alive — to propagate on distant shores (which her colonies perchance yet people) her dark and mystic creeds,"27 adding, "From Egypt came all the knowledge of the world; from Egypt came the love of Athens, and the profound policy of Crete."

> Your modern nations owe their greatness to Egypt — Egypt her greatness to her priests. Rapt in themselves, coveting a sway over the nobler part of man, his soul and his belief, those ancient ministers of God were inspired with the grandest thought that ever exalted mortals. From the revolutions of the stars, from the seasons of the earth, from the round and unvarying circle of human destinies, they devised an august allegory; they made it gross and palpable to the vulgar by the signs of gods and goddesses, and that which in reality was Government they named Religion. Isis is a fable — start not! — that for which Isis is a type is a reality, an immortal being; Isis is nothing. Nature, which she represents, is the mother of all things — dark, ancient, inscrutable, save to the gifted few. "None among mortals hath ever lifted up my veil," so saith the Isis that you adore; but to the wise that veil *hath* been removed, and we have stood face to face with the solemn loveliness of Nature. The priests then were the benefactors, the civilized of mankind; true, they were cheats, impostors if you will.28

It seems highly likely that Madame Blavatsky had read this passage. As we have seen, a similar reference to the veil of Isis occurs in *Zanoni*, which she no doubt recalled when thinking of a title for her magnum opus *Isis Unveiled*. As we shall see later, Mika Waltari's *The Egyptian* similarly exposes the priests of Egypt as impostors but also genuinely concerned with the treatment of sickness. Arbaces is less critical, however, asking, "If they had not deceived their kind they could not have served them? The ignorant and servile vulgar must be blinded to attain their proper good; they would not believe a maxim, they revere an oracle."29 Bulwer also expresses much the same analysis of religion to that of Fyodor Dostoevsky (1821–1881). As Dostoevsky's Grand Inquisitor explains in *The Brothers Karamazov* (1880), it is the job of priests to teach "the value of complete submission! And until men know that, they will be unhappy. Who is most to blame for their not knowing it, speak? Who scattered the flock and sent it astray on unknown paths? But the flock will come together again and will submit once more, and then it will be once for all. Then we shall give them the quiet humble happiness of weak creatures such as they are by nature.... We shall show them that they are weak, that they are only pitiful children, but that childlike happiness is the sweetest of all."30

Also like the Grand Inquisitor, Arbaces believes that such delusions ensure "the welfare and harmony of mankind."31 In this respect, Arbaces resembles the later historical figure of Cagliostro, whom many regard as a charlatan but whose main aim was to aid and improve humanity. Arbaces points out that the ancient Egyptians "asked belief; they returned the gift by civilization. Were not their very cheats a virtue?"32 The mystical approach to comparative religion taken by Madame Blavatsky was again inspired by Arbaces when he puts forward the opinion that Egyptian myths "have furnished to credulous nations the materials of many creeds. They have travelled to the vast plains of India; they have mixed themselves up in the visionary speculations of the Greek; becoming more and more gross and embodied, as they emerge farther from the shadows of their antique origin, they have assumed a human and palpable form in this novel faith; and the believers of Galilee are but the unconscious repeaters of one of the superstitions of the Nile."33

So much for the philosophical element of the novel. Bulwer's most elaborate descriptions are also inspired by Egyptian settings. The entrance to Arbaces' house, for example, is flanked by two sphinxes, a detail reminiscent of the far grander avenue of sphinxes in the temple of Karnak. Lit by the moon, Arbaces' sphinxes "gave an additional and yet more solemn calm to those large, and harmonious, and passionless features, in which the sculptors of that type of wisdom united so much of loveliness with awe."[34]

When the character Apæcides first arrives at this gloomy mansion, he is greeted in just the same way that Zita Johann's Helen Grosvenor is welcomed into the mansion of Karloff's Im-ho-tep in *The Mummy*: a slave answers the door who "without question or salutation, motioned to him to proceed."[35] Once inside, Apæcides sees a house decorated in elaborate Egyptian style with more sphinxes and hieroglyphics, but also with less specific magical apparatus and theatrical lighting effects:

> A small tripod stood at a little distance, from the incense in which the smoke slowly rose. Near this was a vast globe, depicting the signs of heaven; and upon another table lay several instruments, of curious and quaint shape, whose uses were unknown to Apæcides. The farther extremity of the room was concealed by a curtain, and the oblong window in the roof admitted the rays of the moon, mingling sadly with the single lamp which burned in the apartment.[36]

Eight chapters later, we find Arbaces in his pyramidical observatory, which flanks the house:

> A table, on which lay a scroll, filled with mystic figures, was before him. On high, the stars waxed dim and faint, and the shades of night melted from the sterile mountain-tops; only above Vesuvius there rested a deep and massy cloud, which for several days past had gathered darker and more solid over its summit.[37]

Arbaces's preoccupation with astrology has, of course, its parallel with that of Queen Tera in *The Jewel of Seven Stars*, who arranges her reincarnation along astrological lines. Mr. Trelawny points out that

> "there can be no doubt whatever that astronomy was an exact science with the Egyptians at least a thousand years before time of Queen Tera. Now, the stars that go to make up a constellation change in process of time their relative positions, and the Plough is a notable example. The changes in the position of stars in even forty centuries is so small as to be hardly noticeable by an eye not trained to minute observances, but they can be measured and verified. Did you, or any of you, notice how exactly the stars in the Ruby correspond to the position of the stars in the Plough; or how the same holds with regard to the translucent places in the Magic Coffer?"
> We all assented. He went on:
> "You are quite correct. They correspond exactly. And yet when Queen Tera was laid in her tomb, neither the stars in the Jewel nor the translucent places in the Coffer corresponded to the position of the stars in the Constellation as they then were!"
> We looked at each other as he paused: a new light was breaking upon us. With a ring of mastery in his voice he went on:
> "Do you not see the meaning of this? Does it not throw a light on the intention of the Queen? She, who was guided by augury, and magic, and superstition, naturally chose a time for her resurrection which seemed to have been pointed out by the High Gods themselves, who had sent their message on a thunderbolt from other worlds. When such a time was fixed by supernal wisdom, would it not be the height of human wisdom to avail itself of it? Thus it is"—here his voice deepened and trembled with the intensity of his feeling—"that to us and our time is given the opportunity of this wondrous peep into the old world, such as has been the privilege of none other of our time; which may never be again."[38]

Arbaces, though not planning resurrection, none the less dares to hope for a glittering future, despite warnings to the contrary from the stars: "*Again* do the stars forewarn me," he says. "Some danger, then assuredly awaits me.... And, at no distant date from this, comes the peril: but I cannot, of a certainty, read the day and hour. Well! if my glass runs low, the sands shall sparkle to the last. Yet, if I escape this peril — ay, if I escape — bright and clear as the moonlight track along the waters glows the rest of my experience."[39] Arbaces also anticipates the surprise feature of Linderhof, one of King Ludwig II of Bavaria's castles. Linderhof famously has a table that appears from beneath the floor fully laid for a banquet; so too has Arbaces' palatial residence, along with invisible music which would no doubt have brought a smile of recognition from Ludwig's protégé, the composer Richard Wagner, who placed the orchestra under the stage of his Festival Theatre at Bayreuth, rendering it similarly "invisible."

> Suddenly, as they stood in one hall, which was surrounded by draperies of silver and white, the Egyptian clapped his hands, and as if by enchantment, a banquet rose from the floor — a couch or throne, with crimson canopy, ascended simultaneously at the feet of Ione, — and at the same instant from behind the curtains swelled invisible and softest music." [40]

Arbaces's private temple is also suitably theatrical. Hung with black draperies, and furnished with a similarly upholstered couch, it is dominated by a small altar on which stands a bronze tripod. A granite column to one side of this supports a colossal head of Isis carved from black granite. When a blue flame rises from the tripod, Arbaces parts the curtain behind the altar, revealing an aperture which then acts as a kind of magic mirror in which visions are conjured up. Bulwer was very keen to impose a threatening character on Egyptian decor in general, obviously quite different to the way in which the ancient Egyptians themselves regarded their art. When Ione visits Arbaces to procure the love potion from him, she is frightened by Arbaces's exotic surroundings. She regards the hieroglyphical inscriptions fearfully, along with "the faces of the mysterious images, which at every corner gazed upon her — the tripod at a little distance — and, above all, the grave and remarkable countenance of Arbaces himself."[41] Finally, when Arbaces eventually visits the Witch of Vesuvius, she refers to him as "Hermes," the name the Greeks gave to Thoth, the great physician and magician, whom Bulwer suggests lives on in the form of his colorful villain. Such a linkage also reflects Bulwer's interest in Rosicrucianism and Masonry, as both cults were, as we have seen, indebted to the influential occult writings found in the *Divine Pymander of Hermes Trimegistus*.

Several film versions of Bulwer's novel (some of them from the silent era) attest to its literary significance, and while obviously being principally concerned with evocations of the Roman architecture and its ultimate destruction, the character of Arbaces and the Isis cult over which he presides gave the set designers of some of these films an opportunity to indulge in Egyptian decor. Hollywood's version of the tale, directed by Ernest B. Schoedsack and Merian C. Cooper in 1935, eschewed this element altogether, however, along with Bulwer's plot and characters. Arbaces doesn't appear at all. Rather more interesting, from our point of view, was Sergio Leone's 1960 version, *Gli ultimo giorni di Pompei*, starring Steve Reeves. Ramiro Gómez and Aldo Tommasini's set designs included an impressive Isis temple, with a statue of the goddess flanked by two black sphinxes, reminiscent of the entrance to Arbaces' home in Bulwer's novel. Fernando Rey provided an effectively saturnine Arbaces complete with the leopard skin robes of his priestly office. When Vesuvius erupts he attempts to save the treasure he has secured at the foot of the statue of Isis. Isis topples over, however, and crushes him to death as the temple collapses around him, and this pleasure-ground of the Roman empire is buried under volcanic ash.

Mummy movies are also very much tales of empire, eloquently expressing the imperialist desire to dominate and exploit the exotic, along with the repressed guilt that accompanies such a desire. That is probably why stories with an Egyptian theme that were written earlier in the 19th century lack that important element of threat: the guilt simply hadn't had time to ferment into the heady brew it had become by the late–Victorian period. Mummy tales by writers who came from outside the British Empire, such Edgar Allan Poe, whose story "Some Words with a Mummy" was written in 1850, are often lacking in menace or even Egyptian *mood*. There is no real sense of mystery in Poe's tale either, and what tension Poe does build up prior to the reanimation of his mummy is undermined by the satirical dénouement of the story. Poe uses his mummy as a means of criticizing then-contemporary American society and culture. Alemistakeo, Poe's typically punning name for his reanimated ancient Egyptian, expresses nothing but amused, sometimes bad-tempered contempt for the modern world, but he doesn't wreak vengeance on anyone. Alemistakeo does, however, complain about having been desecrated, and that was a what connects this tale to the horrors that were to follow:

> What am I to think of your standing quietly by and seeing me thus unhandsomely used? What am I to suppose by your permitting Tom, Dick, and Harry to strip me of my coffins, and my clothes, in this wretchedly cold climate?[42]

This justified sense of outrage has a great deal in common with that expressed by the various Keepers of the Tomb who populate Universal and Hammer mummy movies. But Alemistakeo was also the prototype for Ramses the Damned, the immortal, stunningly handsome and highly intelligent mummy in Anne Rice's novel *The Mummy — or Ramses the Damned* (1981). Like Alemistakeo, he is presented as an observer and critic of "contemporary" society (Edwardian in this case), as is demonstrated during the conversation in chapter eleven of the book, in which he converses with the daughter and various English friends of the man who discovered his tomb. In the course of the conversation he tackles Edwardian social inequality, is accused of being a Marxist, defends his own reputation as a fair Pharaoh, and counters the suggestion that slaves were forced to build the pyramids, all the while dunking large slices of bread in his soup and asking for more.

If "Some Words with a Mummy" was fundamentally satirical in its purpose, Poe was far more atmospherically Egyptian in his masterpiece "Ligeia" (1838). The references to ancient Egypt here are sparing but highly effective in adding an aura of mystery and occult wisdom to the title character. As the narrator recalls, "I saw not then what I now clearly perceive, that the acquisitions of Ligeia were gigantic, were astounding."[43] Like a mummy herself, Ligeia is dead at the beginning of the story. Poe makes this abundantly clear in such sepulchral and resonant lines as "Ligeia, the beloved, the august, the beautiful, the entombed."[44] In the first paragraph, he refers to "the wan and the misty-winged *Astophet* of idolatrous Egypt"[45] — a coinage of Poe's own creation, as there is no Astophet in the Egyptian mythology. What matters to Poe is the resonance of the words he uses, not necessarily their historical accuracy. Astophet is probably a conflation of Asthoreth, the Egyptian goddess of love, and "Tophet" a kind of hellish underworld associated with the worship of Moloch. Love, hell and death are thus conveyed in a single word, and given a mystic gloss by its Egyptian connotations.

Later, Poe creates the classic juxtaposition of rural England with Egyptian menace, which Hammer were to be the first to put on film in Terence Fisher's *The Mummy*. Ligeia dies and the narrator, crushed "into the very dust with sorrow," purchases an abbey "in the wildest and least frequented portions of fair England."[46] This he repairs and fills with exotic furnishings, artifacts and artworks which include "solemn carvings of Egypt," and around the angles of the chamber in which is situated the bridal couch ("of an Indian model, and low, and sculptured of solid ebony") are positioned gigantic sarcophagi "of black granite, from the tombs of the kings over against Luxor, with their aged lids full of immemorial sculpture."[47] It is against this setting that "this hideous drama of revivication"[48] is enacted. Ligeia, a woman of immense willpower, comes back from the dead to inhabit the body of her rival, the Lady Rowena, whom the narrator marries after Ligeia's death. This story is, to all intents and purposes, the basis of Bram Stoker's *The Jewel of Seven Stars*, with its very similar drama of astral possession and reincarnation with a similarly (if admittedly far more overt) Egyptian theme.

In *The Tomb of Ligeia*, Roger Corman's 1964 film adaptation of Poe's story, the Egyptian subtext of "Ligeia" is focused entirely on two conversations involving Vincent Price's Verden Fell. The first concerns a fox that has been killed after a hunting scene. Lady Rowena's father (played by Derek Francis) shows it to Fell, who eerily explains that it belongs to the species "Vulpis Pelida, peculiar to Upper Egypt and the Nubian desert. In Egyptian art it is found at the feet of Astophet, goddess of ill-omened marriages as her pet." Ligeia, it transpires, kept the fox as her own pet. Later, John Westbook's Christopher Gough walks around Fell's odd mausoleum of a home, passing by a blue mummy case to admire an Egyptian bust. At this moment, Fell appears at the top of a flight of steps and explains that the bust is made of wax:

> FELL: It's a reproduction. I managed to make it myself. You see, I am loathe to open ancient tombs — rob a nation of its treasure and call it archeology.
> GOUGH: It's quite good really.
> FELL: Thank you.
> GOUGH: Twentieth Dynasty?
> FELL: No, twenty-first, but a Delta dynasty and little known and less remembered. You can tell by the eyes. The eyes! They confound me. There's a blindness, a mindless sort of malice in some Egyptian eyes. They do not readily yield up the mysteries they hold.

Poe's other references to Egypt in his other works are no less evocative but less obvious. As in "Ligeia," Poe's tale of an elaborate suicide pact in "The Assignation" (1834) also contains a significant reference to "the huge carvings of untutored Egypt,"[49] which decorate the ornate and treasure-filled palazzo of a fabulously wealthy aesthete who eventually kills himself. "The Conversation of Eiros and Charmion" (1839) has nothing to do with ancient Egypt beyond the echo, in its title, of the names of Cleopatra's handmaidens in Shakespeare's *Antony and Cleopatra*, Charmian and Iras. However, this subtle Egyptian aura casts a suitably mystical atmosphere over an apocalyptic tale describing the "disenchanted frenzy of mankind"[50] as the world ends. Similarly, "The Sphinx" (1846) has only its title in common with things Egyptian, but this nonetheless contributes an important connotation and consequent atmosphere to a tale about a death's head moth. Escaping a cholera epidemic that is raging in New York, the narrator is filled with gloomy thoughts of death. Having always believed in omens, he looks up from the book he is reading one day and stares out of the window "upon some living monster of hideous conformation, which very rapidly made its way from the summit to the bottom."[51] What has actually happened is an optical illusion:

he observes a moth at only 1/16 of an inch from his eyes and so it appears much larger against the perspective of the view; but as an allegory of the cholera epidemic, the magnified insect is truly terrifying and has about it something of the murderous unstoppability of the sphinx in the W. B. Yeats poem, "The Second Coming" (1921) with its blank and pitiless gaze and slow moving thighs.

Poe's influence on French literature, via Charles Baudelaire's translations, was immense, inspiring, as it did, the symbolist and decadent writers at the end of the 19th century. Gustave Flaubert (1821–1880) essayed both naturalism, in *Madame Bovary,* and symbolist decadence in his immense psychological fantasy, *La Tentation de Saint Antoine* (1874), in which Isis herself makes a personal appearance. Before her arrival, however, Flaubert, who had visited Egypt himself in 1849–50, indulged in a lavish description of ancient Alexandria:

> Monuments quite various in their architecture crowd close together. Egyptian pylons loom over Greek temples. Obelisks emerge like lances between red brick battlements. In the middle of squares appear the pointed ears of a Hermes or a dog-headed Anubis. Antony can see mosaics in courtyards, and carpets hanging from beams in the ceilings.
>
> With a single glance he takes in the two ports (the Great Harbour and the Eunostus), as round as two circuses, and separated by a mole which links Alexandria to the craggy island from which rises the tower of Pharos, quadrangular, five hundred cubits high and in nine stories — with its mass of black charcoal smoking at the summit.[52]

Flaubert's Isis later continues:

> Egypt lay beneath us, monumental and serious, long as a temple corridor, with her obelisks on the right, her pyramids on the left, her labyrinth in the middle — and everywhere avenues of monsters, forests of columns, heavy pylons flanking gates always crowned with the earth's globe set between two wings.[53]

Isis describes "stairways leading down to halls in which were pictured the joys of the good, the tortures of the wicked, and everything that takes place in the third invisible world. Ranged along the walls, the dead in painted coffins waited their turn; souls exempt from migrations continued in deep drowsiness until the stirring of another life."[54] The settings before which Elizabeth Taylor would later charm Richard Burton in *Cleopatra* can certainly claim part of their ancestry in Flaubert's sumptuous prose here.

France and Britain competed with each other during the 19th century to create the ultimate ancient Egyptian fantasy. With a man so well traveled in and inspired by Africa, it was inevitable that ancient Egypt fascinated the British writer H. Rider Haggard (1856–1925). His major contribution to ancient Egyptian fiction was *Cleopatra*, which was published in the same year as Henty's "Boy's Own" adventure, *The Cat of Bubastis* (to be discussed later). His earlier, and most famous novel, *She*, which first appeared two years earlier, in 1887, also has significant Egyptian elements in it, though the principal action takes place in an unspecified location in Central Africa. Most of the Egyptian aspects in *She* are imparted, significantly, in England before the adventure begins. This juxtaposition of "familiar" Victorian England with strange, archaic and exotic Egypt was unfortunately cut from Hammer films' adaptation of the story (directed by Robert Day in 1965), which begins the adventure in Africa. Though the presence of Peter Cushing and Bernard Cribbens provides the essential Englishness required, it's not quite as successful as beginning in England — specifically Cambridge University — itself. Rider Haggard was an important early example of a writer who helped consolidate the habitual contrast between ancient Egypt

Ursula Andress as Ayesha in *She* (dir. Robert Day, 1965).

with modern Britain, which forms the basis of so many Egyptian mummy fantasies. Haggard's background was, of course, rooted firmly in the British Empire, and the Empire's fascination with the exotic and Oriental was always a mixture of allure, desire and terror. Attracted by what it could exploit from foreign cultures and countries, it was also subconsciously aware of the violent consequences of so doing, and it was the role of such fiction to help exorcise these repressed fears. Haggard's *King Solomon's Mines* (1885), Sax Rohmer's Fu Manchu novels, and (even earlier than both) Wilkie Collins's tale about the sinister allure of an Indian diamond in *The Moonstone* (1869), all combine images of exotic treasure and luxury with the terror of vengeful foreigners.

The ancient Egyptian elements of *She* really only concern the origins of a character who had died many centuries before the adventure begins — and that character is actually of Greek rather than Egyptian extraction. His name is Kallikrates, High Priest of Isis, who flees Egypt and the wrath of Nectanebo II, the last native pharaoh of Egypt. Like Imhotep and Kharis in future mummy movies, Kallikrates has broken his vows and fallen in love with the Princess Amenartas of the Royal House of the Pharoahs. It was Haggard, therefore, who invented this essential and much-used fictional motif of the fallen High Priest, which he consolidated in *Cleopatra*. In that novel, another High Priest, by the name of Harmachis, falls in love with Egypt's famous queen, with fatal consequences.

In the opening chapters of *She* we learn from a potsherd that is deciphered by Major Holly and Leo Vincey in Cambridge, that Amenartas and Kallikrates made their way, as man and wife, to the domain of Ayesha, She-who-must-be-obeyed—the ageless Queen who has been made immortal by a sacred flame somewhere in the vast center of the African continent where she rules over the long-lost kingdom of Kôr. (Haggard entertainingly fakes his historical documents, presenting them in ancient Greek, demotic, black-letter Latin text and black-letter old English, along with an illustration of the hieroglyphs on Kallikrates scarab, which he translates as "Royal Son of Ra.") Ayesha falls in love with Kallikrates, and furious with jealousy over his love for Amenartas, she slays him and banishes his wife. Consequently regretting her violent action, she waits through the centuries until the day when Kallikrates will return to her; and it is, of course, the handsome Leo Vincey who turns out to be Kallikrates, reincarnated in the body of a Victorian gentleman. At the beginning of the tale, he inherits an ebony case from his father. This is decorated with sphinxes and contains Kallikrates's scarab insignia along with the potsherd of Amenartas. With these antiquities, he embarks on the perilous journey to discover the domain of She.

During the course of their journey, Vincey, Holly and his valet, Job, encounter a tribe called the Amahagger, whom Haggard suggests may also have had contact with the ancient Egyptians. With regard to the Amahagger's vases, Holly says:

> These vases are of a very ancient manufacture, and of all sizes. None such can have been made in the country for hundreds, or rather thousands, of years. They are found in the rock tombs, of which I shall give a description in their proper place, and my own belief is that, after the fashion of the Egyptians, with whom the former inhabitants of this country may have had some connection, they were used to receive the viscera of the dead.[55]

And not only the Amahagger, but also Ayesha herself point out that the long-lost people of the Kingdom of Kôr may have been the fathers of the first Egyptians.[56]

> The people of Kôr never embalmed their dead, as did the Egyptians, but their art was greater than the art of the Egyptians, for, whereas the Egyptians disemboweled and drew the brain, the people of Kôr injected fluid into the veins, and thus reached every part.[57]

Ayesha herself is a great chemist, suggesting another connection with the Land of Khem. Holly's footnote adds that "chemistry appears to have been her only amusement and occupation. She had one of the caves fitted up as a laboratory, and, although her appliances were necessarily rude, the results that she attained were, as will become clear in the course of the narrative, sufficiently surprising."[58] The Temple of Truth at Kôr is also compared to the temple of Karnak at Thebes, and when Amenartas curses Ayesha for having killed her husband, she uses understandably Egyptian terms of reference:

> And she, the swart Egyptian—she cursed me by her gods. By Osiris did she curse me and by Isis, by Nepthys and by Anubis, by Sekhet, the cat-headed, and by Set, calling down evil on me, evil and everlasting desolation.[59]

While Egyptian color may be peripheral to the actual plot of *She* it nonetheless provides a very significant element of exoticism, which adds mythical resonance to the tale, much as the use of Wagner's music was used for "Arthurian" resonance in John Boorman's *Excalibur* (1981). The art direction of Robert Jones and Don Mingaye for Hammer's vision of Ayesha's palace, and, even more so, the costumes of Jackie Cummins for the soldiers who guard it, presented a mélange of Imperial Roman and Assyrian with rather less of an Egyptian element, though the influence is there, as it should be.

This approach followed the 1935 film adaptation of *She*, directed by Lansing C. Holden and Irving Pichel. Aline Bernstein and Harold Miles' costumes for that, in many ways superior version, blended Assyrian with Aztec influences. Complete with a medieval headdress and crown, Helen Gehagen's hypnotically imperious immortal queen, Hash-a–Motep, went on to influence Walt Disney's Wicked Queen in *Snow White and the Seven Dwarfs* (dir. William Cottrell et al,1937). The first two syllables of "Hash-a–Motep" in fact more closely resemble Haggard's instruction to pronounce the name "Ayesha," in his sequel of that name, as "Assha." The opposite of a democrat, Hash-a–Motep happily sends slaves to their deaths, just as Ursula Andress would do in 1965, but in real life, Helen Gehagen eventually gave up acting to become a liberal Democratic politician in the House of Representatives. Oddly, the screenplay of the 1935 *She* changed the location from Africa to the North Pole, with consequent shots of ice deserts rather than sandy ones. These, along with the sensational sets, anticipated the Himalayan setting of Shangri-La in *Lost Horizon* (dir. Frank Capra, 1937). We are a long way from ancient Egypt as the sacred flame leaps spectacularly to life at the end of the film, but in Haggard's book, the Egyptian imagery even accompanies the grand finale, when Ayesha tempts Vincey to join her in her immortal state:

> Like that old Sphinx of Egypt shalt thou sit aloft from age to age, and ever shall they cry to thee to solve the riddle of thy greatness that doth not pass away, and ever shalt thou mock them with thy silence![60]

However, in terms of the development of Egyptian fantasy, *She* was very much a warm-up for Haggard's masterpiece in the genre, *Cleopatra*.

Beginning with a prologue in which an Egyptologist penetrates the tomb of the High Priest, Harmachis, we are presented with a classic horror image, much used in subsequent movies: that of a man who appears to have been buried alive.

> One glance at his face was enough to tell a doctor how he had died.... Without entering into particulars, I will only say that I hope I shall never see such another look as that which was frozen on this dead man's face.[61]

The narrator somewhat hypocritically complains about the "shameless Arabs"[62] who pillage tombs before justifying his own pillage of Harmarchis' papyri (which forms the subsequent narrative). The famous Boulak Museum also gets a mention with regard to this. (The narrator, understandably, keeps silent about his actions to avoid the museum's interest in his exploits.) As we have seen, Haggard visited this institution himself during a tour of Egypt in 1887 and was guided though the exhibits by the celebrated Emile Brugsch. "It is impossible to begin to tell you the impression that all this has made upon me," he confessed.[63] Haggard also visited Sir Henry Bulwer, the High Commissioner for Cyprus, who was an elder brother of Edward Bulwer-Lytton, which adds another (though admittedly somewhat inconsequential) link to the development of Egyptian fantasy. It was also during this tour that he began to work on *Cleopatra*. The story of this romance is a simple but powerful one, interlacing epic history with magic. Cleopatra herself sums up the plot at the very end of the novel:

> It is a strange tale, and now that all is done it may well be told. This Harmarchis was of the ancient race of the Pharaohs, and, having, indeed, been crowned in secret at Abydos, was sent hither to Alexandria to carry out a great plot that had been formed against the rule of us royal Lagidæ. He came and gained entry to the palace as my astrologer, for he was very learned in all magic ... and a man beautiful to see. Now this was his plot — that he should slay me and be named Pharaoh. In truth it was a strong one, for he had many friends in Egypt, and I had few. And on that very night when he should carry out his purpose, yea, at the very hour, came Charmion yonder, and told the plot to me; saying that she had chanced upon its clue. But, in after days — though I have said little thereon to thee, Charmion — I misdoubted me much of that tale of thine; for by the Gods! to this hour I believe that thou didst love Harmarchis, and because he scorned thee thou dids't betray him; and for that cause also hast all thy days remained a maid, which is a thing unnatural.
> Harmarchis I dared not slay, lest his great party should rise in fury and cast me from the throne. And now mark the issue. Though he must murder me, in secret this Harmarchis loved me, and something thereof I guessed. I had striven a little to draw him to me, for the sake of his beauty and his wit; and for the love of man Cleopatra never strove in vain. Therefore when, with the dagger in his robe, he came to slay me, I matched my charms against his will, and need I tell you, being man and woman, how I won? Oh never can I forget the look in the eyes of that fallen prince, that foresworn prince, that discrowned Pharaoh, when, lost in the poppied draught, I saw him sink into shameful sleep whence he might no more wake with honour![64]

Harmachis eventually has his revenge on the Egyptian queen, and Haggard suggests that it was the High Priest who, by magical means, filled Cleopatra with fear at the battle of Actium and made her flee. Harmarchis also engineers Antony's demise and administers the poison which Cleopatra drinks.

Perhaps the most interesting aspects of this always-engaging novel are the magical elements, the first of which takes place in the shrine of Isis, which is filled with a hundred effigies. Harmarchis is then shown a series of magical pictures which depict "the struggle between the Good and Evil Powers."

> I saw that man was created vile, but Those who are above took pity on him, and came down to him to make him good and happy, for the two things are one thing. But man returned to his wicked way, and then the bright Spirit of Good, who is of us called Osiris, but who has many names, offered himself up for the evil-doing of the race that had disthroned him. And from him and the Divine Mother, of whom all nature is, sprang another spirit who is the Protector of us on earth, as Osiris is our justifier in Amenti.
> For this is the mystery of the Osiris.
> Of a sudden, as I saw the visions, these things became clear to me. The mummy cloths of symbol and of ceremony that wrap Osiris round fell from him, and I understood the secret of religion, which is Sacrifice.[65]

During this initiation into the mysteries, Harmarchis also dies and his spirit encounters Isis in a mystical region beyond life. It's not hard to trace the Masonic elements of these scenes, for symbolic death, concomitant with spiritual birth (or insight), is also a part of Masonic ritual. A useful parallel to this idea occurs at the beginning of Mozart's *Die Zauberflöte*, in which Tamino falls unconscious having been terrorized by a serpent. Both Tamino and Harmarchis return to life having become "self-conscious" after their initiation into the Mysteries.

"And we went forth." Illustration by R. Caton Woodville for H. Rider Haggard's *Cleopatra* (London: Longmans, Green, 1914). In his autobiography, *The Galanty Show* (London: Cecil Woolf, 1980), Montague Summers recalled how Haggard's novel "ran through *The Illustrated London News* in 1888. The story was immensely helped by Caton Woodville's admirable illustrations" (p. 43).

Isis speaks to Harmarchis, revealing herself to be "Nature's self."

> I breathe in all that breathes. I wax and wane in the changeful moon: I grow and gather in the tides: I rise with the suns: I flash with the lightning and thunder in the storms. Nothing is too great for the measure of my majesty, nothing is so small that I cannot find a home therein. I am in thee and thou art in Me, O Harmarchis.[66]

Harmarchis collapses as the great hall "burst open and crumbled into flakes of fire." Then, a "great wind blew: there was a sound as the sound of Worlds rushing down the flood of Time — and I knew no more!"[67] Confirming the Masonic elements in Haggard's conception here, an old priest then says, "Come forth, thou who hast passed the fire and learned what lies behind the darkness — come forth, O newly-born!"[68]

We then move from mystical Masonic ritual to distinctly Victorian imperialist values, when Hamarchis is given his heavy burden to dispatch Cleopatra:

> And how can a man die better than in a great endeavor to strike the gyres from his Country's limbs so that she again may stand in the face of Heaven and raise the shrill shout of Freedom, and, clad once more in a panoply of strength, trample under foot the fetters of her servitude, defying the tyrant nations of the earth to set their seal upon her brow?[69]

This is Haggard's translation into Egyptian of Horace's line "Dulce et decorum est pro patria mori" ("It is sweet and fitting to die for one's country"), which was to become so tragically called upon 25 years after the first publication of *Cleopatra* with the outbreak of the first world war. Indeed, the Longman's "Silver Library" edition of the novel, from which this book has been quoting, appeared in March 1914.

Haggard has been criticized for his somewhat misogynistic views with regard to Ayesha in *She* and his description of Cleopatra is no less negative, but no less sumptuous for all that:

> About her rounded neck was a broad collar of gold studded with emeralds and coral. Round her arms and wrists were bracelets of gold studded with emeralds and coral, and in one hand she held the holy cross of Life fashioned of crystal, and in the other the golden rod of royalty. Her breast was bare, but under it was a garment that glistened like the scaly covering of a snake, everywhere sewn with gems. Beneath this robe was a skirt of golden cloth, half hidden by a scarf of the broidered silk of Cos, falling in folds to the sandals that, fastened with great pearls, adorned her white and tiny feet.[70]

To impress her, Harmachis, a singularly handsome fellow himself, enhances his natural allure by ostentatiously adorning himself with magicians' robes:

> I arrayed myself in a long and flowing robe, after the fashion of a magician or astrologer. I placed a cap on my head, about which were broidered images of the stars, and in my belt a scribe's palette and a roll of papyrus written over with mystic spells and signs. In my hand I held a wand of ebony, tipped with ivory, such as is used by priests and masters of magic.[71]

Like the art director of a film, Haggard presents lavish and elaborate descriptions to the imagination of the reader:

> So we passed ... into the resting-place of Cleopatra. It was beautiful beyond imagining — beautiful with many coloured marbles, with gold and ivory, gems and flowers — all art can furnish and all luxury can dream of were here. Here were pictures so real that birds might have pecked the painted fruits; here were statues of woman's loveliness frozen into stone; here were draperies fine as softest silk, but woven of a web of gold; here were couches and carpets such as I never saw. The air, too, was sweet with perfume, while through the open window places came the far murmur of the sea.[72]

Amid such surroundings Harmachis performs the old trick of turning his staff into a snake. Suitably impressed, Cleopatra and Harmachis become enamored of each other and together they set about raiding one of the great pyramids of its treasure by means of a secret passage of which only Harmachis is aware. It is there that they encounter the hideous grey bat mentioned in chapter one. Daunted but not deterred, they rip open the mummy to discover and then remove the jewels secreted within the wrappings.

After the failure of his attempt to assassinate Cleopatra, and his subsequent exile (living in the tomb of Rameses III as also mentioned in chapter one), Harmarchis returns to Cleopatra's court to exert his final vengeance. The queen is testing poisons on her slaves as she is contemplating suicide, a subject which engaged so many 19th-century painters. Haggard also enjoys the horror element here:

> Meanwhile the man stood, his hands to his head. Presently he began to tremble, and then fell, shrieking, to the ground. Anon he was on his feet again, clutching at his bosom, as though to tear out the fire in his heart. He staggered, with livid, twisted face and foaming lips, to where Cleopatra lay watching him with a slow and cruel smile.[73]

Cleopatra asks Harmachis, who is disguised as Olympus the physician, to prepare a poison for her. This is somber music to the High Priest's ears:

> Death shall cure thy ills, and I will brew such a wine as shall draw him down a sudden friend and sink thee in a sea of slumber whence, upon this earth, thou shalt never wake again.[74]

Harmachis also privately compares Cleopatra to a poisonous plant that has twined itself about the giant strength of Antony.

Two final magical events bring the novel to a close. A vision of Isis appears to Harmachis, who "passing over the edge of the world, sought her home in space, to be no more known of men."[75] And in Cleopatra's final moments, the ghosts of all those murdered by her appear before her. "Then her face sank in with terror, her great eyes grew pale, and, shrieking, Cleopatra fell and died: passing, with that dread company, to her appointed place."[76]

Henty's adventure story *The Cat of Bubastis* is a fairly straightforward example of its kind and typical of Henty's particular approach of pitting his young heroes against adversity. The plot concerns the tribulations of Chebron, the son of the Egyptian priest Ameres, who accidentally kills the sacred cat of Bubastis. Ironically, this cat had been selected to serve its totemic role from the house of Ameres himself where it was the family's pet. Chebron has no alternative but to flee in the company of a young foreign prince, Amuba, who had previously been captured by the Egyptians but is later adopted by Ameres. Tragically, the outraged mob kills the priest in revenge for the son's sacrilege and then kidnap his daughter. Amuba later encounters no less a personage than Moses, who emphasizes the novel's major theological concern: that behind all the gods of ancient Egypt lies one true God. Thus does Moses suggest that the God of the Israelites is actually the same as that of the Egyptians. In fact, Henty mentions this idea much earlier in the novel when he has Ameres express the opinion:

> Osiris and Isis, the six other great gods, and the innumerable divinities whom the Egyptians worshipped under the guise of deities with the heads of animals, were in themselves no gods at all, but mere attributes of the power, the wisdom, the goodness, the anger of the one great God — a God so mighty that his name was unknown, and that it was only when each of his

attributes was given an individuality and worshipped as a god that it could be understood by the finite sense of man.[77]

This is a controversial view to say the least, but it does have much in common with that held by Akhnaten, who tried to replace Egyptian polytheism with the one god Aton, not that Henty seems to be aware of that.

The Cat of Bubastis also has one or two rather effective set pieces which help to point the way towards later Hollywood epics. Pointing out to his Victorian audience that "Egyptians were unacquainted with the use of knives and forks," he describes vegetarian banquets accompanied by music, after which a mummy was paraded before the diners as a kind of *memento mori* before they were entertained by dancers, jugglers and acrobats. Hardly an aid to good digestion, this custom was, in fact, mentioned by Herodotus, Henty's source here:

> In social meetings among the rich, when the banquet is ended, slaves bring round to the several guests a bier on which there is a wooden image of a corpse, carved and painted to resemble nature as nearly as possible. As it is shown to each guest in turn, the attendant says, "Gaze here, and drink and be merry; for when you die, such will you be."[78]

Henty would no doubt also have been influenced by Edwin Long's celebrated painting, *An Egyptian Feast*, only 12 years old at the time of the novel's publication. It too was directly influenced by Herodotus, depicting, as it does, a Egyptian hall of positively Hollywood epic proportions, the mummy case being pulled before the wealthy diners by a team of slaves.

Henty also includes an elaborate funeral procession in *The Cat of Bubastes*, which may have influenced Terence Fisher (who grew up with this kind of literature, after all) when filming the processional scenes in *The Mummy*:

> First came servants bearing tables laden with fruit, cakes, flowers, vases of ointment, wine, some young geese in a crate for sacrifice, chairs, wooden tables, napkins, and other things. Then came others carrying small closets containing the images of the gods; they also carried daggers, bows, sandals, and fans, and each bore a napkin upon his shoulder. Then came a table with offerings and chariot drawn by a pair of horses, the charioteer driving them as he walked behind the chariot. Then came the bearers of a sacred boat and the mysterious eye of Horus, the god of stability. Others carried small images of blue pottery representing the deceased under the form of Osiris, and the bird emblematic of the soul. Then eight women of the class of paid mourners came along beating their breasts, throwing dust upon their heads, and uttering loud lamentations. Ameres, clad in a leopard skin, and having in his hands the censer and vase of libation, accompanied by his attendants bearing the various implements used in the services, and followed by a number of priests also clad in leopard skins, now came along. Immediately behind them followed the consecrated boat placed upon a sledge, and containing the mummy-case in a large exterior case covered with paintings. It was drawn by four oxen and seven men.[79]

Knowing the ghoulish tastes of his young (mostly male) audience well, Henty obliges by providing all the gory details of embalming:

> First, an official called a scribe marked on the side of the corpse where an aperture should be made; this was cut by another person, who after doing so fled, pursued with execrations and pelted with stones, as although necessary the operation was considered a dishonorable one and as an injury to a sacred body.
>
> Through this aperture the embalmers removed the whole of the internal organs, which, after being cleansed and embalmed in spices, were deposited in four vases, which were subsequently placed in the tomb with the coffins. Each of these vases contained the parts sacred to a separate

deity. The body was then filled with aromatic resin and spices, and rubbed for thirty days with a mixture of the same ingredients. In the case of the very wealthy the whole body was then gilt; in other cases only the face and portions of the body. The skin of the mummy so preserved is found to be of an olive color, dry and flexible as if tanned; the features are preserved and appear as during life, and the teeth, hair of the head, and eyebrows are well preserved.[80]

Sir Arthur Conan Doyle's celebrated tale "The Ring of Thoth" (1890) concerns an ancient Egyptian priest who drinks an elixir of life, regrets it when his beloved dies and then spends centuries in trying to find the antidote. It is often quoted as one of the main sources of John L. Balderston's screenplay for *The Mummy* in 1932, and, as we shall see, it does have many things in common with it, but from the point of view of plot, *The Mummy* is actually an inverted version of Conan Doyle's tale. Karloff's Im-ho-tep wants to revive his lost beloved and continue his revivified existence on earth, not end it. Sosra, the Egyptian of Conan Doyle's tale, wants to die and join his loved lost one in the afterlife. Classically, Conan Doyle's tale of foreign menace begins in familiar territory (at least familiar to his original readers). We begin in Gower Street, near the British Museum in London's Bloomsbury district. We stay there only long enough, however, for Conan Doyle to mention that his hero, John Vansittart Smith, resides at No. 147a (as opposed to Sherlock Holmes's fictional 221-B Baker Street). Though the action rapidly moves to the Louvre museum in Paris, Conan Doyle's descriptions of it are very reminiscent of the Egyptian galleries in the British Museum, and his opening reference to Vansittart Smith's London address is surely designed to suggest this. So, too, is the scene in which Smith finds himself accidentally alone in the museum after closing time "with the dead men of a dead civilisation."[81]

Sosra has secured a position as caretaker to enable him to perform his ritual when the visitors have departed, and Conan Doyle's description of him can't have been lost on Jack Pierce, Universal's make-up artist extraordinaire, when he was designing Karloff's make-up for Ardeth Bey in *The Mummy*:

> There was no suggestion of pores. One could not fancy a drop of moisture upon that arid surface. From brow to chin, however, it was cross-hatched by a million delicate wrinkles, which shot and interlaced as though nature in some Maori mood had tried how wild and intricate a pattern she could devise.[82]

Also like Sosra, Karloff lights a lamp and squats "in Eastern fashion"[83] over the mummy of his beloved while performing his ritual. This, Vansittart Smith observes and interrupts. Sosra, however, is not malevolent (though he admits he would have killed Smith if he had interrupted him before he found the Ring of Thoth, which contains the antidote for which he seeks). Sosra is motivated solely by love and agrees to tell Smith his melancholy tale. He takes him to his modest concierge quarters, situated at the foot of a "winding, stone stair"[84] that leads to a door which gives access to the street. Though not winding, the off-limits staircase in the Petrie Museum exudes a similarly sinister mood, but as the Petrie Museum was not in existence when Conan Doyle published "The Ring of Thoth," there is, sadly, no possibility of it also having influenced the tale.

Conan Doyle's other mummy tale, "Lot 249" (1894), is the probable source of the means used in Universal's subsequent movies to revive the mummy. Rather than incantations, *The Mummy's Hand*, *Tomb*, *Ghost* and *Curse* all rely on a fluid made from Tana leaves, which Dr. Petrie in *Ghost* explains is an extinct plant. "Smells like clover," Banning remarks, sniffing a leaf. Only three are needed, suitably brewed, to keep Kharis alive when the moon

Mystical pick-me-up: John Carradine administers a brew of sacred Tana leaves to Lon Chaney, Jr.'s, thirsty Kharis in *The Mummy's Ghost* (dir. Reginald LeBorg, 1944).

is full. Although Conan Doyle doesn't mention the name of the plant, Bellingham, the student who revives the unnamed mummy in "Lot 249," seems to use the same means. He has concocted a "balsamic resin" from "palmate leaves," explaining that "it's the sacred plant—the plant of the priests." At the end of the story, when Bellingham's college chum forces him to destroy the monstrous mummy, he is also forced to burn the leaves as well: "We must have no more devil's tricks. In with all these leaves! They may have something to do with it,"[85] he insists, having previously made the xenophobic comment, so typical of the time in which the tale was written, "You'll find that your filthy Egyptian tricks won't answer in England."[86]

Whereas "The Ring of Thoth" consolidated the idea of a long-lost love spanning the centuries, "Lot 249" provided the model of the reactivated mummy as a terrifying monster:

> He could hear a swift, dry patter behind him, and could see, as he threw back a glance, that this horror was bounding like a tiger at his heels, with blazing eyes and one stringy arm outthrown. Thank God the door was ajar."[87]

Like the movies that were to follow in the footsteps of Conan Doyle's horrible mummy, its reanimator, Bellingham, has been using it as a personal Golem, to remove his own enemies. On January 15, 1967, the BBC screened a TV adaptation of the story starring Reginald Barratt, Edmond Bennett and Keith Buckley. Christopher Matthews, who would go on to appear in Hammer's *Scars of Dracula* (dir. Roy Ward Baker, 1970) and *Scream and Scream Again* (dir. Gordon Hessler, 1970) also took part.

More often experienced in Massenet's operatic adaptation, Anatole France's novel *Thaïs* (1890) is set in Alexandria and concerns the attempts of a priest, Paphnutius, to convert the courtesan Thaïs to Christianity. Early in the novel, Paphnutius encounters the statue of a sphinx on his missionary pilgrimage along the banks of the Nile:

> After walking six days, he came to a place called Silsile. There the river runs in a narrow valley, bordered by a double chain of granite mountains. It was there that the Egyptians, in the days when they worshipped demons, carved their idols. Paphnutius saw an enormous sphinx carved in the solid rock. Fearing that it might still possess some diabolical properties, he made the sign of the cross, and pronounced the name of Jesus; he immediately saw a bat fly out of one of the monster's ears, and Paphnutius knew that he had driven out the evil spirit which had been for centuries in the figure. His zeal increased, and picking up a large stone, he threw it in the idol's face. Then the mysterious face of the sphinx expressed such profound sadness that Paphnutius was moved. In fact, the expression of superhuman grief on the stone visage would have touched even the most unfeeling man. Therefore, Paphnutius said to the sphinx—
> "O monster, be like the satyrs and centaurs our father Anthony saw in the desert, and confess the divinity of Jesus Christ, and I will bless thee in the name of the Father, the Son, and the Holy Ghost."
> When he had spoken a rosy light gleamed in the eyes of the sphinx; the heavy eyelids of the monster quivered and the granite lips painfully murmured, as though in echo to the man's voice, the holy name of Jesus Christ; therefore Paphnutius stretched out his right hand, and blessed the sphinx of Silsile.[88]

Sphinxes were also to become an important motif for Oscar Wilde (1854–1900). His then-contemporary story, "The Sphinx Without a Secret" (1894), concerns a woman with a "mania for mystery"[89] who pretends to live a much more interesting life than she actually does. But it was Wilde's long poem, "The Sphinx" (1894), which gathered together the exotic connotations of ancient Egypt that were hovering over Europe at the time and atomized their decadent perfume over succeeding generations. Basically an excuse for complex rhyming and Egyptian imagery, some lines from "The Sphinx" were spoken with aesthetically sinister locution by Hurd Hatfield in the title role of Albert Lewin's 1945 film adaptation of *The Picture of Dorian Gray*:

> In a dim corner of my room for longer than my fancy thinks
> A beautiful and silent Sphinx has watched me through the shifting gloom.
>
> Inviolate and immobile she does not rise she does not stir
> For silver moons are naught to her and naught to her the suns that reel.
>
> Red follows grey across the air, the waves of moonlight ebb and flow
> But with the Dawn she does not go and in the night-time she is there.
>
> Dawn follows Dawn and Nights grow old and all the while this curious cat
> Lies couching on the Chinese mat with eyes of satin rimmed with gold.[90]

During the course of his great aesthetic hymn to opulent oriental mystery, Wilde brings in references to hieroglyphs (which rhyme with not-very Egyptian hippogriffs and basilisks), Isis and Osiris, Horus, Antony and Cleopatra, Thoth, the pyramids, the Nile, hippopotami, crocodiles, snakes, palms, jewels, Ammon, Nubian slaves, Memnon and "Dog-faced Anubis"— a veritable roll call of ancient Egyptian symbolism, much raided by later screenwriters.

As previously discussed with regard to its film adaptation, a sphinx appeared for rather different reasons four years later in *Cæsar and Cleopatra*, Bernard Shaw's attempt to outdo Shakespeare in 1898. Act One begins in the desert where Caesar interrogates this sphinx which, much to his surprise, answers back; but this is no mystical phenomenon. The

The tomb of Oscar Wilde in Père Lachaise cemetery, Paris. Designed by Sir Jacob Epstein.

mysterious voice of the sphinx is soon revealed to be that of Cleopatra who is hiding in it. Before that happens, though, Cæsar eloquently philosophizes before it:

> Hail, Sphinx: salutation from Julius Cæsar! I have wandered in many lands, seeking the lost regions from which my birth into this world exiled me, and the company of creatures such as I myself. I have found flocks and pastures, men and cities, but no other Cæsar, an air native to me, no men kindred to me, none who can do my day's deed, and think my might's thought. In the little world yonder, Sphinx, my place is as high as yours in this great desert; only I wander, and you sit still; I conquer, and you endure; I work and wonder, you watch and wait; I look up and am dazzled, look down and am darkened, look round and am puzzled, whilst your eyes never turn from looking out — out of the world — to the lost region — the home from which we have strayed. Sphinx, you and I, strangers to the race of men, are no strangers to one another.[91]

Shaw put a great deal of himself into his portrayal of Cæsar, which differed from Shakespeare's characterization, largely because Shaw based his Cæsar on what he had read about him in Theodor Momsen's *History of Rome* (1854–1856), whereas Shakespeare had relied on Plutarch's *Lives of the Roman Emperors*. Shaw also wanted his Cæsar to be a mouthpiece not only for his own ideas about democracy but also his belief in the power of the Will. As Shaw's biographer Michael Holroyd put it, Cæsar is "an expression of Shaw's conviction that love may be replaced by a beneficent Will that overcomes fear of death by being used up with work-fulfillment in life."[92] However, as the opening monologue before the sphinx in the first act of the play demonstrates, Cæsar, like Shaw, often found himself preaching in the wilderness. Shaw's Cleopatra is presented as a spoiled, silly girl who requires the political instruction of Cæsar and, as a consequence, is again a very different figure from the sophisticated schemer of Shakespeare (let alone of Rider Haggard and Elizabeth Taylor!).

Shaw's main aim in depicting his version of the relationship between Cæsar and Cleopatra was to demonstrate that it was political acumen rather than love that attracted Cleopatra to the Roman ruler. She can learn from him, and does. Cæsar, like Shaw, was of the opinion that sensible government and political clemency were far more important than love. By setting his play in ancient Egypt, he aimed to make the point that little has changed in the underlying motivations of human beings despite the so-called advances of civilization. In 1912, he added a striking prologue, set in the temple of Ra in Memphis, in which Ra himself refers contemptuously to the modern audience in the theatre as "ye compulsorily educated ones."[93] "Are ye impatient with me? Do ye crave for a story of an unchaste woman? Hath the name of Cleopatra tempted ye hither? Ye foolish ones; Cleopatra is as yet but a child that is whipped by her nurse." The traditional allure of the story is not Ra or Shaw's concern. We are light years away from the world of Rider Haggard. As Ra makes plain, Shaw's parable is as much about the contemporary world as that of ancient Egypt, for, as he points out, "men twenty centuries ago were already just such as you, and spoke and lived as ye speak and live, no worse and no better, no wiser and no sillier."[94]

In such a didactic play the decorative Egyptian elements are indeed largely superfluous. The main motivation behind the spectacular splendors of Pascal's film version was the need of the British film industry to compete with Hollywood and to satisfy all those traditional audience expectations from which Shaw actually wanted to distance his play. This, ironically, is made quite clear right from the start; but an Egyptian mood was very much in the air, and no doubt Shaw was responding to that even if only on a subconscious level. The movie may have died, but its death was only the end of the beginning....

Six

Fiction and Fantasy, Part 2

Richard Marsh, the *nom-de-plume* of Richard Bernard Helmann (1857–1915), published his Egyptian thriller-mystery *The Beetle* in 1897, the same year as Bram Stoker's *Dracula*. Originally more popular than Stoker's vampire classic, it may also have influenced Stoker's *The Jewel of Seven Stars* in its fusion of recognizable London locations and domestic situations with ancient Egyptian malevolence. Also, both novels share a pivotal interest in the ancient Egyptian scarab. Indeed, their titles similarly refer to such a talisman. In Stoker's tale it is a blood-red ruby jewel. In Marsh's, scarabs form the decoration of carpets, adorn the heads of statues of Isis, and, most impressively of all, are the shape into which the mysterious Egyptian villain is able to transform herself. The plot is revealed in four successive narratives written from the differing perspectives of the novel's four principal characters, after the manner of Wilkie Collins. In essence the story is fairly straightforward. A British politician, Paul Lessington, has been accidentally ensnared by a cult of Isis while traveling in Egypt when still a young man. Having spent two months of hypnotized captivity in the temple of this cult, he eventually breaks free and attacks the houri who lured him there in the first place. In revenge for this outrage, the houri follows him to London with the aim of disgracing and ultimately destroying him. As a "Child of Isis," she is able to transform herself into the shape of a scarab beetle, and in this form she also terrorizes various other characters. Having kidnapped the heroine, Marjorie Lindon, the houri is chased by the heroes on a specially hired steam locomotive. Marjorie is rescued, but the strange Egyptian disappears inconclusively at the end, leaving a lingering perfume of mystery.

The emphasis here is on mystery, detection and pursuit, but the Egyptian element adds an important element of occult exoticism which was very much a part of its time. Conan Doyle's *The Sign of the Four* similarly uses Indian exoticism to color a Sherlock Holmes story of stolen treasure and a pact between four convicts (the "four" of the title) during the Indian Rebellion in 1857. Conan Doyle's novel appeared in 1890, only seven years before *The Beetle*. It's revealing to compare Conan Doyle's description of Thaddeus Sholto's exotically furnished rooms in Upper Norwood, along with a scene from "Lot 249," with Marsh's descriptions of the Egyptian temple to which Lessington is lured in *The Beetle*. Conan Doyle describes Sholto's rooms thus:

> The richest and glossiest of curtains and tapestries draped the walls, looped back here and there to expose some richly-mounted painting or Oriental vase. The carpet was of amber and black, so soft and so thick that the foot sank pleasantly into it, as into a bed of moss. Two great tiger-skins thrown athwart it increased the suggestion of Eastern luxury, as did a huge hookah which

stood upon a mat in the corner. A lamp in the fashion of a silver dove was hung from an almost invisible golden wire in the centre of the room. As it burned it filled the air with a subtle and aromatic odour.[1]

Conan Doyle's description of the student Bellingham's Oxford rooms in "Lot 249" is a positive riot of Egyptiana:

Walls and ceiling were thickly covered with a thousand strange relics from Egypt and the East. Tall, angular figures bearing burdens or weapons stalked in an uncouth frieze round the apartments. Above were bull-headed, stork-headed, cat-headed, owl-headed statues, with viper-crowned, almond-eyed monarchs, and strange, beetle-like deities cut out of the blue Egyptian lapis lazuli. Horus and Isis and Osiris peeped down from every niche and shelf; while across the ceiling was a true son of Old Nile, a great, hanging-jawed crocodile, was slung in a double noose.[2]

Marsh's temple to Isis is similarly extravagant:

The walls and roof were of bare stone — as though the whole had been hewed out of the solid rock. It seemed to be some sort of temple, and was redolent with the most extraordinary odour. An altar stood about the center, fashioned out of a single block of stone. On it a fire burned with a faint blue flame — the fumes which rose from it were no doubt chiefly responsible for the prevailing perfumes. Behind it was a huge bronze figure, more than life size. It was in a sitting posture, and represented a woman. Although it resembled no portrayal of her I have seen, either before or since, I came afterwards to understand that it was meant for Isis. On the idol's brow was poised a beetle. That the creature was alive seemed clear, for, as I looked at it, it opened and shut its wings.

If the one on the forehead of the goddess was the only live beetle which the place contained, it was not the only representation. It was modeled in the solid stone of the roof, and depicted in flaming colours on hangings which here and there were hung against the walls. Wherever the eye turned it rested on a scarab. The effect was bewildering.[3]

Each descriptions emphasizes perfume, draperies and Eastern luxury. Indeed, throughout Marsh's tale the image of the scarab beetle is found on carpets and rugs. It is all pervading. Both Conan Doyle and Marsh juxtapose their orientalisms with late–Victorian London, and, as with Sax Rohmer's Fu Manchu (who first appeared in 1912), the East in general is represented as both alluring and dangerous — a stance that clearly identifies the shared ethics and entrenched assumptions of writers active at the height of the British Empire. As Marsh implies in his description of the idol of Isis quoted above, there is no historical reality in his representation of Egyptian mythology. The scarab was not a particular emblem of Isis, and she was not normally portrayed with a scarab beetle on her headdress in ancient Egyptian art, as Marsh describes here. She was certainly never worshipped by means of human sacrifice as Lessington observes during his two-month incarceration in the sinister temple. (The human sacrifices in *The Beetle,* incidentally, are accompanied by the sound of harps, which suggests a distant echo of Europe's fascination with the harpers in Bruce's tomb):

On the right was the majestic seated figure of a goddess. Her hands were crossed upon her knees, and she was naked from her waist upwards. I fancied it was meant for Isis. On her brow was perched a gaily-appareled beetle — that ubiquitous beetle! — forming a bright spot of colour against her coppery skin — it was an exact reproduction of the creatures which were imaged on the carpet. In front of the idol was an enormous fiery furnace. In the very heart of the flames was an altar. On the altar was a naked white woman being burned alive.[4]

A cinematic equivalent of this image, though one that looks to Borneo rather than Egypt, is referred to (though not actually seen) in Hammer's *The Reptile* (dir. John Gilling,

1966) in which Jacqueline Pearce, who plays the daughter of an anthropologist, Dr. Franklyn (Noel Willman), has been transformed into a shape-shifting snake-woman by another sinister cult. Gilling's film obviously inhabits the same narrative tradition here, and, what is more, Gilling completely *understands* its conventions. As we have seen, post-modernism had undermined that context by the time of Stephen Sommers' remake of *The Mummy* in 1999. Having said that, there are some specific connections between Sommers' film and Marsh's novel. One of the recurring "horrors" in *The Beetle* is the sensation experienced by several characters of feeling a beetle crawling under their bed sheets, creeping over their limbs and touching their faces. Sommers' film includes similar physical horror when showing the audience several occasions when scarab beetles literally get under the skin of more than one character and working their way up to their unfortunate victims' brains. (A particularly nasty example of this happens to Omid Djalili's character, Warden Gad Hassan, who ends up banging his brains out against a cave wall to escape his excruciating agony.)

Marsh also suggests that the Egyptians believed in the transmigration of souls, which, as we know, was also contrary to their elaborate burial rituals. But all these discrepancies are there to serve the basic element of the plot that "the priests of Isis — or some of them — [were] supposed to assume, after death, the form of a — scarbaeus." Marsh seems quite aware that this wasn't the case, as he makes a character who is supposedly knowledgeable about Egyptology admit that he has "never heard of it."[5]

As for the sinister priest of Isis who initiates the action of *The Beetle*, Marsh introduces an element of gender ambivalence that is equally forward looking. Many villains are presented in terms of a male/female duality, a state of affairs which a Jungian psychologist would no doubt explain in terms of animus and anima, the male and female counterparts of the psyche. These female accomplices usually represent the negative aspects of the anima. Lady Macbeth is a strong prototype for this kind of wicked female accomplice. So, too, is Kundry, whom the magician Klingsor, in Wagner's opera *Parsifal*, forces to his will. Similarly, Fu Manchu has his sadistic daughter, and Dracula has his brides, but Marsh's High Priestess first appears to us as a hideous *male* figure, lying in bed in a dark room.

British readers soon had another Egyptian adventure to thrill them. First serialized in the *Windsor Magazine* between June and December 1898, Guy Boothby's *Pharos the Egyptian* appeared in the same year as Shaw's *Cæsar and Cleopatra*, but that is its only similarity to Shaw's play. It takes a totally different approach to ancient Egypt and reveals how the ancient mummy of Ptahmes, Chief of the Pharaoh Merenptah's magicians, was condemned to perpetual life by Pharaoh because he failed to defeat Moses' magic and prevent the death of the Pharoah's firstborn. Having suffered the indignity of having had his mummy case stolen in the 19th century, Ptahmes now takes his revenge on the descendent of the man who was responsible, and, in a more general flare of fury, on all the countries that have committed similar sins of sacrilege. His method involves infecting a British artist with a plague bacillus and using him as a horseman of his own created apocalypse. This unfortunate then unwittingly infects the whole of Europe until he destroys himself in the final pages. It is, of course, quite possible that Don Houghton had this tale in mind when scripting Hammer's *The Satanic Rites of Dracula* (dir. Alan Gibson, 1973), in which much the same thing happens.

Though Conan Doyle's short stories "Lot 249" and "The Ring of Thoth" are the two most well-known principal inspirations for Universal's 1932 *The Mummy*, Boothby's tale can also stake a claim to that distinction, as, like "The Ring of Thoth," it also features a speaking (and particularly malevolent) mummy who, free of bandages, walks around in modern society. Foreigners simply aren't to be trusted in Boothby's world. Even in the prologue to the tale, in which a manuscript is delivered into the hands of a stalwart member of the British aristocracy, the messenger is described in vaguely anti–Semitic terms as displaying "a servility that, thank God! is scarcely English."[6]

The story proper begins by introducing us to a Victorian artist by the name of Cyril Forrester, who obviously works in a style similar to that of Poynter, for he has just completed a massive canvas depicting ancient Egypt in the days of its greatest magnificence:

> It represented Merenptah, the Pharaoh of the Exodus, learning from the magicians the effect of his obstinacy in the death of his first-born son. The canvas showed him seated on his throne, clad in his robes of state. His head was pushed a little forward, his chin rested in his hand, while his eyes looked straight before him as though he were endeavoring to peer into the future in the hope of reading there the answer to the troubled thoughts inside his brain. Behind him stood the sorcerers, one of whom had found courage to announce the baneful tidings.[7]

There is, of course, no evidence that Merenptah *was* the Pharaoh of Exodus, though he certainly existed. We do know that Ptahmes was, in fact, a royal scribe and an attendant of the temple of Ptah under Tuthmosis IV and/or Amenhotep II. Not that this matters very much in a tale that uses Egyptology merely as an atmospheric device. As far as the story is concerned, it is significant that the artist, Forrester, has painted Merenptah, for he is soon to meet Ptahmes in the (presumably rather crumbling) flesh on a windy night beneath Cleopatra's Needle on London's Embankment. Outraged on hearing this sinister Egyptian laugh when a man committing suicide hurls himself into the Thames, Forrester accosts him and thus begins his diabolical association with a villain who, like Boothby's more famous Dr. Nikola, can often be friendly and charming but remains, beneath such guile, a fiendish force of evil.

Forrester attends a soirée at which he again encounters Pharos, this time in the company of the old man's "daughter"—a glamorous violinist who is, in fact, under the Egyptian's hypnotic influence. Later, he encounters Pharos again when he breaks into the artist's studio. This room has been decorated in Egyptian style with curios that Forrester has inherited from his Egyptologist father:

> It was as if the quaint images of the Gods, which decorated the walls, were watching me with almost human interest, and even the gilded face upon the mummy case, in the alcove at the farther end, wore an expression that I had never noticed on it before. It might have been saying, "Ah, my nineteenth-century friend, your father stole me from the land of my birth, and from the resting-place the gods decreed for me; but beware, for retribution is pursuing you, and is even now close upon your heels."[8]

Such decor in a Victorian domestic setting may well have lingered in Bram Stoker's memory when he came to describe the curio-infested interiors of Abel Trelawny's Kensington home in *The Jewel of Seven Stars*. It's also useful here to be able to date the idea of an Egyptian curse to a time before the furor of Tutankhamen in the 1920s. Forrester's vague fears of such a thing are soon to be made much more definite when Pharos appears. He intends to steal the mummy case and restore it to Ptahmes's tomb. Before he does, however, he utters a particularly virulent curse upon the head of the unfortunate painter:

> "Thy father, was it, wretched man," he cried, shaking his skeleton fist at me, while his body trembled like a leaf under the whirlwind of his passion, "who stole this body from its resting-

place? Thy father, was it, who broke the seals the gods had placed upon the tombs of those who were their servants? If that be so, then may the punishment decreed against those guilty of the sin of sacrilege be visited on thee and thine for evermore." Then, turning to the mummy, he continued, as if to himself, "Oh, mighty Egypt! hast thou fallen so far from thy high estate that even the bodies of thy kings and priests may no longer rest within their tombs, but are ravished from thee to be gaped at in alien lands. But, by Osiris, a time of punishment is coming. It is decreed, and none shall stay the sword!"[9]

It would appear then, that it was actually Boothby, rather than Marie Corelli, who was the true originator of the Egyptian curses that motivate the plots of so many subsequent mummy movies. Pharos certainly sounds very like George Pastell's Mehemet Bey in Hammer's 1959 *Mummy* film, when he accuses Westerners of desecration:

Your father was, I know, an ardent Egyptologist, one of that intrepid band who penetrated to every corner of our sacred land, digging, delving, and bringing to light such tombs, temples, and monuments as have for centuries lain hidden from the sight of man. For my own part, as you may have gathered from my tirade just now, my sympathies do not lie in that direction. I am one who reverences the past, and would fain have others do so.[10]

Having initiated this important element of future mummy movie history, Boothby then anticipates the Biblical epic (no doubt himself inspired by the epic paintings of British Royal Academicians) with descriptions of Biblical Egypt that are among the most evocative passages in the novel:

From the crowds that congregated round these mighty edifices, and from the excitement which prevailed on every hand, it was plain that some great festival was about to be celebrated. While I watched, the commencement of the procession made its appearance on the farther side of the river, where state barges ornamented with much gold and many brilliant colours were waiting to carry it across. On reaching the steps it continued its march towards the temple. It was preceded by a hundred dancing girls clad in white, and carrying timbrels in their hands. Behind them was a priest bearing the two books of Hermes, one containing hymns in honour of the Gods, and the other precepts relating to the life of the King. Next came the Royal Astrologer bearing the measure of Time, the hour-glass and the Phoenix. Then the King's Scribe, carrying the materials of his craft. Following him were more women playing on single and double pipes, harps, and flutes, and after the musicians the Stolistes, with the sign of Justice and the cup of Libation. Next walked twelve servants of the temple, headed by the Chief Priest, clad in his robes of leopard skins, after whom marched a troop of soldiers with the sun glittering on their armour and accoutrements. Behind, the runners were carrying white staves in their hand, and after them fifty singing girls, strewing flowers of all colours upon the path. Then, escorted by his bodyguard, the Royal Arms bearers, and seated upon his throne of state, which again was borne upon the shoulders of the chief eight nobles of the land, and had above it a magnificent canopy, was Pharaoh himself, dressed in his robes of state and carrying his scepter and the flagellum of Osiris in either hand. Behind him were his fan-bearers, and by his side a man whom, in spite of his rich dress, I recognized as soon as my eyes fell upon him. He was none other than the servant whom Pharaoh delighted to honour, his favorite, Ptahmes, son of Netruhôtep, Chief of the Magicians, and Lord of the North and South. Deformed as he was, he walked with a proud step, carrying himself like one who knows that his position is assured. Following Pharaoh were his favourite generals, then another detachment of soldiers, still more priests, musicians, and dancing girls, and last of all a choir robed in white, and numbering several hundred voices.[11]

There are other aspects of Boothby's novel that are worth noting. One character, an Egyptologist called Sir George Legrath, has "the reputation of being one of the best-dressed men in London"[12] and as such reminds one of the sartorial real-life Egyptologist, John Gardner

Wilkinson. There are also scenes in the Great Pyramid involving bats ("the heat was stifling, and more than once foul things, that only could have been bats, flapped against my face and hands and sent a cold shudder flying over me"[13]) and echoes ("at last my fortitude gave way, a clammy sweat broke out upon my forehead, and remembering that Pharos was in the building, I shouted aloud to him for help. My voice rang and echoed in that ghastly chamber till the reiteration of it well-nigh drove me mad"[14]). Neither can Boothby resist having his hero forced to drink an hallucinogenic opiate at the foot of the sphinx at Giza. It's all there in Boothby's fantastic novel, waiting to terrorize millions of moviegoers in the 20th-century.

The royal dynasties of ancient Egypt were first put into historical order by Manetho, an Egyptian priest historian who lived during the third century B.C. Bram Stoker mentions Manetho in *The Jewel of Seven Stars*, claiming that even so respected an authority was unaware of one of the most interesting rulers of ancient Egypt — Queen Tera. Even Manetho, with "all the lore of the priesthood for forty centuries behind him, and with the possibility of access to every existing record, could not even find her name."[15] That was apparently because the reputation of Stoker's queen was so appalling to the priests of her time that they erased her name from every monument. A similar fate was suffered by the genuinely historical figure of Akhnaten. Tera, of course, was wholly the product of Stoker's imagination. As the explorer Corbeck explains in chapter 14 of Stoker's text:

> See how the priests of her time, and those after it tried to wipe out her name from the face of the earth, and put a curse over the very door of her tomb so that none might ever discover the lost name.[16]

All that the priests allowed to remain inscribed over the entrance to Tera's tomb were the sinister words: "Hither the Gods come not at any summons. The 'Nameless One' has insulted them and is for ever alone. Go not nigh, lest their vengeance wither you away!"[17] — a classic curse from a mummy's tomb indeed. (Imhotep is even referred to as the "nameless one" by Rachel Weisz's character Evy Canahan in the remake of *The Mummy* in 1999.) When describing Trelawny's residence, filled, as it is, with Tera's precious relics, Stoker may well have had in mind the extensive collection of Egyptian curios that cluttered the Dublin home of Sir William Wilde (father of Oscar), whom he knew well. It had been Sir William who had campaigned to have Cleopatra's Needle (which he had seen lying beside Pompey's Pillar in Egypt) brought to England. He had also wrenched a mummy from its tomb at Saqqara and had it shipped back home to Ireland[18] — so it's not hard to imagine Stoker being influenced by such tales when he wrote his own Egyptian romance.

As in *Dracula*, Stoker was very concerned that *The Jewel of Seven Stars* should present his readers with a familiar modern world. To emphasize the strangeness of the ancient world, not only do Queen Tera's artifacts fill a "modern" bedroom but her spirit also insidiously possesses the body of the "modern" heroine, Margaret. Stoker takes care to describe the London locales of his story just as precisely as he did in *Dracula*, and with similar effect. The hero, Malcolm Ross, lives on Jermyn Street, just off London's Piccadilly. Famous for its shirt makers, boot makers and Floris and Co., perfumers to the Court of St. James, it was also inhabited by the magician Aleister Crowley, who lived at No. 93, but not until long after Stoker's death (so, sadly, that "magical" connection could not have been in his mind). Most of the action takes place in Trelawny's palatial mansion on Kensington Palace

Six • *Fiction and Fantasy, Part 2* 165

"Tomb at Sakkara, arched with stone, of the time of Psammitichus, or Psamatik, II, whose name occurs in the roof to the left, and in other places." From J. Gardner Wilkinson, *The Ancient Egyptians — Their Lives and Customs* (London: John Murray, 1854).

Road "nearer Notting Hill than Kensington" and a "truly fine house"[19] according to Ross's description of it. One of the most exclusive addresses in London, Kensington Palace Road is sometimes known as "Billionaires Row." Today, the average cost of a home on this road in around £18 million, so, as one might expect, many of them are now ambassadorial residencies. This is appropriate as Trelawny is himself immensely rich; so rich, in fact, that he has been able to transport the contents of an ancient Egyptian tomb to his private London address. Trelawny, as his name suggests, is also a Cornishman and enjoys the use of his estate on the coast of that county of England, where the terrifying yet also oddly ambivalent dénouement of the story occurs.

So much for the English locations of Stoker's novel. The Egyptian elements are also meticulously researched, as we have already seen. Stoker provides an impressive list of distinguished Egyptologists when discussing hieroglyphs, which stand as testament to his own reading on the subject:

> It was only when the work was taken up and followed by Young and Champollion, by Birch and Lepsius and Rosellini and Savolini, by Mariette Bey and by Wallis Budge and Flinders Petrie and the other scholars of their times that great results ensued, and that the true meaning of hieroglyphic was known.[20]

Stoker not only contrasts East with West and ancient with modern but also opens the book with a dream sequence which he contrasts with pressing, urgent reality. This latter juxtaposition anticipates the conflict between rationality and magic that motivates the narrative as a whole. As the novel opens, Ross is asleep and dreaming of Margaret Trelawny, whom he has only just met. Suggesting the novel's theme of reincarnation, Ross explains that "it is in the arcana of dreams that existences merge and renew themselves, change and yet keep the same, like the soul of a musician in a fugue."[21] This opening scene may also be a veiled reference in this passage to a line from Budge's translation of *The Egyptian Book of the Dead*. This was a book Stoker knew and possessed, so an unconscious echo of it may have made its impact on a small detail at this early stage in the story. Disturbed by the sound of his front doorbell being furiously rung in the middle of the night, Ross says, "All at once the gates of Sleep were thrown wide open."[22] This suggests the lines "Open are the double doors of the horizon/Unlocked are its bolts" from Budge's translation. They also open Philip Glass's minimalist opera, *Akhnaten*, from 1984.

Summoned by Margaret to assist in the strange events of the night on Kensington Palace Road, Ross hurries to her assistance. Trelawny has been attacked, his wrist is bleeding and he remains unconscious. We later learn that the astral spirit of Queen Tera and that of her "Familiar" (a large cat) are responsible. Tera wants to open the safe in Trelawny's room in which he keeps the magical ruby talisman — the jewel of the novel's title. This jewel is a crucial element in the resurrection ritual performed at the end of the story, a fact of which Trelawny is well aware, so he keeps the key to this safe on a bangle around his wrist. This prevents Tera from gaining access to the safe, though not without some determination on her part — hence the wound. It is also suggested in these early chapters that Margaret herself, under the influence of Tera's spirit, is responsible for these attacks upon her own father (an interpretation spelled out, incidentally, in Mike Newell's film). Trelawny is also given a certain sinister quality of his own, reminiscent of Count Dracula. As Margaret puts it, her father can be stern and frightening, even more so when he is being polite. The effect is particularly unnerving "when he is slow and deliberate, and the side of his mouth lifts up to show the sharp teeth."[23] It's true that Trelawny does end up sacrificing his own daughter in his relentless quest to resurrect the ancient queen with whom he has become so completely obsessed, so there is indeed a certain vampiric quality about him in that respect; but rather more disturbing, as we have seen, is the fact that Margaret and Tera are basically the same being, a duality which has a disturbing implication of incest when it comes to the relationship of father and daughter. Throughout the novel there are indications that such an incestuous relationship might help explain the deeper psychological thrust of the story. Margaret dies when her mother dies in childbirth, but is miraculously resurrected when Trelawny enters Tera's tomb at exactly the same moment. As Ross speculates, Margaret might not be an individual at all "but simply a phase of Queen Tera herself; an astral body obedient to her will!"[24] He is horrified by the idea "that there was no Margaret at all; but just an animated image, used by the Double of a woman of forty centuries ago to its own ends!"[25]

Trelawny came to the same conclusion, which is why he sent Margaret away from him during her childhood. He is very definitely obsessed — perhaps "in love" — with Tera. To love one's own daughter in such a way might have been too much of a temptation for conventional morality to withstand. Various subsequent comments seem to confirm this interpretation: "Fathers are naturally a little jealous in such matters as a daughter's choice,"[26] Trelawny confesses, when Ross broaches the possibility of a future engagement between himself and Margaret. Trelawny's otherwise quite reasonable comment takes on a slightly more charged meaning in the context of its utterance. A few pages later, it's suggested that Trelawny loves Margaret as he loved his own wife: "How he must have loved her mother!" Ross reflects. "It was the love of her mother's child, rather than the love of his own daughter, that appealed to him."[27] Margaret both physically resembles Tera and also reflects her mother's "tender and thoughtful"[28] nature. Is it significant that father and daughter "had only come to know each other when the girl was grown up"[29]— i.e., when it was "safer" to love her, if incest is indeed safer than pederasty, at least from a genetic if not a moral point of view. As if to clinch this interpretation, Ross observes Margaret's "gesture of passionate love and admiration"[30] as she stoops to kiss her father's hand. Trelawny later adds, "I knew well that the spirit of her mother is within her. If, in addition, there be the spirit of that great and wondrous Queen then she would be no less dear to me, but doubly dear."[31] As we have already seen, subsequent film versions of the story have emphasized the Oedipal subtext in their own ways.

Whereas Theohpile Gautier had fantasized about a mummy's foot, Stoker makes the severed hand of Tera's mummy the macabre fetish object in his story. Later, however, we are shown the perfectly preserved body of the queen in a scene that implies the necrophiliac admiration of a group of men for a perfectly preserved and naked body in a way that would have been quite impossible to publish at the time in a field other than fantasy; but it is Tera's severed hand that symbolizes Tera's power, and it is the hand that is responsible for the murder of various Arab bearers, as we learn in a flashback section of the story set in Egypt.

> Within, on a cushion of cloth of gold as fine as silk, and with the peculiar softness of old gold, rested a mummy hand, so perfect that it startled one to see it. A woman's hand, fine and long, with slim tapering fingers and nearly as perfect as when it was given to the embalmer thousands of years before. In the embalming it had lost nothing of its beautiful shape; even the wrist seemed to maintain its pliability as the gentle curve lay on the cushion. The skin was of a rich creamy or old ivory colour; a dusky fair skin which suggested heat, but heat in shadow. The great peculiarity of it, as a hand, was that it had in all seven fingers, there being two middle and two index fingers. The upper end of the wrist was jagged, as though it had been broken off, and was stained with a red-brown stain.[32]

Stoker also describes a magic coffer, which only opens at the climax of the story when the light of the seven lamps are correctly aligned with it. A magical process then begins, from which Stoker skillfully distances the reader by placing his narrator, Ross, a little way away from the action. (He must control the lighting of the cavern in which the Great Experiment takes place.) All Ross can see rising from its eventually opened lid, therefore, is "a faint greenish vapour which floated in the direction of the sarcophagus as though impelled or drawn towards it."

> It was evident now that the mummied body has some attraction for it; and also that it had some effect on the body, for the sarcophagus slowly became illumined as though the body had begun to glow. I could not see within from where I stood, but I gathered from the faces of all the four watchers that something strange was happening....
>
> I saw something white rising up from the open sarcophagus. Something which appeared to my tortured eyes to be filmy, like a white mist. In the heart of this mist, which was cloudy and opaque like an opal, was something like a hand holding a fiery jewel flaming with many lights. As the fierce glow of the Coffer met this new living light, the green vapour floating between them seemed like a cascade of brilliant points — a miracle of light!"[33]

But a storm wind bursts open a shutter and disturbs the ritual. Black smoke pothers from the Coffer and Ross can make nothing out save, eventually, a "movement of something white where the sarcophagus was."[34] He gropes his way through the darkness and picks up what he thinks is Margaret's body. Carrying her upstairs, he lays her down in the hall of the house before going in search of matches to illumine the scene. When he returns, Margaret's body has vanished. Only Tera's robe and the Jewel of Seven Stars remain. Returning to the cellar, he realizes his mistake. Margaret, her father, and Doctor Winchester (who was also present at the ritual) are all dead. The body he carried must, therefore, have been that of the resurrected queen, though whether she is good or evil is left to the reader (and the circumstantial evidence) to decide. The horrific glassy stare of Margaret's eyes through her fingers suggests that what she saw being resurrected really was evil, as Stoker has been implying all along. This stark image was nicely transferred to the screen at the end of *Blood from the Mummy's Tomb* when Margaret/Tera stares out from her mummy-like bandages in the hospital after the cellar (in which that film's climax was enacted) has collapsed on all involved.

As Stoker keeps reminding us, the number seven was of great importance to Queen Tera. Seven is, of course, a magical number often invoked in magical stories (and even non-magical ones: there were, of course, *Seven Brides for Seven Brothers* [dir. Stanley Donen, 1954], and *Seven Samurai* [dir. Akira Kurosawa, 1954] as well *The Legend of the Seven Golden Vampires* [dir. Roy Ward Baker, 1974], not to mention Ingmar Bergman's *The Seventh Seal* [1957] and Nathan Juran's *The 7th Voyage of Sinbad* [1958]). In Egypt, seven was the symbol of eternal life not least because multiples of seven rule the incubation periods of many animals, including humans (the duration of pregnancy in women is 280 days, the multiple of which is 7 × 40), but also, of course, it was due to the very many "magical" implications of that number, too numerous to go into here. Stoker provides his own catalogue of seven's significance:

> Seven was to her a magic number; and no wonder. With seven fingers on one hand, and seven toes on one foot. With a talisman of a rare ruby with seven stars in the same position as in the constellation which ruled her birth, each star of the seven having seven points — in itself a geological wonder — it would have been odd if she had not been attracted to it. Again, she was born, we learn in the Stele of her tomb, in the seventh month of the year — the month beginning with

the Inundation of the Nile. Of which month the presiding Goddess was Hathor, the Goddess of her own house, of the Antefs of the Theban line — the Goddess who in various forms symbolizes beauty, and pleasure, and resurrection. Again, in this seventh month — which, by later Egyptian astronomy began on October 28th, and ran to the 27th of our November — on the seventh day the Pointer of the Plough just rises above the horizon on the sky at Thebes.[35]

Oscar Wilde's wife, Constance, was known to be a member of the magical Order of the Golden Dawn, and Stoker had courted Constance before finally marrying Florence Balcombe. Whether Stoker was personally involved in the Golden Dawn remains unknown. (It is usually regarded as unlikely.) However, there remains a curious reference to an Egyptian god at the beginning of the ninth chapter of *The Jewel of Seven Stars*, which perhaps suggests a veiled reference to that organization. Corbeck, having lost the sacred lamps that are so important an element in the reincarnation ritual, is overcome with delight when they are discovered in Margaret's bedroom, having been magically transported there by Queen Tera's astral body. In a heated conversation with a policeman, Corbeck asks, without giving an answer, the following mysterious question: "Perhaps you can tell me what the figure of Ptah-Seker-Ausar holding the Tet wrapped in the Sceptre of Papyrus means?"[36] This is a very curious question to insert, even more so as Corbeck leaves it unanswered. It might suggest that Stoker included such an obscurity for the delectation of a reader who knew what he was talking about, and it may help to establish a connection between the novel and the Golden Dawn, even if in a rather tenuous way. Ptah-Seker-Ausar was a genuine Egyptian composite God, said to be the husband of Sekhmet. A funerary god who fashioned the bodies which were inhabited by souls in the afterlife, Ptah-Seker-Ausar was therefore of particular relevance to the story of Stoker's novel, and it's highly likely that Stoker consulted Budge's 1901 book, *Egyptian Magic*, for information about Ptah-Seker-Ausar, whom Budge describes as follows:

> Under the heading of "Magical Figures" must certainly be included the so-called Ptah-Seker-Ausar figure which is usually made of wood; it is often solid, but is sometimes made hollow, and is usually let into a rectangular wooden stand which may be either solid or hollow. The three gods or trinity of Ptah, Seker (Socharis), and Ausar (Osiris), are intended to represent the god of the sunrise (Ptah), the god of the night sun (Seker), and the god of the resurrection (Osiris). The name Ptah means "Opener," and is usually applied to the sun as the "opener" of the day; and the name Seker means "He who is shut in," that is to say, the night sun, who was regarded as the sun buried temporarily. Now the life of a man upon earth was identified with that of the sun; he "opened" or began his life as Ptah, and after death he was "shut in" or "coffined," like it also. But the sun rises again when the night is past, and, as it begins a new life with renewed strength and vigour, it became the type of the new life which the Egyptian hoped to live in the world beyond the grave. But the difficulty was how to obtain the protection of Ptah, Seker, and Osiris, and how to make them do for the man that which they did for themselves, and so secure their attributes. To attain this end a figure was fashioned in such a way as to include the chief characteristics of the forms of these gods, and was inserted in a rectangular wooden stand which was intended to represent the coffin or chest out of which the trinity Ptah-Seker-Ausar came forth. On the figure itself and on the sides of the stand were inscribed prayers on behalf of the man for whom it was made, and the Egyptian believed that these prayers caused the might and powers of the three gods to come and dwell in the wooden figure. But in order to make the stand of the figure as much like a coffin as possible, a small portion of the body of the deceased was carefully mummified and placed in it, and it was thought that if the three gods protected and preserved that piece, and if they revivified it in due season, the whole body would be protected, and preserved, and revivified. Frequently, especially in the late period, a cavity was made

in the side of the stand, and in this was laid a small roll of papyrus inscribed with the text of certain Chapters of the Book of the Dead, and thus the deceased was provided with additional security for the resurrection of his spiritual body in the world to come. The little rolls of papyrus are often inscribed with but short and fragmentary texts, but occasionally, as in the case of the priestess Anhai, a fine large papyrus, inscribed with numerous texts and illustrated with vignettes, was placed inside the figure of the god, who in this instance is in the form of Osiris only. It seems that the Ptah-Seker-Ausar figure was much used in the late period in Egypt, for many inscribed examples have been found which are not only illegible, but which prove that the artist had not the remotest idea of the meaning of the things which he was writing. It is possible that they were employed largely by the poor, among whom they seem to have served the purpose of the costly tomb.[37]

Stoker's cryptic reference to Ptah-Seker-Ausar therefore not only has relevance to the novel's main theme but may also have been a tribute to Budge, who was, incidentally, a Cornishman and so also a probable model for Abel Trelawny. There is an unsubstantiated rumor that Budge was another member of the Golden Dawn, an organization that in part based its own rituals, in part, on Egyptian religion. Even if Stoker and Budge weren't members of the Order, we do know that John Brodie-Innes (1848–1923) was, and not only did Brodie-Innes call *The Jewel of Seven Stars* "not just a good book but a great book," he also added that "it seems to me in some ways that you have a clearer light on some problems which some of us have been fumbling in the dark after for long enough."[38] Significantly, Brodie-Innes dedicated his novel *The Devil's Mistress* (1915): "To the memory of my dear friend the author of *Dracula* to whose help and encouragement I owe more than I am at present at liberty to state." This equally cryptic comment was no doubt intended to suggest something more than mere admiration, but what? A shared esoteric wisdom of some sort? Perhaps so, especially when we recognize that Stoker had other connections with the Golden Dawn. His novel *The Lair of the White Worm* was illustrated by another member of the Order, Pamela Colman Smith (1878–1951)[39] and Stoker was also on friendly terms with W. B. Yeats. It seems likely, therefore, that there was some kind of link between the Golden Dawn and the esoteric elements of *The Jewel of Seven Stars;* but the link between Egyptian fiction and the occult became even more significant in the writings of Aleister Crowley, the most infamous Golden Dawn member of all.

In "Across the Gulf" (1912), Crowley presents himself as the priest Ankh-f-n-khonsu, who begins his career as a High Priest of the Veiled One (Isis) in Thebes in the Twenty-Sixth Dynasty. A Magus prophesies that the boy will become a priestess, and in order to bring this about, Ankh-f-n-khonsu is encouraged to be as effeminate as possible. He is dressed in female clothing and surrounded with all possible luxury, including Negro slaves and his own harp-player. Crowley's description of the chambers in which the boy is quartered certainly are cinematic:

> Large it was and lofty; and there were sculptured pillars of malachite and lapis-lazuli and of porphyry and yellow marble. The floor was of black granite; the roof was white marble. On the Southern side was my couch, a softness of exotic furs. To roll in them was to gasp for pleasure. In the centre was a fountain of pure gold.[40]

Ankh-f-n-khonsu dislikes all this, however, and rebels, indulging in a variety of boyish activities, such as holding his breath under water, climbing pillars and pulling the head off one of the soldiers who keeps guard over him. Then he finds his male nature responding to the charms of the goddess he should be worshipping in a rather more chaste manner.

This "Veiled One" becomes a living goddess at the times of its "Assumption" and can destroy men with a flash of her eyes. Ankh-f-n-khonsu finds himself falling in lust with the goddess, in a way comparable to the hero of Oscar Wilde's "Charmides," the eponymous hero of which similarly makes love to a statue. It is instructive to compare Crowley's prose here with Wilde's poem, which first appeared in 1890.

> Ready for death with parted lips he stood,
> And well content at such a price to see
> That calm wide brow, that terrible maidenhood,
> The marvel of that pitiless chastity
> Ah! well content indeed, for never wight
> Since Troy's young shepherd prince had seen so wonderful a sight.
>
> Ready for death he stood, but lo! the air
> Grew silent, and the horses ceased to neigh,
> And off his brow he tossed the clustering hair,
> And from his limbs he threw the cloak away
> For whom would not such love make desperate,
> And nigher came, and touched her throat, and with hands violate
>
> Undid the cuirass, and the crocus gown,
> And bared the breasts of polished ivory,
> Till from the waist the peplos falling down
> Left visible the secret mystery,
> Which to no lover will Athena show,
> The grand cool flanks, the crescent thighs, the bossy hills of snow.[41]

Some 20 years after Wilde's poem, Crowley combined this poem's main idea with a stronger dash of sadomasochism no doubt derived from Swinburne, but also charged with Crowley's own libidinous energy:

> Blinded I was with the glory of her face; I should have fallen; but she caught me to her, and fixed her divine mouth on mine, eating me up with the light of her eyes. Her mouth moaned, her throat sobbed with love; her tongue thrust itself into me as a shaft of sunlight smites into the palm-groves; my robes fell shriveled, and flesh to flesh we clung. Then in some strange way she gripped me body and soul, twining herself about me and within me even as Death that devoreth mortal man.[42]

Having consummated their mutual passion, the temple, unfortunately, bursts into flames and falls into ruins. A new age of Osiris is rapidly inaugurated with the words "Equinox of the Gods!"—a development that Crowley/Ankh-n-f-khonsu explains as follows:

> Through Isis man obtains strength of nature; through Osiris he obtains the strength of suffering and ordeal, and as the trained athlete is superior to the savage, so is the magic of Osiris stronger than the magic of Isis....
> Just as thousands of years later was my secret revolt against Osiris—for the world had suffered enough!—destined to bring about another Equinox in which Horus was to replace the Slain One with his youth and vigor and victory.[43]

Ankh-n-f-khonsu attempts to be a dutiful High Priest of the new god. A splendid new temple, of which any film production designer would have been proud, is erected, but Ankh-n-f-khonsu is still infatuated with the Veiled One. Osiris now expresses his displeasure with him, and a whirlwind lifts him out of the temple, depositing him in the desert. Expelled from Thebes, Ankh-n-f-Khonsu wanders in exile. Eventually, he returns to Thebes where he discovers that a new High Priestess of Isis has been installed. They fight to the death in a sadomasochistic, necrophiliac free-for-all of jealousy and rage and, once the rival High Priestess has been slain, Ankh-n-h-Khonsu goes mad before wandering to Memphis, where he seeks the Magus who foretold that he was to be the High Priestess of Isis and of whom he now demands: "Read me the riddle of my life!"

Ankh-n-f-Khonsu now builds a temple to himself and believes he has become Osiris. He appoints a Nubian slave as his High Priest, and a great deal of slaughter follows, due to the people of Memphis who take up against him. The Nubian is one of those killed. Anhk-n-f-Khonsu then attempts a little magic in the manner of the mummy movies that still lay some years beyond Crowley's tale. He slaughters four more girls and fills the Nubian's veins with their blood, and then touches him with his wand. This reanimates the slave long enough to perform a ritual which confirms that Ankh-f-n-Khonsu has now truly become Osiris. He ventures into Memphis and brings death and devastation to all who dwell there by casting the power of his eyes at all who cross his path. But the priest is still enamored of Isis and chastises himself in an attempt at self-purification. Crowley's description of this process makes Swinburne read like Mrs. Hemans. Ankh-n-f-Khonsu smears his limbs with honey and lets rats gnaw at him; he makes love to a leprous corpse and tortures his slaves as a way of thinking up new tortures for himself—all of which are carefully described in Crowley's most rodamontine Sadean manner.

Ankh-n-f-Khonsu then returns to Thebes where there is now a new High Priestess of Osiris who has appointed a stupid boy as her own priest. Ankh-n-f-Khonsu promptly becomes infatuated with the High Priestess and together they arrange to kill the boy priest. A sumptuous banquet is arranged, which is strongly reminiscent of the stage designs of Leon Bakst and José Maria Sert for Richard Strauss's decadent ballet *Die Josephslegende*—a work commissioned by Diaghilev only a few months before the outbreak of World War I in 1914. It, too, has elements of Egyptiana about it, as we shall discover in the following chapter. But Crowley's banquet is even more decadent:

> Indeed, as the hangman took out the corpse, we fell back and lay there among the waste of the banquet, the flagons overturned, the napery awry, the lamps extinct or spilt, the golden cups, chased with obscene images, thrown here and there, the meats hanging over the edge of their bejeweled dishes, their juice staining the white luxury of the linen; and in the midst ourselves, our limbs as careless as the wind, motionless.[44]

After the banquet, the boy priest, drunk with lust, claims that he will give anything if he is granted a kiss from the High Priestess. This she agrees to and then demands that the boy give way to a new High Priest in the shape of Ankh-n-f-Khonsu. Outraged, the boy hurls his ring of office to the floor, and as a punishment for this he has his tongue cut out just as Tom Tyler's Kharis in *The Mummy's Hand* was to suffer. Crowley's executioner pulls out the tongue "with his pincers, saying 'With this tongue didst thou frame a blasphemy against the Holy One, the Bride of Osiris.'"[45]

Karloff's Im-ho-tep escaped this particular atrocity as he has need of his tongue to speak the considerable amount of lines given to him later in the film. Arnold Vosloo's Imhotep negotiates the difficulty of having had his tongue cut out as well by replacing it with someone else's tongue once he's been resurrected. He then goes on to steal the unfortunate man's eyes, before "assimilating" them into his own rotting remains. It's certainly a way of having the best of both worlds, but Karloff managed to be much more frightening without anywhere near as much gratuitous violence, while Lee, being 100 percent himself rather than a CGI image for half the time, was much more convincingly threatening. According to Marcus Hearn and Alan Barnes, a much more graphic depiction of Lee's tongue being cut out was filmed for the continental version of *The Mummy* but never materialized in any final prints.[46]

Crowley had no such qualms. Finally installed as the new High Priest of Osiris, Ankh-n-f-Khonsu cleanses the temple by subjecting all his priests to the Four Elements test. Those who survive being thrown into the air from the top of a tower are drowned. Those who survive drowning are buried alive in the earth, and those who survive that are burned. But the Age of Osiris must, in time, give way to the Age of Horus:

> So I, in this year v of the Equinox of the Gods [1908] wherein Horus took the place of Osiris, will by the light of this my magical memory seek to understand fully the formula of Horus — Ra Hoor Khuit — my god, that ruleth the world under Nuit and Hadit. Then as Ankh-f-an-khonsu left unto me the stèla 666 with the keys of that knowledge, so also may I write down in hieroglyph the formula of the Lady of the Forked Wand and of the Feather, that shall assume his throne and place when the strength of Horus is exhausted.[47]

Aleister Crowley thought himself not only a great writer but also one of England's two greatest poets ("for we must not forget Shakespeare," he conceded[48]). Public opinion, however, unfortunately disagreed with him during his lifetime. His equivalent in Germany was Hanns Heinz Ewers (1871–1943) who had an interest in the occult and macabre that marked him out as a similar personality. Indeed, he was a long-standing friend of Crowley and kept in regular correspondence with him. For years after World War II, Ewers was remembered more for his support of the Nazi party than his voluminous writings. It was this dubious enthusiasm which sent his reputation reeling into the outer darkness, despite being subsequently banned by Goebbels, and if people remembered Ewers's books, it was usually for his story "The Spider" (1908) and his novel, *Alraune* (1911); but like Crowley, Ewers's literary reputation is now being revived. From our point of view, it is his 1913 tale "The Tophar Bride" which is of most interest, for it predates several mummy movie themes. The story (if not its telling) is quite simple: an enthusiast of embalming abducts the narrator's girlfriend, kills her, embalms and mummifies her and then passes the result off as a sensational Egyptological discovery. A Tophar bride, we are told, is the name the ancient Egyptians gave to a widow who willingly submits herself to being buried alive in her deceased husband's tomb. Not only does this tale feature another example of live mummification, it also draws on Stoker's idea of a perfectly preserved corpse, and points the way towards Joan Collins being entombed alive (though hardly willingly) in *Land of the Pharaohs*. Ultimately, it plays into the hands of *Carry on Screaming*, as the embalmer of Ewers's tale abducts more than just one girl, and subjects them to his mummification process for profit, much as Kenneth Williams' Dr. Watt transforms young ladies into shop-window mannequins in his immense "frying tonight" vat.

Ewers was never as successful in England as he was in Germany and America. Far more to British taste (though not so very different from either Crowley's or Ewers' exotic evocations) were the adventure stories of Sax Rohmer. With the profits of *The Mystery of Dr. Fu Manchu* in 1913, Rohmer (a.k.a. Arthur Henry Sarsfield Ward) indulged in a honeymoon to Egypt where he visited the famous Meidum pyramid (which he always preferred to spell as "Mêydûm"). Escorted through its sinister passages by the then custodian of the Cairo Museum, Rex Engelbach, Rohmer was so impressed by the experience that it went on to

"The Duke of Connaught Ascending the Pyramid of Cheops, Cairo — From a Sketch by Our Special Artist, Mr Herbert Johnson," from *The Graphic*, October 21, 1882.

inform significant elements in not only *Brood of the Witch Queen* but also his story "The Death-Ring of Sneferu" in *Tales of Secret Egypt*. Much admired by H. P. Lovecraft, *Brood of the Witch Queen*, despite its somewhat lame title, was once known as the scariest story ever written, and it certainly has sufficient elements of the grotesque and supernatural to grip the reader today, with its exotic perversity. If Dr. Fu Manchu was one of the inspirations for Ian Fleming's Dr. No, Rohmer's Egyptian fantasy exerted no small influence upon the adventures of Indiana Jones, and it also helped establish some of the conventions of mummy movies as well.

We've already seen how *Brood of the Witch Queen* elaborated some of the misconceptions of earlier travelers in Egypt, such as the belief that the pyramids were used as temples for the practice of black magic, as well as the general prejudice Rohmer shared with writers (such as Dennis Wheatley) that what was foreign could rarely be good (especially if its was oriental). *Brood of the Witch Queen* concerns the fiendishly criminal career of one Antony Ferrara, who is actually a reanimated mummy. The novel's hero, Dr. Cairn, explains how Ferrara came into the world:

"When his adoptive father, Sir Michael Ferrara," resumed the doctor, beginning to pace up and down the library — "when Sir Michael and I were in Egypt, in the winter of 1893, we conducted certain inquiries in the Fayûm. We camped for over three months beside the Méydûm Pyramid. The object of our inquiries was to discover the tomb of a certain queen. I will not trouble you with the details, which could be of no interest to anyone but an Egyptologist, I will merely say that apart from the name and titles by which she is known to the ordinary student, this queen is also known to certain inquirers as the Witch-Queen. She was not an Egyptian, but an Asiatic. In short, she was the last high priestess of a cult which became extinct at her death. Her secret mark — I am not referring to a cartouche or anything of that kind — was a spider; it was the mark of the religion or cult which she practiced. The high priest of the principal Temple of Ra, during the reign of the Pharaoh who was this queen's husband, was one Hortotef. This was his official position, but secretly he was also the high-priest of the sinister creed to which I have referred. The temple of this religion — a religion allied to Black Magic — was the Pyramid of Méydûm."[49]

Cairn reveals how he and Sir Michael Ferrara discovered the tomb of Hortotef and performed a magical ceremony that brings the mummy of his child (the product of a union between Horotef and the Witch Queen) back to life:

"Already, you are discrediting the story! Ah! I can see it! but let me finish. Unaided, we performed this process upon the embalmed body of the child. Then, in accordance with the directions of that dead magician — that accursed, malignant being, who thus had sought to secure for himself a new tenure of evil life — we laid the mummy, treated in a certain fashion, in the King's Chamber of the Méydûm Pyramid. It remained there for thirty days; from moon to moon -"
"You guarded the entrance?"
"You may assume what you like, Rob; but I could swear before any jury, that no one entered the pyramid throughout that time. Yet since we were only human, we may have been deceived in this. I have only to add, that when at the rising of the new moon in the ancient Sothic month of Panoi, we again entered the chamber, a living baby, some six months old, perfectly healthy, solemnly blinked up at the lights which we held in our trembling hands!"
Dr. Cairn reseated himself at the table, and turned the chair so that he faced his son. With the smoldering cigar between his teeth, he sat, a slight smile upon is lips.
Now it was Robert's turn to rise and begin feverishly to pace the floor.
"You mean, sir, that this infant — which lay in the pyramid — was — adopted by Sir Michael?"
"Was adopted, yes. Sir Michael engaged nurses for him, reared him here in England, educating him as an Englishman, sent him to a public school, sent him to —"
"To Oxford! Antony Ferrara! What! Do you seriously tell me that this is the history of Antony Ferrara?"
"On my word of honour, boy, that is all I know of Antony Ferrara. Is it not enough?"
"Merciful God! it is incredible," groaned Robert Cairn.[50]

Back in England, Ferrara sets about terrorizing those who stand between him and his plans to secure wealth and power at the expense of others. These plans involve a sinister lotus with egg-shaped buds, salamanders, spiders, the disembodied hands of the Witch Queen herself, and a host of fiendish horrors, which mark this novel as one of the most gripping of all Egyptian fantasies.

Rohmer's collection of Egyptian short stories in *Tales of Secret Egypt* alternates tales of romance and adventure with supernatural stories about Egyptian tombs and relics. The penultimate tale, "In the Valley of the Sorceress," has various things in common with Stoker's *The Jewel of Seven Stars*, not least in the title, which feminizes the title of Stoker's tenth chapter. The queen in Rohmer's story is the famous historical figure of Hatasu (or, as she is more usually known, Hatshepsut). Rohmer suggests that Hatasu, like Queen Tera in

Stoker's novel, was dishonored by the priests of her time due to her practice of black magic, and that this is why her name was erased from all the monuments that bore it. Archeologists, in fact, assume that this was carried out by her jealous and ambitious nephew, Tuthmosis III, who eventually succeeded her. It's certainly true that her name was removed and replaced by that of Tuthmosis, and that Hatasu's mummy was stolen, probably when her tomb was destroyed. The mummy of her consort, whom Rohmer spells as Sen-Mût, also disappeared and his sarcophagus was destroyed. (It's assumed that Tuthmosis III murdered this beautiful and powerful queen, who dressed like a man and has been compared to Queen Elizabeth I of England.)

So, Rohmer certainly knew his Egyptian history, and to lend further credibility to his story, he mentions the American lawyer and archeological financier Theodore M. Davis, who, as we have seen, played an important role in the excavations in the Valley of the Kings. (Rohmer refers to this its Arabic name of Bibân el-Mulûk). In 1906, Davis wrote a book about the tomb of Hatshepsut, whom he referred to rather confusingly as Hatshopsitu. Rohmer's story is set two years after the publication of Davis' book, and is told by one Edward Neville, Assistant-Inspector of Antiquities, who receives a series of letters from his friend Condor for whom Davis' excavations apparently held little interest. Condor is much more concerned with exploring an area a little higher up, where he is convinced he will find the mummy of Hatasu. As Condor begins work, an Arab girl, apparently in great distress, appears from nowhere. The next thing that Neville hears is that all 50 of Condor's native diggers have disappeared, along with the Arab girl. Condor assembles a new, smaller team and begins again. Once more, the Arab girl appears and pleads with him to take her down the Nile to escape the vengeance of her tribesmen who, if they found Condor with her, would also kill him. The next time Neville hears about Condor is when he is informed that Condor has been bitten by a cat and has died, raving mad, in a Cairo hospital, trying to scratch anyone who approached. His eyes gleamed like a cat as well.

Neville now decides to continue Condor's search and similar events occur to him. One night he is disturbed by the howling of dogs who have been unnerved by the arrival of the same Arab girl with the "beautiful and evil face."[51] She pleads with Neville as she had pleaded with Condor, and Neville realizes that "this siren of the wilderness was playing upon me as an accomplished musician might play upon a harp."[52] He repulses her, accusing her of being an impostor and sends her away with enough money to reach the oasis in which she claims to seek refuge. Contemptuously, the Arab girl departs, but the following night Neville is visited by two luminous glittering green eyes like those of a cat or perhaps a jackal — or ... what? He aims at them with his pistol but misses.

Next, his native workers grow restive, eventually deserting the site as before, and Neville is perplexed to find that their work of excavation has been mysteriously filled in. With the help of his headman, Hassan es–Sugra, he begins to dig again, only to find, the following morning, that the same thing has happened. The shaft they had been excavating has been mysteriously filled in once more, but by whom? Hassan es–Sugra then flees, and Neville is left to repeat the work by himself, but after a terrible nightmare in which he sees blazing green eyes and "lithe, slinking shapes ...— cat shapes, ghoul shapes, veritable figures of the pit"[53] he wakes the next day to find his excavation work refilled for the third time. Obviously, the spirit of Queen Hatasu has no intention of allowing anyone to meddle with her tomb.

Rohmer's fascination with magic, ancient Egypt and cats was to return on a rather larger scale in his novel *The Green Eyes of Bâst* in 1919, but before we explore that, there are three more tales concerning ancient Egypt in *Tales of Secret Egypt*, which are also worth exploring. We've already encountered "The Death-Ring of Sneferu" with regard to its frightening moment in a dark pyramid. Sneferu himself was the first king of the fourth dynasty, and he built three famous pyramids, including the famous Meidum example. The story concerns the search for the ring of the title, which eventually brings its promised threat of death to the man who finds it. The narrator, who is also in search of it, is therefore saved by the other man's momentary success—momentary because he is soon bitten by a viper. The most frightening image in the story is a vision experienced by a psychic girl:

> "I see a long line of dead men," she whispered, quaking in a kind of chant; "they are of all the races of the East, and some are swathed in mummy wrappings; the wrappings are sealed with the death-ring of Pharaoh. They are passing me slowly, on their way across the desert from the Pyramid of Mêydûm to a narrow ravine where a tent is erected. They go to summon one who is about to join their company...."[54]

As the narrator adds, "I doubt if I possess the temperament which enables one to contemplate with equanimity a number of dead men promenading in their shrouds."[55]

If "In the Valley of the Sorceress" was a kind of homage to *The Jewel of Seven Stars*, "The Whispering Mummy," the sixth story in the collection, is a parody of its reincarnation theme. It concerns an artist who takes a girl to his studio because she resembles the face of a mummy casket he has included in his painting. The Egyptian who loves this girl avenges himself by abducting her and employing a henchman to whisper through a tube that the girl is dead. The artist is thus made to believe that the spirit of the girl lives on. When he discovers the truth, he wants to complete his picture but is told that she had been banished, as her presence "disturbs the peace of the city."

Finally, the seventh story, "Lord of the Jackals," tells how a man is saved from the wrath of a Bedouin by a wizard who sets thousands of jackals on him. Its basic theme perhaps inspired Noel Langley's even more disturbing (though not Egyptian) 1950 tale "Serenade for Baboons" (in which much the same thing happens, though with baboons rather than jackals, as the title would suggest). Rohmer's description of a desert Simoom is a masterly example of vivid economy:

> My God! it was a demon which sought to blind me, to suffocate me, and which clutched at my throat with strangling fingers of sand! This, I told myself, was the danger which I might have avoided by quitting the camp before sunrise.[56]

He excels here in his description of the wizard's summoning call:

> Again he uttered that uncanny, that indescribable cry. It was not human. It was not animal. Yet it was nearer to the cry of an animal than to any sound made by the human species. His eyes gleamed with an awful light, his spare body had assumed a strange significance; he was transfigured.
> A third time he uttered the cry, and out from one of those openings in the rock which I have mentioned, crept a jackal."[57]

The jackals bring death as surely as Anubis, but it was really Egyptian cats that fascinated Rohmer most, as his next novel demonstrated to thrilling effect. In *The Green Eyes of Bâst* (1920), Rohmer provides a wholly different story inspired by the celebrated cat goddess of the ancient Egyptians. The story has certain major themes in common with Val

Lewton's RKO film *Cat People* (dir. Jacques Tourneur, 1942), for both are concerned with feline transformation. The Lewton film leaves some ambiguity in its story of a Serbian girl who thinks she is cursed in this way. Rohmer, however, leaves nothing to the imagination. The first chapter introduces us to the green eyes in question, glimpsed in a moonlit garden. Later he describes an Egyptian image of a cat dating from the fourth century B.C., which is found in the home of a murdered baronet, Sir Marcus Coverly. Chapter seven suggests that Rohmer knew Henty's book well, as it's subtitled "The Cat of Bubastis." He also quotes from Gaston Maspero's book, *Egyptian Art*, when explaining the mythology of Bâst:

> She sometimes filled a gracious and benign rôle, protecting men against contagious diseases or evil spirits, keeping them off by the music of her sistrum; she had also her hours of treacherous perversity, during which she played with her victim as with a mouse, before finishing him off with a blow from her claws. She dwelt by preference in the city that bore her name, Poubastit, the Bubastis of classical writers.[58]

Subsequent chapters introduce an Eurasian occultist, Dr. Damar Greefe, whose clean-shaven face resembles that of Anubis. (Rohmer nonetheless carelessly refers to Anubis as "the hawk-headed god of Ancient Egypt."[59]) Greefe is first seen in the library of Friar's Park, a "former monastic house," where every available foot of wall space is filled with laden bookcases:

> The volumes were nearly all old, and many of them were in strange, evidently foreign bindings. Items of chemical apparatus and cases of specimens were visible also, as well as an amazing collection of Egyptian relics strewn about the place in the utmost disorder.[60]

The hint of alchemy is not surprising, given the connection of that science with Egypt, but Greefe's equipment is, in fact, used for a different kind of research. Greefe is as diffident and guarded in conversation as George Pastell's Mehemet Bey in Terence Fisher's *The Mummy*, but we do learn that he is the personal physician of a certain Lady Coverly, now a widow. It appears that Greefe lives the life of a pariah at Lady Coverly's expense, who never appears in public. As the chapter closes, the narrator observes that there are a number of *Bubastite cats* in the good doctor's collection. Subsequent chapters bring in further murders and a sinister nubian mute called Cassim, who turns out to be Greefe's servant. We are ushered through deserted chambers in Friar's Park and, as mystery piles on mystery, Rohmer skillfully leads us to the eventual dénouement in which Dr. Greefe explains his interest in *psycho-hybrids* (a condition which one might equate to lycanthropy). It transpires that the pregnant Lady Coverly once visited, with her husband, Sir Burnham, the Egyptian city of Zigazig during the time of the ancient Feast of Bâst. Zigazig is roughly in the same place as the ancient city of Bubastis, and during the night Lady Coverly was visited by one of the large cats that inhabit the place, "the result of which was an illness of a kind very dangerous to one in her delicate state of mind."[61] When Lady Coverly is eventually delivered of her child, Dr. Greefe, by arrangement with Sir Burnham, abducts it before she sets eyes on it, for both know what kind of monster it is. The child, whom Greefe calls Nahémah, turns out to be just the kind of *psycho-hybrid* he has been hoping to study. She is described as having features of a "perfect *Ancient Egyptian regularity*.... Her eyes, during the day, were those of a handsome native woman — almond-shaped and of a wonderful amber colour. At night they were green."[62] Even as a young girl she is an agile climber. During the "Sothic month" her catlike nature becomes increasingly murderous. Greefe blackmails Sir Burnham, threatening to introduce Nahémeh to her brother unless Sir Burnham provides money to finance his researches. He sets up home with Nahémeh and his servant Cassim in a house on the Friar's Park estate, living there with them much as Mehemet Bey and Kharis live in their unholy alliance in the comfortable house which Peter Cushing's John Banning visits in *The Mummy*. Nahémeh forces Greefe to poison her brother and when Sir Burnham dies, she insists on his heir, Sir Marcus Coverly, being dispatched as well by means of a poison gas fiendishly attached to a telephone. Taking feline delight in the crime, she leaves an image of Bâst on Sir Marcus' body. Ultimately she destroys Greefe as well, who is killed by his own poison.

Movies have frequently presented Bast as a sinister god, which is an over-simplification of how the ancient Egyptians regarded her. Not only does David Manners' Frank Whemple refer to Bast as "the goddess of *evil sendings*" in *The Mummy* (1932) but director Seth Holt makes a statue of Bast look particularly malevolent in the scene in *Blood from the Mummy's Tomb* when the spirit of Tera terrorizes Rosalie Crutchley's Helen Dickerson. These, and other examples one could mention, are further evidence of how Egyptian imagery has been imbued with wholly Western characteristics, in this case the European folklore that equates black cats with bad luck.

H. P. Lovecraft also seems to have anticipated Karloff's Im-ho-tep in his story "The Last Test," written in collaboration with Adolphe de Castro and first published in 1928. A sinister Tibetan called Surama features in this tale, of whom one of the other characters says that "a Pharaoh's mummy, if miraculously brought to life, would form an apt twin for this sardonic skeleton." Surama has "parchment-like skin" and "burning black eyes,"[63] which create a death's-head effect. Jack Pierce's mummy make-up for Karloff does seem reminiscent of this image, though the tale has nothing further to do with Egypt. Lovecraft also collaborated on an Egyptian fantasy with the great escapologist, Harry Houdini, in 1924, and it was far more grotesque than anything in Universal's *The Mummy*, released eight years later. Lovecraft, in fact, ghostwrote the story for Houdini. Entitled either "Imprisoned with the Pharaohs" or "Under the Pyramids," it again exploits the old misconception that the pyramids were originally sinister temples. The story describes how Houdini is hurled into the Temple of the Sphinx and discovers that the "blood-congealing legends" of reanimated composite mummies fashioned by "decadent priests" are true:

> The mummies without souls ... the meeting-place of the wandering ... the hoards of the devil-cursed pharaonic dead of forty centuries ... the composite mummies led through the uttermost onyx voids of King Khephren and the ghoul-queen Nitocris I heard their creaking joints and nitrous wheezing above the dead music and the dead tramping.[64]

The idea that there can be soulless mummies (Imhotep and Kharis clearly are not soulless) had previously been explored by August Strindberg (1849–1912) in his curious chamber play, *A Ghost Sonata* (1907), in which he uses the image of an Egyptian mummy to represent the withered wife of a bankrupt colonel. Strindberg's mummy lives in a cupboard and squawks only inanities such as "Pretty Poll" until she addresses the real villain of the piece, the corrupt usurer, Jacob Hummel, whom she accuses of being a robber of souls:

> You robbed me of mine with your false promises; you murdered the consul they buried today, you strangled him with your notes of hand; and now you have stolen the student's soul for a feined debt of his father, who never owed you a penny."[65]

The prolific novelist and short-story writer E.F. Benson (1867–1940) originally had ambitions to be an archeologist and spent several winters in Egypt on behalf of the Egyptian

Exploration Fund. He was there during the winter of 1895–6, excavating the Temple of Mut at Karnak, clearing earth and working on a scale plan of the temple.[66] According to his biographers, Geoffrey Palmer and Noel Lloyd, Benson's nightmares at this time were dominated by the fear of ancient gods ambushing him from behind the cover of palm trees on the banks of the Nile. Far worse was actually to befall him in Egypt: a very nasty case of typhoid fever and a close shave with a black cobra, which he very nearly trod on in his hotel.[67]

Benson's fascination with Egypt and the occult led to several stories on this theme, the two most well-known being a novel, *The Image in the Sand* (1905), and a story, "Monkeys," from *More Spook Stories* in 1934. The Temple of Mut features in the former, which is set in Luxor and concerns an attempt by Sir Henry Jarvis to contact the spirit of his dead wife. With the help of an occultist called Henderson, who possesses an amulet with occult power, they aim to release the spirit of King Set-nekht and force it to assist them in contacting Sir Henry's wife. Unfortunately, Sir Henry's psychic daughter ends up being possessed by the evil spirit of the Egyptian king and is thereafter terrorized by Henderson. Henderson is eventually dispatched by Sir Henry's faithful servant, Abdul, both of whom are drowned near Greenwich pier; but despite this grisly dénouement, Ida is not released from Set-nekht's spirit.

"Monkeys," written much later, is related to J. Sheridan Le Fanu's tale "Green Tea" (1869) as it concerns the malevolent appearance of a monkey—several, in fact. To begin with, we are not sure if the monkeys are hallucinations or not. The first one appears to an overworked physician, Dr. Hugh Morris, who believes in nothing beyond medical facts. His friend, an Egyptologist called Jack Madden, has rather different ideas, and makes a point of reinterring the mortal remains of any mummies he discovers, not wishing to incur the wrath of their dematerialized owners. One evening, Madden and Morris observe a monkey limping around Morris's garden, and Morris attempts to operate on the unfortunate creature, having discovered that one of its vertebrae has been fractured. Unwilling to risk this tricky operation on a human being, he has no hesitation in the case of the monkey and binds the broken vertebra with wire. It dies, of course, but the experiment is deemed instructive. Unfortunately, the doctor now begins to hallucinate and sees a monkey on the anesthetized body of his next patient. Morris visits a nerve specialist, who insists he take a holiday.

Madden, meanwhile, has returned to Egypt, which gives Benson the opportunity to indulge in descriptions of the country he had grown to know well. Madden then receives a telegram from Morris, explaining that he would like to visit him by way of convalescence. They meet again in Egypt and Morris is present at the excavation of an hitherto-untouched tomb. The mummy they discover is guarded by four stone monkeys. Morris, who previously has had little interest in antiquities, is now fascinated to discover that the spine of the mummy, when revealed, shows evidence of exactly the same operation he performed on the monkey. So intrigued is Morris by this evidence of advanced surgery in ancient times, he snaps off the relevant vertebrae and takes them back to England with him, but, as one would expect, he pays the price for such sacrilege and is visited by a huge ape, which murders him and mutilates his body in exactly the same way that the inscriptions of the tomb of the mummy prophesied. When Madden returns to the tomb and disinters the mummy, he finds that the missing vertebrae have been restored to it.

E. F. Benson was so prolific an author it's sometimes hard to accept that he wrote all his novels himself. He did, of course, but Joan Grant (1907–1989) always claimed that her novels were written by someone — or something — else. As her friend Dennis Wheatley expressed it, "She lay in a trance on a sofa, her spirit away from her body while she spoke slowly of her experiences in the distant past."[68] She also claimed to know nothing about ancient Egypt, despite the considerable amount of detailed information about its cultural practices and religious beliefs in her novels, the most famous of which is *Winged Pharaoh*, published in 1937. Whatever the underlying reality of her creative process, her "Far Memory" novels about life in ancient Egypt have some things in common with her predecessors in the field of Egyptian fiction. Her style of writing often takes the form of elaborate lists, which, when they focus on aesthetics, resemble the decadent/aesthetic approach of Oscar Wilde. Anatole France also employed this listing technique in *Thaïs* when Paphnutius consigns all of Thaïs's belongings to the flames:

> Then, seizing by armfuls the sparkling robes, the purple mantles, the golden sandals, the combs, strigils, mirrors, lamps, theorbos, and lyres, he threw them into the furnace, more costly than the funeral pile of Sardanapalus, whilst, drunken with the rage of destruction, the slaves danced round uttering wild yells amid a shower of sparks and ashes.[69]

Similarly, Grant has Sekeeta, the heroine of *Winged Pharaoh*, list her ivory combs, carved with the seal of the Winged Pharaoh (a symbol demonstrating that she has passed her priestly initiation and graduated as an adept of extrasensory perception). We also read about the jars of salves and unguents, the alabaster flasks of scented oils, her silver hand mirrors with ivory handles, and her cosmetics, etc. On a more esoteric level, this listing technique extends to describing her clothing and adornments, in particular the symbolism of the five-rayed pectoral, its its copper symbolizing the *ba,* the silver the *nam,* the electrum the *za* and the gold the *maat*— all representative, of course, of those subdivisions of the ancient Egyptian soul which one of Dennis Wheatley's characters in *The Ka of Gifford Hilary* confesses to find very confusing, as we have already seen. Grant takes a great deal of time and trouble to explain these metaphysical matters. Sekeeta's father, whom we eventually learn is no less a personage than Pharaoh himself, teaches her about such things before she is sent to the temple to become an initiate in the higher mysteries. Wheatley's racial prejudice is also evident in *Winged Pharaoh*. When Sekeeta describes the people of Zuma (who eventually declare war on her father), she describes them as having hooked noses, with impure skin "not clear-cut like ours, not as though cleanly carved in stone, but as if they were was images that had begun to melt in the sun."[70] The pharaoh's name is Za-Atet, a name which, perhaps unsurprisingly, does not appear in Manetho's lists of royal kings and dynasties. Za-Atep is, unfortunately, killed repelling the enemy, and Seeketa is sent off to the temple to become an initiate whilst her brother remains behind to prepare the way for brother and sister eventually to rule as joint Pharaoh.

Grant's ultimate message is that death brings freedom from the body and is not to be feared. If we learned to embrace death rather than resist it, and looked forward to the life to come, we would, apparently, all be much happier. She provides a parable to this effect concerning a man who sits on a scorching rock at noonday. He sees the shade of trees beside a pool but runs farther into the desert. When he hungers he ignores the platter of food beside him and licks the rock instead. Grant is also keen to point out that the process of dreaming allows us to leave our bodies and influence the lives of others, another idea Wheatley agreed with and included in several of his own occult novels.

During her initiation, Sekeeta learns to read the memory of her past lives, along with such philosophical insights as the idea that time is not a straight line but a circle. Her initiation ordeal has much in common with what we read about in *The Life of Sethos* and, later, in the seventh chapter of Rider Haggard's *Cleopatra* concerning the initiation of the priest Harmarchis. Sekeeta experiences a rather un–Egyptian place of torture in a kind of hell, and then visits the places of records, of weather, of melody, perfume, prayer, teaching and peace before undergoing the seven great ordeals, which include those of earth, air, fire and water, the final ordeal confronting her with a pit of vipers.

On her graduation from the temple she returns to rule Egypt with her brother, and we are given many descriptions of her duties: granting audiences, settling disputes and receiving tributes. There's a scene reminiscent of that moment in Shakespeare's *Henry V* where the king walks abroad before the battle of Agincourt and receives some home-truths from his subjects. The same things happens to Sekeeta when she secretly encounters one of the priests from the temple who has never realized her exalted position. Thinking Sekeeta a servant, he blames the queen for treating her so severely that their meetings must be short and infrequent.

Another war follows, and Sekeeta bears the priest's child, which survives a plague. The child is cared for by Sekeeta's brother, so tenderly that she feels remorse for having been jealous of the woman who gave birth to Pharaoh's child. Compassion and understanding, hence, win the day.

Winged Pharaoh was unexpectedly popular when it first appeared and rapidly went into many editions, inspiring several sequels (though no movies): *Eyes of Horus* told the story of a rebellion against the malevolent god Set by a group of freedom fighters who restore Egypt to the ways of Isis and Osiris. *Lord of the Horizon* continued this story in similar vein. Grant's books don't fit comfortably into the tradition of Egyptian fiction charted so far, as they are more concerned with her own ideas of spiritual truth than with sensational plots centered on magic. They are the literary equivalent to the mystical texts concerning ancient Egypt that were apparently dictated by spiritual forces to H. C. Randall-Stevens or "translated" by Jean Terrasson. Like Randall-Stevens, and, indeed, the likes of Rider Haggard and Bram Stoker, she is quite unconcerned by the anomaly that her belief in reincarnation — the very pivot of her tales — wasn't shared by the ancient Egyptians themselves. Dennis Wheatley was convinced that it was impossible to believe that *Winged Pharaoh* is not true memory "divinely granted."[71] His approach to incorporating Egyptian myth and locale into his own fiction, however, made no such claims.

It might seem eccentric to place Thomas Mann between Joan Grant and Dennis Wheatley, but they were, of course, contemporaries and, more to the point, the third novel in Mann's tetralogy, *Joseph and His Brothers* (1938), was set in Egypt and has much in common with the aesthetics of Egyptomania discussed so far. Mann's conception of a series of novels recounting the Biblical story of Joseph occurred to him in 1923, the year after Howard Carter's sensational discovery, but it was actually the request of the painter Hermann Ebers who triggered the idea when he asked Mann to write the preface to a series of pictures based on the Joseph tale. Mann was also aware of Goethe's remark in *Dichtung und Wahrheit*, that the Bible should have devoted more time to this "highly attractive" story. From that tiny seed would eventually grow the 1207 pages (in the English-language edition) of his massive mythical opus, the overall approach of which has much in common with Wagner's four-part music-drama, *Der Ring des Nibelungen*. Germany, of course, had its own Egyptomania. The famous statue of Nefertiti is only the most famous artifact in the Egyptian Collection of the Berlin Museum. Germany also has its own illustrious Egyptologists, including Georg Ebers, whose novel *Eine ägyptische Königstochter* we have already encountered. Another Egyptian novel, *Kleopatra*, appeared in 1894, five years after Rider Haggard's *Cleopatra*. Both works helped popularize the subject of Egyptology in 19th-century Germany, but Ebers was also more scholarly in his approach to the subject, his complete works extending to 25 volumes. He also discovered the celebrated Ebers Papyrus, one of the two oldest medical documents in the world.

Neither did German music and cinema escape from Egyptomania. As we shall see in the next chapter, two of Richard Strauss's stage works, *Josephslegende* (1914) and *Die ägyptische Helna* (1928), contain Egyptian elements; and, as we have already seen, Ernst Lubitsch's *Eyes of the Mummy* was one of the first films to explore the subject. Mann's descriptions of Egypt are also remarkably cinematic in his emphasis of visual details. He, too, cannot resist contemplating the sphinx at Giza, which "had lain there so long that no man could say when and how it had come out of the rock — drifts of sand slanted up to its breast and hid one of the paws. The other paw, still free, was the size of three houses." He describes the "inscrutable head, with the stiff neckcloth, the immortal brow, the eroded nose which gave it a somewhat roguish air, the rocky vault of its upper lip, the wide mouth which seemed to be shaping a sort of calm and primitive and sensual smile. The clear, wide-open, intelligent eyes, intoxicated from deep draughts of time, gazed eastwards as they had ever done."[72]

In the mighty prelude to his four-part literary cycle Mann aimed to take the reader back to the dawn of time. Just as Wagner depicted the creation of the world in the Prelude to *Das Rheingold*, Mann wonders if it was Set himself who built the mighty sphinx:

"From the days of Set"; the people of Egypt had many uses for the phrase, for with them the origins of everything went back in undemonstrable ways into that darkness.[73]

The words "older," "earlier" and "again," he says, are the leitmotifs of Egypt herself, a land so steeped in a past of "profound, mythical and theological character."[74]

Bruce's harpers also make their presence felt in a scene describing dancing girls: "Harp players knelt, with their faces turned heavenwards, sang and played, while behind them other singers clapped out the time, during the offering of the incense."[75] But it is really in his description of pharaonic palaces that Mann competes with later Hollywood spectaculars. These palaces have

papyrus and lotus colonnades, gold-tipped obelisks, colossal statues, turreted gates with sphinx avenues leading to them from the bank. Their doors and flag-poles were gilded, and light flashed from them that dazzled the eyes, till the painted scenes and inscriptions on the buildings, the cinnamon red, the plum-colour, the emerald green, the ochre yellow, and the azure blue all swam together into one confused sea of colour.[76]

Inhabiting a very different literary world, Dennis Wheatley nonetheless published his own Egyptian fantasy, *The Quest of Julian Day*, the year after *Joseph in Egypt*. It begins with the hero, Julian Day, seeking revenge on those who destroyed his career in the Diplomatic Service. This eventually leads him to the quest of the book's title: a search for fabulous buried treasure lost to the world for over 2,000 years. He encounters a present-day Egyptian princess, spends the night in the Tomb of the Sacred Bulls in Alexandria, gets involved with drug smuggling in Cairo's City of the Dead, and has later to fight for his life while trapped in a pharaoh's tomb in the Valley of the Kings. As usual, Wheatley provides his readers with far more historical information than is strictly necessary for such a thriller. Chapter 15, for example ("The Ancient Valley"), provides a two-page potted history of Egyptian dynasties, and follows this up with an account of the Akhnaten story, followed by a visit to his tomb ("hardly worth a visit,"[77] according to Day, who complains about the poor state of the wall paintings). In chapter 18 ("The Green-Eyed Monster") Wheatley takes us to Hatshepsut's temple at Deir el Bahari and provides us with another thoroughly researched account of history before embarking on an excursion to the Valley of the Nobles "which is in some ways more interesting than the Valley of the Kings."[78] These tombs, fortunately, impress Wheatley's hero rather more than did those of Akhnaten's.

Unlike Sax Rohmer, Wheatley describes the ancient Egyptians as a "cultured, kindly people, much like ourselves."[79] However, the climax of the Egyptian adventure is kept for chapter 20 ("Buried Alive") in which Day is trapped in the oval tomb-chamber of Thothmes III, having been "coshed" by the servant of his jealous lover, Oonas. In the silent darkness of the place he understandably suffers a panic attack, letting out a scream of terror that reverberates around the place; but reason eventually triumphs and, again, Wheatley inverts the habitual demonic associations other writers might previously have not been able to resist. Day realizes that the silence is natural, and the tomb is "just an empty room with attractive decorations on its walls."[80] Even so, he prays to Thothmes and asks for forgiveness just to be on the safe side. He does, however, encounter several bats. After a cigarette, he sings songs to himself to keep his spirits up (the rather incongruous "Flat-Foot Floogy" and "Mademoiselle from Armentières").[81] He also decides to write a denunciation of Oonas on the back of an old bill he finds in his pocket. He then turns somersaults, munches fruit-drops, chews tobacco, and smokes more cigarettes to fill the time, after which he falls asleep, only to awaken in the pitch black surrounding him, hoping against hope that Oonas will return to remove what Day hopes she will assume to be his dead body. He will then frighten his enemies by making them think he is a ghost, and hope that in their panic they will leave the gates at the entrance of the tomb unlocked. Everything works out exactly as planned — but that's the advantage of fiction over real life.

Also in the 1930s (1935, to be precise), the American writer Mary Butts published her idiosyncratic *Scenes from the Life of Cleopatra*. She regards her heroine very much from a contemporary (1930s) perspective, even quoting the lyrics of "Tea for Two" at one point and asking the reader to imagine an ancient Egyptian equivalent, but the novel takes on an extra layer of resonance when one remembers that Butts and her husband, the modernist poet and publisher John Rodker, had attended magical "ceremonies" at Aleister Crowley's Abbey of Cefalù in Sicily (in fact, despite its awesome name, a distinctly shabby and even more insanitary single-story edifice). Crowley was dismissive of both the wife and the husband. Of Rodker's poetry, Crowley sniped that it was no more than "incoherent ramblings, strung together and chopped at irregular intervals into lines."[82] Even worse, he referred to Mary Butts contemptuously as a "red-haired maggot"[83] and accused them of merely "playing at Magick."[84] Rodker was, however, well-versed in the history of the occult, and commissioned, among other works, Montague Summers' magisterial English translation from the Latin of the *Malleus Malleficarum,* along with A. E. Ashwin's translations of Nicolas Remy's

Demonolatry and Francesco Maria Guazzo's *Compendium Maleficarum*. Whatever practices she and her husband indulged in at the Abbey of the Great Beast, Butts's fascination with the occult can certainly be traced in passages such as these from her Cleopatra novel:

> In isolation, in antiquity, with ceremonies reckoned by the moon; in privacy, in stillness, at a hidden shrine; before a God, secret to the priests, whose name was a secret from them — was evoked the destruction of her [Cleopatra's] house.
> With ceremonies like those of exorcism, ridding and avoidance, with stench for incense and super-valerian burned, with invocation to the God on hither side of his nature, and evocation of him in a shape of horror, ran the prayers.[85]

Perhaps Butts learnt of such occult ceremonies in Sicily. Certainly such dubious activities were suspected by the locals, Crowley's unsavory reputation eventually reaching the ears of Mussolini, no less, who eventually evicted him in 1923.

During the World War II, Egyptian fantasy became firmly identified with the kind of mummy movies that were being made by Universal Studios in Hollywood. No one bothered to make a film adaptation of Thomas Mann's epic, nor Wheatley's rather faster-paced adventure. Hollywood preferred to exploit ancient Egypt in rather cruder ways, presenting mummies as mindless automata. Whatever the merits of these films, there was no doubt that Egyptian fantasy was by then primarily a cinematic phenomenon; but this wasn't the end of the line for Egyptian fiction as a whole. Indeed, the experiences of the war, the horrors of Naziism and the general sense of *Weltschmerz* all made themselves felt in Mika Waltari's most famous novel, *The Egyptian*, published to great acclaim in 1949. It was turned into the rather underrated 1954 film co-starring Edmund Purdom in the title role. Set during the reign of Akhnaten, it tells the story of Sinuhe, the physician, "He Who Is Alone." During his early life as a novice in the temple an event occurs that profoundly shakes him. Arbaces in Bulwer's *The Last Days of Pompeii* had exposed the trickeries of religion as a necessary evil. So, too, in *The Egyptian*, Sinuhe discovers that a priest has pretended to be the voice of the god Ammon in order to punish one of Sinuhe's misdemeanors, Sinuhe recognizes the voice and is profoundly disillusioned. Shocked and horrified, he loses his faith.

Waltari then describes Sinuhe's adventures with the Babylonian courtesan, Nefer-nefernefer, who seduces him with her charms to give her not only his own property and wealth but also that of his parents. "Do you know why Bast, the goddess of love, is portrayed as a cat?" she asks, adding that a woman are also like cats with sharp claws beneath their velvet paws.

Destitute, Sinuhe then works in a mortuary as a corpse-washer. His fellow workers squabble over which one is to have sex with the female corpses, as living women are not available to such untouchable men. Sinuhe buries his dishonored parents in a pharaoh's tomb in the Valley of the Kings. Jackals cry out in the night as Sinuhe discovers a red scarab jewel, reminiscent of Queen Tera's ruby scarab but without its magical properties. Having said that, it does seem to bring Sinuhe and his comical servant, Kaptah, good luck. Even more grotesque is the stranger Sinuhe then encounters, a man with no nose or ears, reminiscent of Lon Chaney's Erik, in *The Phantom of the Opera*. These early scenes are really about as close to the Gothic strand in Egyptian fantasy that Waltari is prepared to travel, his interest being historical rather than macabre, though as in all the best historical fiction, he is keen to use the genre to comment on his own time, and its mood of weariness and pessimism spawned by the World War II.

Waltari presents Akhnaten as a well-meaning despot, whose determination to overthrow the god Ammon in favor of the peace-loving Aten provokes an uprising. Pharaoh is booed in public. "Hatred dropped poison into his love, and his fanaticism grew."[86] He is presented as a peace-loving aesthete who is so lucent in his own clarity that he does not comprehend the darkness of others. Akhnaten refuses to have anything to do with the uncomprehending people of Thebes and founds his own city with its own temples dedicated to the new god. As with so many who aim to achieve utopia, Akhnaten ends up creating the opposite. Sinuhe, who has by now become Pharaoh's brain surgeon, wants to believe that Akhnaten is right but recognizes the dangers of such aloof idealism. Waltari's description of the Pharaoh's obsession with architecture has ominous parallels with Hitler's similar preoccupations. "He constantly vexed his architects and master builders with drawings and explanations though they understood their business better than he."[87] Like an Egyptian Albert Speer, Sinuhe confesses his love for the Pharaoh, even though Pharaoh is mad, because his madness is more beautiful than the wisdom of other men.

But the real parallel with the barbarism of Naziism occurs when Egypt is forced into war with the Hittites, a people whose name has obvious similarities to that of Hitler, and whose leader, King Suppiluliuma (who never appears in the novel), is an embodiment of tyranny and violence. Here the peaceful idealism of Akhnaten seems to suggest the misguided appeasement policies that led to the Second World War. It takes the courage and realism of Ahknaten's chief commander, Horemheb (a kind of Egyptian Winston Churchill), to save Egypt from itself and its enemies by encouraging Akhnaten to take direct military action. Waltari's description of the eventual hubris of the Hittites, which turns the tide of Egypt's fortunes, can also be read as a kind of ancient Egyptian Stalingrad:

> Had the Hittites been more circumspect, had they envisaged a possible reverse, they might yet have saved one half of their chariots and inflicted a heavy defeat on the Egyptians. They might have wheeled and returned through the breeched barricades, but they could not understand that it was they who were defeated, being unaccustomed to that condition.[88]

Though the character of Sinuhe is actually an anachronism, dating from a period long before that of Akhnaten, many of the other characters are exactly who one would expect. We read of Pharoah Amenhotep and his cunning wife, Taia. Taia claims that she and Amenhotep's High Priest Eie invented the god Aton in order to depose Ammon, and thus increase the power of her son, Akhnaten; but she had no expectation of the way events would unfold. We also encounter Akhnaten's wife, Nefertiti, along with the languid Tutankhamen, who succeeded Akhnaten and, ironically, became the most famous Egyptian ruler of all.

Ancient Egypt, of course, continued to inspire many authors in the latter half of the 20th century, but none quite so successfully recaptured the spirit of the classic Victorian and Edwardian stories (alongside the imaginings of Universal and Hammer films) as Anne Rice in her only attempt in this genre. *The Mummy* (1989) perhaps took its cue from the character of Adam Beauchamp in Hammer's *The Curse of the Mummy's Tomb*. Handsome and witty (Jeanne Roland's Annette Dubois finds him amusing, at least), Beauchamp, like Ramses the Damned, is immortal and almost as well preserved. Both are presented as human beings rather than bandaged automatons. Ramses the Great is a beautiful, blue-eyed, sexually voracious, ravenous, highly intelligent and generally sympathetic character who also happens to be immortal. An elixir of life flows in his veins. It has turned his eyes vivid blue and is the cause of his eternally libidinous energies. He need never sleep. He rapidly absorbs information. He is endlessly curious about Edwardian life. Once exposed to the sun's rays he comes back to life, intent not on avenging the desecration of his tomb but, rather, the Egyptologist who discovered his mummy, for this Egyptologist has been murdered by a dissolute, gambling and inebriated nephew for financial gain. The mummy witnessed the crime and the first thing he does when he comes fully to life in the Egyptologist's library in Edwardian London is attempt to strangle the nephew. He fails, but later in the book the nephew is, appropriately, murdered and mummified by a gang of black-market forgers. Before that happens, Ramses can't stop himself from reviving a mummy's hand by means of his elixir of life. This comes horribly back to life like Queen Tera's severed hand in *Blood from the Mummy's Tomb* (to say nothing of Thing in *The Addams Family*) before Ramses manages to cut it into little pieces and hurl it into the sea. He then, much more catastrophically, revives the damaged mummy of Cleopatra herself, with whom he had been in love centuries before. Resurrected (only in part, to begin with) and mentally deranged, Cleopatra sets off on a murder spree, snapping the necks of handsome young men like breadsticks. This is rather hard to square with Rice's simultaneous aim to clean up Cleopatra's image by claiming that there was much more to her than the sex symbol familiar to millions today. Rice eventually kills off the unfortunate queen when the car in which she is traveling collides with an express train; but, of course, it is not the end of her at all. Like Ramses, Cleopatra is immortal. Nothing can destroy her, a fact which Rice seemed intent on pursuing, as the novel ends with the words "THE ADVENTURES OF RAMSES THE DAMNED SHALL CONTINUE." Sadly, to date, they haven't.

Rice's presentation of the resurrected Ramses as a witty and intelligent character is derived from Poe's portrayal of Alemistakeo in "Some Words with a Mummy," but if one were to single out one paragraph from this hugely entertaining tribute to two centuries of Egyptian fantasy, it would have to be what Rice has to say about the allure of Egypt itself towards the end of the novel. Elliot, Lord Rutherford, the charming, now arthritic past lover of the Egyptologist who discovered Ramses, explains that the attraction of ancient Egypt is that it transports us away from the boredom and hopelessness of everyday life. It is precisely the mystery that is the attraction. Whereas a genuine archeologist is concerned with the facts of the matter, the writers of Egyptian fantasy are inspired by quite the opposite, and despite the immense amount of understanding we now have of ancient Egyptian life and beliefs there's still plenty of room for supposition and mystery.

Seven

Music

A major element in all movies — but particularly the fantasy and historical epic — is, of course, their musical scores; but long before the cinema was invented, composers were experimenting in ways that anticipated the style and requirements of film music. Similarly, the subject matter of opera and ballet often had much in common with that favored by later film studios. The genres pertinent to this book grew out of a musical past as much as from the world of 19th-century fiction and visual art. In the case of opera and ballet those three disciplines naturally combined, and, as we shall see, much that came to characterize "Egyptian" music was based on just as many misunderstandings as the stories and stage settings of such entertainments. The "Egyptian" music provided for European Orientalist entertainments owes little to genuine ethnic musical traditions, instead relying for its effect on a lexicon of Orientalist musical clichés that have been applied to many different kinds of exotic locations: India, China, Arabia, Egypt: it actually makes very little difference, musically speaking, for the musical signifiers of the "exotic" were largely interchangeable. As Derek B. Scott has pointed out, the Bacchanal in Saint-Saëns' opera *Samson et Dalila* (1877), an opera set in Bablyon, was originally called "Marche turque."[1]

What all Orientalist composers were looking for was a way of signifying the cultural differences of "the other." They weren't interested in being ethno-musicologically correct, but looked instead for musical symbols that were alien to (but able to be incorporated into) traditional Western style. Orientalism in music began in the 18th-century with a style of music that became known as "Turkish." This was because it apparently imitated the musical style of Turkish military bands which the Viennese heard during the siege of their city in 1683. In fact, few people heard this music at all, and the "Turkish" sound was based on vague memories, hearsay and a strong dose of European imagination. Orientalism, in fact, was the creation of Europeans who felt the need, for various political, moral and psychological reasons, to identify and "contain" what was alien to their own culture and, therefore, in various ways posed a threat to them. It was just the same reasoning that created the literary (and later cinematic) Egyptian fantasy. Like the novels and stories discussed in the last two chapters, musical Orientalism reached its expressive peak at the turn of the 19th-century, after which its vocabulary went, basically unchanged, into the film score. The only "exotic" style Mozart could draw upon was the "Turkish" style, which he did to great effect in his opera *Die Entführung aus dem Serail* (*The Abduction from the Seraglio,* 1782). The famous "Rondo alla Turca" that concludes Mozart's Piano Sonata in A major, K331, is another well-known example. Significantly, this rondo is in a minor key, another of the ways in which the exotic is often characterized. Other characteristics of "Turkish" style are march time, a regular, tramping rhythm, and jarring *acciaccaturas* (i.e., decorative notes that have no time value themselves, usually lying a semitone or tone above the melody note. These are played almost simultaneously with it to create a dissonant effect). Played on the piano all this sounded novel enough at the time to qualify for being categorized as being "exotic," but when orchestrated with plenty of percussion effects it sounded even more so. Therefore, one might expect to find such "Turkish" music in Mozart's "Egyptian" opera, *Die Zauberflöte* (1791), but it is noticeable by its absence. This wasn't because it was "Turkish" rather than "Egyptian," for, as Edward Said has explained, Orientalism makes no real distinctions between the two. Perhaps the underlying Masonic seriousness of the opera dissuaded Mozart from employing such superficial "effects," but even so, there is much in the text and settings of this work that is of significance to what followed, as we shall see.

Die Zauberflöte, which from now on I'll be referring to as *The Magic Flute*, is technically what the Germans call a *Singspiel*, or singing play, as there are also lengthy sections of purely spoken dialogue. *Singspiel* was a popular form of entertainment in its day, and it's significant that the premiere of *The Magic Flute* took place in a popular theater in the outskirts of Vienna, which was frequented by ordinary people rather than aristocrats and courtiers. Its audience was, indeed, more like that of a modern cinema audience, and with its spectacular stage effects, exotic scenery and often pantomimic action *The Magic Flute* has all the ingredients of a popular movie — a kind of 18th-century *Indiana Jones* film in some ways. The various trials undergone by the characters might also be compared with the experiences endured by the cast of the 1999 remake of *The Mummy*. Of course, *The Magic Flute* had its extremely serious side as well, but there were also plenty of laughs, slapstick and variety along the way. What's more, it was all in German, which made it much more appealing to Mozart's original German-speaking audience of ordinary people. Mozart longed to escape from the courtly confines of *opera seria* with its Italian libretti and worthy classical subject matter, for he was, at heart, a populist. His classical musical style, however, was nowhere near as influential on subsequent Egyptian film fantasy as the work of later Romantic composers. The latter exploited a much more "exotic" vocabulary of musical effects that was appropriated by and was far more appropriate to the popular Romanticism of commercial films with an Egyptian theme. However, the text of *The Magic Flute* was indeed influential on this later development, not least because of the Egyptian set designs it inspired.

Mozart's opera tells how the hero, Tamino, attains spiritual enlightenment under the guidance of the High Priest, Sarastro (whom some commentators have suggested was based on Cagliostro). The Queen of the Night, whom we at first are led to believe is a force for good, tells Tamino that her daughter, Pamina, has been abducted by Sarastro. She charges Tamino with the task of rescuing Pamina, and presents him with a magic flute to help him. To his companion, Papageno, she presents a set of magic bells and together they set off to find Sarastro's temple. We later learn that the Queen of the Night is quite the opposite of a good character and that Sarastro is the opposite of evil. Tamino and Pamina then undergo the trials that will initiate them into Sarastro's magical Masonic circle of enlightenment, and Papageno also finds his own true love in Papagena, who has been disguised up till then as an old woman. The Queen of the Night is vanquished by the rays of light and wisdom that emanate from Sarastro, and everything ends in happiness, love and understanding.

Among the various sources for this Masonic Egyptian opera (Mozart and his librettist

Emmanuel Schikaneder (1751–1812) were both Freemasons themselves) was, as we've seen, Terrasson's *The Life of Sethos*. There are various notable parallels between Schikaneder's libretto and Terrasson's novel, and throughout the second act of the opera the stage directions call for Egyptian decorations. The act opens in a palm grove in which there are 18 seats, and standing on each seat is a pyramid. In the subsequent transformation we are shown a temple described as bring "in the Egyptian style." Later, the priests carry small lamps in the shape of pyramids. Schikaneder's stage directions went on to inspire the magnificent designs of the architect Karl Friedrich Schinkel for a Berlin production in 1813. Though we don't know exactly what the first production looked like, the first edition of the score also included an engraving with vaguely Egyptian designs and Masonic symbols by Ignaz Alberti. *The Magic Flute* was, or course, composed before ancient Egypt was anywhere near as well understood, let alone discovered, as it became in the 19th century, so the imagery used here is rather more eclectic But if we look to Terrasson's *Life of Sethos*, we find many examples of Egyptian decor that would no doubt have informed what Schikaneder (who obviously knew the book) had in mind for the first production. The priests with their pyramidal lanterns in *The Magic Flute*, for example, would seem to have been inspired by this passage from Terrasson's novel:

> While this and the like hymns were repeating, the priests (in robes of linen, with chaplets of lotus on their heads, and sandals of the plant papyrus on their feet) were continually offering sacrifices on three triangular altars placed before the triple statue.[2]

The libretto's frequent references to Isis and Osiris, and the various temples we are shown also derive from passage in *Sethos*, such as this one:

> In the middle of the sanctuary, upon a very high pedestal, and all on one single piece of cast metal, were placed these three deities, in such sort, that Osiris, whose image was the highest, held Isis standing before him, and she Horus in the same manner: For what Strabo says of the temples of Egypt being without statues, or at most having only the figure of some animal in the middle of them, is not to be understood of the times antecedent to the invasion of Cambyses. The head of Osiris was encircled with a radiant sun. Isis was crowned with a bushel, and had her face covered with a veil. Under her left arm she held an urn bowed downwards, and at her feet lay the bird Ibis. And Horus was described holding his finger upon his lips.[3]

It is also revealing to compare what Mozart's High Priest, Sarastro, has to say in his hymn "O Isis und Osiris" in Act II, with a similar prayer in Terrasson's *Life of Sethos*. Sarastro asks the gods to protect Tamino and Pamina as they undergo their initiation trials. He sings (in my translation of the original German text):

> O Isis and Osiris, hear us;
> Give wisdom to this pair.
> Lead their path away from temptations,
> Give them patience in times of danger.
> Let them be victorious in their trial,
> But if they fail and Death should claim them
> Take them to your abode.[4]

Here is Lepsius's translation of a similar invocation to Isis in *The Life of Sethos*:

> Isis, great goddess of the Egyptians, pour down thy spirit upon thy new votary, who has gone thro' so many perils and laborious trials to come before thee: Make him victorious also over his

Opposite: Title page of the first edition of *The Magic Flute*, 1791. Engraving by Ignaz Alberti.

passions, by rendering him tractable to thy laws, that he may be worthy to be admitted to thy mysteries.[5]

The initiation trials endured by Sethos in the novel, and Tamino, in *The Magic Flute*, also have much in common. Once inside the temple, Sethos reads an inscription engraved in black letters on white marble:

> *Whoever goes thro' this passage alone, and without looking behind him, shall be purified by fire, by water, and by air; and if he can vanquish the fears of death, he shall return from the bowels of the earth, he shall see light again, and he shall be entitled to the privilege of preparing his mind for the revelation of the mysteries of the great goddess Isis.*[6]

In *The Magic Flute*, Tamino encounters three men in armor who say much the same thing:

> He who walks this path full of troubles will be purified through fire, water, air and earth; if he can overcome the terror of death he will soar heavenwards from the earth. He will then be enlightened and dedicate himself the mysteries of Isis.[7]

Perhaps the three armed men of *The Magic Flute* were Schikaneder's version of the Anubis-headed priests encountered by Sethos in this passage from the novel:

> One of these three men said to the candidate; We are not posted here to stop your passage: Go on, if the gods have given you the courage: but if you be so unfortunate as to return, we shall then stop your passage: As yet you may go back, but from this moment you'll never get out of this place, unless you go on, without turning or looking back.[8]

The trials of earth, fire and water endured by Tamino also have their origin in *Sethos*. Early in the novel, Sethos enters a subterranean chamber beneath a pyramid and must pass over a grate of red-hot iron. Then, he must cross a canal of Nile water that is fed by a waterfall, and finally work out how to cross a chasm by means of two gigantic wheels that operate a drawbridge — this latter is a particular test of courage, even though no actual harm can come to him. Schikaneder's stage directions for scene 28 in Act II of *The Magic Flute* are surely indebted to the imagery in *Sethos*:

> Two high mountains. From one mountain, the rushing and roaring of a waterfall may be heard; the other spits out fire. Through a grill in each mountain, the fire and water can be seen — where the fire burns the horizon should be red as hell, while a thick mist lies on the water. There are rocks all over the stage, which is divided into two separate parts, each enclosed within an iron grate. Tamino is lightly clothed, without sandals. Two men in black armour accompany Tamino; on their helmets, flames burn. They read him the inscription, illuminated from within, on a pyramid high up in the centre, above the grills.[9]

The number three is of great importance to the story. It is reflected in the three-fold chord Mozart employs throughout, along with the key signature of E-flat (comprising three flats) in which the overture is composed. The solemnity of the music for the priests certainly creates the appropriate atmosphere for a Masonic rite, but, unlike the "Turkish" music we find in *The Abduction from the Seraglio*, there is no comparable "Egyptian" music in *The Magic Flute*. Such local color had to wait, in musical terms, until the 19th century when Romanticism broke free from the classical style that predominated in the 18th century and composers began to experiment with different forms of national music. Having said that, *The Magic Flute* remains the foundation stone of all the Egyptian operas, ballets and concert music that followed.

The next significant ancient Egyptian moment in opera (but, again, rather more because of the set designs than the actual music) took place twenty-seven years after *The Magic Flute*, when Rossini's *Mosè in Egitto* (*Moses in Egypt*) was premiered in 1818 at the San Carlo Opera House in Naples. This venue might seem rather more formal than the popular vaudeville theater in Vienna which hosted the premiere of *The Magic Flute*; but fully to understand the comparisons between 19th-century Italian opera and popular film, we have to appreciate that, for Italians at this period, going to the opera house was very much like going to the cinema in the first half of the 20th century. Nearly every Italian town had its own opera house, big or small, just as most towns in the 1940s in Britain and America had their own cinemas. Audiences went every week regardless of what was on, though the demand was always for something exciting if not too avant-garde. In the Italy of Rossini's time, there literally wasn't anywhere else to go for amusement. Operas were funded by rich noblemen or impresarios who fulfilled the same kind of role as a film producer. The music, like a film score, had to be written very quickly to a libretto chosen for the composer and not the other way round, and opera singers acted much as spoiled film stars behave today. The famous castrati, Luigi Marchesi (1754–1829), for example, refused to sing unless he was able to make his entrance either on horseback or from the top of a hill, with six-foot-tall white feathers decorating his helmet.[10]

The 19th-century Italian opera audiences were far less well behaved than they are today. Other than at premieres, people invariably listened only to certain arias, ignoring much of the rest of the opera while playing cards, eating and drinking, or paying visits to other people in the auditorium. The opera house was also a casino, social club and restaurant (aspects that still cluster around multiplex cinemas today).

Rossini's musical style, though rather different from Mozart's, similarly made no concessions to "exotic" elements. The famous prayer, accompanied by "archaic" harp arpeggios, is about as far as he was willing to go down this road, not that the road really existed at that time, despite the "Turkish" elements exploited by Mozart. The set designs, however, were a different matter, but they were not without their problems at the premiere. The French writer Stendhal (1783–1842) was present at this momentous occasion, but he set out with little enthusiasm for a Biblical opera, complaining, "Whenever I think of the Plagues of Egypt and of Pharaoh, and of the way in which *it came to pass, that at* midnight, *the Lord smote all those that dwelt in the Land of Egypt (Exodus, xii, v. 29)* my memories race back relentlessly to those twelve or fifteen *priests* amongst whom I spent my childhood in the time of the Terror."[11] He continued:

> Thus it came about that I found myself at the *San-Carlo* in no very propitious frame of mind, feeling rather like a man who has been offered a front seat at an *auto-da-fé*....
> The opera opens with the so-called *Plague of Darkness*, a plague which offers any number of facile pitfalls to the unwary dramatic producer, and consequently lends itself to absurdity — all you have to do is to dim the footlights and the overhead battens![12]

However, Rossini's music swept away all of Stendhal's skepticism. Stendhal actually compares it to that of "Haydn at his most sublime."[13] In other words, it has absolutely nothing "Egyptian" about it. Neither were the costume designs what we would think of as typically Egyptian. Moses's costume was modeled on Michelangelo's statue of the same in the church of *San Pietro in Vincoli* in Rome. Having said that, the famously "authentic" costume worn by Charlton Heston in DeMille's *The Ten Commandments* was, in fact, arrived at by accident rather than design.

The subsequent Plague of Fire in Rossini's opera was "a somewhat damp-looking display of fireworks," according to Stendhal, and the "Plague of Heaven-knows-what-else, was received with enthusiasm."[14] So we should never forget that our current obsession with cinematic special effects is nothing new, even though the technology available to achieve them has changed radically. Neither should we be so critical of Hollywood interpolating fiction into its attempts at being historically accurate, for exactly the same kind of thing occurred in *Mosè*. The librettist added a completely fictional love story between Pharaoh and the daughter of Moses' brother, which made a compelling theatrical situation but had no basis whatsoever in the Biblical source.

But perhaps the most striking parallel between Rossini's opera and *The Ten Commandments*, its cinematic offspring, is that both productions included representations of the parting of the Red Sea. DeMille's cinematic version was certainly spectacular; Rossini's was less so. In fact, it was a fiasco. Stendhal explains why:

> Owing to the relative positions of the stage and the auditorium, no theatre is equipped to show the sea except on a back-cloth; but in this instance, it was absolutely essential to produce a sea, by hook or by crook, on the actual front-stage, since the narrative demanded that it should be *crossed!* The stage-technician of the *San-Carlo,* desperately intent upon finding a solution to an insoluble problem, had finished up by producing a real masterpiece of absurdity. Seen from the pit, the "sea" rose up into the air some five or six feet above its retaining "shores"; whereas the occupants of the boxes, who were favoured with a bird's-eye view of the "raging billows," also had a birds-eye view of the little *lazzaroni* whose job it was to "divide the waters" at the sound of Moses' voice! In Paris, no one would have cared a jot; but in Naples, where the *décor* is as often as not a masterpiece of art and skill, there is a certain sensitiveness towards the achievements or failures of this particular aspect of the production.[15]

It was to deflect attention away from this scenic absurdity that Rossini's librettist came up with the idea of introducing it with a Prayer for the Jews, who sing it before their miraculous crossing. Like a film composer altering his score if necessary during the final recording session, Rossini apparently wrote the inspired melody for this Prayer, the most famous part of *Mosè*, in under ten minutes, having been summoned out of bed to do so.[16]

The next composer to advance the Orientalist "Egyptian" cause in music was Hector Berlioz (1803–1869), who, though he admired Rossini, nonetheless criticized his musical style. This criticism admirably sums up the emerging difference between the older, classical style and the newer Romantic one, which would increasingly aim to emphasize local color, orchestral effects and ever greater "realism." The remark occurs in an essay in which Berlioz compares the thunderstorm section in the fourth movement of Beethoven's sixth symphony with the storm music in Rossini's last opera, *William Tell.* Neither of these pieces have anything to do with Egypt, of course, but Berlioz's argument here does have a great deal to do with the change in musical aesthetic that would eventually help make music *sound* Egyptian:

> Unfortunately, the musician is always in evidence; we never lose sight of him in his combinations, even in those which seem the most eccentric. Beethoven on the other hand has known how to reveal himself wholly to the attentive listener: it is no longer an orchestra that one hears, it is no longer music, but rather the tumultuous voice of the heavenly torrents blended with the uproar of the earthly ones, with the furious claps of thunder, with the crashing of uprooted trees, with the gusts of an exterminating wind.[17]

In other words, Beethoven had led the way to create more "realistic," less formulaic music, music which would far more convincingly imitate the sound of a storm (and, from our point of view, would eventually create a more "Egyptian" or "exotic" musical style). Berlioz himself, however, did not travel quite so far in that direction, as his comments above might suggest. There's nothing "Egyptian" about his cantata, *La Mort de Cléopâtre* (1827) other than the subject, but he does attempt to be far more psychologically disturbing than his predecessors — a characteristic that did him no favors when he submitted it, in his attempt to win the coveted Prix de Rome. He failed. When he met one of the judges, he asked why — after all, he had done his best. "That," the judge replied, "is exactly what we have against you. You should not have done your best." What the judge wanted was "soothing" music, but as Berlioz was quick to point out in his amusing account of the affair in his memoirs, it is difficult to write soothing music for a Egyptian queen who is dying in an agony of remorse.[18]

Colorful and Romantic though the work is (with its somber tam-tams and musical evocations of the queen's dying breaths), there are still no concessions to Orientalism in the musical style. However, Berlioz did begin to suggest such effects in the "The Flight into Egypt" from his cantata *L'Enfance du Christ* (1854), and this leads us to the next element in the development of musical Orientalism. This was, in fact, the style of Hungarian gypsy music, which was not, contrary to received opinion, derived from genuine Hungarian folk music. (Franz Liszt confused the two in his hugely influential Hungarian Rhapsodies, and got into trouble for it.) Instead, it was the product of a more cosmopolitan, and, by the 19th-century, commercialized gypsy music that had originally emerged from the Middle East. It is characterized by a particular scale which lies at the heart of all 19th-century (and cinematic) musical Orientalism, no matter what particular country or region is being referred to. Its principal characteristic is the presence of a sharpened fourth in the context of a minor scale. A minor scale flattens the third note of the scale and sharpens the seventh note. This can already sound exotic, but if the fourth note of the scale is also sharpened, a kind of musical shorthand for the "exotic" is created. Its alien quality suggests either fascinating allure or dangerous strangeness — sometimes both, of course. As the West's fascination with (but simultaneous misunderstanding of) the East grew, so too did composers begin to use these musical intervals to help create a musical "other." Of course, the musical cultures of the East weren't the point here. What composers were doing was creating a musical portrait of the East in terms of Western culture. In a sense they were emasculating it, claiming it, and therefore neutralizing it — turning it into a consumable commodity, much as one might decorate a 19th-century Parisian flat with imitation Oriental nicknacks.

Paris rapidly became the world capital of "orientalism," and Egyptiana flourished there. The list of Orientalist, "exotic" operas composed in 19th century Paris is a long one. It includes *Le Roi de Lahore* (1877), *Hérodiade* (1881), *Thaïs* (1894), and *Cléopâtre* (1914), all by Jules Massenet (1842–1912); *L'Africaine* (1864) by Giacomo Meyerbeer (1791–1864); *Lakmé* (1883) by Léo Delibes (1836–1891); *Les Pêcheurs du perles* (1863) and even *Carmen* (1875) both by Georges Bizet (1838–1875). These operas were variously set in India, Africa, ancient Ceylon and 19th-century Spain, but were all using similar techniques to evoke a fantasy of exotic culture. It was a fantasy neatly and constrictively contained in a Western frame that was gilded with sharpened fourths in minor scales. There was "exotic" instrumentation, such as the "archaic" timbres of flutes (indeed, woodwind combinations in general), of harps and of "primitive" percussion. There were also "exotic" (because "novel") timbres, such as the celesta. (Much later the vibraphone and electronic instruments would extend the possibilities of musical Orientalism even further, particularly in the arena of film music). But it is important to stress that all these elements functioned within the parameters of Western harmony and traditional orchestral techniques. As such, it's useful to cling onto Derek B. Scott's observation that the purpose of Orientalism "is not to imitate but to represent."[19]

Other ways of representing the exotic East came when Parisian musicians heard the whole-tone scales of Indonesian musicians at the Paris Exposition in 1889. Liszt had experimented with whole-tone scales some years before in his musical recitation, *Der traurige Mönch*, dating from 1860. Though not intended to be Oriental in their implication in that piece, Liszt's whole-tone scales here were nonetheless used for their "alien," unsettling quality, accompanying, as they do, a supernatural story about a ghostly monk in a storm-blasted tower in Sweden. So the whole-tone scale was already identified as a signifier of "the other." All that was needed to make it "Oriental" was an Eastern setting. In his novel, *The Piano Players*, Anthony Burgess has a silent film pianist explain some of the tricks of the trade to his son. The whole-tone scale is one of them. It made "a kind of South Sea island tune, and you could play any or all of the six notes at the same time and make a nice weird chord of them."[20] Whole-tone scales were also imported into Western music via the Russian musical exoticism of nationalist composers such as Nikolai Rimsky-Korsakov (1844–1908) who sought more exotic musical colorings to reflect not only Russia's continual expansion into Eastern territories, but also in response to the fashion for the exotic that was to lead to the sensational ballets organized by Sergei Diaghilev (1872–1929) at the turn of the century.

The pentatonic scale also became increasingly Orientalized in the 19th century, principally due to its "primitive" connotations already well established through its use in European folk music. The pentatonic scale can sound "English folksy," "Chinese," "Indonesian," even "Egyptian" if necessary. What made it significant was its "difference" from the established diatonic scales of mainstream Western classicism. A similar aesthetic was at work in the Golden Age of Hollywood, which always equated whole-tone and pentatonic scales with the danger of "the other." A classic, Gothic example of this sort of thing occurs in *House of Dracula* (dir. Erle C. Kenton, 1945), in which the composer Edgar Fairchild "infects" Beethoven's "Moonlight" Sonata with such alien tonalities to suggest the hypnotic influence of John Carradine's Count Dracula on a piano-playing victim. Hollywood also associated electronic (and therefore unsettling because non-traditional) instruments with psychological disturbance. Miklós Rózsa's theremin-colored scores for *The Red House* (dir. Delmer Daves, 1947) and *The Lost Weekend* (dir. Billy Wilder, 1945) operate in this manner. Alternatively, electronic timbres suggest the threat of alien invaders from other worlds (such as Bernard Herrmann's score for *The Day the Earth Stood Still* [dir. Robert Wise, 1951]).

But we are leaping ahead in terms of the history of musical Egyptiana, the harmonic and coloristic excesses of which did not reach their peak until the early years of the 20th century. Amid the plethora of Orientalist operas in the latter half of the 19th century, specifically Egyptian settings were relatively rare until the 1890s. The most celebrated of all is surely Verdi's *Aida* of 1871, based on a scenario by the French Egyptologist Auguste Mariette (though his authorship has been disputed by Mary Jane Phillips-Matz, in her biography of Verdi). Mariette certainly designed the costumes, props and sets for the premiere, which very appropriately took place in Cairo on (perhaps less appropriately) Christmas Eve. Charles

L. Kenney's English translation of Antonio Ghislanzoni's *Aida* libretto, issued by Verdi's publishers, Ricordi, includes an introductory passage that explains how Mariette took every care to have the piece "as true to history as scholarly research could achieve,"[22] a phrase which anticipates the hyperbole of a Hollywood press book. Indeed, Hammer Films went to similar trouble to suggest the "authenticity" of their first mummy feature.

The story of *Aida* is standard fare for grand opera and could happily be transposed to any other period or setting. Radames loves the slave girl Aida, but is himself loved by the daughter of Pharaoh. Radames goes off to war and captures Aida's father. Pharaoh gives his daughter to Radames, who (along with Aida) chokes back his tears. Aida's father asks her to extract secret information from Radames, who then gives himself up and is buried alive with Aida. There's nothing new in the concept of falling in love with the wrong person, but the Egyptian context here surely anticipates the illicit love of Conan Doyle's unfortunate Egyptian immortal in "The Ring of Thoth," along with Rider Haggard's priest in *Cleopatra*, both of whom were inspired by Radames's example. We can also trace the live burial of Imho-tep in Karloff's *The Mummy* back to *Aida*'s final grisly scene, via Rider Haggard suggestion that Harmarchis was buried alive at the beginning of *Cleopatra*. In more general cinematic terms, Verdi also invented the concept of the "split-screen," having suggested that the tomb in which Radames and Aida are imprisoned should be shown below the priests, who walk nonchalantly over the temple floor as the lovers die.

If any opera has exploited (and inspired) Egyptomania it is surely *Aida*, productions of which are now advertised (and performed) in the grandest of grand manners, using every theatrical equivalent of Hollywood widescreen magnificence. Each production vies with the other for the most supernumeraries, the most lavish costumes and the biggest processions. It's no surprise that *Aida* is a repertoire piece at the amphitheater at Verona. Verdi, of course, wanted as much spectacle as possible but he also aimed for intimacy and subtlety of characterization. As far as the Orientalism of the music goes, he also demonstrated a significant advance on his predecessors in the ancient Egyptian field, though the score is neither consistently "Egyptian" nor in any way "authentic." Whereas Verdi had made no attempt to portray the Jews in *Nabucco* with any especially Orientalist musical inflections, he did feel the need to characterize his ancient Egyptians in *Aida* with a musical style to represent how different they were from modern Europeans. Of course, the Jews in *Nabucco* were Italians in all but name, as demonstrated in the famous moment when they sing about their captivity in that opera, which became a clarion call for Italian independence. There was no need to characterize them as "the other" in this case. The whole point was that the Jews stood for something that was quite the opposite of "the other." But Verdi's music for the Temple Scene in *Aida* provided an exotic, alluring yet also somewhat unnerving musical symbol of difference, which set the standard for all future musical Orientalisms, and ultimately found its way into later scores for mummy movies. The key element here is the "Egyptian" flattened second note of the E-flat minor scale he employs. Though Verdi uses an E-flat major key signature for this scene, the flattened notes in the melody take us into that traditionally "exotic" world of minor tonality. When he flattens the Fs (the second note of the scale) the Orientalist effect is as immediate as instant soup when hot water is added. All Verdi needed to do to create "instant Egypt" is keep repeating this phrase throughout the scene, accompanied as it is with "archaic" harps, strumming equally "primitive" open fifths. Such music would, of course, be just as at home in an operatic Hindu temple (in fact, a similar approach was taken by Don Banks in his score for Hammer's *The Reptile*, which is set in a Cornish village that's overshadowed by a sinister Oriental cult), but the setting and words sung by the priests help locate the musical gesture in the correct geographical location:

> *A mysterious light from above. A long row of columns, one behind the other vanishing into the distance. Statues of various Deities. In the middle of the stage, above a platform covered with carpets, rises the altar, surmounted with sacred emblems. From golden tripods rise the fumes of incense.*
>
> *RAMPHIS stands at the foot of the altar, surrounded by Priests. The singing of the Priestesses to the sound of the harp is heard from within.*
>
> *Priestesses (within).*
>
> Hail mighty Phtha! that wakes
> In all things breathing life,
> Lo! we invoke thee![23]

Anne Rice found it irresistible to have the heroine of her novel *The Mummy* play a 78rpm recording of *Aida* to the freshly revived, impossibly good-looking mummy of Ramses. Later in the story, she even sends a gathering of other characters to the English Opera House in Cairo to witness a live performance of Verdi's masterpiece.

Victor Massé's operatic adaptation of Gautier's Cleopatra story appeared in 1885 and after that, *fin de siècle* Egyptomania with increasingly Orientalist musical gestures became ever more fashionable. Massenet brought the Egypt of Anatole France's novel, *Thaïs* to the stage in 1894, but this was not an ancient Egyptian opera, the action being set during the period of Byzantine rule. *Thaïs* features a repressed priest, Athanaël (Paphnutius in the original story) who secretly lusts after an Alexandrian courtesan (the Thaïs of the title). He persuades her to convert to Christianity but still can't stop his lustful thoughts. Eventually, Thaïs dies and Athanaël despairs. The exotic setting inspired some Orientalist orchestral music from Massenet, but is mostly remembered today for the very Western "Meditation," which went on to have a separate concert life of its own. It has nothing "Egyptian" about it.

A couple of years later, in 1896, Camille Saint-Saëns, who had already scored a massive Orientalist hit with *Samson et Dalila* in 1877, composed his fifth piano concerto. Begun at Luxor and completed near Cairo during a holiday, it includes a Nubian love song, which the composer said he had heard being sung on his boat as it floated down the Nile. He also tried to imitate the sound of frogs croaking and Nile crickets chirping on the river bank, as well as the sound of a ships' propelor as he set off for other exotic destinations. The fifth concerto soon became known as "Egyptian," though, true to Romantic orientalist principles, it also includes Spanish and Javanese elements.

It was, however, the first years of the 20th century leading up to the World War I when Orientalist Egyptian music reached its peak. The story of Antony and Cleopatra, not least thanks to its representation in Shakespeare's play, has inspired around 70 operas, most of them fairly obscure to contemporary audiences. As was the case with so many 19th-century artists, Massenet was attracted to the subject for the erotic possibilities it offered. His *Cléopâtre* was composed towards the end of his life in 1900 (though not performed until 1914, two years after his death). Timpani beating an ostinato pounded out with "primitive" persistence, Orientalist melodies on wind instruments, and a chorus "ah-ing" in proto–Hollywood fashion provide all the credentials for a late-19th-century Egyptian fantasy, which broke no new ground and demonstrated how Massenet, in the words of the Concise Oxford Dictionary of Opera, continued "to repeat his musical clichés in his later works"[24]—

not that there's really anything wrong with clichés, film music in particular being dependent upon them. The work's most sensationally beautiful moment is Cléopâtre's aria, "J'ai versele poison," in which the despairing Egyptian queen tries to convince her slaves to test poisons for her, assuring them that those who die will be kissed by the Goddess of Egypt. It is the most marvelously seductive combination of eroticism and tenderness, tyranny, sadism and death. Sensuous harps and shimmering strings support the languorous melody here, fully providing the musical counterpart of the French 19th-century paintings that show Cléopâtre engaged in this murderous activity in a variety of different poses.

The history of "Egyptian" music in the 20th century began with a ballet, *Un Nuit d'É-gypte* (*Egyptian Nights*) (1900), by Anton Arensky (1861–1906), which is now more often heard in the orchestral suite version which Arensky made from the full score. Originally written to entertain the Shah of Persia on a visit to St. Petersburg, that performance was canceled because no one had any faith in the music or the libretto. The latter was once again based on Gautier's "One of Cleopatra's Nights." The most Orientalist movement of the suite is known by the title, "Charmeuse des Serpents," and is pretty much the kind of music one would expect from a work written around this time with the title of *Egyptian Nights*. Typically, Arensky arranged this brief (only just over a minute) Orientalist exercise for a sinuous oboe, later joined by a flute, both exploiting the requisite exotic scales. Rather less exotic dances in mainstream late–Romantic, Russian, and even salon style, alternate with more exotic material: a dance for Jews, a dance for warriors, a *pas de deux* (inevitably a waltz), and music for the solemn entrance of Antony. Rimsky-Korsakov, Arensky's teacher, commented rather caustically: "In his youth Arensky had not escaped entirely my own influence; later he fell under that of Tchaikovsky. He will be soon forgotten"[25] — unfair (and untrue) but it is true that Arensky is more often remembered as Rachmaninov's harmony teacher than for his many undemanding though always attractive works.

Nonetheless, *Egyptian Nights* attracted sufficient interest from the choreographer, Mikhail Fokine (1880–1942), who used it as a vehicle for the great Anna Pavlova (1881–1931). Diaghilev saw this production in 1908, and was intrigued by its possibilities, but thought the music too weak to succeed in Paris. After having second thoughts, he conceived the idea of supplementing Arensky's score with music by other composers, and called the whole thing *Cléopâtre*. In this respect, Diaghilev was following basically the same approach as early "silent" films, which were similarly accompanied by means of compiled scores, raided and assembled (often in fairly arbitrary ways) to fit the picture. Diaghilev assured Fokine that the existing choreography could stay the same as music would be chosen to fit it — not that the music Diaghilev had in mind was "Egyptian" even in the vaguest Orientalist manner. For example, he planned to substitute Arensky's overture with the overture from Sergei Taneyev's opera based on the *Oresteia*. Other interpolations included Rimsky-Korsakov's music for Pan in the opera *Mlada*. Glinka's *Ruslan and Ludmila* and Glazunov's ballet *The Seasons* were also interpolated. Even part of Mussorgsky's opera *Khovanshchina* was requisitioned for the resulting mélange. As Diaghilev historian Richard Buckle points out, Diaghilev was unhappy about Arensky's original happy ending (the hunter of Gautier's original tale, now called Amoun, dies after being poisoned by Cleopatra but was then brought back to life by the embrace of his true love[26]). Diaghilev therefore approached Nicolas Tcherepnine (1899–1977), the composer who had provided the music for a previous Diaghilev hit, *Le Pavillon d'Armide*. Leon Bakst (1866–1924) was commissioned to design new scenery depicting immense stone gods flanking the stage, at the back of which a colonnade of somewhat phallic columns revealed the banks of the Nile, illuminated by a purple sky. Diaghilev's other principal set designer, Alexandre Benois (1870–1960), was also responsible for a dramatic touch that anticipated the entrance of so many latter-day movie mummies. He suggested that Cléopâtre should be wrapped in bandages and placed in a mummy case which would then be lifted from a huge sarcophagus before being unwrapped to reveal the queen resplendent in blue wig, gold and glittering jewels. Diaghilev was supremely confident that *Cléopâtre* would be a tremendous success when it opened in Paris in 1909, and it was more than a success — it was a sensation, starring, as it did, four of the greatest ballet dancers of its time: Pavlova, Nijinsky, Karsavina and Fokine himself. Indeed, the exoticism of the work, mainly due to Bakst's intensely colorful sets (emphasizing reds and pinks) and his exotic costume designs, inaugurated the subsequent exotic (and erotic) Orientalist reputation of the Ballets Russes. The combination of color, sex, the erotic convulsions of death, and the barbaric sophistication of tyranny proved irresistible to audiences everywhere, and it is significant to note that these ingredients were precisely the same as those that brought international success to Hammer Films in their heyday in the late 1950s and '60s.

Egyptian art also influenced the choreography of the Ballets Russes. Nijinsky, who rapidly developed into a choreographer as well as the company's leading male star, was fascinated by the hieratic style of ancient Egyptian representations of the human figure. In his choreography for Claude Debussy's *L'Après midi d'un faun* in 1912, Nijinsky insisted that the dancers similarly keep their faces in profile with their bodies facing stage front. Admittedly, this style was designed to suggest the figures on ancient Greek vases, in keeping with the Greek setting of the piece, but the effect simultaneously evoked an "Egyptian" manner in keeping with *Cléopâtre* before it and, indeed, the architectural style of the theater in which *Faune* received its scandalous premiere. Designed by the architect Auguste Perret (1874–1954), the Théâtre des Champs-Élysée was constructed between 1911 and 1913 in an equally scandalous modern style, which eschewed historicist eclecticism in favor of geometric lines, minimal decoration and white reinforced concrete. The starkly sophisticated impact of the façade's three rectangular bays, like so much later modernist architectural design, have much in common with the similarly stark rectangularity of Queen Hatshepsut's temple at Deir al-Bahari. Thanks to these various cultural concatenations, the *style Égyptienne*, once all the rage in Napoleonic France, become highly fashionable again, and continued to be so after the World War I with the Tutankhamen-inspired designs of art nouveau in the 1920s and '30s.

Also in 1912, though not for Diaghilev, Debussy (1862–1918) composed the music for an ancient Egyptian ballet commissioned from him by the notorious Canadian born dancer Maud Allan (1873–1956). She was, in the words of Philip Hoare, a "stage icon of Edwardian sexuality, a siren who exemplified the escapism of the age"[27] and had become famous thanks to her exotic interpretation of Salome in a ballet of her own devising called *The Vision of Salome*, with music by the Belgian composer Marcel Rémy. (Salomania, thanks to the earlier example of Oscar Wilde, vied in popularity with Egyptiomania around this time.) Allan carefully made sure that her Parisian debut in this role in 1907 coincided with a performance there of Richard Strauss's opera on the same subject. The following year she brought the production to London and her impact on audiences there was immortalized by a critic writing for the *Labour Leader*, from whom Hoare quotes in his engaging study of her overall appeal:

> One moment she is the vampire ... next she is the lynx. Always the fascination is animal-like and carnal.... Her slender and lissom body writhes in an ecstasy of fear, quivers at the exquisite touch of pain, laughs and sighs, shrinks and vaults, as swayed by passion.... She kisses the head and frenzy comes upon her. She is no longer human.[28]

Aleister Crowley was an avid fan of Allan's particular art and he commemorated her in his poetry, but the dancer's decadent notoriety unfortunately alerted the guardians of moral rectitude. In 1918 she became involved with a famous libel trial against the British right-wing politician Noel Pemberton Billing (1881–1948), who published an article entitled "The Cult of the Clitoris" in his own news-sheet, *The Vigilante,* accusing Allan of being a lesbian and German spy. A virtual rerun of Oscar Wilde's libel trial against the Marquis of Queensbury in 1895, Allan lost the case after it became embroiled in sexual revelations of a dangerously compromising nature.

Before all that, however, in 1911, Allan had approached Debussy to compose the music for an Egyptian project she had in mind. The story of this originated from an old Egyptian legend that had been translated by Gaston Maspero as "La fille du prince de Bakhtan et l'esprit possesseur" in his *Contes populaires de l'Égypte ancienne* (1882). This tale had originally been discovered by Champollion in the Temple of Khonsu at Thebes, and has something in common with the *deus ex machina* dénouement of Karloff's *The Mummy*, in that the statue of the god Khibsu, god of destiny, nods its head when a princess is successfully exorcised of an evil spirit. Similarly, though for rather different reasons, we have seen how the statue of Isis at the end of *The Mummy* lowers its hand and slays Im-ho-tep with an avenging mystical blast from its ankh. Such an event does have its basis in fact, as statues in ancient Egyptian temples often had moveable limbs, manipulated by the priests, for the purposes of impressing their worshippers.[29] The libretto for what was originally to have been called *Isis* before ending up as *Khamma,* was worked out by to great effect by William Leonard Courtney, a former Oxford academic and subsequent journalist for *The Daily Telegraph*.[30] The story is simple. The enemy has besieged an Egyptian city. In the Temple the enormous black stone statue of the god Amun-Ra is illuminated by the light of the setting sun. The High Priest stands before the statue and worshippers submit their offerings to it. The High Priest then raises his arms in supplication to the god for deliverance, after which Khamma appears and expresses her fear at the situation. By the light of the moon (it's interesting that the stage directions do indeed include that most Debussy-ian phrase, "*clair de lune*") she approaches the statue and performs the first of her three big solo dances before it. The statue raises its arms and in an ecstasy of devotion, Khamma basically dances herself to death (as, indeed, the "chosen one" of Stravinsky's *Sacre du Printemps*, premiered the following year, would also do). By the rosy light of dawn, the doors of the temple open once more and the Grand Priest blesses Khamma's lifeless body.

Debussy thought the whole thing absurd and "childishly simple"[31] but persevered, mainly because of the much-needed cash it offered (20,000 francs, in fact). Like later composers for film, scoring a ballet was one of the most lucrative options open to a composer at that time, but Debussy's relations with Allan became increasingly fraught, the dancer behaving rather like an insensitive film producer with no understanding of how music is composed, still less of Debussy's personal sensibilities; but he never allowed this to interfere with the quality of his music, even though he entrusted the orchestration to his colleague, Charles Koechlin (1867–1950). Ultimately, however, due to the Billing trial and a catalog of alterations and disagreements between dancer and composer, the premiere of *Khamma* took place in a concert performance in 1924 without either Allan or Debussy being involved. Debussy had been dead for six years by that time and Allan had lost interest. Gènevieve Kergrist performed the title role on that occasion. The only person present who had been there from the start was Koechlin. ("We didn't chat," Koechlin recalled of his visits to Debussy in 1913; "we concentrated on my orchestration, which he was happy with, although he warned me that it might be rather difficult to perform."[32])

Traditional Orientalisms, such as the "gypsy" or snake-charmer scale, are kept at a safe distance in this score, though the Orientalist instrumentation and harmonic effect of Debussy's characteristic use of whole-tone scales is certainly in evidence. Unrelated triads and bitonality (playing two keys simultaneously) also make their exotic effect, but the ending is a masterly example of understatement. After the ecstatic music of triumph, a simple theme (*"dans le caractére d'une lamentation"*) accompanies the High Priest's blessing of Khamma's corpse, and trumpets (playing their unrelated triads) sound in the distance before two *ppp* staccato notes bring the piece to a pathetic—almost bathetic end. Debussy was fully aware of the unnerving effect his music would have. He himself was fascinated by the Gothic atmosphere of Edgar Allan Poe (having spent many years on an unfinished operatic adaptation of "The Fall of the House of Usher"), and the music of *Khamma* was intended to cause a *frisson* of fear not so far removed from the intention of later mummy movies. "When will you come and hear the new version of my curious ballet," he wrote to his publisher, "—with its trumpet calls which suggest the revolt and the fire and which send a shiver down your back?"[33]

Debussy made one more foray into the world of ancient Egypt in a work originally written to accompany a recitation of his friend, Pierre Louÿs's *Chansons de Bilitis*. He then arranged these pieces for piano duet, and later for solo piano. Graced with some of the most poetic titles to be found in any collection of piano music, *Six épigraphs antiques* (1914) contains a piece entitled "Pour l'Égyptienne." For this exercise in Orientalism, Debussy does indeed echo past triumphs in the genre, filtered, of course, through his own rather more rarified aesthetic sensibility: we have "primitive" open fifths in the accompaniment, and a sinuous melody exploiting those magical Orientalist intervals.

Meanwhile, back in England, despite the immense literary activity in the field, there was slightly less stirring in the musical tomb of Egyptian fantasy. Gilbert and Sullivan may have tinkered with ancient Japan in *The Mikado* (1885) but they left ancient Egypt alone, and before Elisabeth Lutyens (1906–1983) wrote her *Isis and Osiris* opera in 1969 the most Egyptian offering by an Edwardian composer was provided by Benoit Hollander (1853–1942), the teacher of Hammer Films' resident musical supervisor, Philip Martell (1906–1993). Among his many other compositional projects, Hollander took it upon himself to set Bulwer-Lytton's *The Last Days of Pompeii* to music in 1907. A physician by the name of George H. R. Dabbs adapted Bulwer's text to create the libretto of a "Vocal and Symphonic Poem in Four Parts." Composed, rather prosaically, in Streatham Common, London, the third scene of *Pompeii*, concerning Arbaces, is the most "Egyptian" one, and it opens with a recitative line introduction reminiscent of the Act II prelude in Wagner's *Lohengrin*. This is a suitable model for the Egyptian magician, Arbaçes, as Wagner's Act II prelude is a musical evocation of the sorceress Ortrud. Hollander uses no Orientalisms, however, the musical language echoing middle-period Wagner with its diminished sevenths, tremolos, dramatic dotted rhythms and recitative-style vocal line that attempt to illuminate Dr. Dabbs's somewhat turgid text:

> Stars that look down on us from worlds afar. Priests of the night's deep temple where the Dawn as a young neophyte escapes earth as a tired child returneth where the sun cradled in awful glory leaves the world. And night resumes her dark supremacy. Stars of the night. Ye ghostly ministers that weave the web of human Destiny and move the threads that form the woof of Time — grant Arbaces riches that increase, success in love, success in hate, success in war and peace. Put back Death's shade and from the dial move the shadows back that comes between the sea of life and him.[34]

Granville Bantock (1868–1946), another English Wagnerian who was once more popular in Edwardian England than his contemporary, Sir Edward Elgar (1857–1934), was a master of musical Orientalism, setting the whole of the *Rub'iyat* of Omar Khyyám for choir and orchestra along with incidental music for Wilde's *Salomé*. Ancient Egypt attracted him less, though among his offerings in this field were a ballet, *Aegypt,* from 1892, incidental music to a play about Rameses II, a setting of a poem by his wife, Helena Schweitzer, entitled "Lament of Isis" in 1910, and a choral work from late in his life called *The Sphinx* (1941), all of which are interesting as evidence of a trend far more active in France than in England.

In 1913, another once-fashionable Edwardian composer, Cyril Scott (1879–1970), brought out his piano collection, simply but effectively entitled *Egypt.* It was dedicated to the singer, theosophist and architectural designer, Marie Russak (1865–1945), "That enlightened Seer, who brought back for me the memory of my past Egyptian lives," as Scott put it. As this dedication implies, Scott was also an enthusiastic occultist. He was also harmonically adventurous, anticipating some of the developments of Alexander Scriabin (1872–1915) in Russia and Debussy in France, though no doubt also influenced by them in turn. Rather misleadingly dubbed "the English Debussy" by critics (a term that says rather more about the traditional British lack of self-confidence when it comes to experimental music), Scott's approach is rather more robust than his admiring French counterpart, who nonetheless provided Scott with a glowing testimonial. The Egyptian suite contains five numbers. The first, "In the Temple of Memphis," begins with the expected "primitive" open fifths which we also encounter in the *Indian Love Lyrics* (1902) that were composed by the rather more conventional (though equally Orientalist) Amy Woodforde-Finden (1860–1919). Scott takes these fifths very slowly ("Adagio mysterioso") and decorates them with what the then-contemporary critic, A. Eaglefield Hull, identified as being "suggestive of double flutes," while "the whole-tone steps impart an indefinable weirdness."[35] The second piece also opens with a tranquil whole tone passage, and Eaglefield Hull pinpoints that key aspect of Orientalist aesthetic here (the irrelevance of locale), by suggesting that the third piece, "By the Waters of the Nile," looks "as though it were closely related to the 'Chinese chopsticks' figures" of Scott's first piano concerto, the "lower harmony here adding a strong quality of Eastern mysticism."[36] The fourth movement, "Egyptian Boat Song," has a "slow languidity full of lotus-land charm." (It is a kind of Orientalized Chopin nocturne.) "The music is wonderfully vivid," Eaglefield Hull adds, "mirages of distant mosques with a luminous haze, rise before the eyes."[37] The "Funeral March of Great Raamses," with its key-change and "emphatic, trumpet-like passage reminds us that this is one of the great among the *kings* of the earth,"³⁸ whilst the final piece "Song of the Spirits of the Nile," apparently dumbfounded him. It begins, in fact, as a study in sixths, such as Scriabin explored, though, unlike Scott, without specific mystical intention. Significantly, the whole collection was published in Germany by Schott, rather than in England (one suspects his English publisher, Elkin, found the whole thing rather too experimental and exotic).

Far less well known than Scott and Bantock, and perhaps even Hollander (who is, after all mentioned on more than one occasion by Bernard Shaw in his music criticism) is the composer Paul Litta (1871–1931), who was born in Stockholm of an Italian father and Swedish mother. Inspired by Shakespeare, his lyric scena, *La morte di Cleopatra*, was published in 1914. If Hollander's *Pompeii* was inspired by *Lohengrin*, Litta's work looks to the rather more advanced harmonic language of Wagner's *Tristan und Isolde*. Utterly forgotten today, this short piece nonetheless provides us with another glimpse of the pervasive Egyptiana of this period — a period that was soon to implode under the weight of its own opulence with the coming of World War I.

No musical work more eloquently demonstrates the mood of overbearing extravagance and apocalyptic self-indulgence — the mood, indeed, of "*après moi, le dèluge*"—than Richard Strauss' ballet for the Ballets Russes, *Die Josephslegende*. This was based on the Biblical story of Joseph and the amorous wife of Potiphar, an ancient Egyptian captain of the guard to whom Joseph was sold as a slave:

> And it came to pass after these things, that his master's wife cast her eyes upon Joseph; and she said, Lie with me. But he refused; and said unto his master's wife, Behold, my master woteth not what *is* with me in the house, and he hath committed all that he hath to my hand: *There* is none greater in this house than I; neither hath he kept back any thing from me but thee, because thou *art* his wife: how then can I do this great wickedness, and sin against God? And it came to pass, as she spake to Joseph day by day, that he hearkened not unto her, to lie by her, *or* to be with her. And it came to pass, about this time, that *Joseph* went into the house to do his business; and *there was* none of the men of the house there within, And she caught him by his garment, saying, Lie with me: and he left his garment in her hand, and fled, and got him out.³⁹

Outraged and humiliated by the "goodly" and "well-favoured" Joseph's repeated refusal to pleasure her, Potiphar's wife informs her husband that Joseph has tried to rape her, and Joseph is imprisoned. This ancient story with eternal relevance inspired Strauss (1864–1949) to compose one of his most sumptuous (and least-regarded) scores. It brought to life the libretto of Hugo von Hofmannsthal (1874–1929) and accompanied the extravagant *décors* of Bakst and José Maria Sert, who decided not to set the ballet in Egypt but, perversely, in Venice. "Too scrupulous an accuracy," Sert insisted, "can but impede the freedom of the imagination."⁴⁰ This might seem to disqualify the work from our overview of Egyptiana, but the extravagance of the affair (and the original Egyptian setting of the story) link it to the overall aesthetic of the ancient Egyptian Hollywood epic. Sert's costumes were inspired by the example of the Venetian Renaissance artist Paolo Veronese (Strauss had called himself "the Tintoretto of music"⁴¹), while the set was of truly epic proportions, consisting of gold walls and a series of immense green and gold Solomonic columns, twisting in alternating directions and creating a sense of tension and magnitude fully matched by Strauss's gargantuan music. The artist Charles Ricketts, no stranger to extravagance himself, was overwhelmed by the somewhat ludicrous extravagance of the experience when the production came to London in June:

At a gesture from Potiphar a burning cauldron is brought on to the stage, Joseph wrapped in chains, and irons heated.

Then the music becomes vulgar beyond belief, a light breaks upon Joseph, the chains fall off, and a golden archangel passes across the upper stage, descends and leads Joseph off to the Savoy Hotel — I believe — to a sort of parody of Wagnerian apotheosis music of the worst type.

If the Russians had not been the inspired interpreters of the thing, it would have been intolerable and fatuous. Karsavina as Potiphar's wife was superb. A creature of gold and marble from the start.... When she strangled herself with her pearl necklace, the act was spontaneous and spasmodic like a moth meeting a flame.[42]

In her study of the world before World War II, Barbara Tuchman used *Die Josephslegende* as the symbol of a civilization about to collapse under the weight of its own political pride, self-indulgence and opulence, its repressed sexual energies and accumulated neuroses exploding in the cataclysm of August 1914. After the war, which broke out only three months after the premiere of Strauss's ballet, such extravagance was distinctly out of fashion amongst the intellectual artists of the period, but Diaghilev's prewar aesthetic didn't die out entirely; it merely shifted into the arena of popular culture. Whilst the Ballets Russes plunged into the world of Dada and neo-classicism, the silent movies took up the Egyptiana that had been abandoned by opera, and silent movie stars such as Theda Bara (1885–1955) donned the Egyptian head-dresses discarded by the dancers. Bara performed the title role in the 1917 film of *Cleopatra,* in which she appeared in even more revealing costumes than Diaghilev's ballerinas. She was billed as the first exotic sex symbol. (She also specialized in playing vampires, a predilection which gave birth to the term "vamp.") The Fox studio publicity machine, which dubbed her "the Serpent of the Nile," claimed she had been born in Egypt, passing her formative years under the shadow of the Sphinx. In fact, she had been born far more prosaically in Ohio. *Cleopatra* is now, sadly, (save for a brief fragment) lost, though several tantalizingly exotic stills of Bara survive to demonstrate the considerable amount she had in common with the rather more high-falutin' dancers of the Ballets Russes.

Musically speaking, Egyptian Orientalism also went out of fashion in the world of so-called "classical" music, though we should not forget two superb late flowerings of the genre in the music of Florent Schmitt (1870–1958), who provided sumptuous and often terrifying music for André Gide's adaptation of Shakespeare's *Antony and Cleopatra*. Schmitt later arranged in the form of two orchestral suites in 1919/20. *Antoine et Cléopâtre* would also have made the ideal score for the later film of *Cleopatra* with Elizabeth Taylor in the title role. The third and fourth movements ("Nuit au palais de la reine" ["Night in the palace of the queen"] and "Orgies et danses") convey exactly the mood of decadent, airless, perfumed opulence and terror required. Significantly, Schmitt later scored a film version of Flaubert's novel *Salammbô* in 1925. His earlier ballet, *La Tragédie de Salomé* (1913), had been performed by Karsarvina herself as part of Diaghilev's 1913 season, during which it had been entirely overshadowed by the famous riot caused by Stravinsky's *Rite of Spring*, but the fact that Schmitt had worked for both Diaghilev and the movies usefully helps cement the close connection between the two art forms.

Egypt continued to inspire composers outside the realm of the cinema, though such works were far more sporadic. Ottorino Respighi (1879–1936) is famous for his *Pines* and *Fountains of Rome* (the former blending the sound-effect of a nightingale with his orchestral magic in much the same way that a film soundtrack would). The first of the four movements of his *Vertrate di chiesa* or *Church Windows* orchestral suite (1925), described the "Flight

"Age cannot wither...." Elizabeth Taylor as the most beautiful woman in the world in *Cleopatra* (dir. Joseph L. Mankiewicz, 1963).

into Egypt" of Mary and Joseph with the infant Christ. This was the same subject that had inspired Berlioz, back in the 1850s, to begin an Orientalist musical tradition that was now really in its last gasp in the concert halls and opera houses of Europe, but which would one day burst out with renewed vigor from the soundtracks of movies. Simultaneous with that development, however, were those immensely successful programmatic concert pieces by the Birmingham-born Albert Ketèlbey (1875–1959). Straddling the genres of film score, palm court teatime music, Lisztian symphonic poem and popular song, these expertly orchestrated examples of musical kitsch were often modeled along Orientalist lines with highly evocative titles such as *In a Persian Market* (1920) and *In the Mystic Land of Egypt*, which appeared in 1931, only one year before Universal's *The Mummy*.

Later 20th-century operas based on ancient Egypt have returned to Mozart's approach, rejecting the intervening Orientalisms of 19th-century music, these being considered either too old-fashioned or just too politically incorrect. Having said that, Samuel Barber's 1966 opera based on Shakespeare's *Antony and Cleopatra* did make one or two nods in the old direction. Cleopatra's aria "Give me my robe" for example, has a tramping accompaniment played by the harp that is a distant echo of the similarly tramping bases we so often find in the exotic Edwardian songs of Amy Woodforde-Finden. There is also a dash of exotica in the little dance that Cleopatra's slaves dance for her in "Give Me Some Music," but Barber, tonal and late–Romantic though he is, gives us neither the full-on orchestral sumptuousness of Florent Schmitt nor the unashamed Orientalisms of Saint-Saëns. Antony and Cleopatra's interchange beginning "I am sick and sullen" might well have applied to the infamously disastrous premiere of the work, which was overwhelmed by director Franco Zeffirelli's baroque extravaganza of a production at the New York Metropolitan Opera House. This wasn't helped by the fact that the stage machinery broke down, the lighting cues were mixed up, the audience could hear desperate stage-hands shouting "Look out for the sphinx" from backstage, and the prima donna of the evening, Leontyne Price, was trapped inside a pyramid (perhaps not as terrible a fate as having to wear the costume in which Zeffirelli imprisoned her). "The bodice is Elizabethan," Zeffirelli explained, "the lines around the neck are more Oriental, and the headdress is modeled on the Egyptian. She will look like one of the greatest widows in the world, like a giant praying mantis."[43] Barber never quite recovered from the ghastly fiasco.

Ancient Egypt also caused problems for one of England's leading composers, though one with a rather different style to the late–Romantic Samuel Barber. Elisabeth Lutyens was an advocate of Schoenberg's serial technique at a time when such avant-garde procedures were frowned on by the British musical establishment of the 1940s and '50s. She was consequently sidelined on the concert platform, though later found enthusiastic disciples in the 1960s among younger composers such as Malcolm Williamson and Richard Rodney Bennett. Even so, she remained somewhat in the wilderness, which was why she wrote film music (for Hammer and Amicus horror films in particular) in order to make ends meet. She never scored a mummy movie, which is a shame, though she did write a full length opera on the legend of *Isis and Osiris*, the troubled production history of which led to its being dubbed *Crisis and Osiris* by all involved in its premiere. This took place at Morley College, London, in 1976, six years after the score's completion. The beauties of Lutyens' modern music for this ancient myth were the diametric opposite of the Orientalisms of the "Egyptian" movie scores that were contemporary with it. Lutyens' music was lost on the critics of this unfortunate production, which had misguidedly taken the decision to take a naturalistic approach with "Egyptian" costumes, though on a tiny budget. (Meirion and Susie Harries report that Seth's mane was "a bush of plumber's hemp, normally used to lag pipes."[44]) Critics complained that the pace was "so funereal as to make *Parsifal* seem like an operatic steeple chase," and compared the production to "a tomb painting brought to life but only just."[45] The music itself is actually much simpler in harmonic style than was often the case with Lutyens' advanced approach and, in order to create a mythic quality, she also employed repetitive phrases, just, indeed, as Sibelius had employed ostinati in his very different but no less mythic tone poems, and as would Philip Glass (born 1937) in his minimalist approach to the story of Akhnaten in 1984.

As was the case with *Isis and Osiris,* Philip Glass partly based his text for *Akhnaten* on passages from the Book of the Dead, the first words of the opera, recited against reiterated arpeggios in the orchestra.

> Open are the double doors of the horizon
> Unlocked are its bolts
> Clouds darken the sky
> The stars rain down
> The constellations stagger
> The bones of the hell hounds tremble
> The porters are silent
> When they see this king
> Dawning as a soul.

The action begins with the funeral of Akhnaten's father, Amenhotep III, and moves through the coronation of the new pharaoh. Dialogue between Akhnaten and Nefertiti is conducted in Egyptian to contrast with the spoken texts in English translation. Act II is concerned with Akhnaten's religious revolution in which he abandons the old gods in favor of Aten, much to the dismay of the priests. Act III depicts the downfall of the Pharaoh, who retreats into the inner world of his own ideals as Egypt falls into disarray around him. His shining city, Akhetaten, is reduced to ruins, the old order is restored, Akhnaten is deposed and his name removed from history. The final tableau shows modern tourists viewing the ruins of Akhetaten as we see the ghosts of Akhnaten and his family walking towards the heavenly land of Ra.

Minimalism, like Mozart's classical style, lends itself to any subject. Just as Mozart remained faithful to the Viennese idiom of his time in operas as diverse in subject matter as *The Marriage of Figaro* and *The Magic Flute*, Philip Glass was equally happy to employ his characteristic minimalist aesthetic to a trilogy of operas about Akhnaten, Einstein and Gandhi, all of which were linked by their shared theme of men who changed the world by means of ideas, but all at different periods and very different places. Glass' approach could well be seen as a return to Mozart's way of doing things: a categoric rejection of Orientalism, which in its own way penetrated the emotional and philosophical essence of Akhnaten's story far more powerfully than any Cook's Tour orientalizm could have achieved. For a start, as mentioned above, the texts drawn upon were authentic documents (Budge's translation of *The Book of the Dead* rubs shoulders with Fodor's Guide to Egypt). The stylization of sets and costumes in the original Stuttgart production, rather than theatrical reconstruction and historical accuracy, in some ways enhanced the strangeness and temporal distance of the story and period while at the same time allowing the story to breathe more freely.

Glass's hypnotic ostinati, their subtle rhythmic variations notwithstanding, do however, conform in some ways to an Orientalist convention. The relentless drumming and repeated staccato choral interjections during the funeral of Amenhotep III are comparable to the "primitive" drumming, repeated rhythmic patterns, and non-developing staccato motifs in Max Steiner's native music for *King Kong* (dir. Merion C. Cooper & Ernest B. Schoedsack, 1933) — and Massenet's *Cléopâtre* for that matter. In this respect Glass's score could be seen as a form of modernized Orientalism, which was entirely lacking in Mozart's rigidly non–Orientalist *Magic Flute* and *Thamos* music.

Glass, of course, is also a successful composer for film, but it is highly significant that, despite the success of *Akhnaten*, he was never approached to score Universal Studio's remake of *The Mummy* in 1999. It was Jerry Goldsmith (1929–2004), a much more likely candidate, who got the job. What Universal wanted was obviously something much more firmly rooted in the post–Romantic tradition of Hollywood film music, a tradition that wasn't worried about employing musical Orientalisms; and this leads me to a brief overview of how ancient Egypt has been represented musically in the movie genres that this book has been excavating.

Universal's first, best and always most iconic foray into the genre of mummy movies, *The Mummy,* had rather more music than its predecessor, *Dracula* (dir. Tod Browning, 1931). The only music in *Dracula* was the extract from Tchaikovsky's *Swan Lake* during the opening main title, but *The Mummy* had music specially composed for it by the uncredited James Dietrich (1894–1984), who supplied scores for over 156 films between 1927 and 1940. Many of those contributions were uncredited, too. Like *Dracula*, *The Mummy* also begins with the famous music from *Swan Lake*, though it's introduced by a short passage from Dietrich as Pogany's model pyramid is swung around to reveal the title. To cover the establishing shot of Hatshepsut's Temple, and take us back to the Field Expedition of 1922 when the film's prologue takes place, Dietrich introduces his main theme, which, as one would expect, contains the oriental sharpened subdominant, signifying the exotic East. Less expected, perhaps — particularly from our music-saturated perspective — is the complete lack of music as Karloff's Im-ho-tep is awakened. This classic scene is no doubt more unnerving without music but no modern director would allow such a shot to take place in the silence Karl Freund permits here.

After the young archeologist, played by Bramwell Fletcher, loses his mind after watching the mummy walk before his eyes, we cut to ten years later, the time of the film's production, and Dietrich repeats his main theme. Not all his cues are Orientalist. (Indeed, not all are by him). The recitative-like passage for lower strings that covers the later cut to the Cairo Museum is a straightforward melodramatic cliché derived from countless 19th-century operatic examples. Karloff himself, in his desiccated guise as Ardath Bey, is announced by a simple bassoon figure that suitably evokes his sinister aura without any exotic signifiers.

When we cut to Zita Johann in her first appearance as Helen Grosvenor, Dietrich provides a suitably orchestrated waltz with Orientalist elements, to suggest the hotel musicians who accompany a tea-dance in the hotel's reception rooms where the action takes place. This is exactly the kind of thing required, and is along the lines of the discretely Oriental "Vision of Salome" waltz (1907) by the British "Waltz King," Archibald Joyce (1873–1964), whose Edwardian success continued into the 1930s, particularly in this kind of situation.

Dietrich's subsequent cues use the conventional melodramatic device of sequential passages

Advertisement for Odhams Photo Engravers from the Christmas 1932 edition of *The Bookman* edited by Hugh Ross Williamson (London: Hodder and Stoughton). Significantly, this first appeared at exactly the same time as *The Mummy*, starring Boris Karloff.

(i.e., small phrases which on each repeat are raised by a tone). These are subjected to a crescendo. In the first Pool of Memory scene, we witness Im-ho-tep staring into the misty waters to observe the death of archeologist Sir Joseph Whemple. Whemple is attempting to burn the Scroll of Life, but Im-ho-tep has other ideas and causes Whemple to die from a heartattack before he can do any damage. This is the most impressive of Dietrich's cues, which returns at the end of the picture, and is derived from the kind of musical sequence often used by Liszt in both his piano music and symphonic poems, to similarly dramatic effect.

Rather more innovative is the use of sound effects in the scene that follows, when Helen visits Im-ho-tep in his creepy residence somewhere in the back streets of Cairo. Instead of music, we hear a curious ringing sound combined with off-screen street noise, which creates a suitable sense of alienation and anticipation. Balderston's screenplay was quite specific about what is required here, calling for "the cracking of the drivers' whips, the jingling of money at the table of the changers established at every corner of the street, the rattling of the brazen vessels of the water-carriers, the moaning of the camels, braying of donkeys, and barking of dogs."[46] Once more we look into the magic mirror and experience, in flashback, how Im-ho-tep was buried alive for having committed the sin of loving Anck-es-en-Amon. It's surprising that Dietrich uses no Orientalist devices in these scenes. Instead he relies on effective though all-purpose melodramatic style; but at the end of the picture Dietrich does send the audience home with that all-important sharpened subdominant.

By the time *The Mummy's Hand* appeared eight years later in 1940, Universal had already begun recycling their monster properties in a rather less poetic manner than in the 1930s. The same recycling approach was applied to the music in this film, which borrowed themes from *Son of Frankenstein* (dir. Rowland V. Lee) that had been composed by Frank Skinner (1897–1968). This was appropriate in a way, because although the villain of *The Mummy's Hand*, played by George Zucco, resurrects the mummy of Kharis with a distillation of Tana leaves rather than a bolt of lightning, the monstrous result is much the same. There's absolutely nothing of the East in these Frankenstein cues, however, even though they successfully evoke the blood-and-thunder approach of this effective follow-up.

After Zucco has made his way across the surprisingly arboreal desert and up a crumbling flight of steps to be inaugurated as the new Guardian of the Tomb, we are treated to the inevitable flashback sequence. As we've seen, Universal saved money by reprising the temple scenes from the original mummy film, intercutting shots of Tyler at appropriate moments, but the studio did find enough money to fund a male choir, which the composer Hans J. Salter (1896–1994) uses effectively during the burial of the princess Ananka. This was the first time a choir was used in a mummy film, and the epic idiom used by Salter here was later developed by Miklós Rózsa (1907–1995) in his scores for Biblical epics such as *Quo Vadis* (dir. Mervyn LeRoy, 1951) and *Ben-Hur* (dir. William Wyler, 1959). A typical snake-charmer melody for flute accompanies Kharis' theft of the sacred Tana leaves, and a tam-tam shudders Orientally as the statue of Isis waves its outraged flail. Kharis is subsequently buried alive to more "ah"s from the male choir, which owes something to the similarly "ah-ing" choir in Maurice Ravel's ballet *Daphnis et Chloe* (1912). By means of these orchestrally expanded and more obviously "Egyptian" Orientalist gestures in the score, Salter actually enhanced the atmosphere of the flashback scenes.

When the two American leads (played by Dick Foran and Wallace Ford) are introduced in a Cairo street, Salter employs an Orientalist idiom derived from Ketèlbey's *In a Persian*

Market. "Palm Court" tea-time music is echoed again later when we cut to the desert where Foran and his hastily assembled team have begun to excavate the tomb. Salter's melody here is somewhat reminiscent of the famous Russian partisan song "Little Field," which was used in the fourth symphony of Soviet composer, Lev Knipper (1898–1974), and it nicely demonstrates how Orientalism also found its way into the mainstream via Russian melody.

Musically speaking, there's very little to add with regard to the three mummy films that Universal released during World War II. *The Mummy's Tomb, Ghost,* and *Curse* transform the mummy into a characterless corpse. Music became increasingly the only means by which to induce any terror or dramatic tension in these sadly lackluster productions. As Salter himself explained, "When I looked at them before scoring they didn't seem to have much fright about them. The challenge in those days at Universal was in creating the sense of terror and suspense, and that is something music can do."[47] However, Salter's later mummy scores introduced little that was new, other than the otherworldly timbre of the Novachord, an early electronic instrument which now came to signify "the other" for modern, Nazi-threatened audiences. Skinner's old theme for *Son of Frankenstein* was reprised so much in these films that it must have seemed to many to have been specially composed for the mummy saga, and all the old Romantic Orientalisms seem to have been replaced by the relentless melodramatic effects, one piled on top of another like a parody of a Tchaikovsky coda (the kind of thing, indeed, that Malcolm Arnold parodied in his *Grand Grand Overture* in 1956), only in Salter's Hollywood Gothic style. The genre desperately needed an injection of imagination and poetry.

Meanwhile, the Hollywood Egyptian epic had musical requirements of its own. Composer Elmer Bernstein (1922–2004) kept the Orientalism of *The Ten Commandments* very much in the background. He did incorporate Orientalist elements in the cues that accompany the dance sequences, such as when slave girls form a circle and toss their plaited hair before Sir Cedric Hardwicke's Pharaoh Sethi. For the rest of his score, Bernstein relied on big tunes and big orchestration but all in mainstream Hollywood style. This at least has the advantage of helping the audience relate to the characters. Not only would they recognize all the big stars who populate this lavish costume drama (Vincent Price, Edward G. Robinson, Charlton Heston, Anne Baxter, etc.), but the mainstream Hollywood scoring was just as familiar. Whereas a mummy film aims to present Egypt as a powerful example of "the other," here, we are encouraged to interpret the drama in universal terms, and identify the similarities between the cruelty and materialism of ancient Egyptian and the evils of contemporary society. (In DeMille's original silent version the parallel was spelled out in the second part, set in the 1920s.) Bernstein's cue for the Exodus scene, for example, could serve just as well for a Western, which is, to some extent, how DeMille approached the Biblical story. He cast the Egyptians as the Indians and the Israelites (the chosen people of God) as the American settlers. This was, no doubt, one of the reasons why the film remained so popular for so long among American evangelicals. Bernstein's heroic march for this scene also used tuned percussion and a great deal of brass, and would not be out of place in a marching band playing Souza in a New York ticker-tape procession. Only the lavish string section indicates that the players have been forced indoors.

Like Bernstein, Dimitri Tiomkin (1894–1979) used a choir for *Land of the Pharaohs*. It sounds rather like a Russian Orthodox church service during the final burial scene — a not unexpected resonance from this Russian-born composer. Despite his association with

Westerns, Tiomkin's score for this Egyptian epic is much more Orientalist than Bernstein's approach with *The Ten Commandments*. Required to supply a great deal of processional music, Tiomkin emphasized fanfare-like motifs for brass, lashings of percussion, march rhythms, and phrases that are repeated as relentlessly as the lashes on the backs of the slaves who build Khufu's pyramid. When Joan Collins' Nellifer presents Pharoah's son Xenon (Piero Giagnoni) with the "magic flute" that eventually lures the snake that kills Pharaoh's first wife, Tiomkin obliges with a suitably oriental "snake-charmer" melody that recurs in various guises later in the score.

The influence of the Hollywood epic was certainly present in Hammer's first foray into Egyptiana with *The Mummy*. There was nothing particularly novel about the excellent score composed for this by Franz Reizenstein (1911–1968), but what *was* new was the adoption of Miklós Rósza's Biblical style in the context of a horror film. Over a pedal base, emphasized by a timpani (much as James Bernard had thundered a bass drum throughout the main title of *Dracula* in 1958) Reizenstein accompanies his main "Egyptian" theme with a wordless chorus straight out of a Hollywood sand-and-sandal epic. The melody exploits the exotic potential of the last three notes of the minor scale with the all-important sharpened seventh and flattened sixth creating the required "Oriental" effect (in this context, at least). Later, Reizenstein enhances the "snake-charmer" potential of these three notes by having them played on the oboe, and indeed, they permeate the score in various guises, following the traditional Orientalist manner. He also exploits the sinister connotations of the augmented fourth, or tritone, known also as "diabolus in musica" or "the devil in music," following the example of James Bernard's Dracula and Frankenstein scores for the company. No one, however, had ever heard such a richly orchestrated score for a mummy movie before. It brilliantly complemented Terence Fisher's opulent colors and Bernard Robinson's elegantly appointed sets in a wholly novel way for the time, adding considerable gravitas to the proceedings.

Reizenstein also employed a handful of other motifs, two of which inhabit moderately more unusual harmonic territory. (Reizenstein was a musical traditionalist in his concert works, so would never have thought of resorting to atonality or serialism.) A quasi-modal theme appears when Stephen Banning (played by Felix Aylmer) and Joseph Whemple (Raymond Huntley) first enter Ananka's tomb early on in the picture, and this modality links it to Rósza's more consistent use of modal themes in, for example, *Quo Vadis*. Reizenstein's modal theme is reprised when we see Kharis, in flashback, violating the tomb of Ananka. We hear it again when Stephen Banning, in a later flashback, encounters the reanimated mummy for the first time. The modal theme is certainly an appropriate way to symbolize the tomb, as it inhabits a more archaic form of scale, predating major and minor, and used for exactly the same reason by Rósza. Reizenstein also exploits trumpet fanfares, which create a comparable (though not quite so rarified) *frisson* to those that appear in Debussy's *Khamma*. More significantly, Reizenstein makes sure to include the Orientalist sharpened subdominant on an improvisatory-like solo line for "snake-charmer" oboe, which only increases the "Egyptian" feeling in Ananka's tomb. When Banning screams and Whemple rushes back inside the tomb to find out what's happened, Reizenstein's score resembles the more melodramatic approach of Dietrich in the first Universal *Mummy* film whenever Karloff imposes his will on his enemies.

There is much more colorful percussion in Reizenstein's score than any mummy film had ever enjoyed before. Tam-tams shiver, snare drums snarl, and timpani terrorize the audience quite as much as the mummy itself. As is so often the case, the film wouldn't be half as unnerving without the music. The year 1959 was relatively early for sophisticated horror film soundtracks in England, the most impressive horror film score before James Bernard redefined the genre, being George Auric's music for *Dead of Night* (dir. Alberto Cavalcanti, Charles Crichton, Basil Dearen and Robert Hamer, 1945). One particular cue of Reizenstein's score, in fact, somewhat resembles the rather dryer, neoclassical idiom of Auric. It occurs when the two comic drivers responsible for delivering Kharis' coffin to George Pastel's Mehemet Bey, are frightened by what they take to be the cry of an escaped lunatic. They urge their horses on, there's an accident, and the coffin slides into a swamp. Reizenstein's music here echoes the scene in Auric's score that accompanies the final montage scene in *Dead of Night*. Both exploit shrill flute registers, staccato phrasing and hollow string timbres; and later in this same cue, Reizenstein highlights the less orthodox interval of the perfect fourth, piling three on top of each other and then repeating the process in a higher pitch. The angularity of these intervals (we are more used to hearing thirds and fifths), especially when layered into chords, is perfect for such a situation, but the same effect was also being explored by Hammer's other composers around this time, such as Richard Rodney Bennett in *The Man Who Could Cheat Death* (dir. Terence Fisher, 1959) and Malcolm Williamson in *The Brides of Dracula* (dir. Terence Fisher, 1960)[48]

A lonely oboe announces Mehemet Bey at the swamp as he prepares to resurrect Kharis, and here perhaps Reizenstein (raised and trained on such music, after all) may have had the equally melancholy cor anglais that opens Act III, scene 1 of Wagner's *Tristan und Isolde* in mind. Who knows? Wagner's aim was to evoke a mood of desolation, and Hammer's swamp is certainly desolate. The oboe subsequently enjoys a quasi-improvisation on the main "Egyptian" theme before tritones appear once more, this time very much to the fore on timpani as the choir wails quietly. When Kharis emerges, we hear another theme, played on glockenspiel, again fashioned from fourths, which rise and fall. These go on to function as a murder motif in much the same way as Richard Rodney Bennett's motif for the elixir of life in *The Man Who Could Cheat Death* (dir. Terence Fisher, 1959). What else is Kharis than a man who achieves exactly that?

For the flashback of Ananka's death and embalming, Reizenstein reprises his main theme, and for the funeral procession itself he provides a solemn funeral march with the dotted rhythm and descending phrases that are traditional to such music. After that, there are no new themes, Reizenstein being content to reprise and vary what he's introduced already, but he creates some imaginative effects along the way, not least being the mystical and grotesquely touching moment when the mummy stares longingly at Yvonne Furneaux's Isobel Banning, whom it believes to be his long-lost love, Ananka, reincarnated. Here, Reizenstein introduces a celesta, combined with strings and a female choir that is reminiscent of the equally mystical writing of Gustav Holst (1874–1934) to represent the qualities of Neptune in *The Planets*.

So evocative was Reizenstein's main theme for *The Mummy*, that Hammer decided to use it again in *The Curse of the Mummy's Tomb* in 1964, but it wasn't destined to be as all-pervasive as James Bernard's famous Dracula theme. This was its only reprise, and it was reserved for the inevitable flashback sequences. Nearly everything else was composed by the excellent Carlo Martelli (born 1935) who brought a slightly more acerbic approach to the film than Reizenstein had to its predecessor, though, like him, Martelli was also a traditionalist. His main theme for *Curse* is based on four notes built around the Oriental association of the minor third. Then an even more Orientalist idea comes along exploiting the expected flattened supertonic and sharpened subdominant. Martelli's exciting scoring emphasizes the shock value of brass and shrill string textures along with the exotic connotations of wind. The result is less like Rózsa's Biblical epic style and much more like the score to an adventure film with horror elements, which in a sense this is, as the horror element is somewhat played down in favor of mystery and suspense. One phrase, as the camera prowls around Bernard Robinson's dusty tomb of Ra-Antef, is actually reminiscent of the leitmoif for Freia's golden apples in Wagner's Ring Cycle opera, *Das Rheingold*. This certainly makes sense, as Freia's apples are what gave the gods of Valhalla the gift of immortality — and immortality is what *The Curse of the Mummy's Tomb* is all about.

Martelli also reorchestrated excerpts from established 19th-century Orientalist masterpieces for the scenes in which the mummy is "road-showed" by the American impresario Alexander King (played by Fred Clark). The appearance of Rimsky-Korsakov's *Scheherzade* and "The Procession of the Sardar" from Ippolitov-Ivanov's *Caucasian Sketches* serves to emphasize Edward Said's observation that Orientalist music isn't trying to be accurate, as its principal concern is to "characterize the Orient as alien."

Martelli also provides suitable belly-dancing music, awash with shimmering tambourines for a scene that dwells on the charms of just such a creature, and on board the ship that takes the protagonists back to England, they (and we) are entertained by the Martelli's arrangement of Jacques Offenbach's "Barcarolle" from *The Tales of Hoffmann* (1851).

One year before the release of *The Curse of the Mummy's Tomb,* Alex North (1910–1991) scored the Elizabeth Taylor *Cleopatra* epic. Like Tiomkin and many others, North created exotic connotations by means of percussion, but like Bernstein before him, he didn't overdo the Orientalisms. In fact, his themes could happily serve many a non–Egyptian tragic romance. Unusually, however, he includes a harpsichord to lend an antique signification to the proceedings alongside the more traditional use of harps to suggest this quality. Flutes also inject "snake-charmer" connotations. For Cleopatra's entry into Rome, surely the film's most spectacular scene, North does nod in the direction of older melodic clichés, but colors the scoring of the scene with the unusual timbre of a prepared piano. Ostinati again play their "primitive" part, particularly during the dance of the Isis-winged maidens who precede the appearance of Cleopatra on her massive sphinx.

Don Banks (1923–1980) was wholly responsible for the music in Hammer's next Egyptian fantasy, *The Mummy's Shroud* (dir. John Gilling, 1967). The main title theme, replete with choir, harp glissandi and shimmering cymbals, is certainly epic in intent but it restricts itself to the general Orientalism of a minor key. Banks's approach does include some Oriental touches, but many of his cues here could just as successfully work in *The Evil of Frankenstein* (dir. Freddie Francis) and *The Reptile* (dir. John Gilling), which, of course, he also scored in 1964 and 1966, respectively. One subtle touch does rather nicely evoke the profound sense of homesickness suffered by Michael Ripper's character, Longbarrow, the put-upon secretary of the insufferable Stanley Preston (John Phillips). As Longbarrow explains to Preston's son (David Buck) that he's off to book a passage home to England, we hear the desolate sound (to some Western ears at least) of a muezzin call. There's no dramatic need for this

Mummy's milk. Eddie Powell takes a break to advertise for the Milk Marketing Board during the filming of *The Mummy's Shroud* (dir. John Gilling, 1967).

to be heard, but it was quite correctly felt to emphasize Longbarrow's excitement at leaving a country in which he feels so uncomfortable. (He's constantly sweating, but the discomfort is even more a psychological one.) Even his name suggests the difference between Egyptian culture and his own culture back in England: in Egypt there are dusty tombs; in England we have long barrows. The most significant line in the film is spoken with touching subtlety by Ripper as he explains to his employer that "it will be nice to see the shady lanes of the old country again. It's been a very long time for me." If anything conveyed the essential fear of "the other" it's surely this. Home is very definitely not in Egypt, and that is why any evidence of "abroad"—particularly wandering mummies and men wearing the fez—is treated with such suspicion in this genre.

Hammer's last mummy movie, *Blood from the Mummy's Tomb*, was immeasurably enhanced by Tristram Cary's evocative Orientalist score. Cary was originally chosen because of his affinity with electronic music. It was felt that the frequent shots of the night sky and constellations might benefit from accompaniment with "sci-fi" electronic music, but in fact Cary used only a traditional symphony orchestra, though many of his cues were inexplicably cut, and what remained was often reprised over scenes for which he had provided different music. The starry skies featured the traditionally mystic timbres of harps and woodwind, and sometimes high-pitched strings which gave a suggestion of the electronic textures for which he was so wellknown at the time. Most of his Orientalist themes are ruminations on minor tonalities, especially the flattened sixth and sharpened seventh of that tonality. Flutes again bring an element of the snake-charmer to the proceedings and subtle percussion effects hark back to the "exotic" aspect of "Turkish" music. The music throws a sonic veil of mystery and magic over the film, though it also delivers the required shocks for the horror sequences and brings the film to a shuddering close as single notes on the harp usher in the final tam-tam and cymbal-shrouded chord.

After such a series of variations on a basic theme, there was little that composer Jerry Goldsmith could add to his score for *The Mummy* in 1999, nor was there any need to, as Universal had no intention of allowing their composer to take Philip Glass's approach or any approach other than a traditionally Orientalist one. During the prologue, by far the best sequence in the film, Goldsmith exploits the Orientalist associations of the minor scale with sharpened fourths on sombre brass. The inevitable percussion ostinati predominate, and with the appearance of the voice-over narration ("Thebes—City of the Living, crown jewel of Pharaoh Seti I") the melody is transferred to the equally inevitable flute. As Pharaoh's wife, Anck Su Namum (Patricia Velasquez) walks through a pair of immense golden curtains, Goldsmith emphasizes the classic snake-charmer connotations of a minor third and sharpened fourth, for well over one hundred years a signifier of the exotic East, but which has a great deal more to do with the West.

Conclusion

I return to the pond in the woods where we began, but no bubbles rise from its murky depths. The mallard ducks float undisturbed on its tranquil waters. The shadows are there, but they are only effects of light. The woods are quite safe. Exotic dangers lurk only in my own, much influenced imagination. There are, of course, no words of Thoth (or anyone else for that matter) that can raise the dead, even if the dead indeed lay submerged beneath those somber waters. The old house in the park has actually been converted into luxury flats. A well-known athlete is one of the residents. We've even passed each other occasionally, but no one wearing a fez can be seen, and no menacing silhouette emerges through the curtain of trees that surround me.

There are, of course, plenty of real terrors in the world, but there are no curses from the tomb to worry me. Even so, the consequences of history live on. Whatever the benefits or drawbacks of a multi-cultural society, there's no doubt that the problems of the contemporary world are the result of past injustices: the pillage of imperialism, the exploitation of commercialism, the inequalities of colonialism. The insensitivities and greed of the past still haunt the present, and in more powerful ways today than a century ago.

"Your father believes that Tera is a force for evil and he's spent these years trying to find the root of that force while trying to keep the evil bottled up," said James Villiers as Corbeck in *Blood from the Mummy's Tomb*. It's a very colonial problem: steal the resources of another nation and then try to control the social consequences. Professor Fuchs in that film is in love with the idea of an Egyptian queen who has taken over the body of his own daughter. The incestuous result is another neat metaphor for imperialist paternalism, which pretends to care for the people it subjugates but is really only interested in exploiting it.

For a while, Sax Rohmer's Fu Manchu came spectacularly to life in the person of Osama bin Laden and his Al Qu'ida organization. That Fu is Chinese rather than Egyptian (or, indeed, Saudi) makes very little difference to the Western Orientalist mentality, as Rohmer's Egyptian villains demonstrate. The differences in such a context are merely matters of *style*. "The world shall hear from me again," Fu always intoned after his many (but only ever apparent) destructions. Fortunately, bin Laden cannot now say the same, though suicide bombers aplenty remain at large, as does the West's profound fear and distrust of the East. Surely, such a dangerous state of affairs can best be defused by realizing that this Fu Manchu complex, as we might term it, is the reverse side of a coin minted long ago in European culture. Having said that, contemporary terrors, no matter how shocking, remain prosaic, but the fictions of yesterday retain their magic, despite — perhaps because of the florescence of 24-hour rolling news and a global economy in which everything is shown to be inextricably inter-related. There is no cultural autonomy anymore — hence the decline of the colonial fantasy (of which the mummy genre was a part). The appeal of ancient Egyptian fantasy lay in its ability to exorcise guilt whilst simultaneously allowing its readers to escape into

Publicity poster from the 1920s, with "mystical" Egyptian elements, for the American illusionist Grover George (1887–1958).

the more manageable world of make-believe, where terrors could be overcome. After a thrill of exotic menace, the comfort of familiarity — the "shady lanes of the old country," as Michael Ripper's Longbarrow so movingly put it — was always restored. We do not have that luxury anymore. As W. Somerset Maugham put it at the end of his long creative life, "To imagine is to fail; for it is the acknowledgement of defeat in the encounter with reality." Reality is so all-pervasive these days that fantasy is dying fast. Reality is the new fantasy — perhaps even more implausible than the wildest imaginings of Bram Stoker. It is, indeed, a new form of entertainment, but we surely cannot find any emotional nourishment in it. Reality has so undermined our ability to fantasize that films are unable to resist a knowing wink at their own subterfuge. There can be no narrative conviction under such circumstances.

As for history — all history is, after all, only an interpretation of the past, which, if it is to be in any way useful must prove the old adage that *plus ça change....* Cheops, as played by Jack Hawkins at least, was much like anyone else (on a rather grander scale admittedly) when it came to power. He wanted to keep it, to preserve his wealth, to imagine he could take it with him. We still interpret the past in our own terms, as the recent television series *Rome* (2005–2007), with its scheming, cynical Cleopatra (Lyndsay Marshal), proved in spectacular though perhaps less glamorous fashion than in the days of Claudette Colbert and Elizabeth Taylor.

In the final scene of Philip Glass's opera *Akhnaten*, tourists wander through the ruins of Akhetaten, Akhnaten's once-great city of the sun. The Scribe, now dressed as a 20th-century tour guide, explains:

> There is nothing left of this glorious city of temples and palaces. The mud brick buildings have long since crumbled and little remains of the immense stone temples but the outlines of their floor plans. In addition to the tombs and ruins of the city, there are several *stelae* scattered around the plain which mark the limits of the land belonging to the city — most of them are too widely scattered to visit and are also in bad condition

The tourists eventually leave and the ghosts of Akhnaten and his associates sing mournfully as they move in a procession towards the heavenly land of Ra.

Ancient Egypt is now more than ever a tourist location. Commercialized, misrepresented, fictionalized, Orientalised — it has been almost completely reinvented by the West. This is the main point of Shadi Abdel-Salam's *The Night of Counting the Years*. Ancient-Egypt has become a commodity. Mummy movies, Egyptian epics, ballets, operas, paintings, adventure stories, horror stories, historical romances, even occult fantasies all attest to that. Amusement arcades now advertise the possibility of the treasures one might win within by filling their windows with reproduction Egyptian artifacts. Replica treasures from Tutankhamen's tomb are road-showed. Images of ancient Egypt sell digital cameras and even home insurance. In a confused conflation of influences, one recent British television commercial featured a caricature of an Italian tenor rise from the sarcophagus in an ancient Egyptian tomb). The Egyptian business man Mohamed Al-Fayed, so desperate for British citizenship, was even dubbed "The Phoney Pharaoh" by the satirical magazine *Private Eye*. Ancient Egypt has become what we in the West want to make of it. Our own fears have raised mummies from the dead and we have invested ancient artifacts with our own desires. Of course, Western civilization has been reinventing the ancient world in its own image for centuries. Georgian aristocrats borrowed Palladio's misunderstanding of Greek and Roman

An "Egyptian" display in the window of a contemporary amusement arcade.

architecture for their stately homes, and Georgian developers transformed classical architecture into rows of terraced housing in cities like Bath. One might even claim that contemporary Egypt is exploiting its cultural past just as much as any Westerner. Egypt depends on tourism like no other industry. But surely none of this need spoil our enjoyment of Egyptiana and mummy movies, ancient epics and what one might term Egyptian kitsch, providing we explore its development and acknowledge its misrepresentations. The ghosts of Akhnaten and the ancient past still haunt us, and no matter how much Egyptologists attempt to redress the balance by revealing historical truth, our fantasies of ancient Egypt might be said to have been of much more psychological use to us, as they have most of all helped us to define and explain ourselves.

Filmography

The Vengeance of Egypt (1912)
The Wraith of the Tomb (dir. Charles Calvert, 1915)
Die Augen der Mummie Ma— a.k.a. *The Eyes of the Mummy* (dir. Ernst Lubitsch, 1918)
Cleopatra (dir. J. Gordon Edwards, 1917)
The Ten Commandments (dir. Cecil B. DeMille, 1923)
The Phantom of the Opera (dir. Rupert Julian, 1925)
The Mask of Fu Manchu (dir. Charles Brabin, 1932)
The Mummy (dir. Karl Freund, 1932)
The Ghoul (dir. T. Hayes Hunter, 1933)
The Invisible Man (dir. James Whale, 1933)
The Black Cat (dir. Edgar G. Ulmer, 1934)
The Bride of Frankenstein (dir. James Whale, 1935)
She (dir. Lansing C. Holden and Irving Pichel, 1935)
The Last Days of Pompeii (dir. Ernest B. Schoedsack and Merian C. Cooper, 1935)
The Mummy's Hand (dir. Christy Cabanne, 1940)
The Mummy's Tomb (dir. Harold Young, 1942)
The Mummy's Ghost (dir. Reginald Le Borg, 1944)
The Mummy's Curse (dir. Leslie Goodwins, 1944)
Caesar and Cleopatra (dir. Gabriel Pascal, 1946)
The Egyptian (dir. Michael Curtiz, 1954)
Valley of the Kings (dir. Robert Pirosh, 1954)
Abbott and Costello Meet the Mummy (dir. Charles Lamont, 1955)
The Ten Commandments (dir. Cecil B. DeMille, 1956)
Land of the Pharaohs (dir. Howard Hawks, 1956)
The Mummy (dir. Terence Fisher, 1959)
Gli ultimo giorni di Pompei (dir. Sergio Leone, 1959)
Il sepolchro dei re a.k.a. *Cleopatra's Daughter* (dir. Fernando Cerchio, 1960)
Nefertiti, regina del Nilo a.k.a. *Nefertiti, Queen of the Nile* (dir. Fernando Cerchio, 1961)
Cleopatra (dir. Joseph L. Mankiewicz, 1963)
Carry on Cleo (dir. Gerald Thomas, 1964)
She (dir. Robert Day, 1965)
Carry on Screaming (dir. Gerald Thomas, 1966)
The Curse of the Mummy's Tomb (dir. Michael Carreras, 1964)
The Mummy's Shroud (dir. John Gilling, 1967)
Blood from the Mummy's Tomb (dir. Seth Holt, 1971)
Dr. Phibes Rises Again (dir. Robert Feust, 1972)

The Spy Who Loved Me (dir. Lewis Gilbert, 1977)
Warlords of Atlantis (dir. Kevin Connor, 1978)
Death on the Nile (dir. John Guillermin, 1978)
The Awakening (dir. Mike Newell, 1980)
Raiders of the Lost Ark (dir. Steven Spielberg, 1981)
Sphinx (dir. Franklin J. Shaffner, 1981)
Young Sherlock Holmes (dir. Barry Levinson, 1985)
Stargate (dir. Roland Emmerich, 1994)
Bram Stoker's Legend of the Mummy (dir. Jeffrey Obrow, 1997)
Talos the Mummy (dir. Russell Mulcahy, 1998)
Prince of Egypt (dir. Brenda Chapman/Steve Hickner, 1998)
The Mummy (dir. Stephen Sommers, 1999)
Bubba Ho-Tep (dir. Don Coscarelli, 2002)
Chemical Wedding (dir. Julian Doyle, 2008)

Television

Mystery and Imagination—"The Curse of the Mummy" (dir. Guy Verney, 1970)
Doctor Who—"Pyramids of Mars" (dir. Paddy Russell, 1975)
Sexton Blake and the Demon God (dir. Roger Tucker, 1978)
The Tomorrow People—"The Rameses Connection" (dir. Roger Gartland, 1995)

Chapter Notes

Introduction

1. Bram Stoker, *The Jewel of Seven Stars* (Far Thrupp: Alan Sutton, 1996), p. 75.
2. Sax Rohmer, *Brood of the Witch Queen* (London: C. Arthur Pearson, 1919), p. 146.
3. Howard Carter, *The Tomb of Tutankhamen* (London: Sphere, 1972), p. 38.
4. *Ibid.*
5. Thomas Mann, *Joseph and His Brothers*, trans. H. T. Lowe-Porter (New York: Alfred A. Knopf, 1966), pp. 32–33, "Tales of Jacob."
6. Rohmer, *Brood of the Witch Queen*, note 2, p. 170.
7. Wagner was concerned that his father was the Jewish actor and artist Ludwig Geyer. With regard to his latent homosexuality, Jean-Jacques Nattiez, in *Wagner Androgyne* (Princeton: Princeton University Press, 1993), p. 191, quotes from Wagner's letter of January 9, 1862, to Peter Cornelius: "*My friend, you must come and live with me, once and for all!...* You will belong to me, as my wife does, and we shall share everything equally together, be it good fortune or failure, everything as a matter of course.... You'll do what you can, as I shall, but always like two people who really belong to each other like a married couple." Cosima Wagner's *Diaries*, also quoted by Nattiez on p. 192 (the entry for January 1, 1882), record one of Wagner dreams in which "he was thrashing a boy, using a tallow candle, which proved to be unsuitable — too soft — for the task, whereupon he woke up!"
8. Richard Wagner, trans. Charles Osborne, *Stories and Essays* (London: Peter Owen, 1973), pp. 38–39.
9. *Ibid.*, p. 39.
10. Cosima Wagner, trans. Geoffrey Skelton, *Diaries*, Vol. 2 (London: Collins, 1978), entry for December 18, 1881.
11. Anthony Sattin, *A Winter on the Nile — Florence Nightingale, Gustave Flaubert and the Temptations of Egypt* (London: Hutchinson, 2010), p. 185.
12. Villiers de L'Isle Adam, trans. M. Gaddis Rose, *Axël* (London: Soho, 1986), pp. 170–171.
13. W. Somerset Maugham, *A Writer's Notebook* (London: William Heinemann/The Book Society, 1949), p. 246.

Chapter One

1. Leslie Halliwell, *The Dead That Walk* (London: Paladin, 1988), pp. 204–205.
2. *Ibid.*, pp. 205–206.
3. Gaston Leroux, *The Phantom of the Opera* (London: Michael O'Mara, 1987), p. 115.
4. Philippa Faulks and Robert L. D. Cooper, *The Masonic Magician — The Life and Death of Count Cagliostro and His Egyptian Rite* (London: Watkins, 2008), p. 90.
5. Philip J. Riley, ed., *The Mummy* — Universal Filmscripts Series, Classic Horror Films, Vol. 7 (Absecon: MagicImage Filmbooks, 1989), scenes L-29–L-42.
6. *Ibid.*, scene A-20.
7. *Ibid.*, scene I-14.
8. *Ibid.*, scenes F-2 and L-61.
9. *Ibid.*, p. 25.
10. Jonathan Rigby, *English Gothic* (Richmond: Reynolds & Hearn, 2000), p.18.
11. Philip J. Riley, ed., *The Mummy* — Universal Filmscripts Series, Classic Horror Films, Vol. 7, note 5, scene C-5.

12. Edward Said, *Orientalism—Western Conceptions of the Orient* (Harmondsworth: Penguin, 1985), pp. 71–72.
13. Rohmer, *Brood of the Witch Queen*, p. 170.
14. *Ibid.*, p. 154.
15. Halliwell, *The Dead That Walk*, note 1, p. 218.
16. Marjorie Deans, *Meeting at the Sphinx* (London: MacDonald, 1946), p. 42.
17. Michael Holroyd, *Bernard Shaw, Vol. 3—The Lure of Fantasy* (London: Chatto & Windus, 1991), p. 476.
18. Deans, *Meeting at the Sphinx*, note 16, p. 107.
19. *Ibid.*, p. 95.
20. *Ibid.*, pp. 94–95.
21. Herbert van Thal, ed., *Fanfare for Ernest Newman* (London: Arthur Barker, 1955), p. 45 (Martin Cooper, "Giacomo Meyerbeer").
22. Christopher Lee, *Lord of Misrule* (London: Orion, 2003), p. 181. Lee also recalled (on pp. 181–182) the physical discomfort of the role: "I'd been most horribly bruised and battered and bashed on this film, bursting through real glass windows, and a door someone had bolted from the inside without telling me so that I'd almost dislocated my shoulder, and had had explosive charges detonated on plates set within my bandages to give the illusion of my being peppered with a shotgun."
23. Halliwell, *The Dead That Walk*, p. 229.
24. Dez Skinn, ed., *Hammer's Halls of Horror* magazine, no. 22 (London: Top Sellers, July 1978), p. 8 ("The Mummy," adapted by Steve Moore [script] and David Jackson [artwork]).
25. Morris Bright & Robert Ross, *Mr Carry On* (London: BBC Worldwide, 2000), p. 140.
26. Kenneth Williams, *Diaries* (London, HarperCollins, 1993), entry for November 10, 1974, p. 483: "Saw myself in 'International Cabaret.' I look lean and intellectual in the way Peter Cushing looks ... the voice tends towards the *posh* and the face is often severe and aesthetic [sic] when it should be smiling and jolly. The general impression of my performance is someone superior being forced to pander to the inferior, and that is roughly the truth of the situation." Williams found filming *Carry on Screaming* very uncomfortable. On January 19, 1966, pp. 271–272, he "did stuff with Oddbods—all that revolting mummy make-up, and teeth. Made me feel sick." On February 7, pp. 272–273: "The shot was me, backing away from the reincarnated Pharaoh and falling into a great trough of dough, struggling out again and then falling into the vat wit the monster. It wasn't pleasant. The dough stuck into hair *everywhere* and it was the devil's own job to remove it."
27. *To the Devil ... The Death of Hammer*. DVD documentary in *The Hammer Collection*, Studio Canal B000HN31KQ. Interview with Christopher Wicking.
28. John Garforth, *Sexton Blake and the Demon God* (London: Mirror Books, 1978), p. 137.
29. Roderick Grierson and Stuart Munro-Hay, *The Ark of the Covenant* (London: Weidenfeld and Nicolson, 1999), p. 20.
30. *Ibid.*, p. 17.
31. Alan Baker, *Invisible Eagle—The History of Nazi Occultism* (London: Virgin, 2000), p. 97.
32. Grierson and Munroe-Hay, *The Ark of the Covenant*, note 29, p. 22.
33. *Ibid.*, p. 303.

Chapter Two

1. John Romer, *Valley of the Kings* (London: Michael Joseph, 1981), p. 29.
2. Thomas Mann, trans. H. T. Lowe-Porter, *Joseph and His Brothers* (New York: Alfred A. Knopf, 1966), p. 11 ("Tales of Jacob").
3. Carter, *The Tomb of Tutankhamen*, p. 128.
4. Exodus, chapter 5, verse 2.
5. *Ibid.*, chapter 1, verses 7–11.
6. *Harvard Magazine*, July-August 2003, http://harvardmagazine.com/2003/07/who-built-the-pyramids (research by Richard Redding of University of Michigan Museum of Natural History).
7. Deborah Manley, *The Nile—A Traveller's Anthology* (London: Cassell, 1991), p. 79.
8. G. A. Henty, *The Cat of Bubastes—A Tale of Ancient Egypt* (London & Glasgow: Blackie, 1889), p. 82.
9. *Ibid.*, pp. 85–86.
10. John Romer, *Valley of the Kings*, note 1, p. 80.
11. *Ibid.*, 82.

12. H. C. Randall-Stevens, *Atlantis to the Latter Years* (Jersey: Knights Templars of Aquarius, 1966), p. 89.
13. Rohmer, *The Romance of Sorcery* (Whitefish: Kessinger, 2003), p. 12.
14. Rohmer, *Brood of the Witch Queen*, pp. 123–124.
15. *Ibid.*, p. 115.
16. Romer, *Valley of the Kings*, note 1, p. 81.
17. Rohmer, *Brood of the Witch Queen*, note 14, p. 136.
18. Alan Moorehead, *The Blue Nile* (London: New English Library, 1980), p. 20.
19. Manley, *The Nile — A Traveller's Anthology*, note 7, p. 80.
20. H. Rider Haggard, *Cleopatra* (London: Longmans, Green, 1914), p. 177.
21. *Ibid.*, p. 190.
22. Rohmer, *Brood of the Witch Queen*, note 14, p. 129.
23. *Ibid.*, p. 138.
24. Romer, *Valley of the Kings*, note 1, p. 21.
25. Moorehead, *The Blue Nile*, note 18, p. 26.
26. Frank McLynn, *Napoleon* (London: Jonathan Cape, 1997), p. 169.
27. Romer, *Valley of the Kings*, note 1, p. 39.
28. Stoker, *The Jewel of Seven Stars*, pp. 99–100.
29. *Ibid.*, p. 14.
30. http://www.drhawass.com/blog/press-release-tunnel-seti-i-tomb.
31. Rohmer, *Brood of the Witch Queen*, note 14, p. 124.
32. Stoker, *The Jewel of Seven Stars*, note 28, p. 207.
33. *Ibid.*, p. 206.
34. Lord Byron, *Byron's Poetical Works* (London: Virtue, 1855), p. 210 ("Don Juan," Canto I, stanza CCXIX).
35. *Ibid.*, p. 147 ("English Bards and Scotch Reviewers").
36. Haggard, *Cleopatra*, note 20, p. 267.
37. Thomas Mann, trans. H. T. Lowe-Porter, *Joseph and His Brothers*, note 2, p. 509 ("Joseph in Egypt").
38. Sax Rohmer, "The Death-Ring of Sneferu," in *Tales of Secret Egypt* (New York: McKinlay, Stone & Mackenzie, 1919), p. 47.
39. Sax Rohmer, "Breath of Allah," in *Tales of Secret Egypt*, note 38, p. 114.
40. Manley, *The Nile — A Traveller's Anthology*, note 7, p. 81.
41. Romer, *Valley of the Kings*, note 1, p. 126.
42. Peter Berresford Ellis, *H. Rider Haggard — A Voice from the Infinite* (London: Routledge & Kegan Paul, 1987), p. 121.
43. Aleister Crowley, *The Confessions of Aleister Crowley*, eds. John Symonds and Kenneth Grant (London: Arkana, 1989), p. 394.
44. Aleister Crowley, *The Equinox of the Gods*, http://hermetic.com/crowley/equinox-of-the-gods/eqotg7.html, chapter 7, section VII, 3 "The People."
45. Rohmer, "The Death-Ring of Sneferu" in *Tales of Secret Egypt*, note 38, p. 56.
46. Romer, *Valley of the Kings*, note 1, p. 151.
47. www.dailymail.co.uk/sciencetech/article-1083945/Mystery-screaming-mummy.html.
48. Romer, *Valley of the Kings*, note 1, p. 161.
49. *Ibid.*, pp. 162–163.
50. Mika Waltari, *The Egyptian*, trans. Naomi Walford (Porvoo/Helsinki/Juva: Werner Söderström Osakeyhtiö, 1979), p. 54.
51. Stoker, *The Jewel of Seven Stars*, note 28, pp. 121–122.
52. Romer, *Valley of the Kings*, note 1, p. 188.
53. Carter, *The Tomb of Tutankhamen*, note 3, p. 31.
54. *Ibid.*, p. 35.
55. *Ibid.*, p. 39.
56. Teresa Hansom, *The Mysterious Miss Marie Corelli — Queen of Victorian Bestsellers* (Thrupp: Alan Sutton, 1999), p. 203.
57. *Ibid.*, p. 200.
58. Marie Corelli, letter of March 24, 1923, to the *New York World*.
59. http://www.qualtestusa.com/KingTutsCurse.html.
60. Carter, *The Tomb of Tutankhamen*, note 3, p. 164.

Chapter Three

1. Philippa Faulks and Robert L. D. Cooper, *The Masonic Magician—The Life and Death of Count Cagliostro and His Egyptian Rite* (London: Watkins, 2008), p. 23.
2. *The Divine Pymander of Hermes Trimegistus—An Endeavour to Systematise and Elucidate the Corpus Hermeticum* (Godalming: The Shrine of Wisdom, 1978), p. 9.
3. *Ibid.*, pp. 10–11.
4. Faulks and Cooper, *The Masonic Magician—The Life and Death of Count Cagliostro and His Egyptian Rite*, note 1, p. 27.
5. *Ibid.*
6. *Ibid.*, p. 6.
7. *Ibid.*, p. 45.
8. *Ibid.*, p. 141.
9. Jean Terrasson, trans. Thomas Lediard, *The Life of Sethos* (London: J. Walthoe, 1738), p. i.
10. Philippa Faulks and Robert L. D. Cooper, *The Masonic Magician—The Life and Death of Count Cagliostro and His Egyptian Rite*, note 1, p. 42.
11. Terrasson, *The Life of Sethos*, note 9, p. 30.
12. *Ibid.*, pp. 70–71.
13. *Ibid.*, p. 153.
14. E. A. Wallis Budge, trans., *The Book of the Dead—The Papyrus of Ani*, http://www.sacred-texts.com/egy/ebod/ebod18.htm, plates VII–X, p. 286.
15. Rossiter, ed., *The Book of the Dead—Papyri of Ani, Hunefer, Anhaï* (Fribourg-Geneva: Liber, 1984), p. 116.
16. Waltari, *The Egyptian*, p. 30.
17. *Ibid.*, p. 43.
18. Marcus Hearn and Alan Barnes, *The Hammer Story—The Authorised History of Hammer Films* (London: Titan, 2007), p 43.
19. Rossiter, ed., *The Book of the Dead—Papyri of Ani, Hunefer, Anhaï*, note 10, p. 59.
20. Budge, trans., *The Book of the Dead—The Papyrus of Ani*, note 9, plate XV, p. 307.
21. Stoker, *The Jewel of Seven Stars*, p. 245.
22. *Ibid.*, p. 241.
23. *Ibid.*, p. 187.
24. Paul Murray, *From the Shadow of Dracula—A Life of Bram Stoker* (London: Jonathan Cape, 2004), p. 227.
25. E. A. Wallis Budge, *Osiris and the Egyptian Resurrection*, Vol. II (New York: Dover, 1973), p. 141.
26. E. A. Wallis Budge, *Egyptian Ideas of the Future Life* (New York: Cosimo Classics, 2005), p. 165.
27. Dennis Wheatley, *The Ka of Gifford Hillary* (Geneva: Heron, 1972), p. 229.
28. *Ibid.*
29. *Ibid.*, p. 306.
30. Sax Rohmer, *Tales of Secret Egypt* (New York: McKinlay, Stone & Mackenzie, 1919), p. 120 ("Breath of Allah").
31. Bernard Bromage, *The Occult Arts of Ancient Egypt* (Wellingborough: Aquarian, 1979), p. 93.
32. Joan Grant, *Eyes of Horus* (London: Diploma Press, 1974), p. 27.
33. *Ibid.*, pp. 27–28.
34. Bromage, *The Occult Arts of Ancient Egypt*, note 26, p. 98.
35. Stoker, *The Jewel of Seven Stars*, note 16, p. 186.
36. Bromage, *The Occult Arts of Ancient Egypt*, note 26, p. 109.
37. Crowley, *The Confessions of Aleister Crowley*, p. 393.
38. *Ibid.*, p. 394.
39. Aleister Crowley, *The Drug and Other Tales*, ed. William Breeze (Ware: Wordsworth, 2010), p. 166 ("Across the Gulf").
40. *Ibid.*, p. 200.
41. *Ibid.*, p. 193.
42. *Ibid.*, p. 200.
43. Peter Washington, *Madame Blavatsky's Baboon* (London: Secker and Warburg, 1993), p. 37.
44. *Ibid.*, p. 38.
45. Edward Bulwer-Lytton (The Right Hon. Lord Lytton), *Zanoni* (London: George Routledge & Sons ["The Stevenage Edition"], undated), p. 13.

46. Edward Bulwer-Lytton (The Right Hon. Lord Lytton), *The Last Days of Pompeii* (London: George Routledge & Son ["The Stevenage Edition"], undated), p. 67.
47. *Ibid.*, p. 10.
48. William Beckford, *Dreams, Waking Thoughts and Incidents*, ed. Robert J. Gemmett (Stroud: Nonsuch, 2006), p. 177.
49. H. P. Blavatsky, *Isis Unveiled, Vol. 2—Theology* (Pasadena: Theosophical University Press, 1988), p. 434.
50. Dez Skinn, ed., *Hammer's Halls of Horror* magazine, no. 21 (London: Top Sellers, June 1978), p. 35 (Catherine O'Brien & Tony Crawley, "Warlords of the Deep").
51. *Ibid.*
52. *Ibid.*, p. 34.
53. Ellic Howe, *Magicians of the Golden Dawn—A Documentary History of a Magical Order 1887–1923* (London: Routledge & Kegan Paul, 1972), p. 2.
54. *Ibid.*, p. 23.
55. *Ibid.*, p. 107.
56. Barbara Belford, *Bram Stoker—A Biography of the Author of* Dracula (London: Weidenfeld & Nicolson, 1996), p. 297.
57. Ellic Howe, *Magicians of the Golden Dawn—A Documentary History of a Magical Order 1887–1923*, note 48, p. 201.
58. Dennis Wheatley, *The Devil Rides Out* (Geneva: Heron, 1972), p. 204.

Chapter Four

1. Liza Picard, *Restoration London* (London: Phoenix, 1998), p. 210.
2. Manley, *The Nile—A Traveller's Anthology*, p. 160.
3. David Watkin & Philip Hewat-Jaboor, eds., *Thomas Hope—Regency Designer* (New Haven: Yale University Press, 2008), p. 34.
4. *Ibid.*
5. *Ibid.*, pp. 35–36.
6. *Ibid.*, p. 36.
7. John Morley, *Death, Heaven and the Victorians* (London: Studio Vista, 1971), p. 44.
8. Watkin & Hewat-Jaboor, eds., *Thomas Hope—Regency Designer*, note 3, p. 36.
9. Charles Dickens, *American Notes* (London: Hazell, Watson & Viney, 1930), p. 70.
10. Michael Snodin, *Karl Friedrich Schinkel—a Universal Man* (New Haven: Yale University Press, 1991), p. 110.
11. Vivien Noakes, *Edward Lear—The Life of a Wanderer* (Far Thrupp: Sutton, 2004), p. 108.
12. *Ibid.*, p. 184.
13. *Ibid.*, p. 183.
14. *Ibid.*
15. *Ibid.*, p. 184.
16. Herman De Meulenaere, *Ancient Egypt in Nineteenth Century Painting* (Knokke-Zoute: Berko, 1992), p. 88.
17. William Gaunt, *Victorian Olympus* (London: Non-Fiction Book Club, 1953), p. 76.
18. *Ibid.*
19. Georg Moritz Ebers, *An Egyptian Princess*, http://www.gutenberg.org/files/5460/5460-h/5460-h.htm, preface.
20. *Ibid.*, preface to fourth edition.
21. *Ibid.*, chapter five.
22. R. J. Barrow, *Laurence Alma-Tadema* (London: Phaidon, 2003), p. 25.
23. *Ibid.*
24. Samuel Carter Hall, ed., *Art Journal* (London, Virtue, 1874), p. 100.
25. Maarten Raven, "Alma-Tadema als Amateur Egyptolog," in *Bulletin van het Rijksmuseum* (Amsterdam: Rijksmuseum, 1980), p. 147.
26. Barrow, *Laurence Alma-Tadema*, note 22, p. 27.
27. Gaunt, *Victorian Olympus*, note 17, p. 79.
28. Victoria Price, *Vincent Price—A Daughter's Biography* (London: Sidgwick & Jackson, 1999), p. 134.
29. Kevin Brownlow, *David Lean—A Biography* (London: Richard Cohen, 1996), pp. 138–139.
30. Marc Gross, "Land of the Pharaohs," in *Film Review*, June 29, 2007, www.filmsinreview.com/2007/06/29/land-of-the-pharaohs.

31. André Pozner, *www.filmreference.com/Writers-and-Production-Artists/Ta-Vi/Trauner-Alexandre.html*.
32. Richard Klemmensen, ed., *Little Shoppe of Horrors*, April 1978, p. 72.

Chapter Five

1. Laurence Irving, *Henry Irving* (London: Faber and Faber, 1951), p. 523.
2. W. MacQueen-Pope, *Carriages at Eleven—The Story of the Edwardian Theatre* (London: Hutchinson, 1947), pp. 42–43.
3. William Shakespeare, *The Oxford Shakespeare*, ed. W. J. Craig (Oxford: Oxford University Press, 1978), p. 985 ("Antony and Cleopatra").
4. Plutarch, *Life of Marcus Antonius*, trans. Sir Thomas North, XXVI.
5. Shakespeare, *The Oxford Shakespeare*, note 3, p. 1011 ("Antony and Cleopatra").
6. Jean Terrasson, *The Life of Sethos—Taken from Private Memoirs of the Ancient Egyptians, Vol. 1*, trans. Thomas Lediard (London: J. Walthoe, 1732), pp. 35–36.
7. *Ibid.*, p. 31.
8. William Beckford, *Vathek*, trans. Herbert B. Grimsditch (London: The Bodley Head, 1953), p. 42.
9. David Stuart Davies, *Return from the Dead* (Ware: Wordsworth, 2004), p. 198 (Jane Webb, "The Mummy").
10. *Ibid.*, p. 199.
11. *Ibid.*, pp. 199–200.
12. *Ibid.*, pp. 196–197.
13. *Ibid.*, p. 202.
14. *Ibid.*, pp. 202–203.
15. *Ibid.*, p. 205.
16. Theophile Gautier, trans. Lafcadio Hearn, *One of Cleopatra's Nights* (San Bernardino: Borgo Press, 1999), p. 11. Influential though Gautier's story was, Pushkin's fragment, "Egyptian Nights," was, in fact, written three years earlier, in 1835. In it, a poet improvises a poem about Cleopatra and her lovers, who are prepared to sacrifice their lives for a night in her arms.
17. *Ibid.*, p. 19.
18. *Ibid.*, p. 6.
19. *Ibid.*, pp. 19–21.
20. *Ibid.*, p. 22.
21. *Ibid.*, pp. 37–38.
22. *Ibid.*, p. 45.
23. *Ibid.*, p. 21.
24. *Ibid.*, p. 7.
25. *Ibid.*, p. 17.
26. Edward Bulwer-Lytton (The Right Hon. Lord Lytton), *The Last Days of Pompeii* (London: George Routledge & Sons ["The Stevenage Edition"], undated), p. 494.
27. *Ibid.*, p. 64.
28. *Ibid.*, pp. 79–80.
29. *Ibid.*, p. 80.
30. Fyodor M. Dostoevsky, *The Brothers Karamazov*, Vol. 1, trans. Constance Garnett (Geneva: Heron Books), p. 266.
31. Bulwer-Lytton (The Right Hon. Lord Lytton), *The Last Days of Pompeii*, note 26, p. 80.
32. *Ibid.*, pp. 80–81.
33. *Ibid.*, p. 144.
34. *Ibid.*, p. 103.
35. *Ibid.*
36. *Ibid.*, p. 104.
37. *Ibid.*, p. 168.
38. Stoker, *The Jewel of Seven Stars*, p. 130.
39. Bulwer-Lytton (Lord Lytton), *The Last Days of Pompeii*, note 26, p. 169.
40. *Ibid.*, p. 182.
41. *Ibid.*, p. 252.
42. Edgar Allan Poe, *The Complete Illustrated Stories of Edgar Allan Poe* (London: Chancellor Press, 1988), p. 527 ("Some Words with a Mummy").
43. *Ibid.*, p. 170 ("Ligeia").
44. *Ibid.*, p. 174.

45. *Ibid.*, p. 167.
46. *Ibid.*, p. 173.
47. *Ibid.*, pp. 173–174.
48. *Ibid.*, p. 179.
49. *Ibid.*, p. 281 ("The Assignation").
50. *Ibid.*, p. 263 ("The Conversation of Eiros and Charmion").
51. *Ibid.*, p. 721 ("The Sphinx").
52. Gustave Flaubert, *The Temptation of St Anthony*, trans. Kitty Mrosovsky (Harmondsworth: Penguin, 1980), p. 77.
53. *Ibid.*, p. 183.
54. *Ibid.*, p. 184.
55. H. Rider Haggard, *She* (London & Glasgow: Collins, 1974), p. 109.
56. *Ibid.*, p. 183.
57. *Ibid.*, p. 190.
58. *Ibid.*, p. 201fn.
59. *Ibid.*, p. 285.
60. *Ibid.*, p. 288.
61. H. Rider Haggard, *Cleopatra* (London: Longman, Green ["The Silver Library"], 1914), p. 7.
62. *Ibid.*, p. 88.
63. Peter Berresford Ellis, *H. Rider Haggard—A Voice from the Infinite* (London: Routledge & Kegan Paul, 1987), p. 121.
64. Haggard, *Cleopatra*, note 61, pp. 313–314.
65. *Ibid.*, p. 60.
66. *Ibid.*, p. 66.
67. *Ibid.*, p. 69.
68. *Ibid.*, p. 70.
69. *Ibid.*, pp. 75–76.
70. *Ibid.*, p. 90. Harmarchis's image of Cleopatra as a "Thing of Flame" (p. 69) is similar to James Whale's intention that the white silk dress worn by Gloria Stuart in *The Old Dark House* (1932) should make her similarly resemble a flame.
71. *Ibid.*, p. 101.
72. *Ibid.*, pp. 106–107.
73. *Ibid.*, p. 290.
74. *Ibid.*, p. 297.
75. *Ibid.*, p. 302.
76. *Ibid.*, p. 323.
77. G. A. Henty, *The Cat of Bubastes—A Tale of Ancient Egypt* (London & Glasgow: Blackie, 1889), p. 72.
78. Mark Bills, *Edwin Longsden Long RA* (London: Cygnus Arts, 1998), p. 112 (George C. Swayne, *The History of Herodotus* quoted).
79. Henty, *The Cat of Bubastes—A Tale of Ancient Egypt*, note 77, p. 158.
80. *Ibid.*, p. 211.
81. Davies, *Return from the Dead*, note 9, p. 230 (Sir Arthur Conan Doyle, "The Ring of Thoth").
82. *Ibid.*, p. 229.
83. *Ibid.*, p. 231.
84. *Ibid.*, p. 234.
85. *Ibid.*, p. 272 (Sir Arthur Conan Doyle, "Lot 249").
86. *Ibid.*, p. 266.
87. *Ibid.*, p. 267.
88. Anatole France, *Thäis*, trans. Robert B. Douglas (London: John Lane, The Bodley Head, 1920), pp. 19–20.
89. Oscar Wilde, *The Complete Works of Oscar Wilde* (London & Glasgow: Collins, 1977), p. 218 ("The Sphinx Without a Secret").
90. *Ibid.*, p. 833 ("The Sphinx").
91. George Bernard Shaw, *Complete Plays of Bernard Shaw* (London: Odhams Press, 1934), p. 237 ("Caesar and Cleopatra").
92. Holroyd, *Bernard Shaw, Vol. 2—The Pursuit of Power*, p. 18.
93. Shaw, *Complete Plays of Bernard Shaw*, note 91, p. 250 ("Caesar and Cleopatra").
94. *Ibid.*, p. 252.

Chapter Six

1. Sir Arthur Conan Doyle, *The Sign of Four* (London: Leopard, 1996), pp. 33–34.
2. Davies, *Return from the Dead*, note 9, p. 250 (Sir Arthur Conan Doyle, "The Ring of Thoth").
3. Graham Green & Hugh Green, *The Penguin Book of Victorian Villainies* (London: Claremont Books, 1995), pp. 632–633 (Richard Marsh, "The Beetle").
4. *Ibid.*, p. 624.
5. *Ibid.*, p. 509.
6. Guy Boothby, *Pharos the Egyptian* (New York and Melbourne: Ward, Lock, 1899), p. 12.
7. *Ibid.*, p. 23.
8. *Ibid.*, p. 49.
9. *Ibid.*, p. 56.
10. *Ibid.*, p. 57.
11. *Ibid.*, pp. 220–221.
12. *Ibid.*, p. 77.
13. *Ibid.*, p. 175.
14. *Ibid.*, p. 42.
15. Stoker, *The Jewel of Seven Stars*, p. 119.
16. *Ibid.*
17. *Ibid.*, p. 89.
18. Belford, *Bram Stoker—A Biography of the Author of* Dracula, p. 63.
19. Stoker, *The Jewel of Seven Stars*, note 15, p. 4.
20. *Ibid.*, p. 86.
21. *Ibid.*, p. 1.
22. *Ibid.*, p. 2.
23. *Ibid.*, p. 5.
24. *Ibid.*, p. 149.
25. *Ibid.*
26. *Ibid.*, p. 106.
27. *Ibid.*, p. 109.
28. *Ibid.*, p. 110.
29. *Ibid.*, p. 114.
30. *Ibid.*, p. 155.
31. *Ibid.*, p. 156.
32. *Ibid.*, pp. 66–67.
33. *Ibid.*, pp. 175–176.
34. *Ibid.*, p. 177.
35. *Ibid.*, p. 120.
36. *Ibid.*, p. 69.
37. E. A. Wallis Budge, *Egyptian Magic* (London: Kegan, Paul, Trench and Trübner, 1901), pp. 84–86.
38. Murray, *From the Shadow of Dracula—A Life of Bram Stoker*, p. 229.
39. *Ibid.*, p. 264.
40. Aleister Crowley, *The Drug and Other Stories*, ed. William Breeze (Ware: Wordsworth, 2010), p. 171 ("Across the Gulf").
41. Oscar Wilde, *The Complete Works of Oscar Wilde* (London & Glasgow: Collins, 1977), p. 755 ("Charmides").
42. Crowley, *The Drug and Other Stories*, note 40, p. 179 ("Across the Gulf").
43. *Ibid.*, p. 182.
44. *Ibid.*, p. 197.
45. *Ibid.*, p. 196.
46. Hearn & Barnes, *The Hammer Story—The Authorised History of Hammer Films*, p. 43.
47. Crowley, *The Drug and Other Stories*, note 40, p. 200 ("Across the Gulf").
48. Crowley, *The Confessions of Aleister Crowley*, p. 35fn.
49. Rohmer, *Brood of the Witch Queen*, p. 194.
50. *Ibid.*, p. pp. 195–196.
51. Rohmer, *Tales of Secret Egypt*, p. 275 ("In the Valley of the Sorceress").
52. *Ibid.*, p. 277.
53. *Ibid.*, p. 288.
54. *Ibid.*, p. 54 ("The Death-Ring of Sneferu").

55. *Ibid.*, p. 55.
56. *Ibid.*, p. 177 ("Lord of the Jackals").
57. *Ibid.*, p. 190.
58. Sax Rohmer, *The Green Eyes of Bast* (London: Cassell, 1924), p. 62.
59. *Ibid.*, p. 129.
60. *Ibid.*, p. 128.
61. *Ibid.*, p. 271.
62. *Ibid.*, p. 274.
63. H. P. Lovecraft, *The Loved Dead* (Ware: Wordsworth, 2007), p. 70 ("The Last Test").
64. *Ibid.*, pp. 61–62 ("Imprisoned with the Pharaohs").
65. August Strindberg, *Plays: One*, trans. Michael Meyer (London: Methuen, 1982), p. 180 ("The Ghost Sonata").
66. Geoffrey Palmer & Noel Lloyd, *E. F. Benson as He Was* (Luton: Lennard, 1988), pp. 53–54.
67. *Ibid.*, p. 59.
68. Joan Grant, *Winged Pharaoh* (London: Sphere [The Dennis Wheatley Library of the Occult, Vol. 22], 1974), p. 7 (Dennis Wheatley's introduction).
69. Anatole France, *Thaïs*, trans. Robert B. Douglas (London: John Lane, The Bodley Head, 1920), pp. 151–152.
70. Joan Grant, *Winged Pharaoh* (London: Methuen, 1943), p. 67.
71. Grant, *Winged Pharaoh*, note 68, p. 7 (Dennis Wheatley's introduction).
72. Thomas Mann, *Joseph and His Brothers*, trans. H. T. Lowe-Porter (New York: Alfred A. Knopf, 1966), pp. 498–499 ("Joseph in Egypt").
73. *Ibid.*, p. 11 ("Tales of Jacob").
74. *Ibid.*, p. 12.
75. *Ibid.*, p. 502 ("Joseph in Egypt").
76. *Ibid.*, p. 515.
77. Dennis Wheatley, *The Quest of Julian Day* (Geneva: Heron Books, 1972), p. 213.
78. *Ibid.*, p. 258.
79. *Ibid.*, p. 259.
80. *Ibid.*, p. 290.
81. *Ibid.*, p. 294.
82. Crowley, *The Confessions of Aleister Crowley*, note 48, p. 879.
83. *Ibid.*, p. 878.
84. *Ibid.*, p. 879.
85. Mary Butts, *Scenes from the Life of Cleopatra* (New York: The Ecco Press, 1974), p. 49.
86. Mika Waltari, *The Egyptian*, p. 233.
87. *Ibid.*, p. 293.
88. *Ibid.*, p. 435.

Chapter Seven

1. Derek B. Scott, "Orientalism and Musical Style," in *Critical Musicology Journal* http://www.sara musik.org/articles/scott.html.
2. Jean Terrasson, *The Life of Sethos—Taken from Private Memoirs of the Ancient Egyptians*, Vol. 1, p. 20.
3. *Ibid.*, p. 18.
4. Emanuel Schikaneder and Carl Ludwig Giesecke, *The Magic Flute*, Act II, scene 20.
5. Terrasson, *The Life of Sethos—Taken from Private Memoirs of the Ancient Egyptians*, Vol. 1, note 2, p. 164.
6. *Ibid.*, p. 155.
7. Schikaneder and Giesecke, *The Magic Flute*, Act II, scene 28.
8. Terrasson, *The Life of Sethos—Taken from Private Memoirs of the Ancient Egyptians*, Vol. 1, note 2, p. 158.
9. Schikaneder and Giesecke, *The Magic Flute*, Act II, scene 28.
10. Francis Toye, *Rossini—A Study in Tragi-Comedy* (London: William Heinemann, 1934), p. 319.
11. Stendhal [Henri Beyle], *The Life of Rossini*, trans. Richard N. Coe (London: John Calder, 1985), p. 319.
12. *Ibid.*
13. *Ibid.*

14. *Ibid.*, p. 321.
15. *Ibid.*, p. 322.
16. *Ibid.*, pp. 323–324.
17. Oliver Strunk, ed., *Source Readings in Music History, Vol. 5—The Romantic Era* (London: Faber and Faber, 1981), p. 71 (Hector Berlioz, "Rossini's 'William Tell'").
18. Hector Berlioz, *The Memoirs of Hector Berlioz*, trans. David Cairns (London: Cardinal/Sphere, 1990), p. 82.
19. Derek B. Scott, "Orientalism and Musical Style," in *Critical Musicology Journal*, note 1, p. 10.
20. Anthony Burgess, *The Piano Players* (London: Hutchinson, 1986), p. 34.
21. Mary Jane Phillips-Matz, *Verdi—A Biography* (Oxford: Oxford University Press, 1992).
22. Antonio Ghislanzoni, *Aida*, trans. Charles L. Kenney (London: Ricordi, undated), p. 3.
23. *The Opera Libretto Library* (New York: Avenel, 1980), pp. 223–224 ("Aida").
24. Harold Rosenthal & John Warrack, eds., *The Concise Oxford Dictionary of Opera* (Oxford: Oxford University Press, 1990), p. 313.
25. Nikolai Andreyevich Rimsky-Korsakov, *My Musical Life*, trans. Judah A. Joffe (London: Eulenberg, 1974), p. 418.
26. Richard Buckle, *Diaghilev* (London: Weidenfeld, 1993), p. 128.
27. Philip Hoare, *Wilde's Last Stand—Decadence, Conspiracy & the First World War* (London: Duckworth, 1997), p.65.
28. *Ibid.*, p. 77.
29. Robert Orledge, *Debussy and the Theatre* (Cambridge: Cambridge University Press, 1985), p. 132.
30. W. L. Courtney, *The Development of Maurice Maeterlinck and Other Sketches of Foreign Writers* (London: Grant Richards, 1904). This volume demonstrates Courtney's familiarity with the decadent/symbolist literary texts of the day. It includes essays not only on Maeterlinck but also on Gabrielle D'Annunzio, J. K. Huysmans, and Russian writers such as Tolstoy and Gorky. Courtney's approach is well-informed but not uncritical of these influential figures.
31. Robert Orledge, *Debussy and the Theatre*, note 29, p. 133.
32. Roger Nichols, ed., *Debussy Remembered* (London: Faber and Faber, 1992), p. 102.
33. Edward Lockspeiser, *Debussy—His Life and Mind, Vol. 2—1902–1918* (London: Cassell, 1965), p. 156.
34. Benoit Hollander/George H. R. Dabbs, M.D., *Pompeii—a Dramatic Vocal and Symphonic Poem in Four Parts for Soli, Chorus, Orchestra and Organ—The Libretto After Bulwer Lytton's Novel* The Last Days of Pompeii (London: Hollander, 1907), pp. 109–111.
35. A. Eaglefield Hull, *Cyril Scott: The Man and His Works* (London: Waverley, 1925), p. 72.
36. *Ibid.*, p. 73.
37. *Ibid.*, pp. 73–74.
38. *Ibid.*, p. 74.
39. Genesis, chapter 39, verses 7–12.
40. Barbara Tuchman, *The Proud Tower—A Portrait of the World Before the War 1890–1914* (London: Papermac, 1997), p. 343.
41. *Ibid.*, p. 316.
42. Richard Buckle, *Diaghilev*, note 26, p. 278.
43. Peter G. Favis, "The Tragedy of Antony and Cleopatra," *New York Times,* January 9, 2009.
44. Meirion and Susie Harries, *A Pilgrim Soul—The Life and Work of Elisabeth Lutyens* (London: Michael Joseph, 1989), p. 258.
45. *Ibid.*, pp. 258–259.
46. Philip J. Riley, ed., *The Mummy*, Universal Filmscripts Series, Classic Horror Films, Vol. 7, scene I-1.
47. Tony Thomas, CD booklet notes for *Hans J. Salter—Music for* Frankenstein/ RTE Concert Orchestra, cond. Andrew Penny (Marco Polo 8.223477).
48. David Huckvale, *Hammer Film Scores and the Musical Avant-Garde* (Jefferson: McFarland, 2008), chapters five and eight.

Bibliography

Baker, Alan. *Invisible Eagle—The History of Nazi Occultism.* London: Virgin, 2000.
Barrow, R. J. *Laurence Alma-Tadema.* London: Phaidon, 2003.
Beckford, William. *Dreams, Waking Thoughts and Incidents.* Edited by Robert J. Gemmett. Stroud: Nonsuch, 2006.
_____. *Vathek,* Translated by Herbert B. Grimsditch. London: The Bodley Head, 1953.
Belford, Barbara. *Bram Stoker—A Biography of the Author of* Dracula. London: Weidenfeld and Nicolson, 1996.
Berlioz, Hector. *The Memoirs of Hector Berlioz.* Translated by David Cairns. London: Cardinal/Sphere, 1990.
Bills, Mark. *Edwin Longsden Long RA.* London: Cygnus Arts, 1998.
Blavatsky, H. P. *Isis Unveiled, Vol. 2—Theology.* Pasadena: Theosophical University Press, 1988.
Boothby, Guy. *Pharos the Egyptian.* New York and Melbourne: Ward, Lock, 1899.
Bright, Morris, and Robert Ross. *Mr Carry On.* London: BBC Worldwide, 2000.
Bromage, Bernard. *The Occult Arts of Ancient Egypt.* Wellingborough: Aquarian, 1979.
Brownlow, Kevin. *David Lean—A Biography.* London: Richard Cohen, 1996.
Buckle, Richard. *Diaghilev.* London: Weidenfeld, 1993.
Budge, Sir E. A. Wallis. *Egyptian Ideas of the Future Life.* New York: Cosimo Classics, 2005.
_____. *Egyptian Magic.* London: Kegan, Paul, Trench and Trübner, 1901.
_____. *Osiris and the Egyptian Resurrection*, Vol. II. New York: Dover, 1973.
Bulwer-Lytton, Edward (The Right Hon. Lord Lytton). *The Last Days of Pompeii* ("The Stevenage Edition"). London: George Routledge, undated.
_____. *Zanoni* ("The Stevenage Edition"). London: George Routledge, undated.
Burgess, Anthony. *The Piano Players.* London: Hutchinson, 1986.
Butts, Mary. *Scenes from the Life of Cleopatra.* New York: The Ecco Press, 1974.
Byron, Lord. *Byron's Poetical Works.* London: Virtue, 1855.
Carter, Howard. *The Tomb of Tutankhamen.* London: Sphere, 1972.
Conan Doyle, Sir Arthur. *The Sign of Four.* London: Leopard, 1996.
Corelli, Marie. Letter of March 24, 1923, to the *New York World*.
Courtney, W. L. *The Development of Maurice Maeterlinck and Other Sketches of Foreign Writers.* London: Grant Richards, 1904.
Crowley, Aleister. *The Confessions of Aleister Crowley.* Edited by John Symonds and Kenneth Grant. London: Arkana, 1989.
_____. *The Drug and Other Stories.* Edited by William Breeze. Ware: Wordsworth, 2010.
Davies, David Stuart. *Return from the Dead.* Ware: Wordsworth, 2004.
Deans, Marjorie. *Meeting at the Sphinx.* London: Macdonald, 1946.
De Meulenaere, Herman. *Ancient Egypt in Nineteenth Century Painting.* Knokke-Zoute: Berko, 1992.
Dickens, Charles. *American Notes.* London: Hazell, Watson and Viney, 1930.
The Divine Pymander of Hermes Trimegistus—An Endeavour to Systematise and Elucidate the Corpus Hermeticum. Godalming: The Shrine of Wisdom, 1978.
Dostoevsky, Fyodor M. *The Brothers Karamazov*, Vol. 1. Translated by Constance Garnett. Geneva: Heron Books, undated.
Ellis, Peter Berresford. *H. Rider Haggard—A Voice from the Infinite.* London: Routledge and Kegan Paul, 1987.

Ewers, Hanns Heinz. *Nachtmahr—Strange Tales*. Newcastle-upon-Tyne: Side Real Press, 2009.
Faulks, Philippa, and Robert L. D. Cooper. *The Masonic Magician—The Life And Death of Count Cagliostro and His Egyptian Rite*. London: Watkins, 2008.
Flaubert, Gustave. *The Temptation of St. Anthony*. Translated by Kitty Mrosovsky. Harmondsworth: Penguin, 1980.
France, Anatole. *Thaïs*. Translated by Robert B. Douglas. London: John Lane, The Bodley Head, 1920.
Garforth, John. *Sexton Blake and the Demon God*. London: Mirror Books, 1978.
Gaunt, William. *Victorian Olympus*. London: Non-Fiction Book Club, 1953.
Gautier, Theophile. *One of Cleopatra's Nights*. Translated by Lafcadio Hearn. San Bernardino: Borgo Press, 1999.
Grant, Joan. *Eyes of Horus*. London: Diploma Press, 1974.
_____. *Winged Pharaoh*. London: Methuen, 1943.
_____. *Winged Pharaoh* (The Dennis Wheatley Library of the Occult, Vol. 22), London: Sphere, 1974.
Green, Graham, and Hugh Green. *The Penguin Book of Victorian Villainies*. London: Claremont Books, 1995.
Grierson, Roderick, and Stuart Munroe-Hay. *The Ark of the Covenant*. London: Weidenfeld and Nicolson, 1999.
Haggard, Sir H. Rider. *Cleopatra* ("The Silver Library"). London: Longmans, Green, 1914.
_____. *She*. London and Glasgow: Collins, 1974.
Hall, Samuel Carter, ed. *Art Journal*. London: Virtue, 1874.
Halliwell, Leslie. *The Dead That Walk*. London: Paladin, 1988.
Hansom, Teresa. *The Mysterious Miss Marie Corelli—Queen of Victorian Bestsellers*. Far Thrupp: Alan Sutton, 1999.
Harries, Meirion, and Susie Harries. *A Pilgrim Soul—The Life and Work of Elisabeth Lutyens*. London: Michael Joseph, 1989.
Hearn, Marcus, and Alan Barnes. *The Hammer Story—The Authorised History of Hammer Films*. London: Titan, 2007.
Henty, G. A. *The Cat of Bubastes—A Tale of Ancient Egypt*. London and Glasgow: Blackie, 1889.
Hoare, Philip. *Wilde's Last Stand—Decadence, Conspiracy and the First World War*. London: Duckworth, 1997.
Holroyd, Michael. *Bernard Shaw, Vol. 2—1998–1918—The Pursuit of Power*. London: Chatto and Windus, 1989.
_____. *Bernard Shaw, Vol. 3—1918–1950—The Lure of Fantasy*. London: Chatto and Windus, 1991.
Howe, Ellic. *Magicians of the Golden Dawn—A Documentary History of a Magical Order 1887–1923*. London: Routledge and Kegan Paul, 1972.
Huckvale, David. *Hammer Film Scores and the Musical Avant-Garde*. Jefferson, NC: McFarland, 2008.
Hull, A. Eaglefield. *Cyril Scott: The Man and His Works*. London: Waverley, 1925.
Irving, Laurence. *Henry Irving*. London: Faber and Faber, 1951.
Lee, Christopher. *Lord of Misrule*. London: Orion, 2003.
Leroux, Gaston. *The Phantom of the Opera*. London: Michael O'Mara, 1987.
Lockspeiser, Edward. *Debussy—His Life and Mind, Vol. 2 1902–1918*. London: Cassell, 1965.
Lovecraft, H. P. *The Loved Dead*. Ware: Wordsworth, 2007.
MacQueen-Pope. W. *Carriages at Eleven—The Story of the Edwardian Theatre*. London: Hutchinson, 1947.
Manley, Deborah. *The Nile—A Traveller's Anthology*. London: Cassell, 1991.
Mann, Thomas. *Joseph and His Brothers*. Translated by H. T. Lowe-Porter. New York: Alfred A. Knopf, 1966.
McLynn, Frank. *Napoleon*. London: Jonathan Cape, 1997.
Moorhead, Alan. *The Blue Nile*. London: New English Library, 1980.
Morley, John. *Death, Heaven and the Victorians*. London: Studio Vista, 1971.
Murray, Paul. *From the Shadow of Dracula—A Life of Bram Stoker*. London: Jonathan Cape, 2004.
Nattiez, Jean-Jaques. *Wagner Androgyne*. Princeton: Princeton University Press, 1993.
Nichols, Roger, ed. *Debussy Remembered*. London: Faber and Faber, 1992.
Noakes, Vivien. *Edward Lear—The Life of a Wanderer*. Far Thrupp: Sutton, 2004.
The Opera Libretto Library. New York: Avenel, 1980.
Orledge, Robert. *Debussy and the Theatre*. Cambridge: Cambridge University Press, 1985.
Palmer, Geoffrey, and Noel Lloyd. *E. F. Benson as He Was*. Luton: Lennard, 1988.
Phillips-Matz, Mary Jane. *Verdi—A Biography*. Oxford: Oxford University Press, 1992.
Picard, Liza. *Restoration London*. London: Phoenix, 1998.
Plutarch. *Life of Marcus Antonius*. Translated by Sir Thomas North. XXVI.

Poe, Edgar Allan. *The Complete Illustrated Stories of Edgar Allan Poe.* London: Chancellor Press, 1988.
Price, Victoria. *Vincent Price—A Daughter's Biography.* London: Sidgwick and Jackson, 1999.
Randall-Stevens, H. C. *Atlantis to the Latter Years.* Jersey: Knights Templars of Aquarius, 1966.
Raven, Maarten. "Alma-Tadema als Amateur Egyptolog," in *Bulletin van het Rijksmuseum.* Amsterdam: Rijksmuseum, 1980.
Rigby, Jonathan. *American Gothic.* Richmond: Reynolds and Hearn, 2007.
_____. *English Gothic.* Richmond: Reynolds and Hearn, 2000.
Riley, Philip J., ed., *The Mummy*—Universal Filmscripts Series. Classic Horror Films, Vol. 7. Absecon, NJ: MagicImage Filmbooks, 1989.
Rimsky-Korsakov, Nikolai Andreyevich. *My Musical Life.* Translated by Judah A. Joffe. London: Eulenberg Books, 1974.
Rohmer, Sax. *Brood of the Witch Queen.* London: C. Arthur Pearson, 1919.
_____. *The Green Eyes of Bast.* London: Cassell, 1924.
_____. *The Romance of Sorcery.* Whitefish, MT: Kessinger, 2003.
_____. *Tales of Secret Egypt.* New York: McKinlay, Stone and Mackenzie, 1919.
Romer, John. *Valley of the Kings.* London: Michael Joseph, 1981.
Rosenthal, Harold, and John Warrack, eds. *The Concise Oxford Dictionary of Opera.* Oxford: Oxford University Press, 1990.
Rossiter, Evelyn, ed. *The Book of the Dead—Papyri of Ani, Hunefer, Anhaï.* Fribourg-Geneva: Liber, 1984.
Said, Edward. *Orientalism—Western Conceptions of the Orient.* Harmondsworth: Penguin, 1985.
Shakespeare, William. *The Oxford Shakespeare.* Edited by W. J. Craig. Oxford: Oxford University Press, 1978.
Shaw, George Bernard. *Complete Plays of Bernard Shaw.* London: Odhams Press, 1934.
Skinn, Dez, ed. *Hammer's Halls of Horror* magazine, no. 21. London: Top Sellers, June 1978.
_____. *Hammer's Halls of Horror* magazine, no. 22. London: Top Sellers, July 1978.
Snodin, Michael. *Karl Friedrich Schinkel—a Universal Man.* New Haven and London: Yale University Press, 1991.
Stendhal [Henri Beyle]. *The Life of Rossini.* Translated by Richard N. Coe. London: John Calder, undated.
Stoker, Bram. *The Jewel of Seven Stars.* Far Thrupp: Alan Sutton, 1996.
Strindberg, August. *Plays: One.* Translated by Michael Meyer. London: Methuen, 1982.
Strunk, Oliver, ed. *Source Readings in Music History, Vol. 5—The Romantic Era.* London: Faber and Faber, 1981.
Summers, Montague. *The Galanty Show.* London: Cecil Woolf, 1980.
Terrasson, Jean. *The Life of Sethos—Taken from Private Memoirs of the Ancient Egyptians, Vol. 1.* Translated by Thomas Lediard. London: J. Walthoe, 1732.
Thal, Herbert van, ed. *Fanfare for Ernest Newman.* London: Arthur Barker, 1955.
Toye, Francis. *Rossini—A Study in Tragi-Comedy.* London: William Heinemann, 1934.
Tuchman, Barbara. *The Proud Tower—A Portrait of the World Before the War 1890–1914.* London: Papermac, 1997.
Wagner, Cosima. *Diaries, Vol. 2—1869–1877.* Translated by Geoffrey Skelton. London: Collins, 1978.
Wagner, Richard. *Stories and Essays.* Translated by Charles Osborne. London: Peter Owen, 1973.
Waltari, Mika. *The Egyptian.* Translated by Naomi Walford. Porvoo/Helsinki/Juva: Werner Söderström Osakeyhtiö, 1979.
Washington, Peter. *Madame Blavatsky's Baboon.* London: Secker and Warburg, 1993.
Watkin, David, and Philip Hewat-Jaboor, eds. *Thomas Hope—Regency Designer.* New Haven and London: Yale University Press, 2008.
Wheatley, Dennis. *The Devil Rides Out.* Geneva: Heron, 1972.
_____. *The Ka of Gifford Hillary.* Geneva: Heron, 1972.
_____. *The Quest of Julian Day.* Geneva: Heron, 1972.
Wilde, Oscar. *The Complete Works of Oscar Wilde.* London and Glasgow: Collins, 1977.
Williams, Kenneth. *Diaries.* London: HarperCollins, 1993.

Websites

Boothby, Guy. *Pharos the Egyptian. Windsor Magazine*, June-December, 1898, *http://homepage.ntlworld.com/forgottenfutures/pharos/pharos00.htm.*
Budge, Sir E. A. Wallis, trans. *The Book of the Dead—The Papyrus of Ani, http://www.sacred-texts.com/egy/ebod/ebod18.htm.*

Crowley, Aleister. *The Equinox of the Gods*, *http://hermetic.com/crowley/equinox-of-the-gods/eqotg7.html*, chapter 7, section VII, 3, "The People."
www.dailymail.co.uk/sciencetech/article-1083945/Mystery-screaming-mummy.html.
http://www.drhawass.com/blog/press-release-tunnel-seti-i-tomb.
Ebers, Georg Moritz. *An Egyptian Princess, http://www.gutenberg.org/files/5460/5460-h/5460-h.htm.*
Gross, Marc. "Land of the Pharaohs," in *Film Review*, June 29, 2007, *www.filmsinreview.com/2007/06/29/land-of-the-pharaohs.*
Harvard Magazine, July-August 2003, *http://harvardmagazine.com/2003/07/who-built-the-pyramids.*
Pozner, André. *www.filmreference.com/Writers-and-Production-Artists/Ta-Vi/Trauner-Alexanre.html.*
http://www.qualtestusa.com/KingTutsCurse.html.
Scott, Derek B. "Orientalism and Musical Style," in *Critical Musicology Journal http://www.saramusik.org/articles/scott.html.*
Thomas, Tony. CD booklet notes for *Hans J. Salter—Music for* Frankenstein/ RTE Concert Orchestra, cond. Andrew Penny (Marco Polo 8.223477).
To the Devil ... The Death of Hammer. DVD documentary in *The Hammer Collection,* Studio Canal B000HN31KQ. Interview with Christopher Wicking.

Index

Numbers in ***bold italics*** indicate pages with photographs.
Film titles are followed by their directors.

À Rebours 5
Abbott, Bud 20, 27
Abbott and Costello Meet the Mummy 22, ***26***
Abd er Rassul, family of 78, 80
Abdel-Salam, Shadi 1, 220
The Abduction from the Seraglio (Mozart) 118, 188, 192
The Abominable Dr. Phibes ***49***
Abu Simnel 29, 72, 75, 115, 119
"Across the Gulf" (Crowley) 100, 170–173
Adam, Ken 48
The Addams Family (dir. Sonnenfeld) 187
Aegypt (Bantock) 203
L'Africaine (Meyerbeer) 195
Die ägyptische Helena (Strauss) see *The Egyptian Helen* (Strauss)
Eine ägyptische Königstochter (Ebers) see *An Egyptian Princess* (Ebers)
Aida (Verdi) 30, 31, 78, 97, 196–198
Ainsworth, Harrison ***114***
Aird, Sir John 124
Akhnaten 54, 59, 63, 64, 72, 81, 82, 86, 153, 164, 185–186, 208, 220
Akhnaten (Glass) 164, 184, 208–209, 220
Alberti, Ignaz ***190***, 191
Alen, William van 126
Alexander I, Tsar 111
Al-Fayad, Mohamed 115, 220
Allan, Maud 200–202
Alma-Tadema, Sir Lawrence 28, 120–124, ***122***, ***123***, 125, 128, 130, ***138***
Ames, Ramsey 23
The Ancient Egyptians—Their Lives and Customs (Wilkinson) ***67***, ***165***
Andress, Ursula ***146***, 148
Antoine et Cléopâtre (Schmitt) 205

Antony and Cleopatra (Barber) 207
Antony and Cleopatra (Shakespeare) 132–134, ***133***, 144, 198, 205
Appion 54
L'Après midi d'un faune (Debussy) 200
Archard, Bernard 49, 50
Arensky, Anton 199
Arnold, Malcolm 212
Asher, Jack 130, 131
Ashton, Roy 129
"The Assignation" (Poe) 144
Atlantis to the Latter Years (Randall-Stevens) 63
Die Augen der Mumie Ma see *The Eyes of the Mummy*
Auric, Georges 24, 214
The Avenging Hand 7
The Awakening 28, 47, 66, 94, 98, 99, 131, 166
Axël 5
Aylmer, Felix 15, 31, 213

Baker, Roy Ward 155, 168
Baker, Tom 49, ***50***, 88, 91
Bakst, Leon 199, 204
Balcombe, Florence 169
Balderston, John L. 12, 13, 18, 19, 59, 86, 154, 211
Balzac, Charles-Louis 70
Bankes, William 75
Banks, Don 198, 215–216
Bantock, Sir Granville 203, 204
Bara, Theda 9, ***10***, 205
Barber, Samuel 207
Barbieri, Giovanni Francesco see Guercino
Barnes, Alan 173
Barratt, Reginald 155
Barrow, R. J. 123
Barry, Amanda ***38***
Barry, Sir Charles 75
Bast 99, ***126***, 178–179, 185
Bateman, James 118
Batman (Television series) 35

Baudelaire, Charles 145
Baxter, Anne 212
Beckford, William 102, 135, 137
Beethoven, Ludwig van 4, 194, 196
The Beetle (Marsh) 159–161
Belmore, Lord 63
Belzoni, Giovanni Battista 39, 71–75, 77, 80, 103, 114, 119
Ben-Hur 211
Bennett, Richard Rodney 207, 214
Benois, Alexandre 200
Benson, E. F. 179–181
Bergman, Ingmar 168
Berlioz, Hector 194–195, 207
Bernard, James 106, 213, 214
Bernini, Gian Lorenzo 109
Bernstein, Aline 148
Bernstein, Elmer 212, 213, 215
Bey, Turhan 23
Bible 2, 28, 29, 52, 53, 54, 59, 60, 61, 70, ***71***, 79, 84, 96, 107, ***107***, ***108***, 123, 124, 132, 162, 163, 182, 193, 194, 204, 212, 213, 215
Biddulph Grange (Staffordshire) 118
Billing, Noel Pemberton 201, 202
Bin Laden, Osama 218
Bizet, Georges 195
Black, Isobel 43, 44
The Black Cat 4, 15–16, ***17***, 18
Blackwood, Algernon 104
Blanchard, Laman ***114***
Blavatsky, Helena Petrovna 101, 102, 103, 106, 140
Blickling Hall (Norfolk) 114
Blood from the Mummy's Tomb 7, 31, 38, 39, 43, 45–47, ***45***, 48, 74, 76, 77, 94, 130, 168, 179, 187, 217, 218
Bogarde, Sir Dirk 27
Bonomi, Joseph (the elder) 114
Bonomi, Joseph (the younger) 77, 114, 115

The Book of the Dead 3, 48, 57, 86, 91–92, 94, 95, 96, 164, 208
The Book of the Law (Crowley) 78, 99–100
Boorman, John 148
Boothby, Guy 38, 56, 161–164
Brabin, Charles 18
Bram Stoker's Legend of the Mummy 48
Brandy, Howard 45
"Breath of Allah" (Rohmer) 77, 96–97
Brecht, Bertolt 24
The Bride of Frankenstein **17**, 18, **20**
The Brides of Dracula 214
Bridgman, Frederick Arthur 125
Brodie-Innes, John William 104, 170
Bromage, Bernard 97–98, 99
Brood of the Witch Queen (Rohmer) 2, 3, 18, 19, 57, 64–65, 73–74, 76, 174–175
The Brothers Karamazov (Dostoevsky) 140
Browning, Tod 11, 13, 46, 209
Bruce, James 67, 68, 72, 75, 160, 183
Brugsch, Emile 78–79, 99, 100, 148
Bryan, John 128, **129**
Brynner, Yul **27**, 28
Bubba Ho-Tep 57
Buck, David 215
Buckle, Richard 199
Buckley, Keith 155
Budge, Sir E. A. Wallis 91, 94–95, 164, 169–170, 208
Bulwer, Sir Henry 148
Bulwer-Lytton, Sir Edward (Lord Lytton) 54, 101–102, 103, 139–140, 142, 148, 185, 202
Burdon, Hugh 45, 46, 131
Burgess, Anthony 196
Burton, James 76, 77, 114
Burton, Richard 37, 38, 145
Butts Mary 184–185
Byrne, Eddie 33
Byron, George Gordon, Lord 74, 75, 135

Cabanel, Alexandre 120
Cabanne, Christy 18, **21**
Caesar and Cleopatra (dir. Pascal) 25, **25**, 28, 68, **68**, 128, **129**, 158
Cæsar and Cleopatra (Shaw) 25, 128, 156, 158, 161
Cagliostro, Count Alessandro 12, 88, 89, 140, 189
Calvert, Charles 7
Cameron, Allan **57**, 131

Campbell, Bruce 57
Capra, Frank 148
Carlton Cinema 126, **127**
Carmen (Bizet) 195
Carnarvon, Lord 82, 84–85
Carné, Marcel 129
Carradine, John 23, 28, **155**, 196
Carreras, Sir James 39
Carreras, Michael 39, **40**, 41, 45, 131
Carreras Building 126, **126**
Carry On Cleo **37**, **38**, 38–39
Carry On Screaming 39, 55, 173, 226n26
Carson, John 88
Carter, Howard 2, 3, 40, 60, 80, 82–83, 85, 103, 127, 182
Carthew, Anthony 93
Cary, Tristram 217
Castro, Adolphe de 179
The Cat of Bubastes (Henty) 61, **62**, 145, 152–154, 178
Cat People 178
Catlett, Mary Jo 48
Cavalcanti, Alberto 214
Cerchio, Fernando 36
Champollion, Jean-François 70, 75, 76, 77, 103, 164
Chan, Jacqui 38
Chandler, Helen 13
Chaney, Lon 10, 11, 15, 185
Chaney, Lon, Jr. 22, **23**, **24**, 129, **155**
Chapman, Brenda 57
Chapman, Mark Lindsay 48
Charisse, Cyd 51
Charlie Chan in Egypt 18
"Charmides" (Wilde) 171
Chemical Wedding 87–88
Chopin, Frédéric 203
Christie, Agatha 48, 78
Christine, Virginia 24, **24**
Church Windows (Respighi) 205, 207
Churchill, Donald 46
Churchill, Sir Winston 124, 186
Clarke, Fred 40, 74, 215
Cleopatra (Alma-Tadema) **138**
Cleopatra (dir. DeMille) 2, 18, **19**
Cleopatra (dir. Edwards) 9, **10**, 205
Cleopatra (dir. Mankiewicz) 2, 25, 37–38, 68, 118, 123, 145, 205, **206**, 215
Cleopatra (Ebers) 183
Cleopatra (Haggard) 66, 75–76, 78, 145, 147, 148–152, **150**, 182, 183, 197
Cleopatra's Daughter 35, 36
Cléopâtre (Diaghilev ballet) 138, 199–200
Cléopâtre (Massenet) 195, 198, 209

Clyde, Jeremy 51
Coe, Peter 24
Colbert, Claudette 18, **19**, 220
Coleridge, Samuel Taylor 127
Coles, George 126, **127**
Collins, Joan 30, **30**, 31, 173, 213
Collins, M. E. & O. H. **126**
Collins, Wilkie 146, 159
The Coming Race (Bulwer-Lytton) 54
Compendium Maleficarum (Guazzo) 185
Conan Doyle, Sir Arthur 77, 85, 154–155, 159–160, 161, 197
Connor, Kevin 51
"The Conversation of Eiros and Charmion" (Poe) 144
Cooper, Merian C. 142, 209
Cooper, Robert L.D. 12, 88, 89
Corelli, Marie 83–84, 163
Cornelius, Peter 225n7
Coscarelli, Don 57, 58
Costello, Lou 20, 27
Cottrell, William 148
Coulouris, George 45, 131
Count Dracula (Television drama) 113
Courtney, William Leonard 201, 234n30
Cox, Rick 48
Cribben, Bernard 145
Crighton, Charles 214
Crowden, Graham 44, 46
Crowley, Aleister 15, 78–79, 82, 87, 88, 99–101, 105, 164, 170–173, 184–185, 201
Crowley, Rose 79, 99
Crutchley, Rosalie 45, 179
Crystal Palace *see* Egyptian Court
Cummins, Jackie 148
The Curse of Frankenstein 31
The Curse of the Mummy 43–44
The Curse of the Mummy's Tomb 39, **40**, **42**, 42, 43, 74, 76, 77, 130, 131, 186, 214–215
Curtiz, Michael 2, 28, **29**
Cushing, Helen 45
Cushing, Peter 22, 31, 33, 38, 39, 45, 51, 55, 56, 93, 145, 179, 226n26

Dabbs, George, H. R. 202–203
Dalziel brothers 124
The Damned (dir. Losey) 27
D'Annunzio, Gabrielle 104, 139, 234n30
Darvi, Bella 28
Daves, Delmer 196
Davis, Ossie 57
Davis, Philip 51
Davis, Theodore M. 82, 176
Day, Robert 39, 145, **146**

The Day the Earth Stood Still 196
Dead of Night 214
Dearden, Basil 214
Death on the Nile 48, 78
"The Death Ring of Sneferu" (Rohmer) 76, 79–80, 174, 177
Debussy, Claude 104, 200–202, 203, 213
Delamotte, W. Alfred *114*
Delgado, Roger 42
Delibes, Léo 195
DeMille, Cecil B. 2, 9, *11*, 18, *19*, 25, *27*, 28, 61, 125, 128–129, 130, 132, 193–194, 212
Demonolatry (Remy) 185
Denon, Dominique-Vivant (Baron de Denon) 69, 70, 110–111, 112, 118, 127
Description de l'Egypte 69, 110, 118, 125
Description of the East (Pococke) 65
The Desert Song 29
The Devil Rides Out (dir. Fisher) 105–106
The Devil Rides Out (Wheatley) 105–106
The Devil's Mistress (Brodie-Innes) 104, 170
Diaghilev, Sergei 138, 172, 196, 199–200, 205
Dickens, Charles 5, 101, 118
Dietrich, James 209, 211, 213
Dillon, Frank *60*
Diodorus Siculus 59
Disney, Walt 148
The Divine Pymander of Hermes Trismegistus 87, 142
Djalili, Omid 161
Dr. Phibes Rises Again! 48
Doctor Who 49–50
Donen, Stanley 168
Doré, Gustave 70, *71*, *108*, 109
Dostoevsky, Fyodor 140
Down, Leslie-Anne 54
Doyle, Julian 87–88
Dracula (dir. Browning) 11, 12, 13, 46, 209
Dracula (dir. Fisher) 31, 213
Dracula (Stoker) 5, 159, 164, 170
Dreier, Hans 18
Drovetti, Bernardino 72
Due notti con Cleopatra (dir. Mattoli) 138
Dynasty 30

Eatwell, Brian 48
Ebers, Georg Moritz 120–121, 183
Ebers, Hermann 182
Eckersberg, Christoffer Wilhelm 125
Edward VII 132
Edwards, J. Gordon 9, *10*

Edwards, Mark 46, 47
Egypt (Scott) 203–204
The Egyptian (dir. Curtiz) 2, 28, *29*, 36, 185
Egyptian (Waltari) 28, 81, 92, 140, 185–186
Egyptian Court (Crystal Palace) 77, 114–115, *116*
Egyptian Hall (Harrods) 115
Egyptian Hall (Piccadilly) 74, 77, 112
Egyptian House (Penzance) *113*
Egyptian Nights (Arensky) 199
Egyptian Nights (Pushkin) 230n16
An Egyptian Princess (Ebers) 120–121, 183
Einstein, Albert 208
Elcock, Charles Ernest 126
Elgar, Sir Edward 203
Elizabeth I 176
Emmerich, Roland 55
L'Enfance du Christ (Berlioz) 195
Les Enfants du Paradis 129
Engelbach, Rex 173
Die Entführung aus dem Serail (Mozart) see *The Abduction from the Seraglio*
Epstein, Sir Jacob *157*
Evelyn, Judith 81
The Evil of Frankenstein 215
Ewers, Hanns Heinz 173
Excalibur 148
Eyes of Horus (Grant) 91, 93, 97, 98, 182
The Eyes of the Mummy 7, 9, 183

Fairbanks, Douglas 127
Fairchild, Edgar 196
Faulks, Philippa 12, 88, 89
Ficino, Marsilio 86
The Finding of Moses (Alma-Tadema) 124
The Finding of Moses (Goodall) 125
Fisher, Terence 2, *32*, 35, *36*, 41, 93, 131, 143, 153, 178, 213, 214
Flaubert, Gustave 145, 205
Fleming, Ian 174
Fletcher, Bramwell 12, 13, 80, 209
Fokine, Mikhail 138, 199
Foran, Dick 20, 22, 211–212
Ford, Harrison *52*
Ford, Wallace 20, 211
Forster, E.M. 23
France, Anatole 155–156, 181, 198
Francis, Derek 51, 144
Francis, Freddie 113, 215
Frankenstein (dir. Whale) 11, 13, 15, 18
Frankenstein (Shelley) 135

Fraser, Brendan 27, 57
Freund, Karl 7, 12, *12*, *31*, 86, *104*, 209
Friberg, Arnold 125, 128
Fu Manchu novels 146, 218
Fuest, Robert 48, *49*
Furneaux, Yvonne 32, 214

Gamal, Samia 30
Gandhi, Mahatma 208
Garbo, Greta 13
Gardner, Helen *9*
Gaskill, Charles L. 9
Gaunt, William 120, 125
Gautier, Théophile 7, 69, 137–139, 167, 198, 199
Geary, Stephen 113
Gebler, Tobias von 89
Gehagen, Helen 148
Gell, Sir William 75, 76
George, Grover *219*
George Augustus Frederick, the Prince Regent 72
Geyer, Ludwig 225n7
Ghislanzoni, Antonio 197
A Ghost Sonata (Strindberg) 179
The Ghoul 4, 14, *14*, 15, 25
Giagoni, Piero 31
Gibbon, Edward 65
Gibson, Alan 56, 161
Gide, André 205
Gilbert, Lewis 24
Gilbert, Sir William S. 202
Gilling, John 41, 43, *44*, 131, 160–161, 215, *216*
Gilmore, Peter 51, 102
Glass, Philip 166, 208–209, 217, 220
Glazunov, Alexander 199
Glinka, Mikhail 199
Godard, Jean-Luc 129
Godwin, Edward William 126
Goebbles, Dr. Joseph 173
Goethe, Johann Wolfgang von 137, 182
Goldsmith, Jerry 209, 217
Golitzen, Alexander 27
Gómez, Ramiro 142
Goodall, Frederick 125
Goodman, John 128
Goodrick-Clarke, Nicholas 54
Goodwin, Harold 41
Goodwins, Leslie 24, *24*
Gorky, Maxim 234n30
Gossett, Lou 48
Granger, Stewart 25
Grant, Arthur 131
Grant, Joan 90, 91, 93, 97, 181
Grant, Lawrence 18
Grauman, Sid 126–127
Graves, Robert 9
Gray, Charles 106
Greaves, John 65
Grebaut, Eugène 80

The Green Eyes of Bast (Rohmer) 177–179
Green Hell 109, 128
"Green Tea" (Le Fanu) 180
Grierson, Roderick 54
Griffith, Hugh 48
Gross, Marc 129
"Guardian of the Abyss" (dir. Sharp) 88
Guazzo, Francesco Maria 185
Guercino 107, *107*
Guillermin, John 48
Gwillim, Jack 40

Hadley, Henry Kimball 137
Haggard, Sir H. Rider 56, 66, 75, 78, 145–147, 148, 150–152, *150*, 158, 182, 183, 197
Halliwell, Leslie 7, 9, 23, 33
Hamer, Robert 214
Hammer House of Horror (Television series) 88
Hardwicke, Sir Cedric 14, 28, 212
Harries, Meirion 208
Harries, Susan 208
Harris, Naomi 56
Harrison, Sir Rex 38
Hatfield, Hurd 156
Hatshepsut 79, 82, 127, 175, 176, 184, 200, 209
Haviland, John 118
Hawass, Dr. Zahi 73, 80
Hawkins, Jack 30, 220
Hawks, Howard 2, 30, *30*, 129, 130
Hawkshaw, Sir John 125
Hawley, Dave 61, *79*
Hay, Robert 77, 114
Haydn, Joseph 193
Hayles, Brian 51, 102–103
Hearn, Marcus 173
Heitfeld, Heinrich 14
Hemens Felicia 172
Henry, Rev. Matthew *53*, 54, *107*
Henty, George Alfred 61, *62*, 63, 145, 152–153, 178
Hérodiade (Massenet) 195
Herodotus 120, 153
Herrmann, Bernard 196
Hessler, Gordon 155
Heston, Charlton 28, 47, 94, 125, 193, 212
Hickner, Steve 57
Highgate Cemetery *112*, 113
Himmler, Heinrich 102, 103
Hitchcock, Alfred 4
Hitler, Adolf 9, 22, 26, 54, 102, 186
Hoare, Philip 200–201
Hodge, Alan 9
Hofmannsthal, Hugo von 204
Holden, Lansing C. 148

Hollander, Benoit 202–203, 204
Holroyd, Michael 158
Holst, Gustav 214
Holt, Seth 7, 45, *45*, 47 131, 179
Hope, Thomas 111–112, 115
Horace 151
Hörbiger, Hanns 102
The Horror of Frankenstein 50
Horus 49, 50, 90, 91, 92, 98, 99–100, 103, 153, 156, 160, 171, 173, 191
Houdini, Harry 179
Hough, John 44
Houghton, Don 161
House of Dracula 196
Howard, Leslie 40
Howard, Ronald 40, 41
Howe, Ellic 103, 104
Howell, Adele Cannon 128
Hull, A. Eaglefield 203–204
Hunt, William Holman 119
Hunter, T. Hayes 4, 14, *14*, 25
Huntley, Raymond 31, 213
Huysmans, Joris Karl 5, 234n30
Hyde, Jonathan 3

The Image in the Sand (Benson) 180
"Imprisoned with the Pharaohs" (Lovecraft/Houdini) 179
In a Persian Market (Ketèlby) 207, 211
In the Mystic Land of Egypt (Ketèlby) 207
"In the Valley of the Sorceress" (Rohmer) 175–176, 177
Indiana Jones films 30, 174, 189
The Invisible Man 15, *16*
Ippolitov-Ivanov, Mikhail 215
Iribe, Paul 9
Irving, Sir Henry 132, *133*
Irving, Laurence 132
Ishmail, Pasha 78
Isis 14, 22, 54, 66, 86, 87, 88, 89, 90, 91, 92, 99, 100, 102, 103, 104, 105, 111, 112, 125, 134, 138, 139, 140, 142, 145, 146, 147, 149, 151, 152, 156, 159, 160, 170, 171–172, 182, 191, 192, 201, 211, 215
Isis and Osiris (Lutyens) 202, 207–208
Isis Unveiled (Blavatsky) 101, 102, 103, 140
Israel in Egypt (Poynter) 61, 124–125, *124*

Jackson, David 35, *36*
Jagger, Mick 50
Jannings, Emil *9*
Jesus Christ 12, 156
The Jewel of Seven Stars (Stoker) 2, 7, 14, 16, 44, 65, 66–67, 73, 74, 78, 81–82, 92, 94–95, 98, *98*, 104, 141, 144, 159, 162, 164–170, 175, 177
Johann, Zita 13, 18, 128, 141, 185, 209
Johnson, Herbert *174*
Jollois, Jean-Baptiste Prosper 70
Jones, Owen 77, 114, 115
Jones, Robert 148
Jory, Victor 29
Joseph and His Brothers (Mann) 59, 182–183
Joseph in Egypt (Mann) 3, 76, 183
Joseph, Overseer of Pharaoh's Graneries (Alma-Tadema) 123, *123*
Josephslegende (Strauss) 172, 183, 204–205
Jowett, Rev. William 63
Joyce, Archibald 209
Julian, Rupert 10, 11
Jung, Carl Gustav 3, 87, 161
Junge, Alfred 14
Juran, Nathan 168
Justice, James Robertson 31

The Ka of Gifford Hillary (Wheatley) 95–96, 181
Karloff, Boris 4, 10, 11, 12, *12*, 13, 14, *14*, 15, 16, *17*, 18, 31, 33, 35, 46, 55, 59, 80, *104*, 105, 128, 141, 154, 172, 179, 197, 201, 209, *210*, 213
Karn, Richard 48
Karnak 13, 93, 119, 140, 147, 180
Karsavina, Tamara 200, 205
Kaszna, Kirt 29
Kellaway, Cecil 20
Kennedy, John F. 57
Kensal Green Cemetery *114*
Kenton, Erle C. 196
Kergrist, Gènevieve 202
Ketèlby, Albert 207, 211
Khamma (Debussy) 201–202, 213
Kier, Andrew 38, 45, 46, 47
King, Louis 18
King Kong 209
King Solomon's Mines (Haggard) 146
Kipling, Rudyard 77
The Kiss of the Vampire 44
Klee, Paul 101
Kleopatra (Ebers) see *Cleopatra* (Ebers)
Knipper, Lev 212
Koechlin, Charles 202
Kosleck, Martin 24
Krampf, Günther 14
Kurosawa, Akira 168

Lacey, Catherine 43
The Lair of the White Worm

(Stoker) 170
Lakmé (Delibes) 195
"Lament of Isis" (Bantock) 203
Lamont, Charles 22, **26**
Lanchester, Elsa **17**, 18, **20**
Land of the Pharaohs 2, 30, **30**, 66, 129, 173, 212–213
Lane, Edward William 76
Langley, Noel 177
The Last Days of Pompeii (Bulwer-Lytton) 101, 102, 139–142, 185, 202–203
The Last Days of Pompeii (dir. Schoedsack/Cooper) 142
"The Last Test" (Lovecraft) 179
Lear, Edward 119
Le Borg, Reginald 22, **155**
Lecomte du Noüy, Jean-Jules-Antoine 120
Ledoux, Claude-Nicholas 118
Lee, Sir Christopher 13, 15, 27, 31, 32, **32**, 33, 35, 39, 55, 56, 87, 93, 94, 99, 105, 106, 173, 226n22
Lee, Rowland V. 211
Lees, Frederick 104
Le Fanu, J. Sheridan 180
Legh, Thomas 70
Leigh, Vivien 25, **25**
Leon, Valerie 45, **45**, 46, 47, 48
Lepère, Jean-Baptiste 70
Lépine, Jean-Antoine 110
Lepsius, Richard 77, 96, 120, 166, 191
Leroux, Gaston 10, 11
LeRoy, Meryvn 211
Lessing, Gotthold Ephraim 4
Lévi, Éliphas 101
Levinson, Barry 54, 55, **55**
Levy, Louis 4, 14
Lewin, Albert 156
Lewis, Brian **34**
Lewton, Val 178
Ley, Willy 54
Liedtke, Harry 9
The Life of Sethos (Terrasson) 89, 90, 134, 182, 191–192
"Ligeia" (Poe) 143–144
Liszt, Franz 4, 195, 196, 211
Litta, Paul 204
Lloyd, Noel 180
Long, Edwin Longsden 125, 153
Lord of the Horizon (Grant) 182
"Lord of the Jackals" (Rohmer) 177
Loren, Sophia 138
Loret, Victor 80, 81
Losey, Joseph 27
Lost Horizon 148
The Lost Weekend 196
"Lot 249" (Conan Doyle) 154–155, 159–160, 161
Louÿs, Pierre 202
Lovecraft, H. P. 174, 179

Low, Andrew **40**, 93, 130
Lubitsch, Ernst 7, **9**, 183
Lucas, George 51
Ludwig II of Bavaria 142
Lugosi, Bela 4, 12, 13, 16, **17**
Lutyens, Elisabeth 202, 207–208

MacGreggor, Scott 130
Machen, Arthur 104
MacQueen-Pope, W. J. 132
Maeterlinck, Maurice 234n30
The Magic Flute (Mozart) 31, 70, 89, 118, 149, 189–193, **190**, 208, 209
Malleus Maleficarum 184
The Man Who Could Cheat Death 214
Manetho 164, 181
Mankiewicz, Joseph L. 2, 118, 123, **206**
Mann, Thomas 3, 59, 76, 182–183, 185
Manners, David 179
Marchesi, Luigi 193
Mariette, Auguste 78 166, 196–197
Marsh, Richard 159–161
Marshal, Lyndsay 220
Marshall, Frank A. **133**
Martell, Philip 202
Martelli, Carlo 214–215
Martin, John 125, 138
The Mask of Fu Manchu 18
Maspero, Gaston 78, 79–80, 82, 110–111, 178, 201
Massé, Victor 137, 198
Massenet, Jules 155, 195, 198, 209
Massey, Daniel 51
Mathers, Samuel MacGregor 103, 104, 105, **105**
Matheson, Richard 105–106
Matthews, Christopher 155
Mattoll, Mario 138
Mature, Victor 28
Maugham, William Somerset 5, 220
Maxwell, Lois 48
Mayock, Peter 50
McCarthy, Joseph 27
Méliès, Georges 7
Mendelssohn, Felix 30
Messel, Oliver 128
Metternich Stele 99
Meulenaere, Herman De 119
Meyerbeer, Giacomo 20, 195
Michelangelo 193
The Mikado (Gilbert and Sullivan) 202
Miles, Harold 148
Mills, Robert 118
Milton, John 137
Mingaye, Don 148

Mohammed Ali Pasha 72, 99, 119
Momsen, Theodor 158
Mondrian, Piet 101
"Monkeys" (Benson) 180
Moonchild (Crowley) 88
The Moonstone (Collins) 146
Moore, Albert 125
Moore, Roger 23
Moore, Steve **36**
Moorehead, Alan 68
Moran, Peggy **20**, 22
Morell, André 42, 130
Morgan, Jacques de 54, 80
Morgan, Terence 40, **42**, 76
Morris, Aubrey 48
La Mort de Cléopâtre (Berlioz) 195
La morte di Cleopatra (Litta) 204
Mosé in Egitto (Rossini) 193–194
Mower, Patrick 44
Mozart, Wolfgang Amadeus 31, 70, 89, 118, 149, 188, 191–193, 207, 208
Mulcahy, Russell 57
The Mummy (dir. Fisher) 2, 15, 23, 31–35, **32**, **36**, 39, 56, 82, 87, 92–94, 99, 106, 129–130, 143, 153, 163, 173, 178, 179, 213–214
The Mummy (dir. Freund) 7, 12, **12**, 13, 18, 19, 59, 76, 86, 88, 92, 93, **104**, 128, 141, 154, 161, 179, 197, 201, 207, 209, **210**, 211, 213
The Mummy (dir. Sommers) 3, 15, 27, 57, **57**, 92, 131, 136, 161, 164, 189, 209, 217
The Mummy! (Webb Loudon) 135–137
The Mummy, or Ramses the Damned (Rice) 143, 186–187, 198
The Mummy's Curse 23, 24, **24**, 154, 212
"The Mummy's Foot" (Gautier) 69, 137, 139
The Mummy's Ghost 22, 23, 24, 28, 154, **155**, 212
The Mummy's Hand 11, 18, 20, **21**, 22, 33, 109, 128, 139, 154, 172, 211–212
The Mummy's Shroud 41–43, **44**, 129, 130, 215–217, **216**
The Mummy's Tomb 22, 23, **23**, 128, 154, 212
Munro, Caroline 48
Munro-Hay, Stuart 54
Murray, Paul 95
Mussolini, Benito 185
Mussorgsky, Modest 199
My Fair Lady 25
The Mystery of Dr. Fu Manchu (Rohmer) 173

Nabucco (Verdi) 197
Napoleon 41, 68, 69, 70, 88, 109, 110, 111, 119, 125, 127, 200
Nassar, Gamal Abdel 33
Nattiez, Jean-Jacques 225*n*7
Nazzari, Amedeo 37
Neame, Christopher 46
Neame, Ronald 128
Nefertiti — Queen of the Nile 36
Negri, Pola 7, *9*
Nelson, Horatio 68
Newberry, Bill 27
Newell, Mike 28, 47, 81, 131, 166
Newton, Sir Isaac 87
The Night of Counting the Years 1, 78, 220
Nightingale, Florence 5
Nijinsky, Vaslav 200
Norden, Frederic Louis 65–66
North, Alex 215
North, Virginia *49*

Obrow, Jeffrey 48
O'Connor, Kevin J. 15
Odell, G. J. 22
Offenbach, Jacques 215
Oland, Warner 18
The Old Dark House 231*n*70
"One of Cleopatra's Nights" (Gautier) 137, 198, 199
Order of the Golden Dawn 103, 104, 169, 170
Osiris 86, 87, 88, 89, 90, 91, 92, 93, 95, 100, 103, 105, 106, 114, 115, 118, 147, 149, 152, 153, 160, 163, 169–170, 171–172, 173, 182, 191
O'Sullivan, Richard 38
Otterson, Jack 128
Owen, Dickie 39, 41, *42*, 42

Paget, Debra 35
Palladio, Andrea 220
Palmer, Geoffrey 180
Pani, Corrado 36
Parker, Eleanor 29
Parsifal (Wagner) 161
Partleton, George 129
Pascal, Gabriel 25, *25*, 26, *68*, 128 *129*, 158
Pastell, George 31 33, 40, 50, 78, 163, 178, 214
Pastimes in Egypt 3000 Years Ago (Alma-Tadema) 120–122, *122*, 123
Pavlova, Anna 199, 200
Paxton, Joseph 115
Pearce, Jacqueline 161
Pêcheurs du perles (Bizet) 195
Pei, Ieoh Ming 127
Perret, Auguste 200
Petrie, Sir William Matthew Flinders 9, 51, 80, 82, 154, 166

The Phantom of the Opera (dir. Julian) 10, 11, 185
The Phantom of the Opera (Leroux) 55
Pharos the Egyptian (Boothby) 56, 161–164
Philae 70, 75
Philbin, Mary 10
Phillips, John 43, 215
Phillips-Matz, Mary Jane 196
Philo 54
Pichel, Irving 148
The Picture of Dorian Gray (dir. Lewin) 156
Pierce, Jack P. 12, 154, 179
Pilate, Pontius 12
Piranesi, Giovanni Battista 88, 109, *110*, 110, 111
Pirosh, Robert 28
Pliny the Elder 61, 63
Plutarch 132, 133–134, 158
Pococke, Richard 65
Poe, Edgar Allan 139, 143–145, 187, 202
Pogany, Willy 86, 127–128, 130, 209
Powell, Eddie 42, *44*, *216*
Poynter, Sir Edward John 28, 61, 124–125, *124*, 130, 162
Presley, Elvis 57
Price, Leontyne 207
Price, Vincent 37, 48, *49*, 128, 144, 212
Prince of Egypt 57
Princep, Val 125
Ptah 13, 97, 122, 162, 169–170, 189
Pugin, Augustus Welby 114, *115*
Purcell, Henry 135
Purdom, Edward 28, 36, 185
Pushkin, Alexander 230*n*16
Putnam, Nina Wilcox 12
Pyramidographia (Greaves) 65
"Pyramids of Mars" 49–51, *50*, 55, 88, 91

The Quest of Julian Day (Wheatley) 183–184
Quibell, James 82
Quo Vadis 28, 211, 213

Rabelais, François 99
Rachmaninoff, Sergei 199
Radcliffe, Ann 135
Raiders of the Lost Ark 52, *52*, 54
Rains, Claude 15, *16*, 25
Rameses I 59, 72, 139
Rameses II 59, 72, 74, 78, 80, 88, 115, 119, 123, 139, 203
Rameses III 68, 75, 78, 80, 152
Rameses IV 71, 77
Randall-Stevens, H. C. 63, 64, 90, 102, 182

Rank, J. Arthur 25
Ravel, Maurice 211
Raven, Maarten 123
Raven, Simon 51
Rebel, Bernard 39
The Red House 196
Reeves, Steve 142
Reizenstein, Franz 2, 213–215
Rémy, Marcel 200
Remy, Nicholas 184
The Reptile 160–161, 198, 215
Respighi, Ottorino 205
Rey, Fernando 142
Rice, Anne 143, 186–187, 198
Richardson, Sir Ralph 14
Richardson, Robert 63, 136
Ricketts, Charles 204
Rigby, Jonathan 15
Rimsky-Korsakov, Nikolai 196, 199, 215
"The Ring of Thoth" (Conan Doyle) 77, 78, 153, 155, 160, 161, 197
Ripper, Michael 39, 43, 215, 217, 220
Rixen, Jean-André 120
Robert le diable (Meyerbeer) 30
Roberts, David 118–119
Robinson, Bernard 50, 130–131, 213, 215
Robinson, Edward G. 212
Robinson, Margaret 130
Robinson, P. F. 112
Robson, Flora 25
Rochegrosse, Georges 120
Rodker, John 184
Rogers, Peter 38, 39
Rohmer, Sax 2, 18, 19, 20, 57, 64, 66, 73, 76, 77, 79, 83, 89, 96, 102, 146, 160, 173–179, 184, 218
Le Roi de Lahore (Massenet) 195
Roland, Jeanne 41, 186
The Romance of Sorcery (Rohmer) 64
Rome (Television series) 220
Romer, John 63, 64, 66, 78, 80
Rossellini, Roberto 129
Rossini, Gioachino 193–194
Rowe, Nicholas 55
Rózsa, Miklós 196, 211, 213, 215
Russak, Marie 203
Russell, Paddy *50*

Sackson, M., Jr. *60*
Sadsy, Peter 113
Said, Edward 18, 189, 215
Saint-Saëns, Camille 188, 198, 207
Salt, Henry 72
Salter, Hans J. 211–212
Samson et Dalila (Saint-Saëns) 188, 198
Sangster, Jimmy 33, 35, 50, 94

Sardou, Victorien 9
The Satanic Rites of Dracula 56, 161
Saville, Peter 113
Scars of Dracula 155
Scenes from the Life of Cleopatra (Butts) 184–185
Schaffner, Franklin J. 54
Schaw, William 88
Schikaneder, Emanuel 118, 191–192
Schinkel, Karl Friedrich 118, 191
Schmid, Christian 56
Schmitt, Florent 205, 207
Schoedsack, Ernest B. 142, 209
Schoenberg, Arnold 207
Schumann, Robert 4
Schweitzer, Helena 203
Scott, Cyril 203–204
Scott, Derek B. 188 196
Scott, Paul 23
Scream and Scream Again 155
Scriabin, Alexander 101, 203
Il sepolcro dei re see *Cleopatra's Daughter*
"Serenade for Baboons" (Streatfield) 177
Sert, José Maria 172, 204
Set (Seth-Typhon) 49, 87, 90, 91, 93, 99, 105, 106, 136, 147, 182, 183
Seti I 73, 74, 75, 76, 77, 78, 80, 86, 136
Seven Brides for Seven Brothers 168
Seven Samurai 168
The Seventh Seal 168
The 7th Voyage of Sinbad 168
Shakespeare, William 132–134, 144, 156, 158, 173, 182, 198, 204, 205, 207
Sharp, Don 44, 88
Shaw, George Bernard 25, 26, 128, 156, 158, 161, 204
She (dir. Day) 39, 145–147, **146**, 148
She (dir. Holden/Pichel) 148
She (Haggard) 56, 145–148, 151
Shelley, Mary 135, 136, 137
Shrapnel, John 87
Sibelius, Jean 208
Sicard, Father Claude 65
The Sign of the Four (Conan Doyle) 159–160
Simmons, Jean 28, 68, **68**
Simpson, Dudley 50
6 épigraphes antiques (Debussy) 202
Skeggs, Roy 46
Skinner, Frank 211
Smelt, Charles 70
Smith, Patricia Colman 170
Snodin, Michael 118

Snow White and the Seven Dwarfs 148
Soane, Sir John 73, 75, 76, 114, 136
"Some Words with a Mummy" (Poe) 143, 187
Sommers, Stephen **57**, 131, 136, 161
Son of Frankenstein 211, 212
Sontag, Susan 10
Souza, John Philip 212
Spader, James 63
Speer, Albert 9, 186
Sphinx (dir. Schaffner) 54
The Sphinx (Bantock) 203
"The Sphinx" (Poe) 144–145
"The Sphinx" (Wilde) 156
"Sphinx Without a Secret" (Wilde) 156
Spielberg, Steven 52, **52**, 54
Spriggs, Elizabeth 56
The Spy Who Loved Me 25, 48
Star Wars 51
Stargate 55, 63
Steiner, Max 209
Stele of Revealing 78, 99, 100
Stendhal (Henri Beyle) 193–194
Stewart, Thomas Somerville 118
Stoker, Bram 2, 5, 7, 14, 16, 18, 43, 44, 45, 46, 47, 48, 56, 65, 66, 70, 73, 78, 81, 82, 83, 92, 94–95, 96, **98**, 104, 131, 144, 159, 162, 164, 166–170, 175–176, 182, 220
Stone, Edward Albert 126
Stowe Landscape Gardens (Buckinghamshire) 109
Strabo 59
Strauss, Richard 172, 183, 200, 204–205
Stravinsky, Igor 201, 205
Strindberg, August 179
Stuart, Gloria 231n70
Stumar, Charles 12
Sullivan, Sir Arthur 202
Summers, Montague **150**, 184
Swinburne, Algernon 100, 171, 172
Szyk, Arthur 22

Tales from the Crypt 113
Tales of Secret Egypt (Rohmer) 76, 77, 79–80, 96, 174, 175, 177
Tallis, John **53**, **107**
Talos the Mummy 57
Taneyev, Sergei 199
Taste the Blood of Dracula 113
Taylor, Elizabeth 25, 37, 38, 68, 118, 145, 158, 202, **206**, 215, 220
Taylor, John Russell 44
Tchaikovsky, Pyotr Ilyich 199, 209, 212

Tcherepnine, Nicolas 199
The Ten Commandments 2, 9, **11**, 25, **27**, 28, 52, 61, 125, 126, 128–129, 132, 193–194, 212, 213
La Tentation de Saint Antoine (Flaubert) 145
Tepes, Vlad 70
Terrasson, Jean 89, 90, 134–135, 182, 191
Tessier, Christien 56
Thaïs (France) 155–156, 181, 198
Thaïs (Massenet) 195
Thamos, König in Aegypten (Mozart) 89, 209
Thesiger, Ernest 14, **14**, 15, 25
Thomas, Gerald **37**, **38**, 38
Thomas, W. L. **124**
Thompson, Carlos 29
Thoth 12, 57, 86, 90, 91, 92, 99, 103, 142, 156
Tiomkin, Dimitri 30, 31, 212–213, 215
Tolstoy, Leo 234n30
The Tomb of Ligeia (dir. Corman) 144
Tommasini, Aldo 142
The Tomorrow People (Television series) 55–56
"The Tophar Bride" (Ewers) 173
Townsend, Jill 47
Trauner, Alexandre 129, 130
Der traurige Mönch (Liszt) 196
Tree, Sir Herbert Beerbohm 124, 132
Trogus, Pompeius 54
Tuchman, Barbara 205
Turner, Joseph Mallord William 119
Tutankhamen 2, 3, 9, 40, 43, 54, 56, 59, 60, 64, 70, 72, 82–84, 93, 103, 127, 162, 186, 200, 220
Twins of Evil 44
Tyler, Tom 11, 20, **21**, 22, 172, 211

Ulmer, Edgar G. 4
Gli Ultimo giorno di Pompei (dir. Leone) 142
"Under the Pyramids" (Lovecraft/Houdini) *see* "Imprisioned with the Pharaohs"
Ustinov, Sir Peter 28, 49

Valley of the Kings 28
Vanbrugh, John 109
Van Sloane, Edward 13, 19
Vathek (Beckford) 102, 135, 137
Velasquez, Patricia **57**, 217
The Vengeance of Egypt 7
Verdi, Giuseppe 30, 78, 97, 196–198
Verney, Guy 44

Veronese, Paolo 204
Villiers, James 46, 76, 131, 218
Villiers de l'Isle Adam, August 5
Villiers du Terrage, Baron Édouard de 70
The Vision of Salome (Rémy/Allan) 200
A Voice Out of Egypt (Randall-Stevens) 63, 90
Vosloo, Arnold 15, 57, 59, 136, 172
Voyage d'Egypte et de Nubie (Norden) 65

Wagner, Cosima 225n10
Wagner, Richard 3, 4, 14, 15, 127, 142, 148, 161, 182, 202–203, 204, 215, 225n8
Walker, Stewart 20
Waltari, Mika 28, 81, 92, 140, 185–186
Warlords of Atlantis 51, 63, 101, 102
Washington, Peter 101
Watkin, David 112
Webb Loudon, Jane 135–137
Weisz, Rachel 164
Wells, H. G. 15
Wells, Jacqueline 18
The Werewolf of London 20
Wescott, Dr. Wynn 103
West, Adam 35
Westbrook, John 144
Whale, James 11, 13, 15, **16**, **17**, 18, **20**, 109, 128, 231n70
Wheatley, Dennis 95–96, 105, 106, 174, 181, 183–184, 185
"The Whispering Mummy" (Rohmer) 177
Whitehouse, Mary 83
Wicking, Christopher 44, 45
Wilde, Constance 103, 169
Wilde, Oscar 100, 156, **157**, 164, 169, 171, 181, 200, 201, 202
Wilde, Sir William 164
Wilder, Billy 196
Wilding, Michael 28
Wilkinson, Sir John Gardner **67**, 68, 75–76, 77–78, 114, 123, 163–164, **165**
William Tell (Rossini) 194
Williams, Kenneth 39, 55, 56, 173, 226n26
Williams, Simon Harvey **113**
Williamson, Malcolm 207
Willman, Noel 161

Winged Pharaoh (Grant) 90, 181–182
Wise, Robert 196
Woodforde-Finden, Amy 203, 207
Woodman, Dr. William Robert 103
Woodville, R. Caton **150**
Woolf, Gabriel 49
The Wraith of the Tomb see *The Avenging Hand*
Wyler, William 211

Yates, Bert 22
Yeats, W. B. 101, 103, 145, 170
Young, Harold 23, **23**
Young Sherlock Holmes 54, **55**, 109

Zanoni (Bulwer-Lytton) 101, 139, 140
Die Zauberflöte (Mozart) see *The Magic Flute*
Zeffirelli, Franco 207
Zucco, George 20, 22, 23, 33, 50, 78, 211

www.ingramcontent.com/pod-product-compliance
Ingram Content Group UK Ltd.
Pitfield, Milton Keynes, MK11 3LW, UK
UKHW051508160725
460855UK00014B/142